ANDY WARHOL

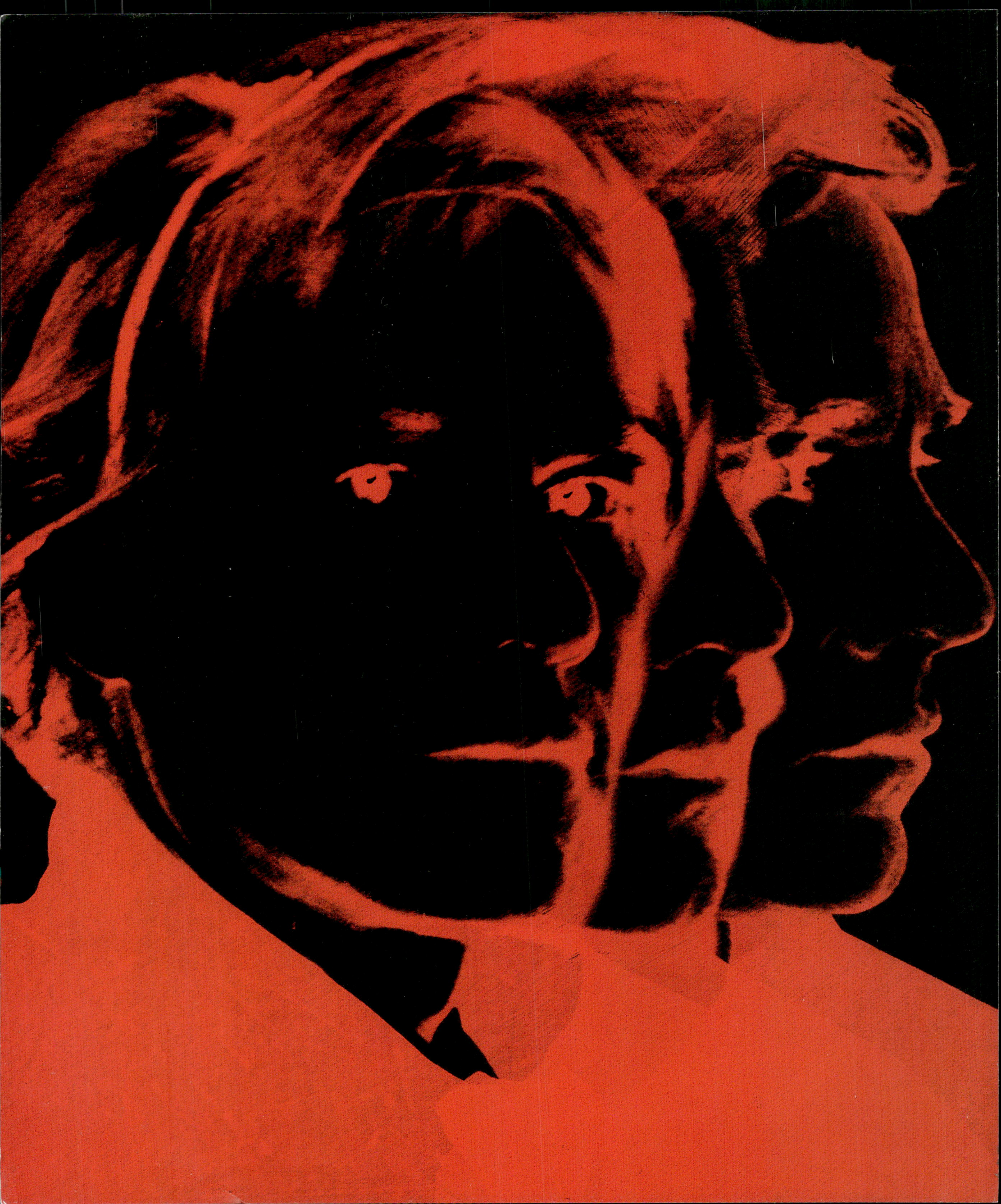

ANDY WARHOL
THE LAST DECADE

Joseph D. Ketner II

with essays by Keith Hartley and Gregory Volk

and contributions by Bruno Bischofberger, Keith Haring, and Julian Schnabel

Milwaukee Art Museum
DelMonico Books·Prestel MUNICH BERLIN LONDON NEW YORK

Published on the occasion of the exhibition
Andy Warhol: The Last Decade
Curated by Joseph D. Ketner II, Lois and Henry Foster Chair in Contemporary Art, Emerson College, Boston

Organized by the Milwaukee Art Museum, Wisconsin

Exhibition itinerary:

Milwaukee Art Museum
September 26, 2009–January 3, 2010

Modern Art Museum of Fort Worth
February 14–May 16, 2010

Brooklyn Museum
June 18–September 12, 2010

The Baltimore Museum of Art
October 17, 2010–January 9, 2011

For DelMonico Books•Prestel:
Designer: Miko McGinty, Inc.
Editor: Elisa Urbanelli
Proofreader: Richard G. Gallin
Indexer: Nancy Wolff
Printing and binding: CS Graphics

Library of Congress Control Number: 2009924750

British Library Cataloguing-in-Publication Data: a catalogue record for this book is available from the British Library; Deutsche Nationalbibliothek holds a record of this publication in the Deutsche Nationalbibliografie; detailed bibliographical data can be found under: http://dnb.ddb.de.

ISBN 978-0-87273-163-9 (paperback)
ISBN 978-3-7913-4344-0 (hardcover)

All works are by Andy Warhol unless otherwise noted.

Published in 2009 by Milwaukee Art Museum and DelMonico Books, an imprint of Prestel Publishing.

Milwaukee Art Museum
700 N. Art Museum Drive
Milwaukee, WI 53202
www.mam.org

Prestel Verlag
Königinstrasse 9
80539 Munich
Germany
Tel: 49 89 24 29 08 300
Fax: 49 89 24 29 08 335
www.prestel.de

Prestel Publishing Ltd.
4 Bloomsbury Place
London WC1A 2QA
United Kingdom
Tel: 44 20 7323 5004
Fax: 44 20 7636 8004

Prestel Publishing
900 Broadway, Suite 603
New York, NY 10003
Tel: 212 995 2720
Fax: 212 995 2733
Email: sales@prestel-usa.com
www.prestel.com

The paper in this book meets the guidelines for permanence and durability of the Committee on Production Guidelines for Book Longevity of the Council of Library Resources.

9 8 7 6 5 4 3 2 1

Front cover: *The Last Supper*, 1986 (detail of plate 78)
Back cover: *Camouflage*, 1986 (detail of plate 72)
Endpapers: *Self-Portraits*, 1986 (details of plates 66 and 67)
Frontispiece: *Self-Portrait*, 1978 (detail of plate 4)
Page 6: *Camouflage*, 1986 (detail of plate 73)
Page 10: *Oxidation Painting*, 1978 (detail of plate 14)

Printed and bound in Singapore

Contents

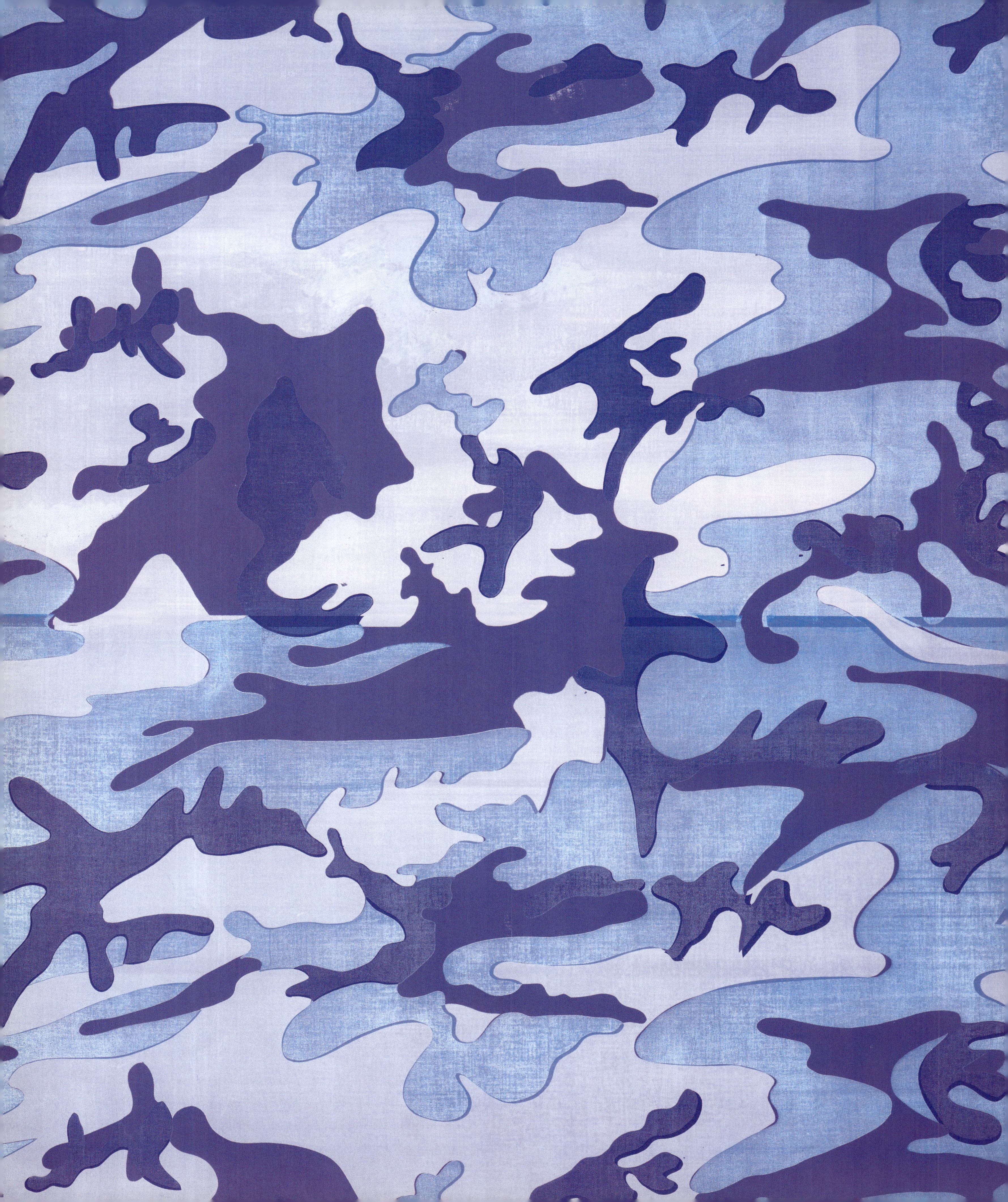

Foreword

Daniel T. Keegan
Director, Milwaukee Art Museum

The Milwaukee Art Museum has a long tradition of presenting important exhibitions of contemporary art. *Andy Warhol: The Last Decade* continues that tradition and continues the Museum's long relationship with Warhol. Mrs. Harry Lynde Bradley, one of Milwaukee's significant collectors of modern art, made the prescient decision to acquire a pair of Warhol's *Campbell's Soup* paintings (1965, figs. 1, 2) early on for her own collection. Then, a few years later, the Museum hosted an exhibition of Warhol's prints (1974) in advance of opening the new Bradley Collection Galleries of Modern Art, which would display Mrs. Bradley's tremendous collection (1975). Perhaps the most significant contribution that Milwaukee has made to Warhol's exhibition history was *Warhol/Beuys/Polke* (1987), curated by then-director Russell Bowman and curator Dean Sobel. The exhibition made searing insights into three of the leading artistic innovators of the day, presenting, for the first time, Warhol in the context of his peers. This novel and smart exhibition attracted the attention of the art world not only for its daring thesis but also, sadly, because it was presented the year that Warhol died.

Again, the Milwaukee Art Museum stands at the forefront of scholarship on Warhol with *Andy Warhol: The Last Decade*, the first museum exhibition in the United States to present Warhol's late work. Joseph D. Ketner II, the Museum's former chief curator, has assembled a significant group of paintings and has forged new research about Warhol's late career. This is no light undertaking. Ketner has added significantly to the illustrious scholarship on Warhol, assembling a group of collaborators, including Keith Hartley and Gregory Volk, who have contributed fresh information on the subject. We are also pleased to reprint essays by Keith Haring, Julian Schnabel, and Bruno Bischofberger. The exhibition *Andy Warhol: The Last Decade* and this accompanying publication challenge preconceived notions of the Pop icon and add a new dimension to his legacy.

This project would not have been possible without the collaboration of Thomas Sokolowski, director of the Andy Warhol Museum, and his staff. Their dedication to the project, many loans to the exhibition, and support for the catalogue brought this project to life. Throughout the project, Ketner has worked in coordination with the Andy Warhol Foundation for the Visual Arts, Inc., under the direction of Joel Wachs. I appreciate their endorsement of the project. I also acknowledge the staff at the Milwaukee Art Museum for their efforts on the exhibition and catalogue: John McKinnon, assistant curator of modern and

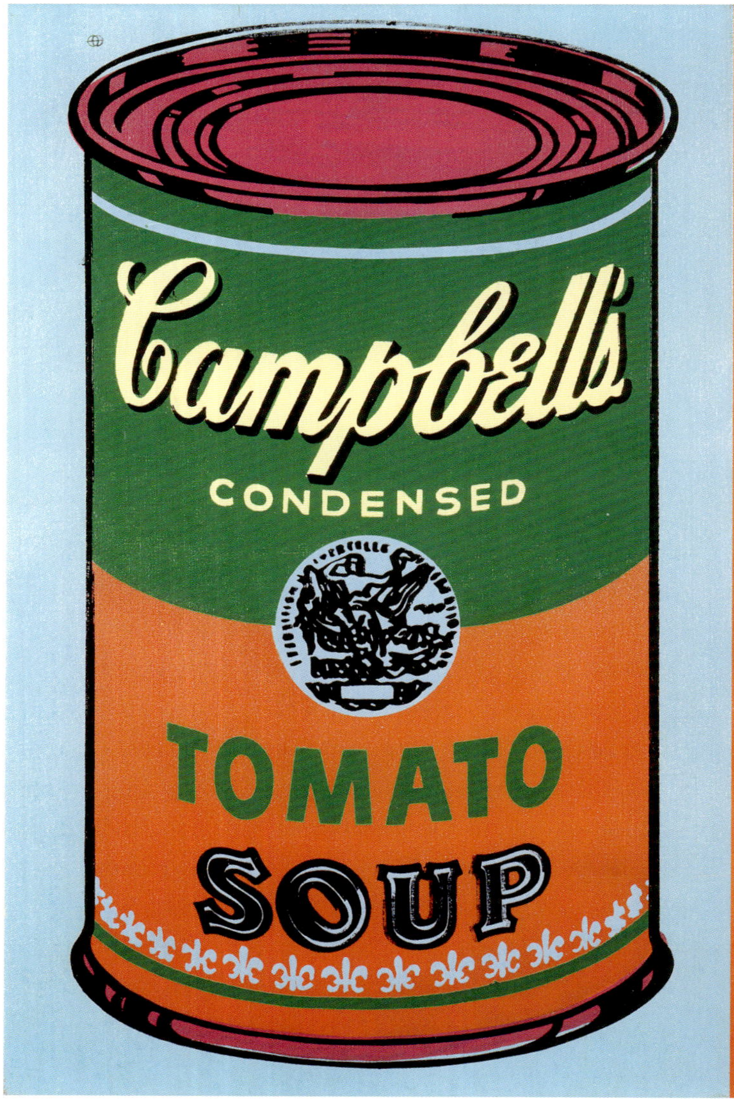

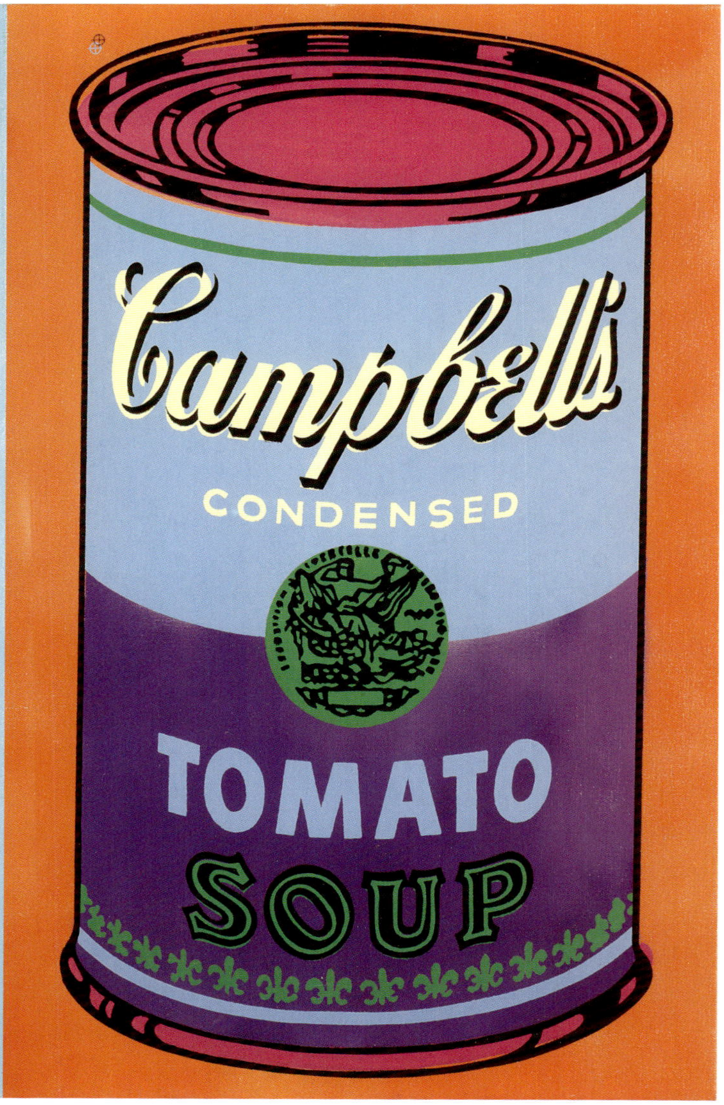

Fig. 1. *Campbell's Soup*, 1965. Acrylic and silkscreen ink on canvas, 36 x 24 in. (91.4 x 61 cm). Milwaukee Art Museum, Gift of Mrs. Harry Lynde Bradley

Fig. 2. *Campbell's Soup*, 1965. Acrylic and silkscreen ink on canvas, 36 x 24 in. (91.4 x 61 cm). Milwaukee Art Museum, Gift of Mrs. Harry Lynde Bradley contemporary art, who coordinated countless details; Laurie Winters, director of exhibitions; Dawn Frank, registrar; Larry Stadler, lead preparator; Jim DeYoung, senior conservator; John Irion, designer; Gwen Benner, director of business enterprises; and many others who helped bring this exhibition to life.

Coordination with other institutions was essential for this exhibition to tour throughout the United States. My colleagues Dr. Marla Price at the Modern Art Museum of Fort Worth, Arnold Lehman at the Brooklyn Museum, and Doreen Bolger at the Baltimore Museum of Art helped disseminate this project to a wider audience. Special gratitude is also extended to the Baltimore Museum of Art for its many loans to the exhibition. We are grateful to all of the generous lenders—both public and private—for allowing us to include their works in this traveling exhibition. They are listed individually on page 217.

Finally, thanks to our wonderful sponsors for their financial support and firm belief in the Milwaukee Art Museum. Their participation was critical for a project of this scale. Sue and Bud Selig, Debbie and Mark Attanasio, Donald and Donna Baumgartner, Christine Symchych, Milwaukee Art Museum's Friends of Art, and an anonymous foundation have all provided generous sponsorship. Additionally, a film program in conjunction with this exhibition is sponsored by the Johnson and Pabst LGBT Humanity Fund at the Greater Milwaukee Foundation. The exhibition in Milwaukee, Fort Worth, Brooklyn, and Baltimore is also supported by an indemnity from the Federal Council on the Arts and Humanities. I express my gratitude to those mentioned here for their combined efforts and to the many others who participated this project. This exhibition marks another significant milestone in the history of the Milwaukee Art Museum and again asserts its longstanding commitment to presenting groundbreaking exhibitions by leading artists of contemporary art.

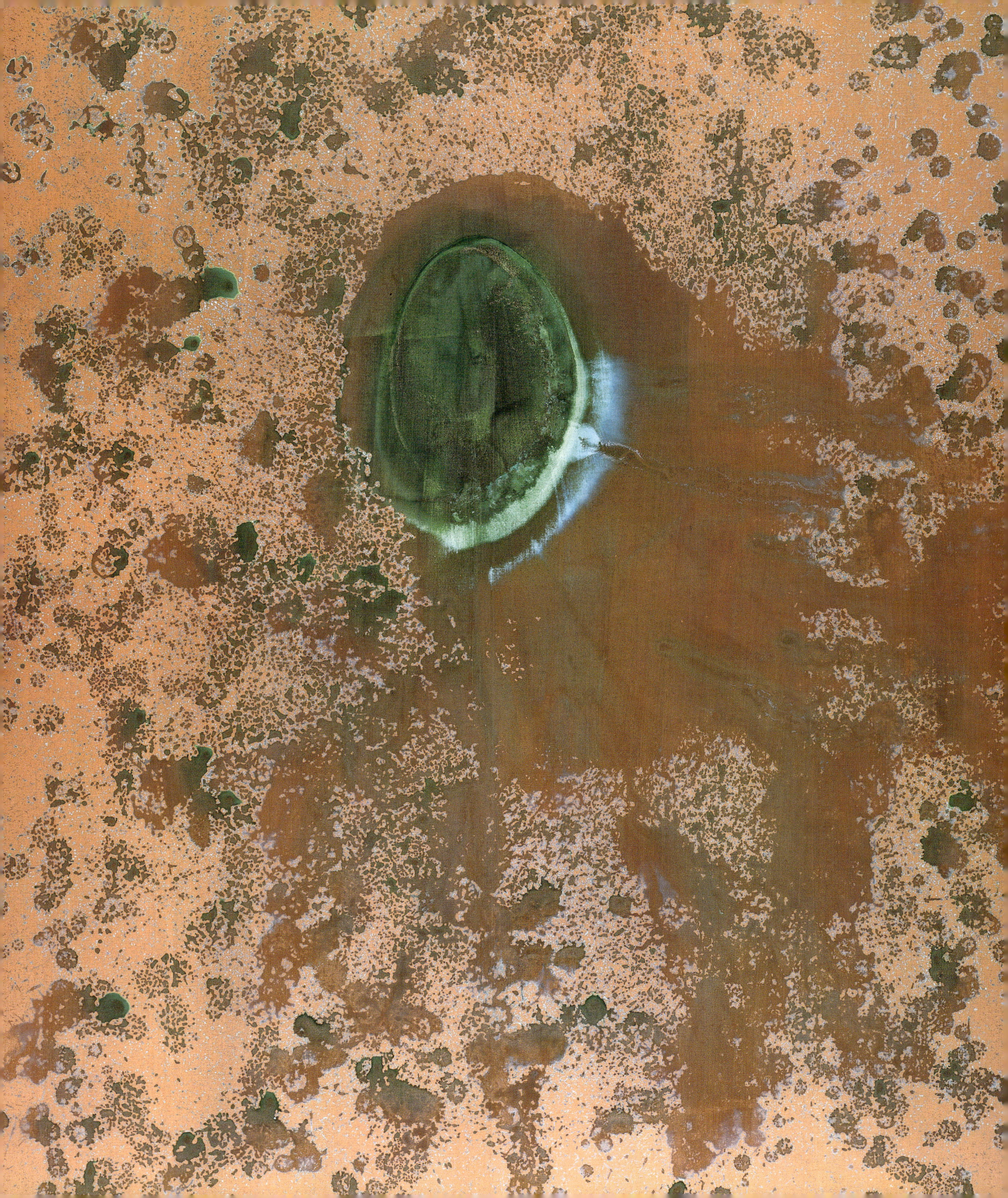

Acknowledgments

Joseph D. Ketner II

Ten years ago I had a revelatory experience similar to that of the biblical Paul struck by a bolt of enlightenment from the heavens and knocked off his horse. I was sandwiched between cabinets in the crowded storage rooms of the Rose Art Museum at Brandeis University when the preparator pulled out a screen, literally a few feet from my nose, on which hung Warhol's almost ten-foot-high *Saturday Disaster* (1964, fig. 55, page 75). As it passed before my eyes, the painting overwhelmed me with a sublime feeling of awe. I had to step back in order to dodge the crashing cars and to take the entirety of the image into my view. At that moment I fully experienced the visceral impact of Warhol's *Disaster* series and knew that I must do a project based on that work. A couple of years later Neil Printz, who had just finished the first volume of the Warhol catalogue raisonné, came to Brandeis at my invitation, as the Henry Luce Foundation Visiting Scholar, to research and write about the university's excellent collection. Printz had worked with Walter Hopps on an exhibition of the *Disasters* at the Menil Collection in 1987. From my experience of being enveloped by a *Disaster* painting and then a series of conversations that ensued with Printz and others, the thesis for this project evolved over the course of a decade.

The late paintings, long ignored or dismissed by the art world, have been receiving more and more attention in recent years. *Andy Warhol: The Last Decade*—the first museum exhibition in the United States to focus on Warhol's late work—will travel to three museums after opening at the Milwaukee Art Museum (MAM): the Modern Art Museum of Fort Worth; the Brooklyn Museum; and the Baltimore Museum of Art. I am grateful to MAM director Daniel T. Keegan for encouraging me to complete this project after I left my post as chief curator at that museum to assume my present position. For recognizing the novelty and incredible opportunity that this show presented, I appreciate the support of Michael Auping, chief curator at the Modern Art Museum of Fort Worth; Arnold Lehman, director, and Charles Desmarais, deputy director, at the Brooklyn Museum; and Jay Fisher, senior curator at the Baltimore Museum of Art. It is especially wonderful to have Baltimore involved in this project, for it possesses large holdings of Warhol's late paintings, acquired under former curator Brenda Richardson, which are featured in this exhibition.

Warhol's late work poses special problems for a traveling exhibition owing to the fact that many of the paintings are extraordinarily large, as well as valuable. I am indebted to the lenders for their willingness to participate in this project. In this regard I am eternally grateful for the generosity of the Andy Warhol Museum in Pittsburgh, around whose unparalleled collection of Warhol's late work this exhibition is built. The Warhol Museum holds the largest collection of the artist's late work, contributed by the Warhol Foundation as part of its enormous contribution to launch the museum. Thomas Sokolowski, the museum's director, and his staff were exceedingly generous in permitting me access to artworks, archives, and information. Equally important are the works lent by Bruno Bischofberger, Anthony d'Offay, José Mugrabi, and Ealan Wingate, each of whom has played an important role in acquiring, presenting, and promoting Warhol's late work. Other institutions have supported this project with loans of monumental paintings, entrusting them to us so that they may be widely seen and known: the Kunsthalle Bielefeld, Germany; and the Museum of Modern Art, New York. In addition, a number of individual collectors, including private lenders who have chosen to remain anonymous, have graciously agreed to part with their cherished works for this landmark exhibition. I extend my thanks to each lender.

Andy Warhol: The Last Decade is a collaborative venture between the Milwaukee Art Museum and the Andy Warhol Museum. Tom Sokolowski performed critical roles beyond lender and colleague to assist in the multitude of issues that arise from a project of this complexity. I appreciate his efforts to help bring it to fruition. Matt Wrbican, the museum's archivist, helped me uncover new materials and information that are published for the first time in this catalogue. The staffs of the two museums have worked closely to coordinate the organization of this exhibition. John McKinnon, assistant curator of modern and contemporary art at MAM, is a valued colleague who has served as the curatorial coordinator for Milwaukee. Heather Kowalski, registrar at the Warhol Museum, and Dawn Frank, registrar at MAM, performed the delicate and laborious process of organizing the shipping, insurance, and complex indemnities necessary to manage this exhibition. And Jim DeYoung, senior conservator at MAM, has worked in tandem with Christine Daulton, conservator at the Warhol Museum, the person most familiar with the care and conservation of Warhol's paintings, accompanying these works to each venue to ensure their safety and preservation.

The ambitious catalogue for this exhibition is also an extended collaboration between the Milwaukee Art Museum and DelMonico Books•Prestel, New York. Under the direction of Mary DelMonico, the editorial control of Elisa Urbanelli, and the magic design of Miko McGinty, this book has come to fruition. Over the past decade, a number of curators, writers, scholars, critics, and students across the United States and Europe have contributed to the ongoing study of Warhol. In seeking new voices and perspectives on the subject, I identified Keith Hartley, chief curator and deputy director of the Scottish National Gallery of Modern Art in Edinburgh, and Gregory Volk, an independent writer working in New York. In recent years Keith and I have become colleagues partly owing to the fact that we were involved in parallel Warhol projects—Keith had worked with Dietmar Elger on his *Warhol Self-Portraits* exhibition for the Sprengel Museum, Hannover (2004), and then on his own exhibition for the Scottish National Gallery (2007), focusing on the museum's fabulous acquisition of a large number of works from the London art dealer Anthony d'Offay (2007). Keith brings a fresh viewpoint to the subject of Warhol's abstraction. This is the fourth time that Gregory and I have worked on books together, previously contributing to catalogues on Roxy Paine (Contemporary Arts Museum Houston, and the Rose Art Museum, Brandeis University, 2002), Yun-Fei Ji (Contemporary Art Museum St. Louis, 2004), and Bruce Nauman (Milwaukee Art Museum, 2006). Gregory brings a unique voice to his subjects, in this case weaving intriguing literary connections among Warhol, Ralph Waldo Emerson, and P. T. Barnum. My own essay is indebted to a host of assistants, interns, and students in Milwaukee and at Emerson College. In Milwaukee I had the good fortune of working with Shannon Dosemagen, Sarah Doty, Anna Gallagher, Andrew Hartzell, Leslie Monagle, Elyse Nelson, and Danielle Paswaters. At Emerson College, two students, Alana Levinson and Anjali Pala, helped me through the research and administrative details of pulling together the manuscripts for this book.

In addition, this catalogue includes two important out-of-print essays by Keith Haring and Julian Schnabel, whose early views on the *Collaborations* and *Shadows*, respectively, convey the depth of their responses to these works when the paintings first appeared. These are published through the courtesy of the Keith Haring Foundation and Julian Schnabel's Studio. The catalogue also records the first-person account of art dealer Bruno Bischofberger, who commissioned the *Collaborations* among Warhol, Jean-Michel Basquiat, and Francesco Clemente. Finally, I was fortunate to be able to draw on my own interviews with Jay Shriver, Warhol's principal studio assistant from 1982 until the artist's death in 1987; Benjamin Liu, also an assistant to Warhol from 1982 to 1987; and Vincent Fremont, the vice president of Warhol Enterprises from 1970 to 1987. These bring to the catalogue the vivid recollections of those who participated in and witnessed this intense period of creativity and production for Warhol. The combination of essays, artist's responses, and first-person accounts realizes the goal to present new ideas from a variety of perspectives, which explore previously little-known work by one of the most significant artistic and cultural innovators of the late twentieth century.

Andy Warhol: The Last Decade is a complex, ambitious, and expensive project. Its sponsors have demonstrated recognition of the importance of the exhibition and its significance to the Milwaukee Art Museum. We deeply appreciate Sue and Bud Selig and Debbie and Mark Attanasio, generous supporters and art collectors who are the major sponsors of this exhibition. I am grateful to Donald and Donna Baumgartner, Christine Symchych—a sponsor of the exhibition who has been very supportive of the Milwaukee Art Museum and me—Milwaukee Art Museum's Friends of Art, and an anonymous foundation. Thank you. A film program in conjunction with this exhibition is sponsored by the Johnson and Pabst LGBT Humanity Fund at the Greater Milwaukee Foundation.

More is written about Andy Warhol than any other artist. Yet, as Charles Stuckey observed, nearly 80 percent of all exhibitions and literature focus on the brief, eight-year Pop phase of Warhol's work. Emulating Warhol's own ambition to continually seek new ideas, I aspired to contribute a new perspective on Warhol. This proved challenging. But, as this exhibition demonstrates, when we examine the last decade of Warhol's career, we witness a mature artist bringing his own oeuvre full circle, sweeping the early images for which he is so well known into a complex dance of painting and printing, abstraction and representation, surface and meaning. In many ways, it is only in the light of the typically Warholian paradox that marks the late work that his early Pop images find their full context—and their profundity. This exhibition and the book that accompanies it aim to shape the discourse concerning Warhol's last decade.

Warhol's Last Decade: Reinventing Painting

Joseph D. Ketner II

I don't paint anymore. I gave it up about a year ago and just do the movies now. I could do two things at the same time but movies are more exciting. Painting was just a phase I went through.

—Andy Warhol, 1966[1]

Benjamin H. D. Buchloh: Are your TV program and your paintings, then, in a sense the extreme opposite poles of your activities as an artist?
Andy Warhol: Yes, we are trying to do two things, but the painting is really exciting.

—May 28, 1985[2]

In 1965 Andy Warhol, at the height of his celebrity as the prince of Pop art, announced that he was abandoning painting, à la Marcel Duchamp, in order to concentrate on making movies. Over the previous few years, using methods of mechanical reproduction to create a pantheon of images that became icons of the mass culture of the era, he had participated in the launch of a new style of art, Pop (figs. 1, 2). With an irreverent attitude toward art and a glorification of glamour, Warhol, paradoxically, fused high art, low culture, high society, and the avant-garde, transforming the art of an age and cultivating a lifestyle of celebrity. At the beginning of his success as a Pop artist, he had expressed a desire to work in not only a diversity of media but also a range of styles: "How can you say one style is better than another? You ought to be able to be an Abstract Expressionist next week, or a Pop artist, or a realist, without feeling you've given up something. . . . I think that would be so great, to be able to change styles. And I think that's what's going to happen, that's going to be the whole new scene."[3] With this statement, Warhol prophesied what would become a primary characteristic of contemporary art practice, where style and medium are by-products of the artistic concept. Yet he was not able to fully realize this liberation of style in his own work until he returned to painting, twenty years after renouncing it. In the process, he reinvented the medium as part of his vast repertoire of visual languages—and as part of a dialogue between the hand and the machine, and between the private Warhol and his public persona.

Throughout the 1960s and 1970s, contrary to his proclamation, Warhol explored an extraordinary spectrum of media—painting, printing, photography, drawing, film, television, music, and fashion. But despite the breadth of his output, by the end of the 1970s he felt trapped by the public's expectations of him to present images of popular culture and to embody fame and social celebrity through mass media. His cinematic work won awards in the world of avant-garde independent film, but it failed to receive the popular acclaim and fortune to which he aspired. The fame of his Factory and its reckless, bohemian lifestyle remained the subject of gossip columns and a locus of chic society, but he had grown weary of the continuous parade of society portrait commissions and physically exhausted by the nightly clubbing on the New York social circuit. The specter of his ultimate demise, looming over him since the failed assassination attempt in 1968, haunted his personal life. In an interview with *Art News* in 1980—appropriately titled, "Gee, What's Happened to Andy Warhol?"—the artist reflected on the previous decade: "The 70s were sort of quiet. . . . I think the 80s are going to be more exciting. . . . In the 70s, nothing really different happened in art."[4] He longed for the stimulation of new ideas and new art, which he rediscovered in painting. Touring the art museums of Paris in the summer of 1977 with Pontus Hulten, the founding director of the Centre Pompidou, motivated Warhol: "I had energy and wanted to rush home and paint and stop doing society portraits."[5] At this point, "just trying to do newer ideas,"[6] he embarked on a period of experimentation that marked the most radical metamorphosis in his work since he adopted the screenprint process in 1962.

In the heat of his cinematic work, Warhol had dismissed painting as "so old fashioned."[7] But from the moment that Warhol pissed on a painting in the seminal summer of 1977, he catalyzed a chemical reaction in his art practice. This act of defiance, complete with its overtly gay sexual overtones, freed Warhol's hand from the pencil, the screenprint, the camera, and the recorder, and thrust his body physically back into the action of making art, the performance of painting. Over the next decade, beginning with the "no-hands" abstraction of the *Oxidation Painting* series (1977–78, pls. 10–15) and the evanescent, screened *Shadows* (1978–79, pls. 16–21), he entered what was for him entirely new territory, abstract art; returned to painting by hand with brushes; and created works with profound personal content and meaning, a radical departure from his Pop imagery of the 1960s and his society portraits of the 1970s. During this period the vitality of the studio was palpable, as one new series of paintings followed another, and one new technique or idea came after another. Mining his own early Pop icons, the artist created the *Retrospective* paintings (1979, pl. 22) and the haunting, painterly *Reversal* series (1978–79, pls. 23, 24). Invoking references to Abstract Expressionism and Color Field, he screened a series of *Yarn* paintings (1983, pls. 25–30) that mechanically re-create Pollock's classic drips, and then followed these abstractions with the *Rorschach* series (1984, pls. 31–35), updating his blotted-line drawing technique into abstract paintings.

Warhol's cooperative ventures with Jean-Michel Basquiat, beginning in the fall of 1982, form the fulcrum of Warhol's late work. They rekindled his love of the paintbrush, as is evident in the *Collaborations* (1984–85, pls. 36–43), opened him to the possibilities of figurative painting and drawing, and expanded the repertoire of styles that he exploited over the last few years of his life. The experience of working in combinations of hand painting and screening with Basquiat, and briefly with Francesco Clemente, spurred Warhol to create his *Black & White Ads* (1985–86, pls. 44–59), which deceptively blur the distinctions between the hand-painted and the mechanically screened image. Finally, in a great flourish of activity in 1986, his last year, Warhol produced three major series: the so-called fright-wig *Self-Portraits* (pls. 60–68), the *Camouflage* paintings (pls. 69–73), and the *The Last Supper* paintings (pls. 74–80), which present a full range of abstract and representational imagery, created by both hand and screenprint.

Warhol's imaginative creativity during the last decade of his career can only be compared to the early 1960s, when Pop art popped and when Warhol participated in challenging the primacy of the artist's mark inherited from Abstract Expressionism. People associated with Warhol during his late period remark on the vitality, energy, and spirit of experimentation surrounding his pursuit of painting.[8] He enthusiastically embraced each new idea, each new body of work, and he labored continuously in their production, working almost daily in the studio to complete his multitude of projects.[9] At that time Warhol created more new series of paintings, in larger numbers and on a vastly larger scale, than during any other phase of his life. But far from a period of "Factory" production, it was a period of extraordinary artistic development for Warhol, during which we witness a dramatic transformation of his style and the introduction of new techniques to address subjects that resonated with personal meaning and significance.

More is written about Warhol than almost any other artist, in both the critical and popular press. Yet the late period of Warhol's career has been only a footnote in this coverage, which overwhelmingly focuses on his Pop art of the 1960s.[10] Although his late paintings were shown in Europe on numerous occasions, they were virtually unknown in the United States.[11] It disturbed Warhol that, despite his public statements that "newer ideas" dominated his return to studio practice, these works found little audience in this country.[12] He was still the subject of social and gossip columns, and he still exhibited his print commissions and his re-creations of Pop imagery. But the late paintings became his personal work, which he created to satisfy his artistic appetite. Finally, in the last year in his life, perhaps as a sign of the changing tide of sentiment toward Warhol's work, galleries and critics in the United States began to give these paintings attention. Two shows appeared in the fall of 1986: *Hand-painted Images, 1960–62* at Dia Art Foundation and *The Oxidation Paintings, 1978* at Gagosian Gallery. Roberta Smith, writing in the *New York Times*, related Warhol's newer works to his earliest hand-painted Pop images and described the *Oxidation Paintings* as "seriously beautiful. . . . They lack his media-oriented edge, but they also seem vastly preferable to those silkscreen celebrities of recent years." Addressing Warhol's position as a painter, she asked the important question in the minds of critics at that moment: "Do they express Warhol's hesitance as a painter, or—equally possible—his underlying disdain for the medium?"[13]

A number of exhibitions appeared shortly after Warhol died in February 1987, including several that presented these late series to the public for the first time. As a memorial Leo Castelli organized an exhibition of seven of the artist's last works, including *Black & White Ads*, *Camouflage*

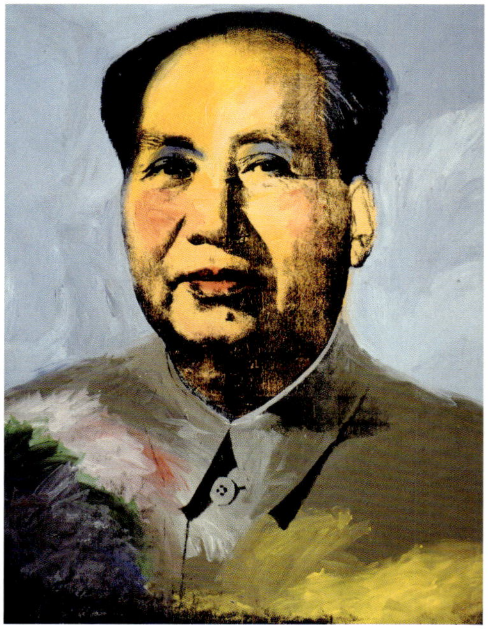

Fig. 3. *Mao*, 1973. Acrylic and silkscreen ink on canvas, 176½ x 136½ in. (448.3 x 346.7 cm). Mr. and Mrs. Frank G. Logan Purchase Prize and Wilson L. Mead funds, 1974.230, The Art Institute of Chicago

paintings, and a work from *The Last Supper* series. With this assembly, Roberta Smith recognized, "More than much of his recent work, these canvases give evidence of Warhol's continued evolution as an artist."[14] Since then the number of exhibitions featuring post-Pop Warhol has steadily reached a crescendo.[15] Most of these are commercial gallery productions rather than museum projects. The few European museums that have tackled the subject have either concentrated on a single series of works or treated the entirety of Warhol's work beginning with *Mao* in 1972 (fig. 3) as a consistent whole. However, there is a clear conceptual and stylistic break between the work of the 1970s and that of the 1980s. Some have proposed that the *Skulls* series (1976, fig. 4) announces the beginning of the late work.[16] Yet it employs the same representational strategy and production technique as the earlier *Mao* and *Hammer and Sickle* series (1976). In fact, Warhol's work does not undergo a radical transformation until he creates the *Oxidation Paintings* in 1977–78, which the artist confirms in his biography was an important transitional moment in his life.

Accordingly, *Warhol's Last Decade* centers on a select body of paintings, beginning with the *Oxidation Paintings* and *Shadows* from 1978, and critically analyzes this work to provide a rubric for understanding the final phase of Warhol's artistic development. Through these works Warhol expresses his personal artistic voice behind the public business ventures of his print commissions, television productions, and fashion engagements. In a spirit of artistic inventiveness he explored the dialectics of abstraction and representation, hand painting and the mechanical image, and surface and meaning. And although he was willing to entrust photography and printing to assistants and workshops, it was clearly important to him that he be the one to execute the painting on these personal works.[17] Through these paintings we witness Warhol grappling with two poles in his work: his role as a creator of mechanically produced imagery and his extraordinary technical facility as a painter and draftsman. Articulating his artistic range, he reveals himself as a mature artist in full command of his entire repertoire.

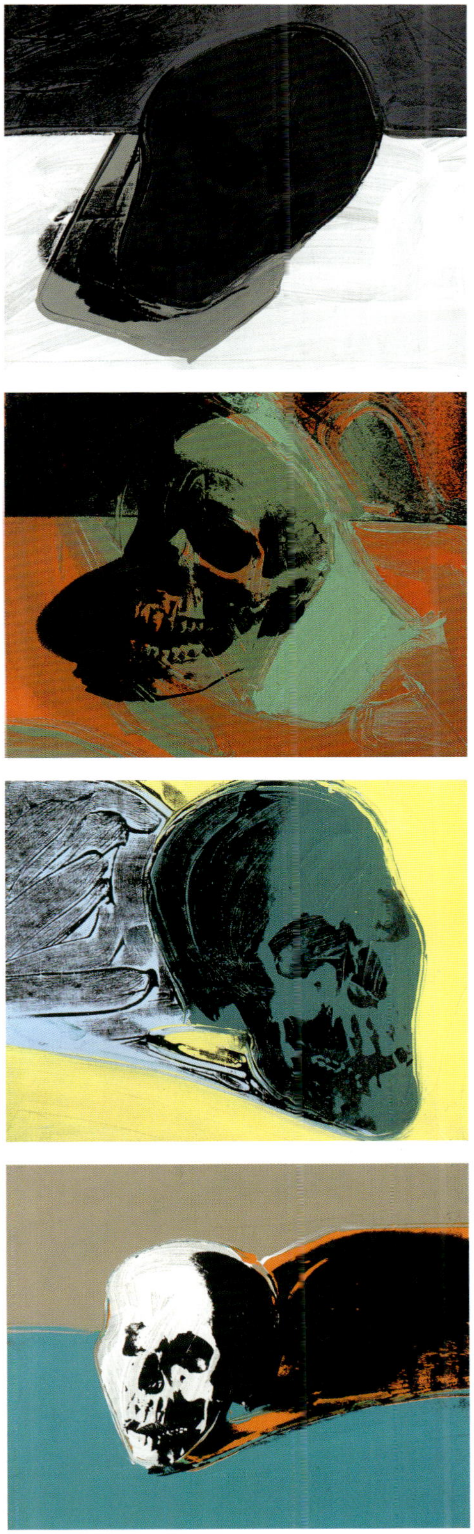

Fig. 4. *Skulls*, 1976. Acrylic and silkscreen ink on canvas, 15 x 19 in. (38.1 x 48.2 cm) each. The Baltimore Museum of Art: Purchase with funds provided by Laura R. Burrows-Jackson, Baltimore, and partial gift of The Andy Warhol Foundation for the Visual Arts, Inc., BMA 1994.25–28

The explosion of artistic innovation and productivity that characterize Warhol's late period was preceded by a brief but intense period of self-doubt, reminiscent of the anxiety he felt when he quit painting in 1965, fearing that he "was running out of things to paint." As he told the dealer

Ivan Karp, "[T]here's nothing left for me . . . I'm a popular character. . . . but I've got no images."[18] The artist's interviews and diary entries beginning in the mid-1970s bear evidence of his eroding self-confidence, during which he reflected on the validity of his art and introspectively sought answers to his anxiety. Throughout his career, Warhol was self-conscious about his artistic reputation and his celebrity. But by the time he turned fifty in August 1978, precisely ten years after the assassination attempt, he was consumed with a mid-life reexamination of himself and his accomplishments. His critical reception was at a nadir, as many in the art world dismissed him as too commercial. Pervasive doubt besieged him: "I wasn't creative since I was shot."[19]

Warhol's critical evaluation of himself is evident in the little-known *Self-Portrait* series that he created in 1978 (pls. 1–4), his first such works since the photo-booth and "mum voyeur" portraits of the previous decade (figs. 5, 6). Compared to the full-faced, jutting-jaw confidence of his youthful photo-booth portrait or the carefully cultivated persona of the voyeur with a furrowed brow—Warhol at the zenith of his celebrity—the multiple exposures of the 1978 negative portraits suggest a confused identity fraught with uncertainty. The reversed images further reinforce the metaphor of the artist examining the deep shadows and dark recesses of his own psyche with piercing eyes. From the same year, Warhol's better-known *Self-Portrait with Skull* (pls. 5, 7) and *Self-Portrait (Strangulation)* (pls. 6, 8) portray the artist reflecting on his own mortality or, as Kynaston McShine aptly phrased it, "Warhol as Hamlet."[20]

Warhol's period of introspection gave way to one of retrospection, during which he revisited and reinterpreted some of his most successful ideas and, simultaneously, experimented with new subjects. He had openly discussed with his friends his desire to make art again, and for Warhol that meant painting. And, given that he matured during the hegemony of Abstract Expressionism, "serious" painting for Warhol meant abstraction. It was clear to everyone in Warhol's studio that he wanted to create abstract paintings—but in his own unique, paradoxical manner. This new direction was almost a reversal of the infamous moment in the early 1960s when Warhol invited his friend the filmmaker

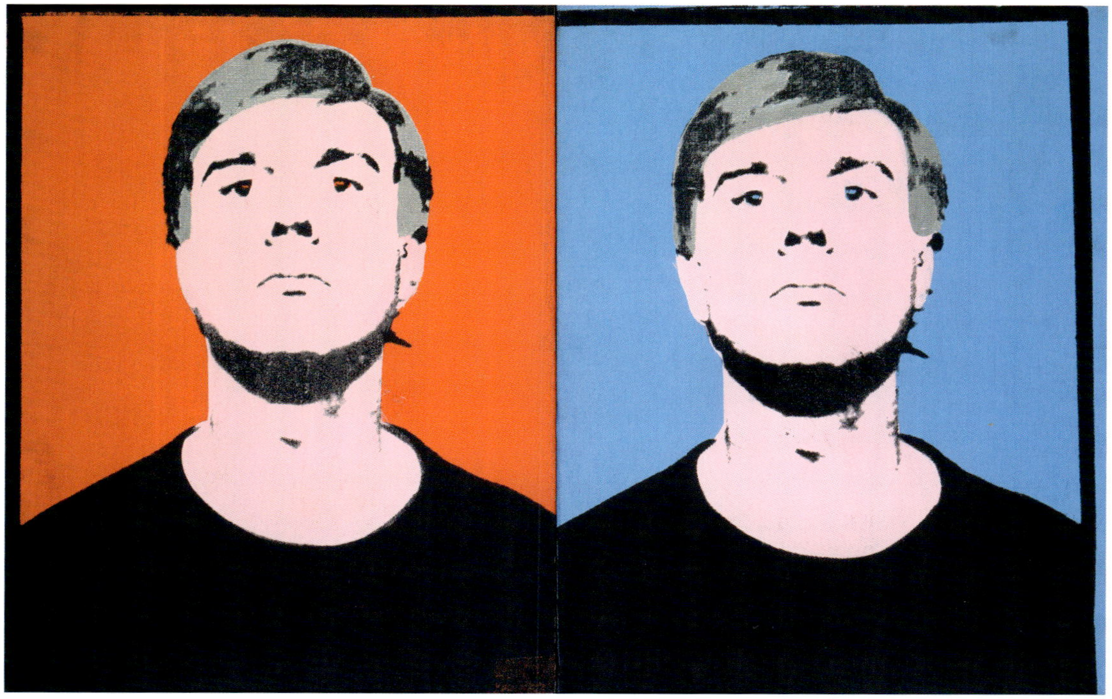

Fig. 5. *Self-Portrait*, 1964. Acrylic and silkscreen ink on canvas, two panels, 20 x 16 in. (50.8 x 40.6 cm) each. VG Bild-Kunst Bonn

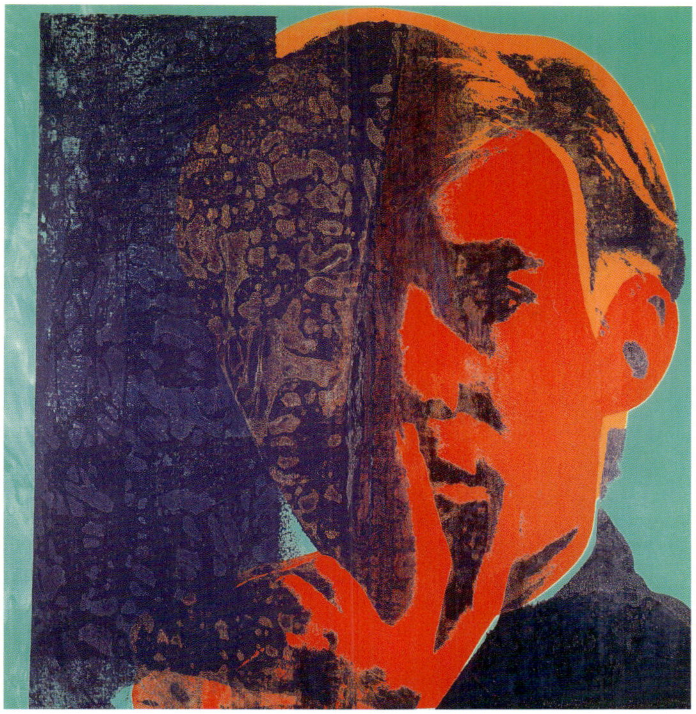

Fig. 6. *Self-Portrait*, 1967. Acrylic silkscreened, brushed, and stenciled on canvas, 72 x 72 in. (183 x 183 cm). Private collection

Emile de Antonio into his studio and showed him two paintings of Coca-Cola bottles, one painted with expressive brushstrokes and the other painted in a tight, cool proto-Pop style (figs. 7, 8). De Antonio belittled the former as "ridiculous" and suggested that he destroy it, choosing the latter and thus, according to legend, launching Warhol into Pop.[21] He had reached the proverbial fork in the road of his career and decided to take one path. Nearly twenty years later the artist returned to this moment and chose to explore both styles.

By this point, Warhol had essentially quit making movies, having finished his last one, *Andy Warhol's Bad*, in 1976. He clearly differentiated his artistic activities from his business enterprises. Warhol Enterprises continued with its business ventures, *Interview* magazine and the continuous stream of portrait commissions, and Warhol had begun new ventures in television and fashion modeling, activities that were essential to marketing his public persona and "to keep the business going."[22] But his principal work at the "office" on Union Square occurred in the studio, where he and his assistant Ronnie Cutrone were busy creating the *Oxidation Paintings* and the *Shadows* in a spirit of active experimentation.[23]

With the *Oxidation Paintings* (pls. 10–15), Warhol made a departure of seismic proportions from his screened Pop images and society portraits.[24] For the source of this idea he reached into his storage bins and pulled out a conceptual work from the early 1960s, a white canvas on which he had urinated. According to Cutrone, Warhol wondered aloud if this long-shelved pun on painting could be revived. He began a variety of chemical experiments to transform this concept of the invisible painting into visually viable artworks.[25] Ironically, the rich gold and acidic green of the oxidizing metallic paints radiate the lushness of the finest Color Field paintings. With their complex, naturally varied color and texture flowing across the surface, the works possess a striking visual presence. Their effect recalls Warhol's early aspirations for painting: "All painting is fact, and that is enough; the paintings are charged with their very presence. The situation, physical ideas. Physical presence—I feel this is the comment."[26] Although he was referring to his early Pop paintings, the same principles apply to the *Oxidation Paintings*. Warhol's parody of Pollock and Color Field painting is obvious in these works. And he was doubtless aware of the reference to Duchamp's *Fountain* (1917) when he turned his studio into a public bathroom,

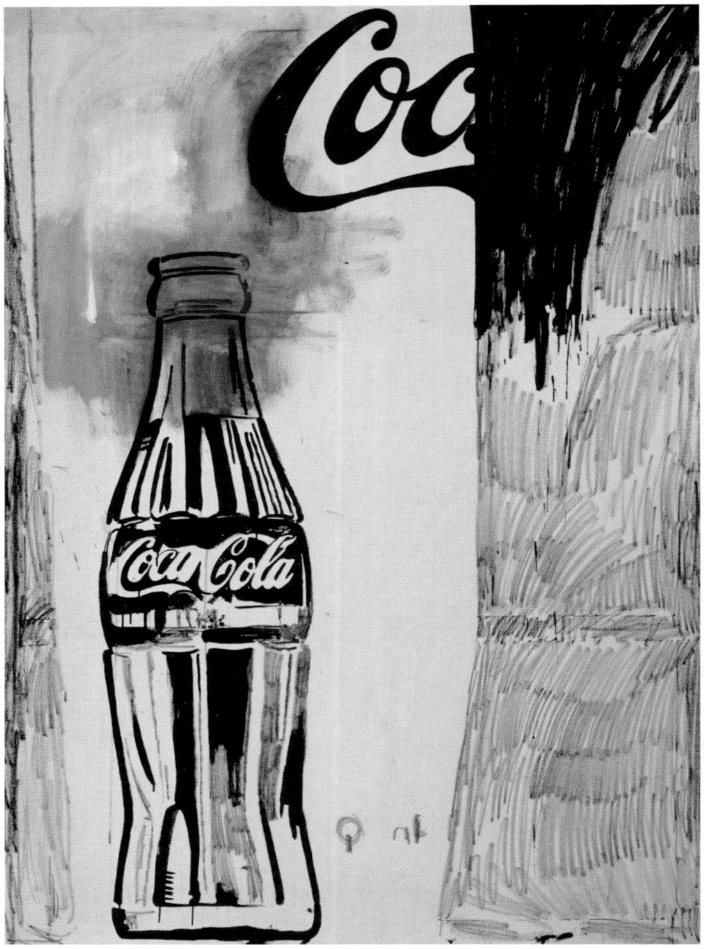

Fig. 7. *Coca-Cola [2]*, 1961. Casein and crayon on linen, 69½ x 52¼ in. (176.5 x 132.7 cm). The Andy Warhol Museum, Pittsburgh; Founding Collection, Contribution Dia Center for the Arts

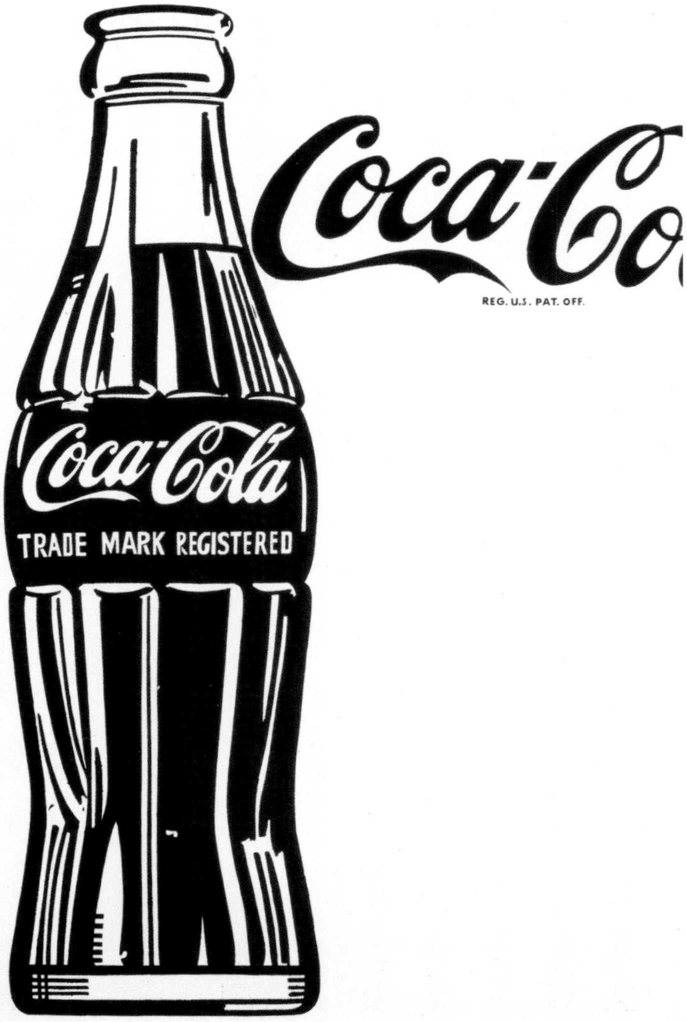

Fig. 8. *Large Coca-Cola*, c. 1962. Acrylic on canvas, 85 x 57 in. (215.9 x 144.8 cm). The Andy Warhol Foundation for the Visual Arts, Inc.

where a parade of men and women lined up to pee on the famous artist's canvases.[27] Although pissing on canvas is an impudent snub on the art form of painting, it could be argued that Warhol simultaneously demonstrated deference to his peers and predecessors among the Abstract Expressionists and Color Field artists with these beatific paintings, showing respect for their work with his description of painting as fact, which sounds remarkably like Clement Greenberg's formalist justification for abstract painting.

Warhol's closest confidants were unnerved when he ventured into abstraction, beseeching him, "But you're Andy Warhol. You have to paint *things* [author's emphasis]." The people closest to Warhol acknowledge that he clearly aspired to be an abstract artist; but, according to Cutrone, "It had to have some kind of sense of reality or humor."[28] Warhol's response was to paint something ephemeral, *Shadows* (fig. 9, pls. 16–21). Whether Warhol or Cutrone conceived this idea is not certain, but Warhol employed the same process that he used for portrait paintings: Cutrone took some Polaroids of stage-lit mat boards, then Warhol selected the image and had acetates made and traced for the screens. As he had done since the *Mao* series, Warhol whipped up a painterly surface with a large mop to create the ground on to which the shadow tracings were screened.[29] The thick impasto of the surfaces give these works the imprimatur of "high art," and the dark shadows lend them the brooding melancholy of profound meaning, providing a stark contrast to the bright colors that project through the shadows. Warhol again achieves the "physical presence" of painting, in this case by using a printing process. In the words of Trevor Fairbrother, the *Shadows* series represents the "inspired marriage of high art and mechanical reproduction."[30] Produced in two groups, these paintings introduced novel images to the history of art and shaped the characteristics of Warhol's work over the subsequent nine years.

A sequence of events in 1979 had a profound influence on the development of Warhol's late work and brought the issues surrounding his critical reception into sharp relief. Heiner Friedrich, a German gallerist recently transplanted to SoHo, proposed an exhibition of Warhol's *Shadows* at his West Broadway gallery in January (fig. 53, page 66). For this installation Warhol conceived of 102 canvases abutting one another in a continuous sequence around the gallery walls, in a manner reminiscent of his 1963 *Elvis* installation at the Ferus Gallery in Los Angeles. Warhol was very anxious about this exhibition, the biggest display of new work in New York since the *Mao* series nearly a decade earlier. He thought "the show looked good" but was nervous about the critical response. "This show will be like all the others. The reviews will be bad—my reviews always are. But the reviews of the party will be terrific."[31] In fact, much to Warhol's delight, quite the

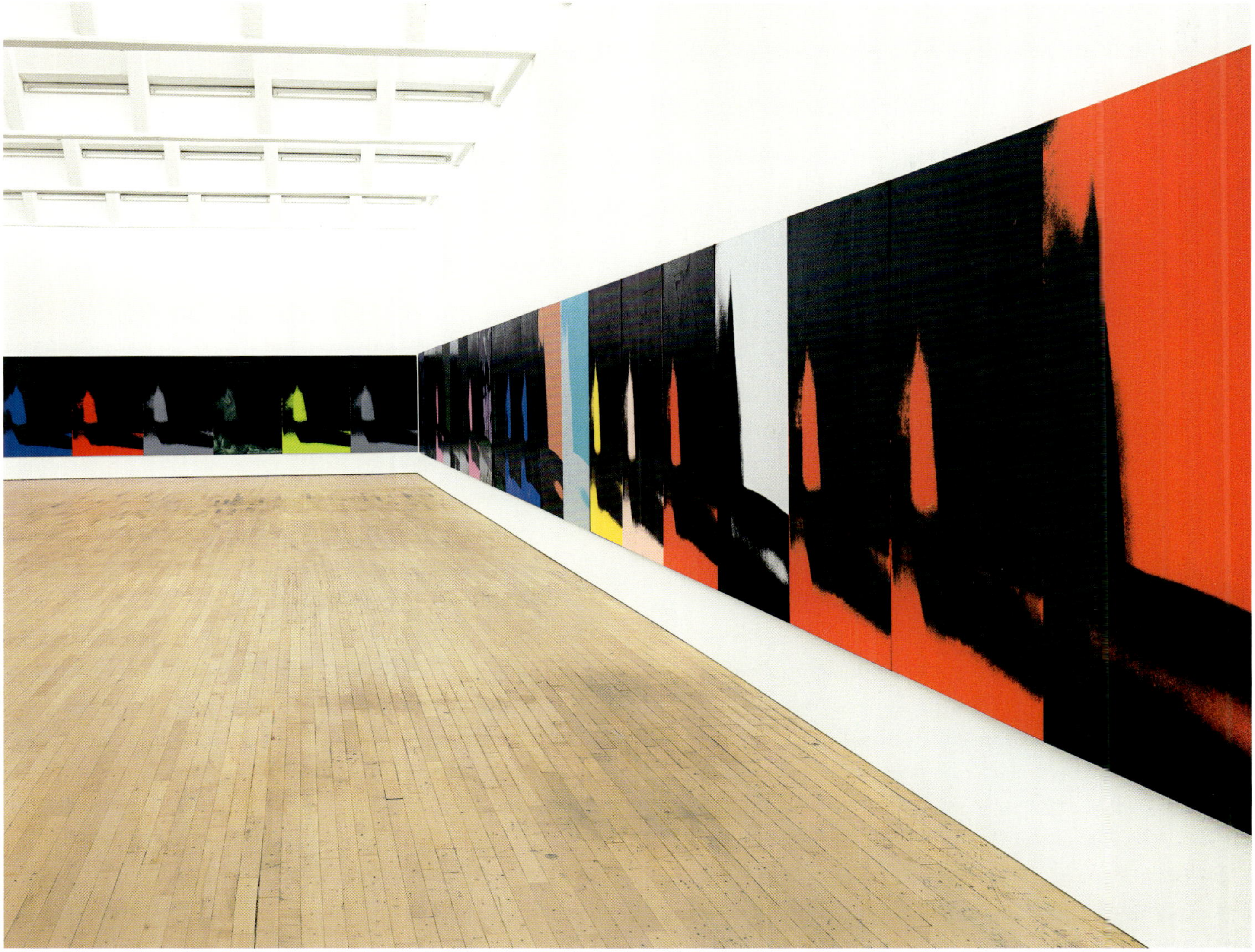

Fig. 9. Installation of *Shadow* paintings at Dia:Beacon, Beacon, New York

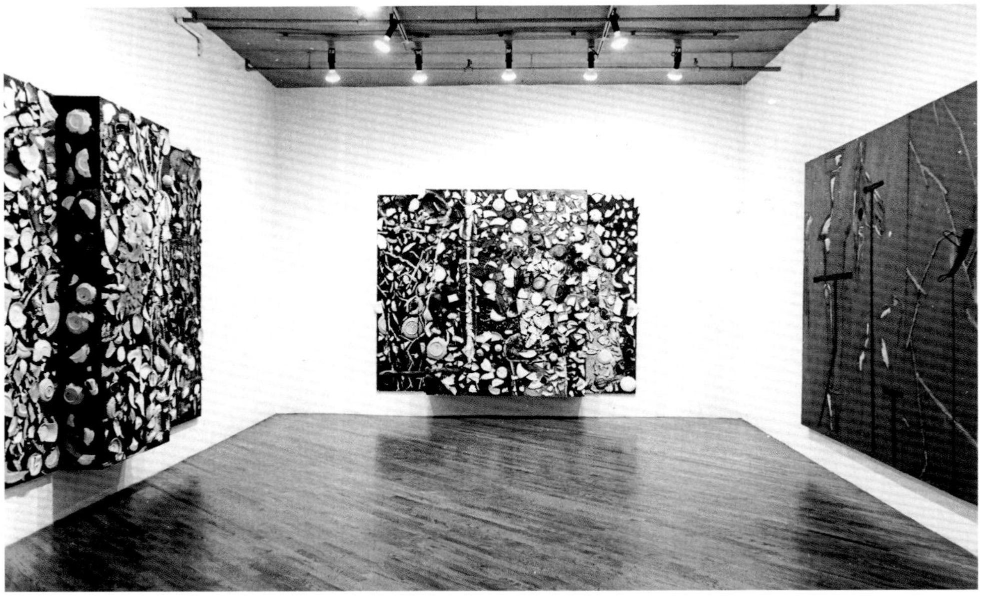

Fig. 10. Installation of *Julian Schnabel* at Mary Boone Gallery, 420 West Broadway, New York, November 10–December 6, 1979

opposite happened. These novel works startled critics, who praised them as "pregnant with signification" and "Warhol's best in recent years."[32]

The accolades buoyed the impressionable artist's fragile ego. With this encouragement, Warhol produced a number of individual paintings titled *Shadows*, in a variety of colors, in black and white, and with diamond dust (pls. 19, 20). Excited by the reception of these works, he continued to solicit new ideas for source material from friends and colleagues. Larry Rivers, a close friend, told Warhol that his dealer had encouraged him to re-create some of his popular "golden oldies," which stimulated Rivers to paint new works.[33] Warhol latched on to this notion and embarked on his *Retrospectives* and *Reversals* (1978–79, pls. 22–24), series in which he mined the iconography of his Pop period, reproducing images such as the Campbell's soup cans, Corn Flakes, cows, Marilyn, and Mona Lisa. The *Retrospectives* parlayed his Pop successes into new compositions that stretched out to be the largest canvases of his career to date; the *Reversals*—negatives of those same subjects—resulted in ghostly specters of his former icons seen through the lens of memory and reconstituted as haunting painterly abstractions.

As Warhol developed his painting practice, the Neo-Expressionists burst onto the New York art scene with the loud splatter of paint flung onto a canvas. First came an exhibition of Julian Schnabel at the Mary Boone Gallery in the fall of 1979 (fig. 10), which was followed by shows of Eric Fischl and David Salle. A new generation of art stars erupted in repudiation of the dogmatic reign of Minimal and Conceptual art and theory. The clamor of excitement around the return to painting infused new life into the art community and invigorated Warhol's painting pursuits. He was impressed with the youthful energy of this generation of painters. He loved their work, but at the same time they challenged him. In his paranoid imagination he feared that they could force him to capitulate his perceived position at the pinnacle of the New York art world.[34]

Warhol's euphoria over the *Shadows* show was short-lived. In November 1979, the Whitney Museum of American Art opened the exhibition *Andy Warhol: Portraits of the Seventies* (fig. 11), which was universally derided by the art community. Portraits of the glitterati of the decade, mixed with monumental images of Mao, lined the galleries (figs. 3, 12, 13). In the catalogue for the exhibition the august art historian Robert Rosenblum knighted Warhol as the "Court Painter to the Seventies" and credited him with single-handedly reviving grand-manner portraiture. He read into the works the psychology of the sitters and snapshots of "a human comedy of our age."[35] Unfortunately for Warhol, the show was received as a human tragicomedy. Critics condemned Warhol's commercialism, chastising him for "swimming in a sea of superficiality" and carrying "an absolute interest in the size of his bank balance." Yet, cognizant of his artistic contributions, the same critics conceded, "Warhol is still a painter of the first rank," and

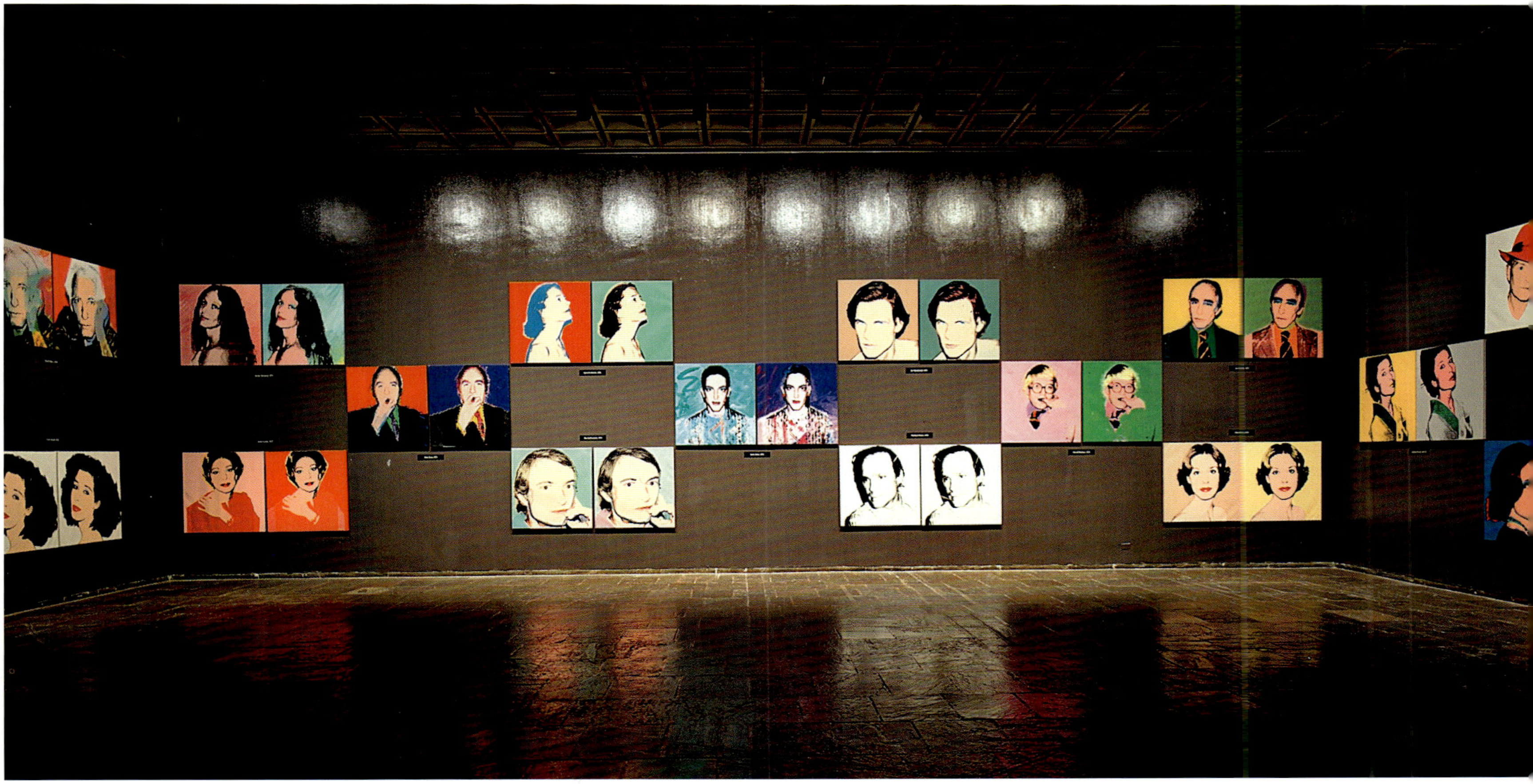

Fig. 11. Installation of *Andy Warhol: Portraits of the Seventies* (November 20, 1979–January 27, 1980) at the Whitney Museum of American Art, New York

Fig. 12. *Liza Minnelli*, 1979. Acrylic and silkscreen ink on linen, 40 x 40 in. (102 x 102 cm). The Andy Warhol Museum, Pittsburgh; Founding Collection, Contribution Dia Center for the Arts

Fig. 13. *Liza Minnelli*, 1979. Acrylic and silkscreen ink on linen, 40 x 40 in. (102 x 102 cm). The Andy Warhol Museum, Pittsburgh; Founding Collection, Contribution Dia Center for the Arts

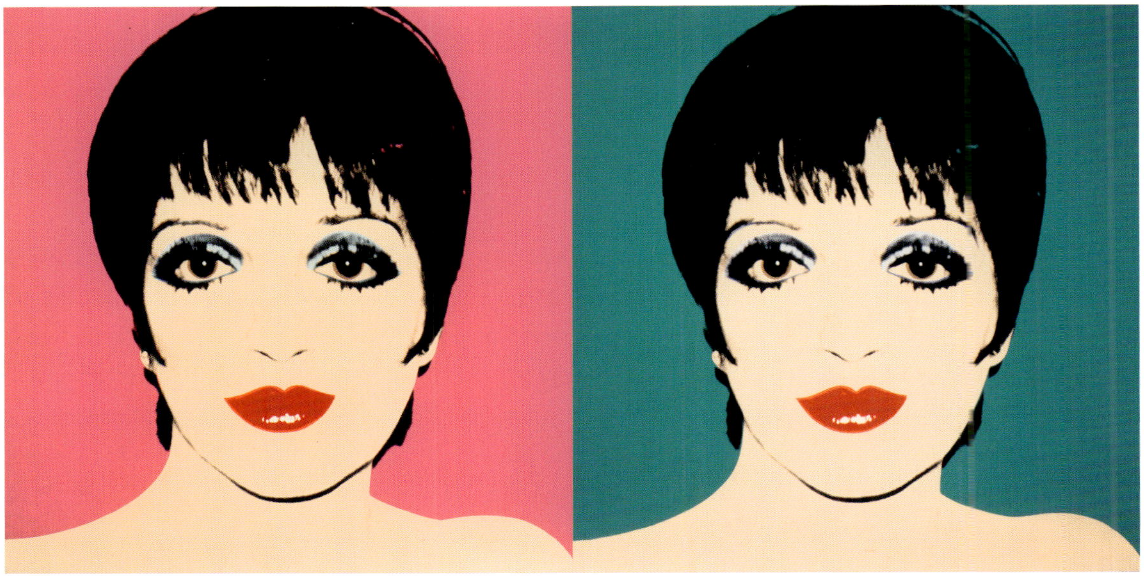

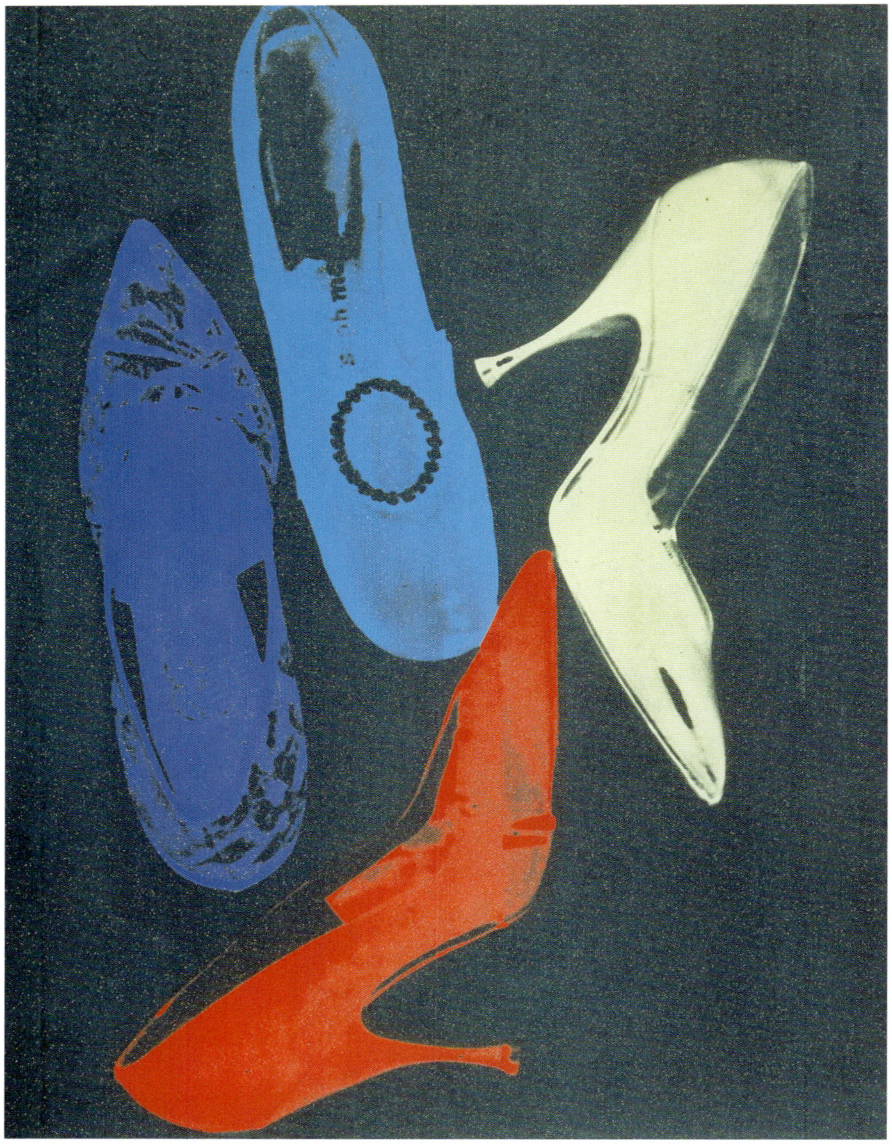

Fig. 14. *Shoes*, 1980. Acrylic, diamond dust, and silkscreen ink on canvas, 70 x 90 in. (177.8 x 228.6 cm). VG Bild-Kunst Bonn

recommended that he "desert his fashionable nonentities and return to the convicts, hammers and sickles and electric chairs."[36] Although Warhol had been hardened by harsh criticism throughout the 1970s, he was deeply affected by their words. The reception of the portrait show cast a pall over Warhol's studio production and dampened the enthusiasm he had developed toward his work in the previous two years.

During the next year, Warhol produced relatively few personal paintings in his studio. But the reviews neither lessened the ever-greater demand among European and American high society for Warhol's portraits nor dampened the social cachet surrounding Warholism. Over the next two years he concentrated his efforts on the commissioned portraits and the release of two books, *Andy Warhol's Exposures* (1979) and *POPism: The Warhol '60s* (1980), for which he did a promotional tour around the country. He also began to perform for Vincent Fremont's television series *Andy Warhol's T.V.* (1980–82). These were successes for Warhol Enterprises. His publications even received rave reviews in the *New Yorker*. But the dismal critical response to the *Portraits* show still weighed heavily on Warhol, who could not understand "why everybody gave my show at the Whitney a bad review."[37]

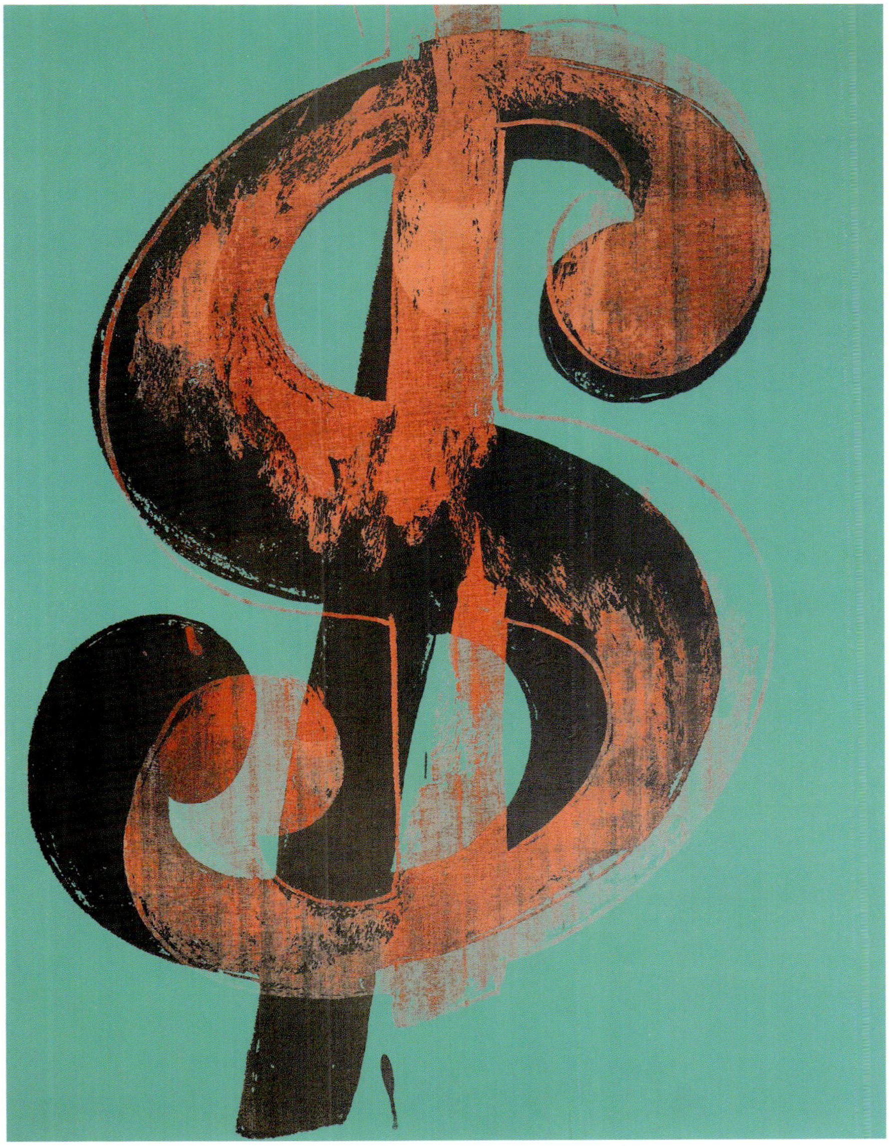

Fig. 15. *$*, 1981. Acrylic and silkscreen ink on canvas, 90 x 70 in. (230 x 178 cm). Mugrabi Collection

At this point, instead of following the path of abstraction in the lauded *Shadows*, Warhol was preoccupied with the idea of reworking his earlier artistic successes by expanding the premise behind the *Retrospectives* and *Reversals*. In 1980 he went "back to [his] roots" as a commercial artist in the 1950s, producing "Diamond Dust" *Shoes* (1980, fig. 14).[38] He bought a large selection of ladies' shoes, scattered them across the floor, and photographed them in tightly cropped arrangements. He then sent the images to his printer, Rupert Smith, to be screened and coated with a glittering surface of diamond dust. Over the next two years, Warhol refreshed versions of his *$* (1981, fig. 15) and revamped the ideas behind the *Hammer and Sickle* series (1976) into his *Guns* and *Knives* (1981–82, figs. 16, 17). He assembled these paintings for an exhibition at the Leo Castelli Gallery in January 1982; however, as Ronnie Cutrone recounts, the guns and knives were edited out at the last minute and the show consisted solely of dollar-sign paintings. In the wake of the Whitney reviews, Warhol must have been devastated when *Artforum* reported, "In recent years his shows have been increasingly disappointing and this latest is the most disappointing yet. . . . Warhol's work has always been empty, but now it seems empty-headed."[39]

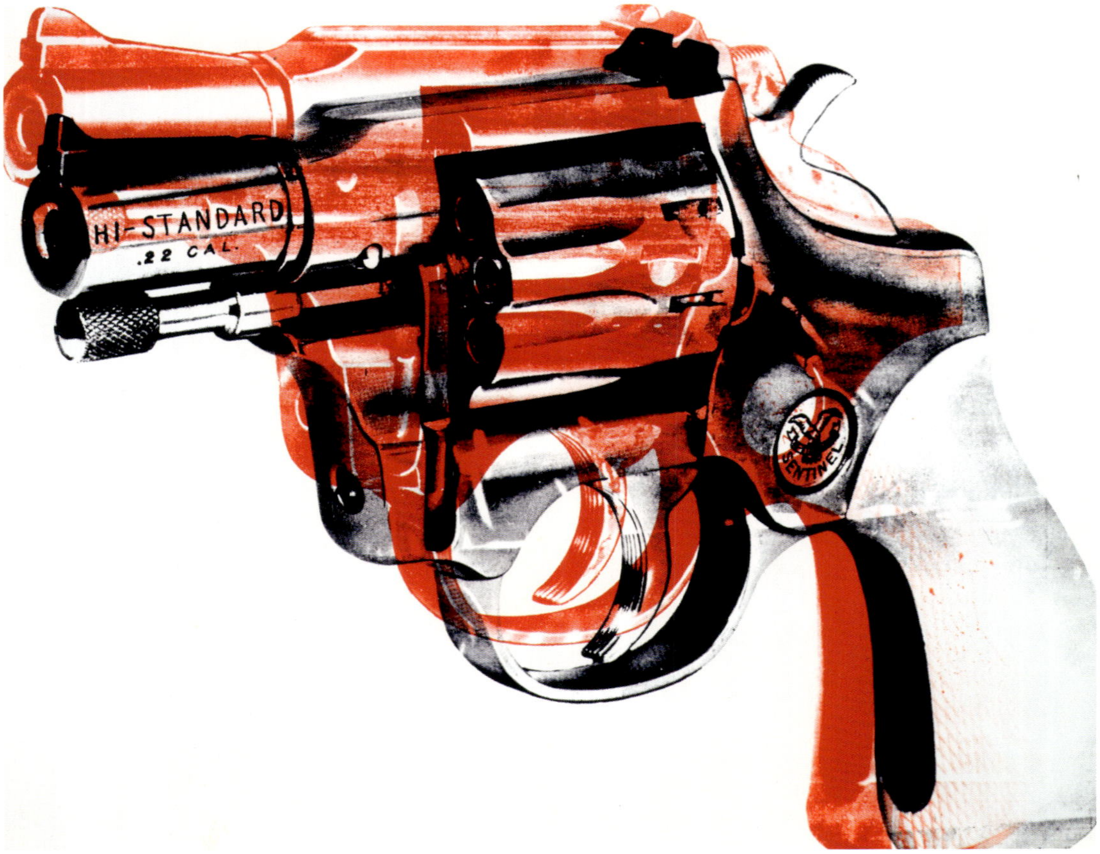

Fig. 16. *Gun*, 1981. Acrylic and silkscreen ink on linen, 70 x 90 x 1¼ in. (177.8 x 228.6 x 3.2 cm). The Andy Warhol Museum, Pittsburgh; Founding Collection, Contribution The Andy Warhol Foundation for the Visual Arts, Inc.

A few months before he read this harsh review, Warhol had experienced another moment of revelation. In November 1981, while touring in Toronto, he saw an exhibition of "masterpieces" by a range of artists from Paul Gauguin to Henry Moore at the Art Gallery of Ontario: "Really impressive . . . I mean, my work looks like nothing compared to that stuff. Oh, I'm getting to hate my—I must be—all I do is tour, everybody else works. I have to get back and do something. I might be well known, but I'm sure not turning out good work. I'm not turning out anything."[40] Stimulated by his Toronto experience he returned to the studio and began to explore new forms of abstraction and new subjects of personal significance. He remarked that he considered his *Guns* and *Knives* as abstract compositions. Yet, they are more than simply formal designs. In creating *Guns* and *Knives* in tandem with *$*, Warhol fulfilled his youthful ambition to create symbols of contemporary society, in this instance conflating issues of money, power, and violence during a time that witnessed the dawning of the neo-conservative Ronald Reagan era and sectarian conflicts around the globe.[41]

Warhol's desire to imbue his late works with meaningful content harks back to an ambition he had early in his career, before he had solidified his public persona as

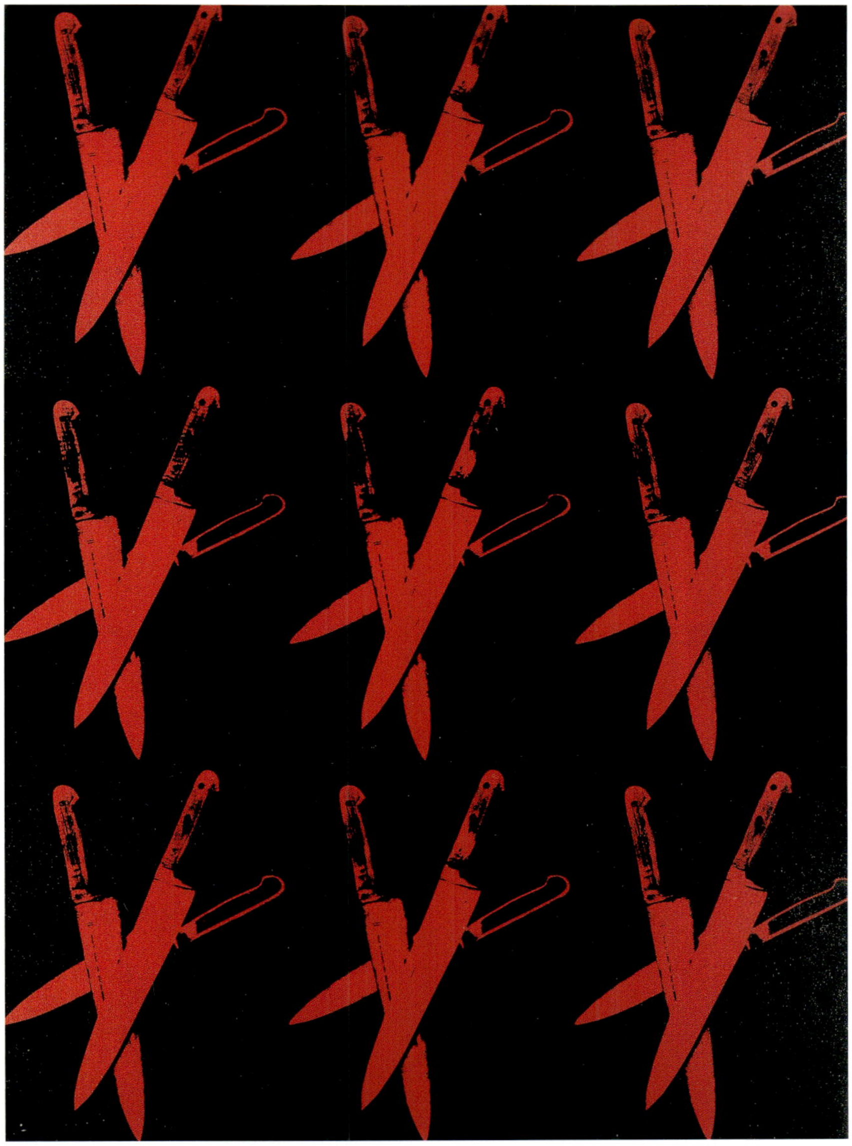

Fig. 17. *Knives*, 1982. Acrylic and silkscreen ink on canvas, $70\frac{7}{8}$ x 52 in. (180 x 132 cm). Mugrabi Collection

the aloof mirror of society, when he aspired to have his Pop images be "a statement of the symbols of the harsh, impersonal products and brash materialistic objects on which America is built today. . . . [T]he practical but impermanent symbols that sustain us."[42] The "gee whiz," "everything is great" Andy was a public mask that protected the personal Warhol, who appeared in his late paintings, asking probing questions and seeking meaning: "What is art? Does it really come out of you or is it a product?"[43]

Warhol continued to seek images that not only functioned as formal abstractions but also were laden with meaning. He created the *Crosses* (1981–82, fig. 18) and *Eggs* (1982, figs. 19, 20) series, which added the metaphor of religion to his images of money and power. Warhol, who was raised in the Eastern Orthodox church, privately practiced Catholicism. Recognizing his religious devotion, we can read the crosses, which surface in his artwork for the first time, as symbols of his faith.[44] The *Eggs* carry similar Christological references to Easter and the rebirth of Christ. Holidays were always very important to Warhol, who produced cards and gifts to be distributed to friends and clients on these occasions, and the Easter greetings he had made early in his career as a commercial artist served as the source of this image.[45] Drawing from his memory of

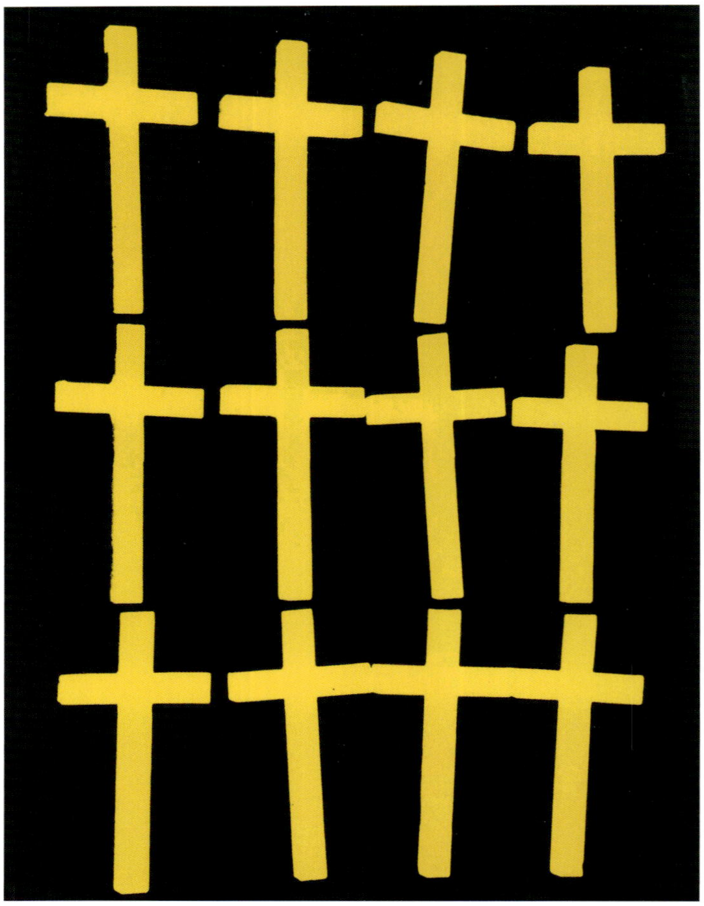

Fig. 18. *Crosses*, 1981–82. Acrylic and silkscreen ink on canvas, 90 x 70 in. (230 x 178 cm). Mugrabi Collection

Fig. 19. *Eggs*, 1982. Acrylic and silkscreen ink on linen, 90 x 70 in. (228.6 x 177.8 cm). The Andy Warhol Museum, Pittsburgh; Founding Collection, Contribution The Andy Warhol Foundation for the Visual Arts, Inc.

Fig. 20. *Eggs*, 1982. Acrylic and silkscreen ink on canvas, 90 x 70 in. (228.7 x 177.9 cm). The Baltimore Museum of Art: Purchase with funds provided by the Fanny B. Thalheimer Memorial Fund; and partial gift of The Andy Warhol Foundation for the Visual Arts, Inc.

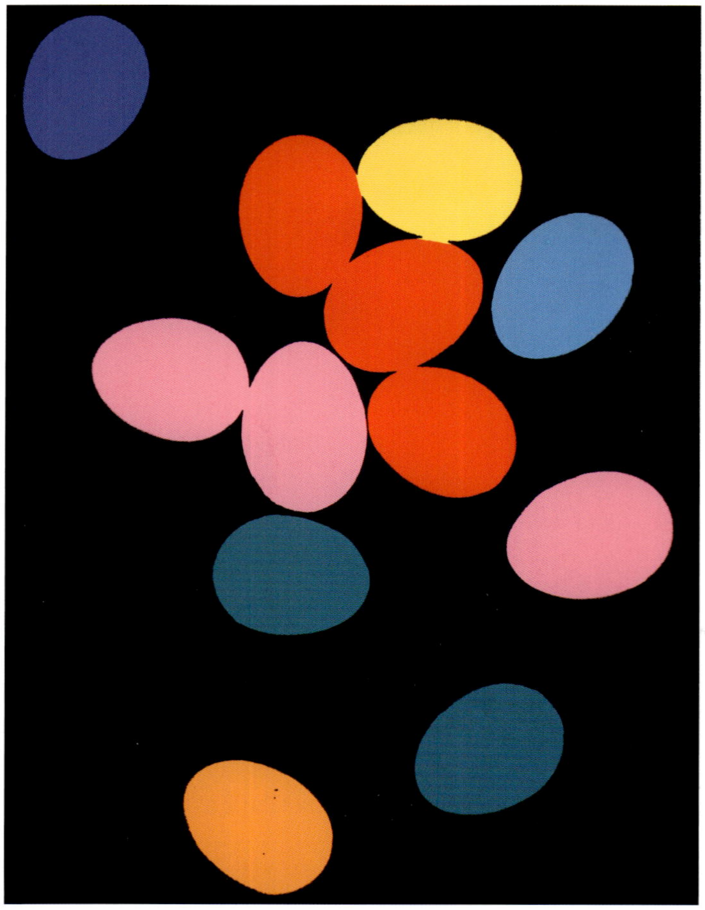

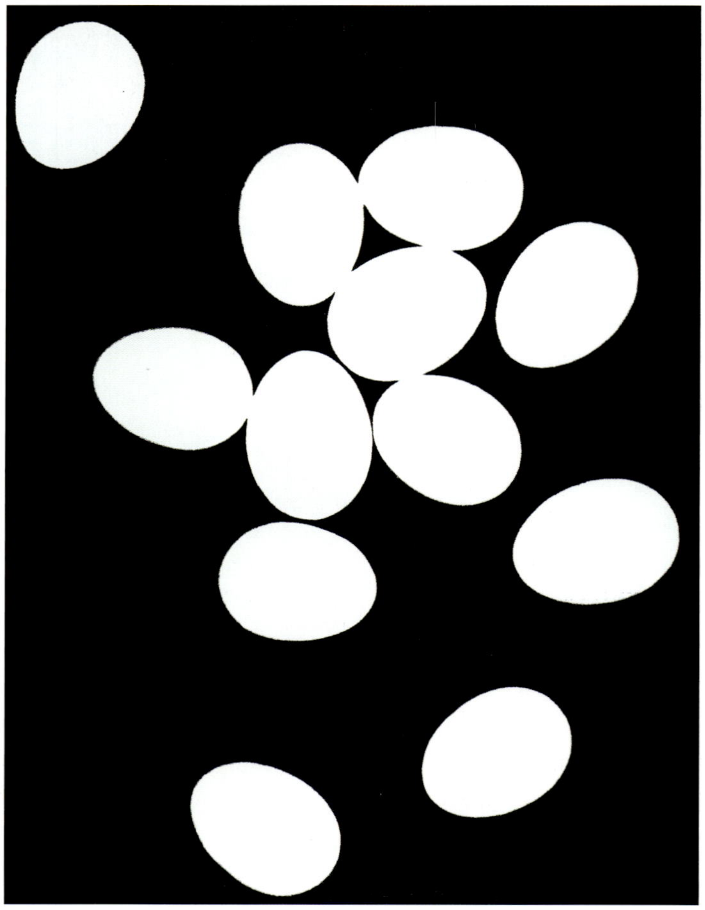

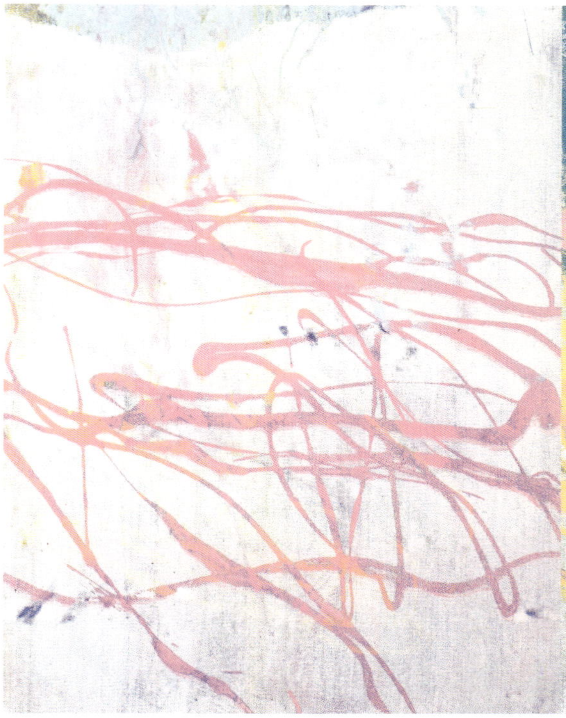

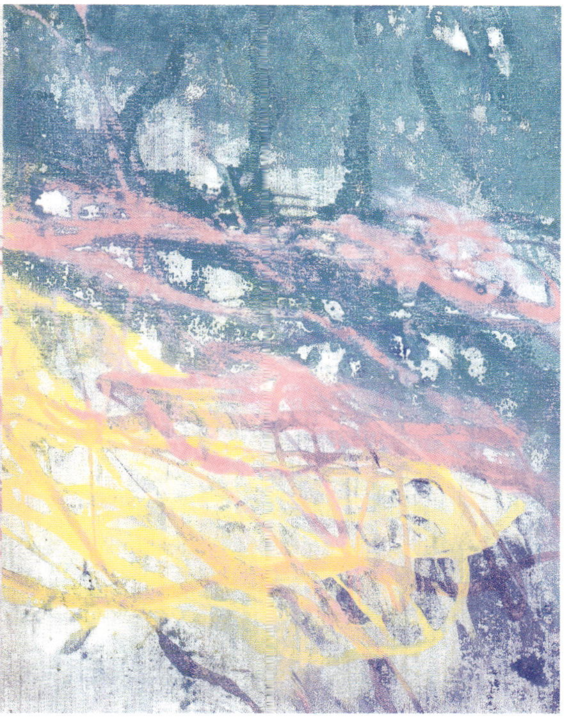

Fig. 21. *Abstract Painting*, 1982. Acrylic and silkscreen ink on canvas, 20 x 16 in. (50.8 x 40.6 cm). Anton Kern Gallery, New York

Fig. 22. *Abstract Painting*, 1982. Acrylic and silkscreen ink on canvas, 20 x 16 in. (50.8 x 40.6 cm). Anton Kern Gallery, New York

these early cards, he reinterpreted the ovals into an abstract arrangement, combining allusions to spiritual rebirth with references to the dot paintings of Larry Poons and Peter Young. All of the works of this period—*$*, *Guns*, *Knives*, *Crosses*, and *Eggs*—were created in the same screenprint technique as the portraits.

At the same time Warhol was searching for new, meaningful imagery, he also explored the potential for abstract gesture as pictorial design, while subverting the manual touch through the mechanical print. In 1982 he produced a series of fifteen small abstractions that appear to be Abstract Expressionist paintings (1982, figs. 21, 22). However, they were created entirely by a series of screens of varying transparency to reproduce the effect of layered paint.[46] No source is known for these images. Warhol may have brushed them as drawings, photographed them, and then made screens for printing. These wonderful little works give insight into the range of Warhol's experiments with abstraction, and they appear to have emboldened him to venture into abstraction for a commissioned "portrait." Filpucci, a Florentine yarn manufacturer, commissioned Warhol to create a series of paintings of its products in 1983. After working in the studio on a variety of abstract arrangements of yarn spools, the artist unraveled the yarn into a scatter across his seamless paper and selected an all-over composition reminiscent of Pollock's drip paintings (pls. 25–30). Rupert Smith gave these screenprints his "rainbow roll" and created a series of brilliantly colored, beautifully decorative Abstract Expressionist canvases.[47] The *Yarn* paintings possess neither the variety of surface incident nor the pointed cynicism of Warhol's previous venture into Abstract Expressionism, the *Oxidation Paintings*; however, they do fully realize the Matissean splendor that was so important to him.

In the works created between 1981 and 1983 Warhol was clearly grappling with his burgeoning ideas about the dualities of representation and abstraction, printing and painting, and surface and meaning. Only after working through these exercises did he once again breach the creative barrier and forge novel images in a novel technique, creating the *Rorschach* series (pls. 31–35), the most significant departure from his mechanically reproduced work since the *Oxidation Paintings*. In his obsessive pursuit of painting Warhol asked his studio assistant, Jay Shriver, for "a new idea." Shriver suggested the old idea of Rorschach tests, which Warhol had done as exercises when he was a student at the Carnegie Institute. Warhol instructed Shriver to make a series of inkblot studies (c. 1983, fig. 23), and intrigued by their mysterious shapes, he enlarged these folded-paper studies into monochrome paintings. Taking advantage of the fact that for the first time he had an entire floor at the Union Square building, he expanded this idea to a monumental scale.[48] He enlisted the whole studio staff. Shriver would prepare one-half of the canvas—sometimes stretching ten to fourteen feet in length—then the crew would fold the canvas and get on their hands and knees to roll the ink, using the large bolts on which the raw canvas was delivered. In essence, this translated Warhol's early blotted-line drawing technique into painting. The physical energy spent laboring over these massive canvases generated a great deal of excitement in the studio. Warhol would duck away from appointments in the "office" to work in the back studio because "he was having so much fun."[49]

The *Rorschach* paintings, by virtue of their monolithic scale, dominate a room. Like their namesake, the tests conceived by the Swiss psychiatrist Hermann Rorschach, Warhol's totemic forms evoke deep mysteries lurking under the surface. Yet they also function as surface design in the form of delicate lacework or richly mottled pools of ink. The gold *Rorschach* paintings, in particular, radiate the opulence of grand gates. After about a year, Warhol moved on from these personal experiments, and they were not exhibited until after his death. However, several were chosen in 1986 for a group exhibition on contemporary abstraction, where they attracted the attention of art critic Robert Nickas, who linked them to the work of the younger painters Peter Halley and Philip Taaffe. Nickas read these paintings simply

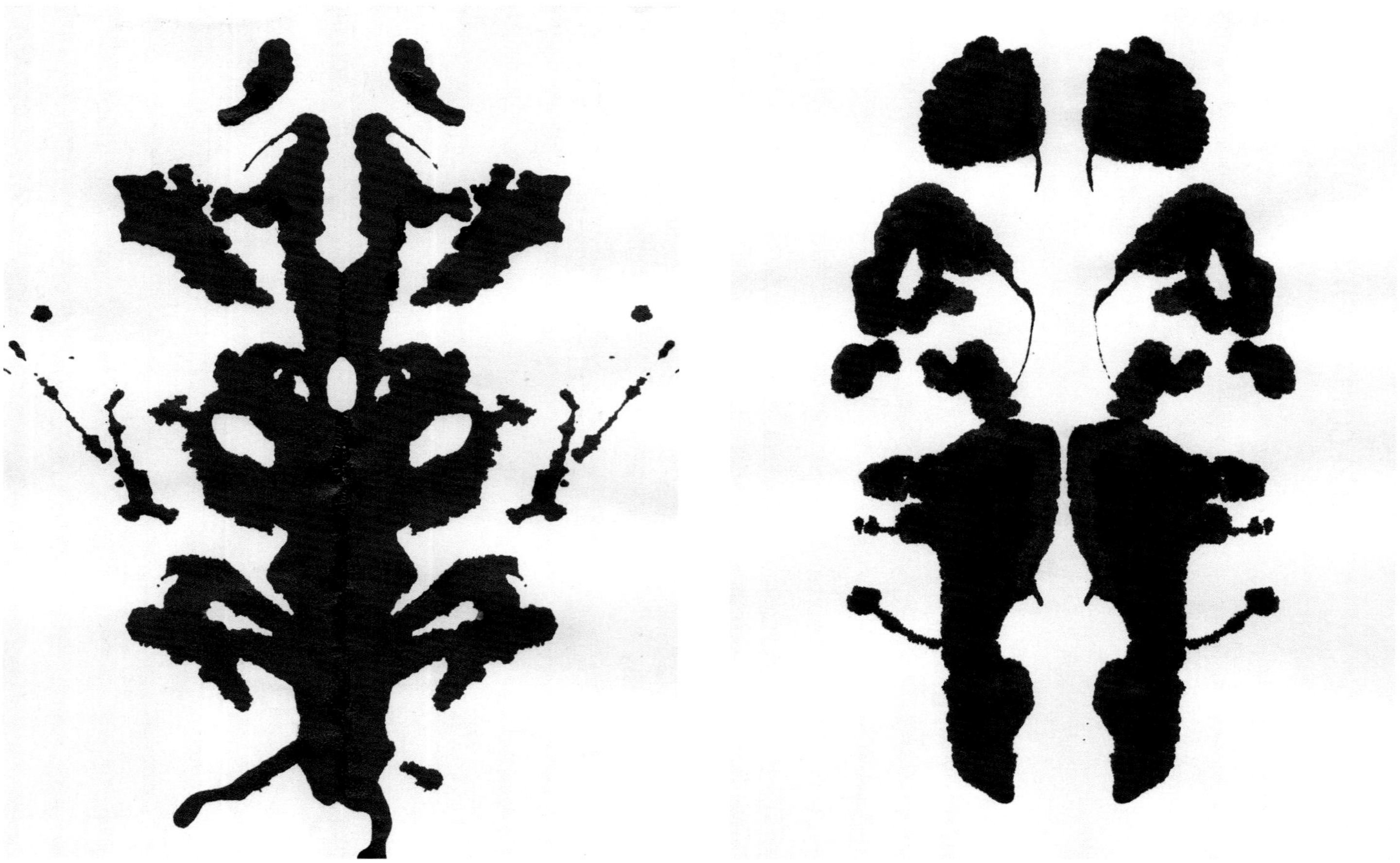

Fig. 23. Four sheets used as source material for Andy Warhol's *Rorschach* series, c. 1983. Archives, The Andy Warhol Museum, Pittsburgh

as meaningless abstract exercises: "There's nothing there. It has no thereness. It is a completely dumb, blank empty painting."[50] Rosalind Krauss picked up on this argument in her essay for the first exhibition of the *Rorschach* series, in 1996, interpreting the paintings as a conscious attempt on Warhol's part to negate the modernist strategy of reduction.[51] However, Warhol clearly states, "[T]he *Rorschachs* is a good idea and doing it just means that I have to spend some time writing down what I see in the *Rorschachs*. That would make it more interesting."[52]

Among artists it is a common practice to make trades with other artists whose work you respect. Warhol had been in the habit of offering portraits in exchange for works by artists that he wished to collect. In October 1982 the Swiss dealer Bruno Bischofberger introduced Warhol to a young painter, Jean-Michel Basquiat, whom he was now representing. Warhol was intrigued to discover that the person he had known as SAMO, the graffiti artist, whom he had helped with a handout of cash on the street corner, was now working with Bischofberger. Warhol took a Polaroid of Basquiat for a portrait, and Basquiat proposed that they shoot a Polaroid of the two of them together. Much to Warhol's surprise, Basquiat's assistant returned that afternoon with a painted double-portrait of Warhol and Basquiat based on the photo.[53] The audacity and facility of the young painter, who claimed that his assistant had painted the picture, impressed Warhol, who returned a portrait of Basquiat screened on to an *Oxidation Painting* (fig. 24). A few weeks later he invited Basquiat back for lunch and encouraged him to paint on to some of his small canvases. The energy of the work so enthralled Warhol that he kept

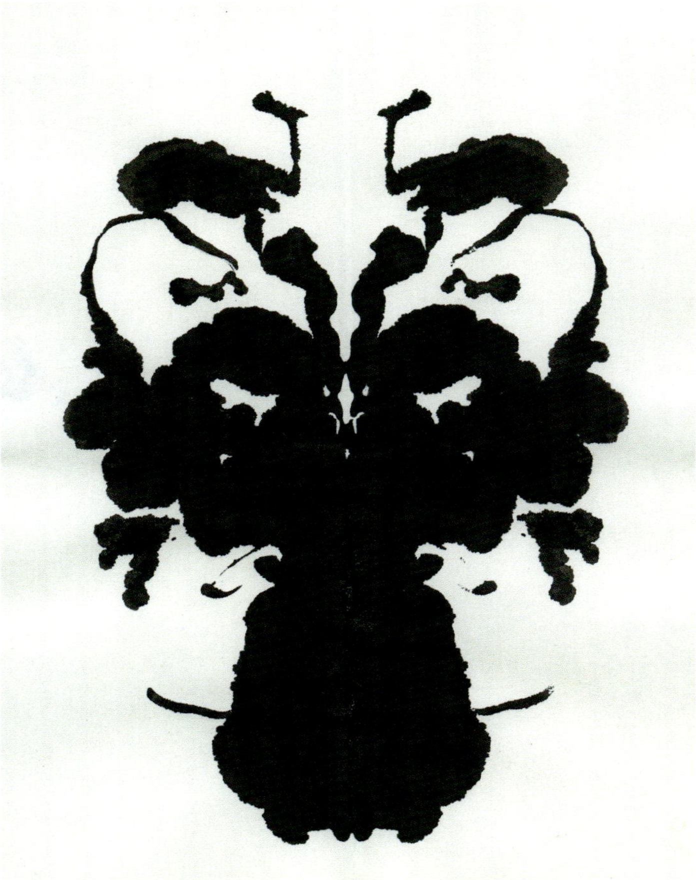

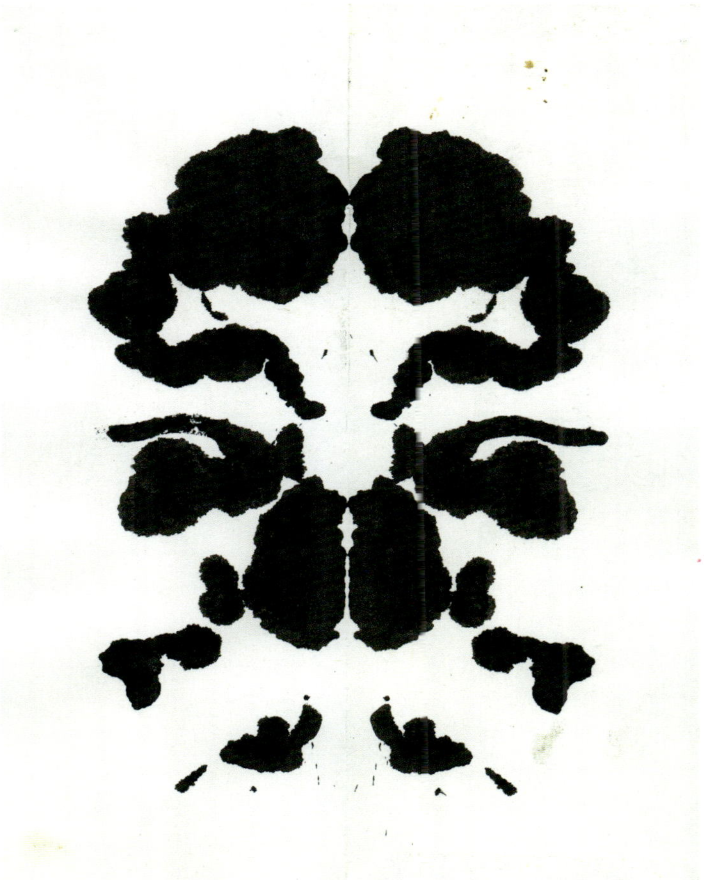

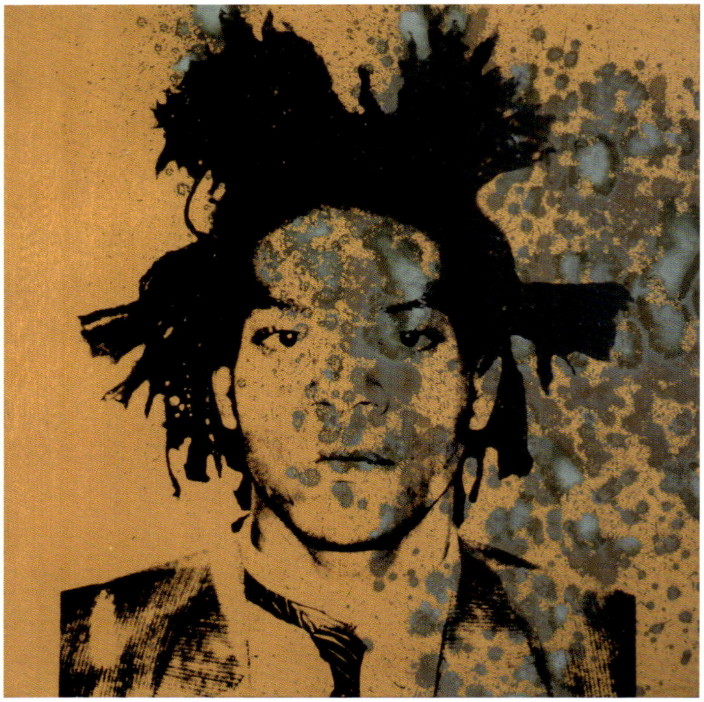

Fig. 24. *Jean-Michel Basquiat*, c. 1982. Acrylic, silkscreen ink, and urine on canvas, 40 x 40 in. (101.6 x 101.6 cm). The Andy Warhol Museum, Pittsburgh; Founding Collection, Contribution The Andy Warhol Foundation for the Visual Arts, Inc.

his assistants after hours to create even larger works for Basquiat to work on the next day. From this catalytic circumstance other collaborations ensued.

The impetuousness of the youthful Basquiat energized Warhol's studio and his social life. The two artists immediately bonded and over the next two and a half years developed a close relationship, painting together in the studio in the afternoon and clubbing at night. Warhol immersed himself in the community of young artists in SoHo, participating in the gallery and studio circuit with Sandro Chia, Francesco Clemente, Keith Haring, Julian Schnabel, and a host of others. He was invigorated by challenging new art and a social set bustling with creative people.[54]

Recognizing the extraordinary potential of the collaborative process, Bischofberger introduced Clemente into the mix and commissioned a series of collaborations among Basquiat, Clemente, and Warhol.[55] Each of the artists started four canvases, which were then circulated to the others for their contributions. The intention was for each to work independently, as in the Surrealist *cadavre exquis*, or exquisite corpse. Bringing together three of the principal painters who were participating in the current revival of the art form was a bold and ambitious idea on the part of Bischofberger. The gallerist aspired to meld three very talented painters with different voices, from three different backgrounds and generations, who would work in syncopation, draw on each other's qualities and strengths, and produce a suite of paintings that spoke with a unique voice. They succeeded in a number of the canvases, including *Alba's Breakfast* (1984, pl. 38). Begun by Clemente, Warhol responded by screening a GE logo and painting an egg still life; and Basquiat completed the work with his "primitive" faces and graffiti scripts. The confluence of Basquiat's attacking brushstroke, Warhol's facile line, and Clemente's lyrical figure results in a unified and mysterious painting.

Bischofberger hosted an exhibition of the *Collaborations* at his gallery in Zurich in the fall of 1984. The critics gave it a lukewarm reception.[56] Calloused by years of bad reviews, Warhol was undeterred in his enthusiasm to continue collaborating with Basquiat. The synergy between them, nurtured over the previous year, had ignited the older artist's creative spark. The resulting transformation in Warhol's work was startling. In the early stages of their collaboration Warhol would screen his logos as a ground on to which Basquiat would paint his snarling faces and coarse graffiti scripts, as in *Arm and Hammer II* (1985, pl. 39). Over the cycle of their collaboration, Warhol departed from his screened grounds and picked up the brush, parlaying his strokes with those of Basquiat. As the relationship matured, the handiwork of the two artists became increasingly indistinguishable, and the two began to adopt each other's techniques. Only Warhol's telltale logos and Basquiat's snarling faces differentiate the work of the artists. In these later canvases, Warhol utilized his virtuoso touch as a foil for Basquiat's dynamically brutal brushwork. And Warhol worked toward this synthesis: "I think those paintings we're doing together are better when you can't tell who did which parts."[57] This quality is most pronounced in *African Masks* (1984, pl. 42),[58] a tour de force of figurative painting. In this remarkable frieze of figures parading across a monumental canvas, one can see the artists working, alternating between black and white faces and totemic forms, sometimes revealing, sometimes concealing the authorship of the handiwork.

The American dealer Tony Shafrazi arranged with Bischofberger to have a selection of the *Collaborations* exhibited at his New York gallery in September 1985. But by that time the relationship between the two artists was beginning to fray. Some people in the art community suggested that Basquiat's friendship with Warhol was ruining the rawness of the younger artist's work. Listening to these voices, Basquiat had become aloof and visited Warhol's studio less frequently. Warhol was concerned. But at the opening he expressed elation that "the paintings looked really great, everyone seemed to like them." His elation turned to despair when the *New York Times* critic panned the exhibition, accusing Basquiat of becoming Warhol's mascot and forcing Warhol to realize, "I guess it's really over."[59] This was a traumatic experience for Warhol. He had grown to cherish the excitement surrounding his creative work and social life with Basquiat.

At the height of his elation with the *Collaborations*, Warhol confessed the obvious: "Jean-Michel got me into painting different, so that's a good thing."[60] And that "good thing" was to work with a paintbrush. Henry Geldzahler unequivocally stated that *129 Die in Jet (Plane Crash)* (1962, fig. 25) was Warhol's last hand-painted picture.[61] But Warhol had never entirely abandoned painting during the two subsequent decades. His major series of the 1970s, beginning with *Mao* (1972, fig. 3, page 16) and continuing through the *Hammer and Sickle* (1976) and *Skulls* (1976, fig. 4, page 17), not only were painted under the screens but also demonstrate a tremendous painterliness, which was achieved by using his trademark mop to lather up the painted surface under the flat screenprints. He also employed this technique with increasing bravura in the portraits throughout the 1970s. In a 1974 interview he claimed that he was "trying to put style" into his portraits by hand painting the backgrounds. He continued to develop his painting "style" through the 1970s and into the 1980s. Beginning with the *$*, he produced brush-painted studies that were then photographed and screenprinted.[62] With the *Collaborations*, after years of screening, mopping, pressing, and pissing to produce his paintings, he had rediscovered, in concert with Basquiat, a viable "style" of figurative painting by drawing with a brush. The *Collaborations* mark not only Warhol's return to hand painting but also his return to figure painting by hand, a complete reversal of his Pop art.

Concurrently with the *Collaborations*, Warhol painted the *Black & White Ads* (pls. 44–59). In this series, he again scanned his past for Pop-styled images culled from newspapers and magazines, which seemed to represent poignant signs of current mass culture and also issues of personal significance. He reproduced ads for retro products like Beatle boots, Mineola motorcycles, and Campbell's soup cans (pl. 45), as well as those for current fads such as fitness, combat boots, and alternative medicines (pls. 44, 47). Yet the most incisive of the *Ads* are his sociopolitical commentaries on the exploding budget deficit, impending nuclear holocaust, and global militarism (fig. 27; pls. 49, 50).[63] And for the first time in his career, in personal pieces that were never shown in his lifetime, Warhol expressed the depth of his religious beliefs in works such as *Heaven and Hell Are Just One Breath Away! The Mark of the Beast*, and *Repent and Sin No More!* (pls. 51–56). The evangelical tone of the ads that Warhol chose to reproduce confirms his religious fervor. This is also evident in his conflation of

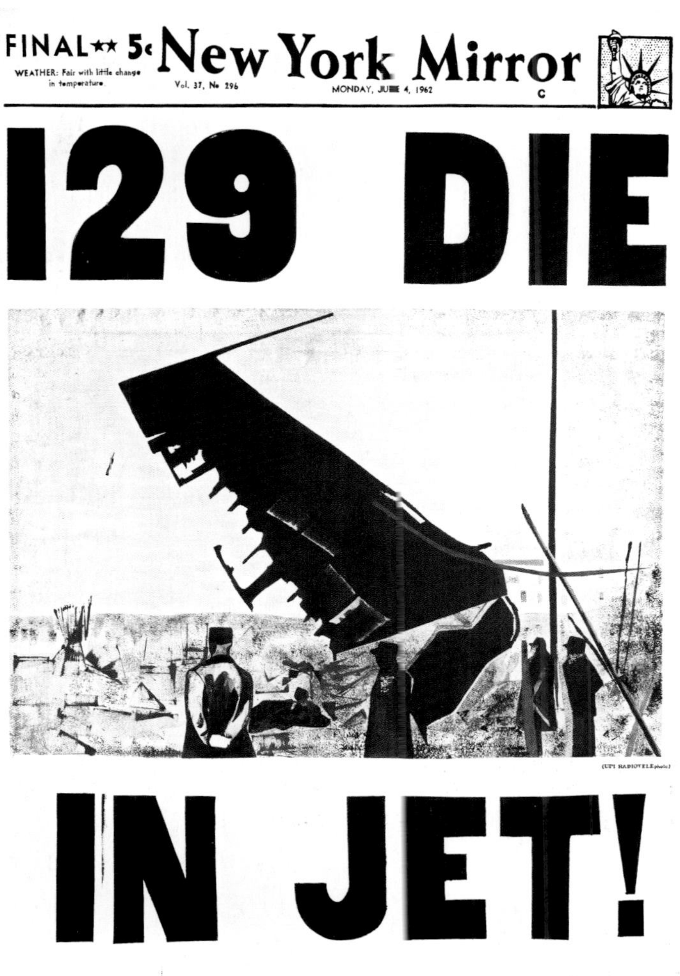

Fig. 25. ***129 Die in Jet (Plane Crash)*, 1962. Acrylic on canvas, 99 x 71⅜ in. (254 x 183 cm). Museum Ludwig, Cologne**

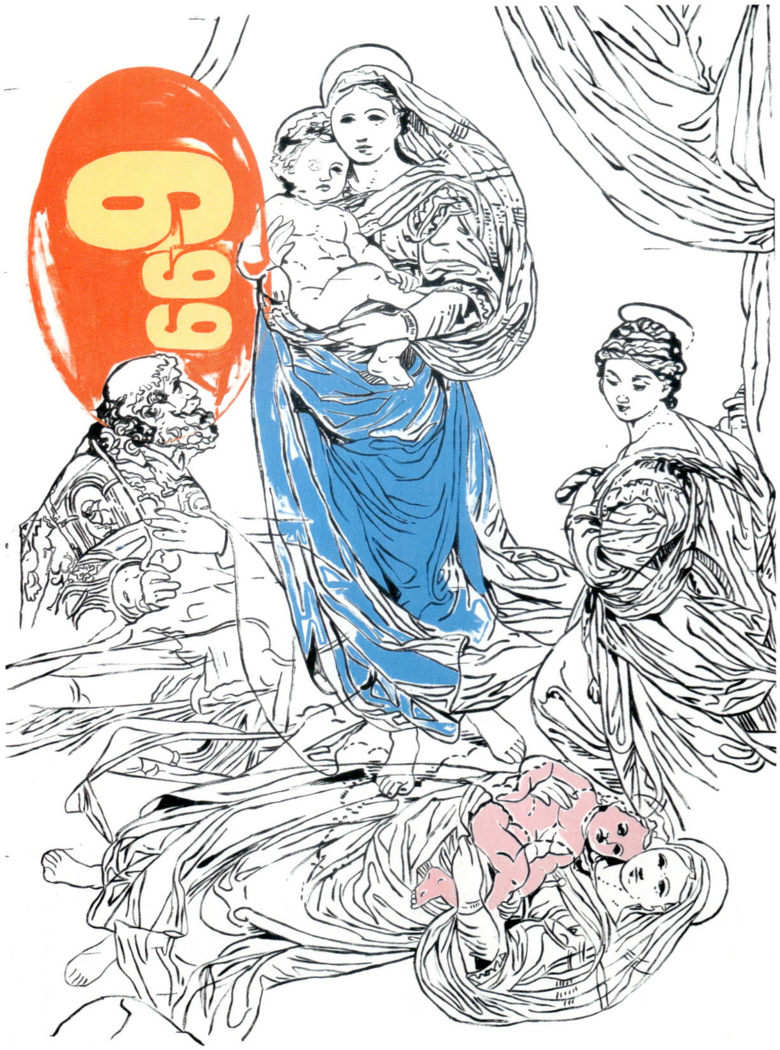

Fig. 26. *Raphael Madonna—$6.99*, 1985. Acrylic and silkscreen ink on linen, 156¼ x 116 in. (396.9 x 294.6 cm). The Andy Warhol Museum, Pittsburgh; Contribution The Andy Warhol Foundation for the Visual Arts, Inc.

a bodybuilding ad and an image of Jesus Christ (pl. 59), where Warhol exhorts the viewer to align themselves with Christ and "Be a Somebody with a BODY." He developed this subject matter into *Raphael Madonna—$6.99* (1985, fig. 26), in which he rearranges Raphael's *Sistine Madonna* (1513–14), a figure of adulation, into a maternal image bearing the Christ child, who commands the adoration of the supplicant saints and angels as the mother of Christ.

Warhol created the *Black & White Ads* using his "patented" Pop process of clipping ads, projecting them, tracing the projections on to paper, and having acetates made that were then screened. However, he also reverted to the technique of executing brush studies, as he had done for *$*, to produce the appearance of brushstrokes and running paint in the finished screens. Warhol's freehand draftsmanship and fluid brushwork enliven the surface of these works, which are essentially silkscreened reproductions of his original drawings. The duality of the hand and machine are at work here. He applied the painting lessons from his *Collaborations* series with Basquiat, which were being executed simultaneously, to create a remarkable group of paintings that exemplify his exploration of the dialectic between hand painting and mechanical reproduction. But he also painted directly on the canvas, tracing over the projection of an ad. The artist relished playing this deception. In works such as *Airborne—We Kill for Peace* (fig. 27) and *The Last Supper (Be a Somebody with a Body)* (pl. 59), Warhol displays his extraordinary touch, exercising the full potential of his fluid brushwork and supple line. The *Double $5/Weightlifter* (pl. 44) is also painted by hand, yet it appears to be a screened image, complete with the

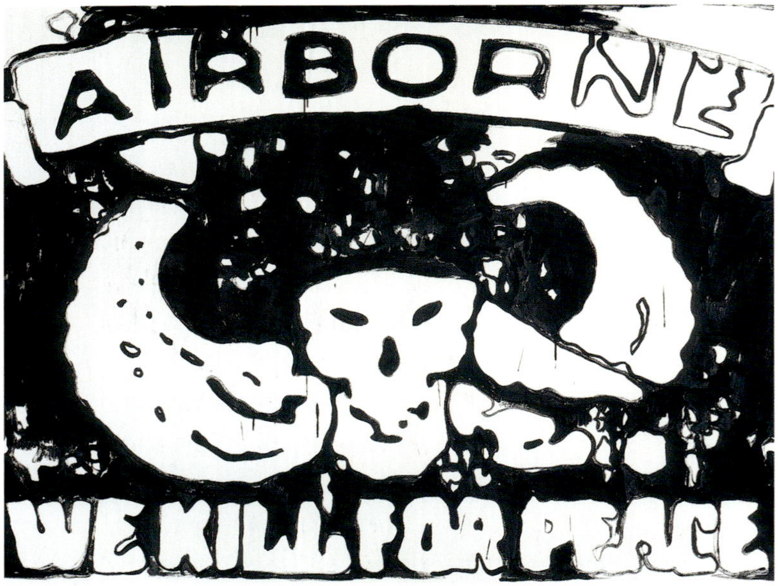

Fig. 27. *Airborne—We Kill for Peace*, 1985–86. Acrylic on canvas, 50 x 68 in. (127 x 172.7 cm). Private collection

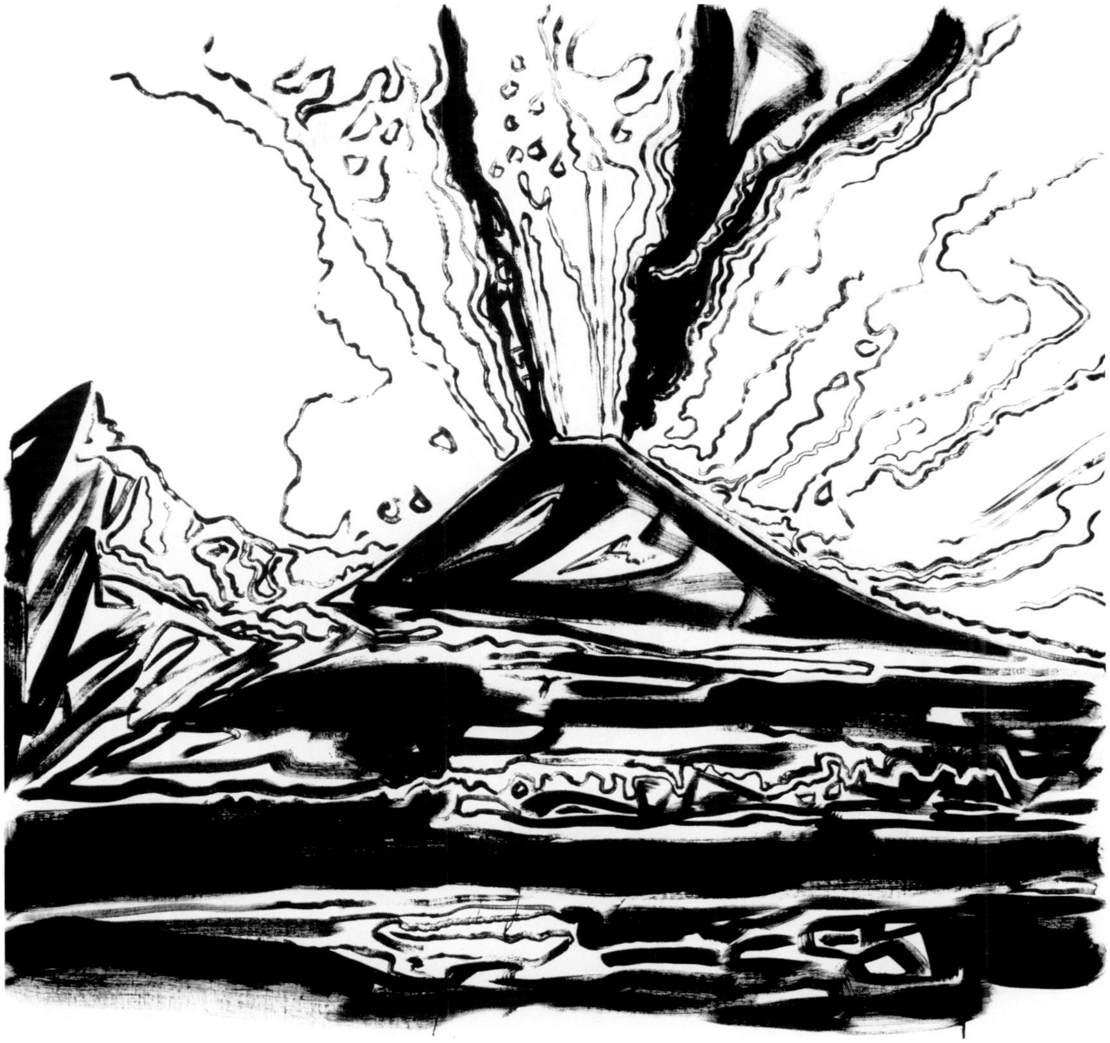

Fig. 28. *Mount Vesuvius*, 1985. Acrylic and silkscreen ink on linen, 78 x 82 in. (198.1 x 208.3 cm). The Andy Warhol Museum, Pittsburgh; Founding Collection, Contribution The Andy Warhol Foundation for the Visual Arts, Inc.

mis-registration lines and drips of his classic Pop screen paintings. On the other hand, his screened version of *Mount Vesuvius* (fig. 28), after Joseph Wright of Derby, conveys the liquid line delicately laid in Warhol's late hand-painted pieces. In these *Ads* Warhol toys mischievously with the illusory potential of hand and mechanical processes, putting a new spin on trompe-l'oeil painting.

The confluence of Warhol's many new painting projects, his active social life, and the demands of his business ventures combined with the multitude of print projects, television productions, and fashion engagements made this period the busiest of Warhol's career. Seemingly self-assured in his art and his business, he exuded an air of calm composure, pursuing his projects with a focused, committed purpose.[64] Yet it was a difficult time for him: his collaborator had left him, his partner was terminally ill with AIDS, and his own health was faltering. Reflecting on mortality, he asked, "Really, what is life about? You get sick and die. That's it. So you've just got to keep busy."[65] Although he obsessed over death and rejection, he hid behind his mask and immersed himself in his work. In his studio Warhol was more prolific from late 1985 through 1986 than during any other single year of his professional practice, producing as much work as some artists do in their entire careers. He worked continuously, finishing the *Collaborations* (1984–85);

painting *Philip's Skull* (1985), *Black & White Ads* (1985–86), *Physiological Diagrams* (1985–86), portraits of *Lenin* (1986), and the *Statue of Liberty* series (1986); and stitching his innovative *Hand-Sewn Photographs* (1986). Warhol's compulsive production culminated in three great series in 1986: the fright-wig *Self-Portraits*, the *Camouflage* paintings, and *The Last Supper* paintings. Each covered a different subject and was created in a different technique, building on the artist's recent experiments with the dualities of abstraction and representation, painting and printing, and surface and meaning.

Among Western artists over the past millennium, Warhol, like Rembrandt van Rijn and Pablo Picasso, created an extraordinary wealth of self-portraits that leave posterity with insights into the artist's identity. Warhol's fright-wig *Self-Portraits* (pls. 60–68), in which the haunting visage of the artist floats in a void, are, arguably, his most widely known. For this commission, from the London dealer Anthony

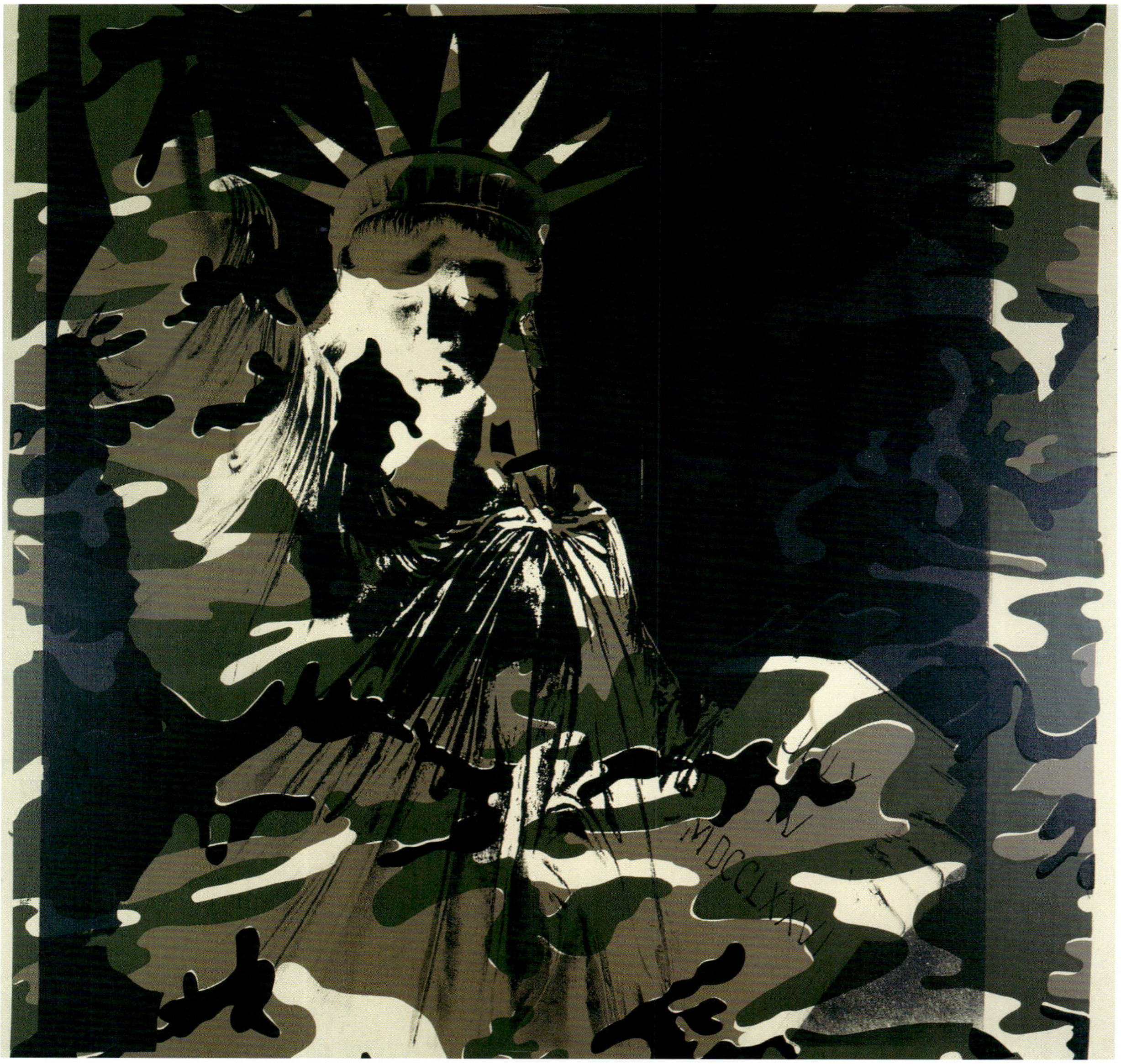

Fig. 29. *Statue of Liberty*, 1986. Acrylic and silkscreen ink on linen, 80 x 76 in. (203.2 x 193 cm). The Andy Warhol Museum, Pittsburgh; Founding Collection, Contribution The Andy Warhol Foundation for the Visual Arts, Inc.

d'Offay, Warhol instructed Benjamin Liu to photograph him in the confined space of the stairwell outside the spacious studio. With a few quick snaps of the Polaroid, the artist had the selection of images that he needed. D'Offay selected the Polaroid with Warhol's hair lying across his forehead, while Warhol preferred the image with a vertical tuft of hair sprouting up from his wig, like Basquiat's Rasta style. But d'Offay insisted, and Warhol produced a series of closely cropped images of his face with his mouth hanging open (pl. 60). In July d'Offay exhibited these portraits in London to great success, selling many of them. But Warhol, ever conscious of his image, was mortified by the paintings. "I mean walking into a room full of the worst pictures you've ever seen of yourself, what can you say, what can you do?" The portraits with his hair sticking up like Basquiat's excited Warhol, and he resolved to continue making more of that image for himself.[66]

Both versions of the *Self-Portraits* present a disturbing image of the artist as a ghostly specter of the bon vivant who vamped around New York with the celebrities and artists of the 1970s and 1980s. They measure the transition in Warhol's life over the years since he made his kaleidoscopic, dizzying self-portraits of 1978 (pls. 1, 2). Although the fright-wig paintings recall Warhol's negative self-image of the earlier period (pls. 3, 4), they are removed from being a staged reflection on his mortality (figs. 5, 6) and embody a direct confrontation with the reality of one's ultimate demise. D'Offay himself compares the self-portraits to death masks.[67]

With the same breath that he produced these daunting *Self-Portraits*, Warhol created the *Camouflage* paintings (pls. 69–73), which are some of his most exuberant Matissean works and an extension of his ideas of taking serial imagery into the realm of abstraction through the repetition of free-form design. Scavenging the studio for more ideas, Warhol asked Shriver what he was painting those days, to which he responded that he was emulating military camouflage. The prospect of extending the principles of printed abstraction in a new direction excited Warhol, as did extending the metaphor of deception that was inherent in camouflage. He and Shriver worked on a number of tracings from a single swatch of mesh camouflage. By cropping and inverting the designs in a range of color combinations, Warhol produced an incredible variety of effects, from traditional army camouflage (pl. 71) to delicate pastel patterns (pl. 73). He proposed using them in an elaborate decorative scheme in which he would hang small camouflage paintings on top of monumental canvases, creating a repetition of pattern in a shallow bas-relief; this scheme was never executed.[68] Camouflage became a favorite motif in Warhol's last year, appearing on *Self-Portraits* (pl. 68), a *Last Supper* (pl. 76), and versions of his *Statue of Liberty* (fig. 29). The device served as a metaphor for not only his deceptive painting practices but also the screen that conceals the private Warhol from his public persona.[69]

Warhol had cultivated a repertoire of religious imagery in his *Black & White Ads* and his *Raphael Madonna—$6.99*. However, only in his final series, *The Last Supper* paintings (pls. 74–80), does Warhol publicly reveal his spirituality. It is a rarity in the history of modern and contemporary art for an avant-garde artist to treat religious subjects with the sincerity of his or her personal convictions. In fact, Warhol's series, the largest of his career, consisting of approximately one hundred works on which he worked for more than a year, is the most ambitious body of religious paintings of the twentieth century.[70] The Greek dealer Alexandre Iolas had purchased a building across from Santa Maria delle Grazie in Milan, the site of Leonardo da Vinci's fresco *The Last Supper* (c. 1495–98), to house his gallery, and he sought an artist to inaugurate the space by referencing Leonardo's fifteenth-century landmark of Western art. No one other than Warhol took his offer, but Warhol eagerly accepted. Although the commission allowed Warhol to go public with his religious beliefs, he denied in a public statement that the works held any personal significance, insisting, "I'm still a commercial artist. I was always a commercial artist.[71]

Initially Warhol struggled with deciding the proper approach to *The Last Supper*.[72] Certainly, he would not work from the original. He always worked from photographic imagery and media as his sources. Even as he reinvented painting, he did so with the intermediary of mechanical reproduction. Ever conscious of his place in the history of art, he did not want to invite comparison with Leonardo by presenting his own paintings. Rather, he differentiated his work through a *double entendre* of replicating reproductions of Leonardo's fresco.

Warhol and his staff rooted around in shops for different models, which they tested. Liu purchased a polychrome three-dimensional plaster model from a neighborhood market, and someone else discovered an engraving in a nineteenth-century encyclopedia of art, both of which Warhol set aside until later (figs. 30, 31). Finally, Shriver found a turn-of-the-twentieth-century chromolithograph (fig. 32) that Warhol deemed to be the ideal source. For the installation in Milan, Warhol produced a suite of screenprints and three large-scale screened paintings (pls. 74, 75), all variations on the chromolithograph. The works were adhered to the wall surface, which has led to the suggestion that Warhol sought to emulate the support structure of Leonardo's fresco.[73]

Despite his public proclamations to the contrary, the subject of *The Last Supper* moved Warhol profoundly. The image of Christ before his disciples possessed him. For an artist who was obsessed with the subject of death throughout his career, the Lord's final repast functioned as the consummate disaster painting.[74] He not only completed his commissioned screenprints for Iolas but also

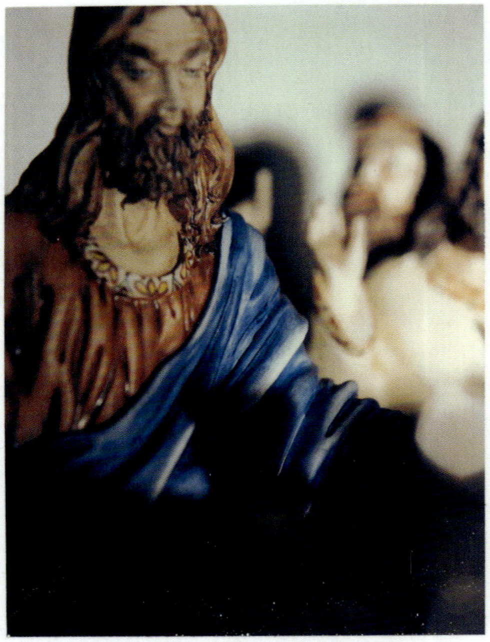

Fig. 30. *Last Supper*, 1985. Polaroid™ Polacolor ER. The Andy Warhol Museum, Pittsburgh; Founding Collection, Contribution The Andy Warhol Foundation for the Visual Arts, Inc.

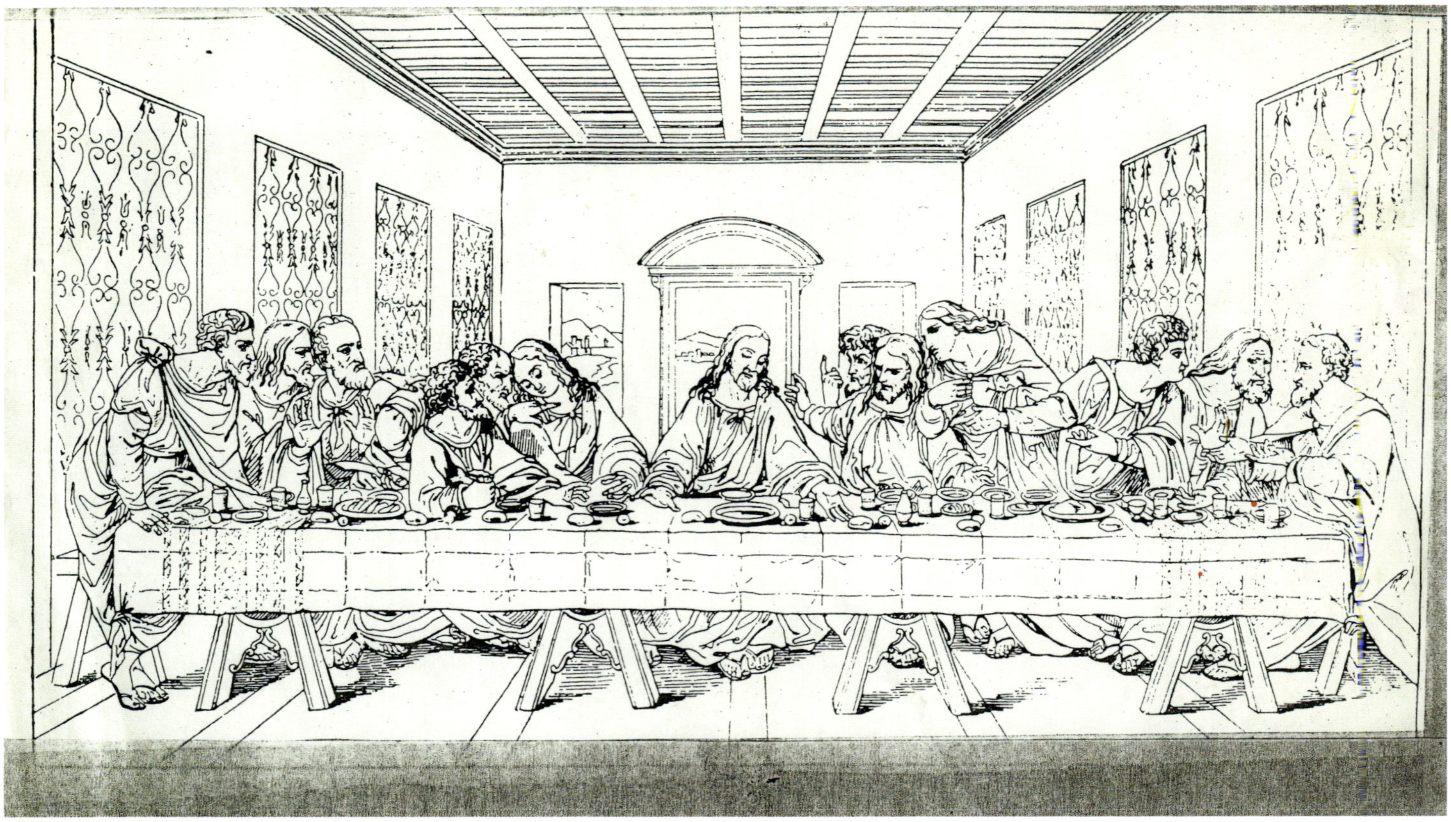

Fig. 31. Photocopy of a line drawing from John Dennison Champlain, Jr., ed., *Cyclopedia of Painters and Paintings*, vol. 10 (New York: Scribner's, 1913), p. 32, used as source material for Andy Warhol's *The Last Supper* series. Archives, The Andy Warhol Museum, Pittsburgh

continued the series, painting vast stretches of canvas by hand in his ballroom studio on 33rd Street. Working evenings and weekends, Warhol returned to the line drawing and projected it on to the wall, tracing the source with an assurance and devotion. Of these works he remarked, "I painted them all by hand—I myself; so now I've become a Sunday painter. . . . That's why the project took so long. But I worked with a passion."[75] In these ventures Warhol's renewed interest in figure painting and his penchant for screened logos coalesced. In *The Last Supper* ("The Big C") (1986, pl. 78), he designed a complex composition in which segments from *The Last Supper* in a variety of scales revolve around a $6.99 price tag and "The Big C," all tied together by his trademark Mineola motorcycles. Warhol's symbols convey salient personal meaning: "The Big C" references Christ, who is surrounded by the fluttering wings of the owl of wisdom in the upper right; it also cues us in to Warhol's fascination with alternative medicines (see his *Physiological Diagram*, 1985, fig. 33). The headline that Warhol used from the *New York Post* asks, "The Big C: Can the Mind Act as a Cancer Cure?"[76] The Dove and General Electric emblems in the painting owned by the Museum of Modern Art (pl. 80) symbolize Christ as the divine light of peace. The import of these symbols indicates a dramatic departure from the interpretation of Warhol as a creator of literal images that mirror society and instead suggests the earlier artist who aspired to craft "symbols that sustain us."[77] In his purest version of *The Last Supper* (pl. 79), from which Warhol purged the logos, he depicted the forms and draperies of Christ and the apostles with a technical virtuosity and on a scale that rank these paintings among the most extraordinary, ambitious drawings of the twentieth century.

Warhol was fully aware of the contradiction inherent in the complete reversal of his artistic goals, from contributing to

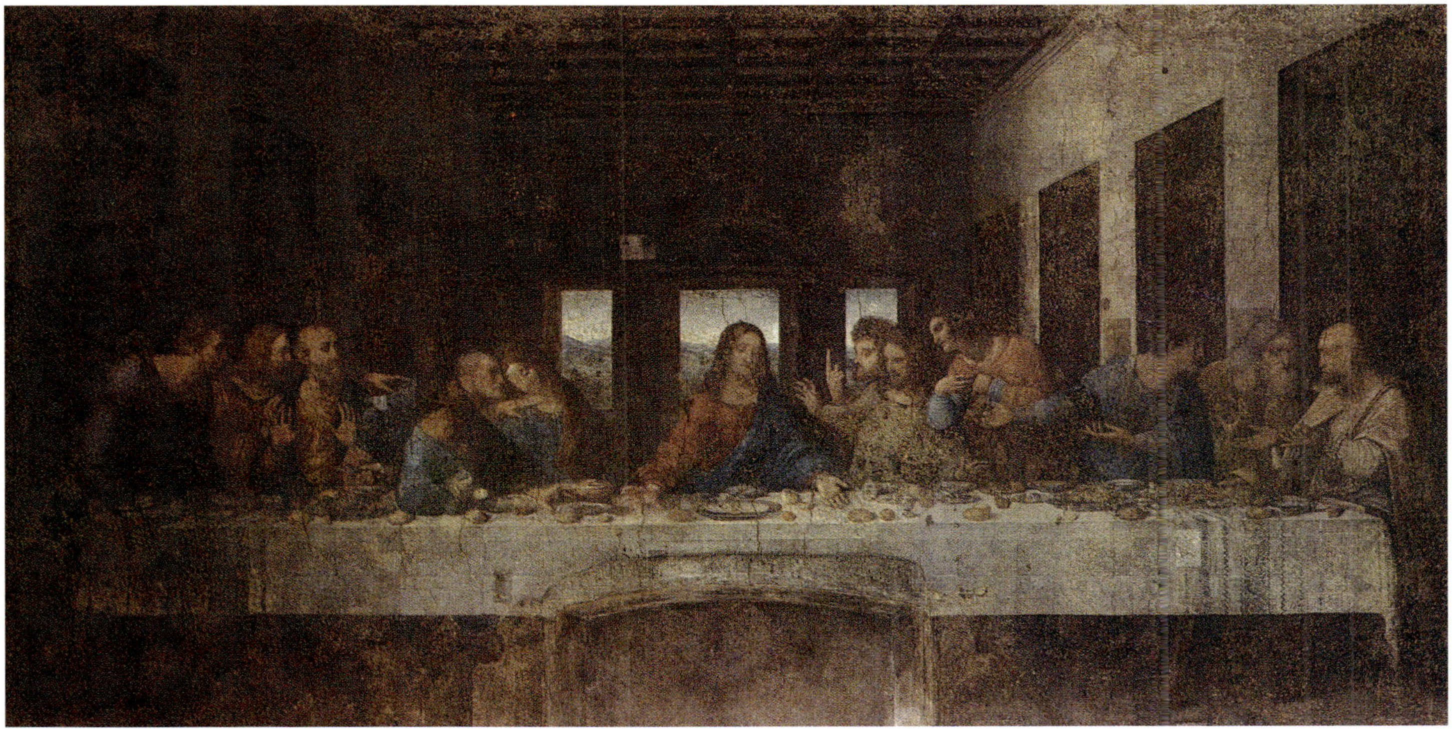

Fig. 32. Chromolithograph used as source material for Andy Warhol's *The Last Supper* series. Archives, The Andy Warhol Museum, Pittsburgh

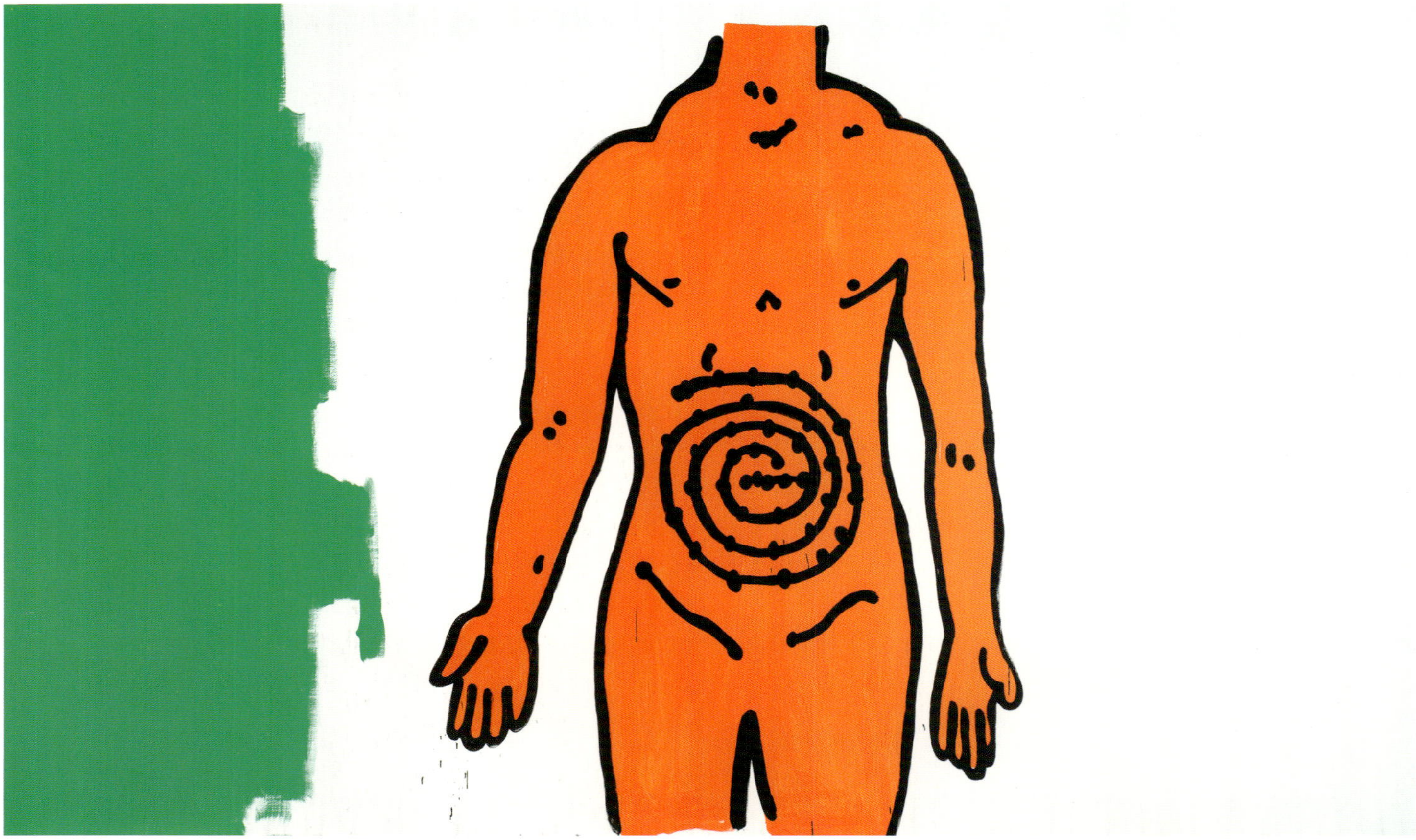

Fig. 33. *Physiological Diagram*, c. 1984–85. Acrylic on canvas, 116 x 200 in. (294.6 x 508 cm). The Baltimore Museum of Art: Purchase with funds provided by Esther and Richard Pearlstone through the Pearlstone Family Fund; and partial gift of The Andy Warhol Foundation for the Visual Arts

the “end of painting” in the 1960s to participating excitedly on the front line of the revival of the medium in the 1980s. The aloof filmmaker who dismissed painting as “so boring” in 1965 had become the earnest innovator who enthused, “I like all paintings; it’s just amazing that it keeps, you know, going on. And the way new things happen and stuff.”[78] Only with a perspective matured by decades of innovation and experimentation could he incorporate painting back into his practice, bringing the artist’s hand and personal content into a dialectic with mechanically produced imagery designed for mass consumption.

In these late works Warhol mined his past. The metaphor of the *Retrospectives* and *Reversals* (pls. 22–24) continually resurfaces in his return to earlier subjects, techniques, and strategies for meaning. These wide-ranging projects—inspired by commissions and assistants as well as self-generated; produced by hired printers or by his own hand; conceived as parodies of painting, painting with artistic aspirations, devotional votives, or simply decoration—are linked by Warhol’s consistent desire to develop new ideas around painting. Although he returned to some earlier and traditional mechanisms, Warhol was able, ironically, to advance his work along the leading edge of contemporary art. It is almost as if he had anticipated the artistic avant-garde of the late 1970s and 1980s by introducing a revival of painting, appropriation, and figuration.

In 1980, when the Neo-Expressionists were exploding on to the New York art scene amid a clamor of excitement around the return to painting, critic Robert Pincus-Witten observed,

> Glitz, glitter, glass seem the real subject of immediate contemporary art. . . . I suppose the real critical issue today is the beauty of the skin deep and the life of the mind as epitomized by Andy Warhol’s *Interview* magazine. In the ’60s, Warhol was a burning critical issue. In the ’70s, Warholism superseded Warhol. In the ’80s, the Return of Andy Warhol.[79]

Pincus-Witten recognized that the celebrity lifestyle cultivated by Warhol was resurgent under the younger art stars. New artists and new money had spawned an unprecedented proliferation in the art market. But Pincus-Witten was not yet aware of what was transpiring beneath the surface of Warholism and behind the doors to the studio at Warhol Enterprises at the time. Warhol was participating in the gestalt of the era, having moved back into painting with a vigor and, as Pincus-Witten predicted, participating in the critical artistic issues of the moment. With the art that ensued from his rush of creative energy, Warhol prophetically prefigured much of the new painting that would appear over the subsequent decades. His late paintings introduced new forms of abstraction and a return to figuration in advance of the Neo-Expressionists and Neo-Geo painters. Oscillating between the mechanical reproduction of appropriated images and hand paintings while navigating a host of media-centric business ventures, he established a model for the cross-media and media-driven art practice that characterizes today’s ahistorical contemporary art world, in which issues of medium, style, abstraction, and figuration are essentially irrelevant.

Notes

1. Andy Warhol in an interview with Gretchen Berg, "Andy Warhol: My True Story," Nov. 1, 1966, in Kenneth Goldsmith, ed., *I'll Be Your Mirror: The Selected Andy Warhol Interviews, 1962–1987* (New York: Carroll & Graf Publishers, 2004), p. 88.

2. Andy Warhol quoted in Benjamin H. D. Buchloh, "An Interview with Andy Warhol," May 28, 1985, in Annette Michelson, ed., *Andy Warhol: October Files 2* (Cambridge, Massachusetts, and London: The MIT Press, 2001), p. 126.

3. Andy Warhol quoted in G. R. Swenson, "What Is Pop Art?" *Art News,* 62 (Nov. 1963), p. 26.

4. Andy Warhol quoted in Paul Gardner, "Gee, What's Happened to Andy Warhol?" *Art News*, 79 (Nov. 1980), p. 73.

5. Andy Warhol, entry for "Wednesday, May 25, 1977—Paris," in Pat Hackett, ed., *The Andy Warhol Diaries* (New York: Warner Books, 1989), p. 45.

6. Andy Warhol quoted in Buchloh, "An Interview with Andy Warhol," in Michelson, *Andy Warhol,* p. 123.

7. Andy Warhol quoted in Ralph Pomeroy, "An Interview with Andy Warhol," *Afterimage*, 2 (Fall 1970), p. 39.

8. Vincent Fremont, vice president of Warhol Enterprises from 1971 to 1987, has repeatedly commented on the energy of this period, most adamantly when he said, "It was not until after Andy Warhol's death that we fully realized there had been an increasing vitality and momentum occurring in his painting during the last years of his life"; quoted in Charles Stuckey, *Andy Warhol: Heaven and Hell Are Just One Breath Away! Late Paintings and Related Works, 1984–1986*, exh. cat. (New York: Gagosian Gallery and Rizzoli, 1992), p. 6. In *Cast a Cold Eye: The Late Work of Andy Warhol*, exh. cat. (New York: Gagosian Gallery, 2006), p. 16, Fremont remarked, "The eighties was a very productive time for Andy artistically." This view is supported by Ronnie Cutrone, who has said in several interviews, "Andy was always experimenting," and that this was a period of great experimentation; quoted in *Andy Warhol: Oxidation Paintings, Piss Paintings*, exh. cat. (Munich: Galerie Daniel Blau, 1998); and in Patrick S. Smith, *Warhol: Conversations about the Artist* (Ann Arbor, Mich.: UMI Research Press, 1988), p. 353. In interviews with the author, Vincent Fremont (Feb. 15, 2007), Jay Shriver, Warhol's painting assistant from 1980 to 1987 (Oct. 29, 2008), and Benjamin Liu, an assistant to Warhol from 1982 to 1987 (Nov. 22, 2008), each confirmed the energy and intensity of activity in the studio during this period. Jay Shriver was amazed that "everything was being done simultaneously," and Benjamin Liu said there were "a lot of cultural activities going on around new art, film, and music."

9. Warhol remarked in several interviews about his commitment to studio work, saying, "I work seven days a week. But I get the most done on the weekends because during the week people keep coming by to talk"; Andy Warhol, "Painter Hangs His Own Paintings," *New York Magazine*, Feb. 5, 1979. And his assistants concurred, with Brigid Berlin confiding to a journalist, "I suspect he's working harder now and painting more than ever"; Gardner, "Gee, What's Happened to Andy Warhol?" p. 73. This was also confirmed in the author's interviews with Vincent Fremont, Benjamin Liu, and Jay Shriver.

10. Judging by the two major retrospectives organized since Warhol's death in 1987, the view of his career is dramatically skewed toward the 1960s Pop art. Charles Stuckey, in *Andy Warhol: Heaven and Hell Are Just One Breath Away!* p. 9, notes that more than two-thirds of the approximately 460 works included in the 1989 exhibition dated from the first eight years of his career; see Kynaston McShine, ed., *Andy Warhol: A Retrospective*, exh. cat. (New York: The Museum of Modern Art, 1989). This trend continued in the exhibition of 2001–02, in which 70 percent of the 240 works displayed dated from before 1968; see Heiner Bastian, *Andy Warhol Retrospective* (London: Tate Publishing; Los Angeles: Museum of Contemporary Art, 2001).

11. The four exhibitions of his late paintings were *Shadows* at Heiner Friedrich Gallery (Jan. 1979)*; Reversals* and *Dollar Signs* at Leo Castelli on West Broadway and Greene Street, respectively (Jan. 1982); *Andy Warhol/Jean-Michel Basquiat Collaborations* at Tony Shafrazi Gallery (Sept. 1985); and *Oxidations* at Gagosian Gallery (Sept. 1986). European galleries and museums presented Warhol in a large-scale retrospective organized in 1978 by the Kunsthaus Zürich; the *Retrospectives* and *Reversals* at Galerie Bruno Bischofberger, Zurich (May–June 1980) and again as the *Warhol '80: Serie Reversal* at the Museum Moderner Kunst/Museum des 20. Jahrhundert, Vienna (Apr.–May 1981); the *Oxidations* at the Documenta 7 in Kassel (1982); the *Zeitgeist* series at the Martin-Gropius-Bau, Berlin (Oct.–Dec. 1982); *Paintings for Children* at Galerie Bruno Bischofberger, Zurich (Dec. 1983–Jan. 1984); *Collaborations* at Galerie Bruno Bischofberger, Zurich (Sept. 1984); *Self-Portraits* at Anthony d'Offay Gallery, London (July–Aug. 1986); and *Il Cenacolo* (*The Last Supper*) at Alexandre Iolas, Milan (Jan. 1987).

12. Buchloh, "An Interview with Andy Warhol," in Michelson *Andy Warhol*, p. 123.

13. Roberta Smith, "Art: A Collaboration, Tim Rollins and K.O. S.," *The New York Times*, Nov. 21, 1986, p. C28.

14. Roberta Smith, "7 of Warhol's Final Paintings," *The New York Times,* July 10, 1987, p. C4.

15. The list of exhibitions that featured Warhol's late paintings after his death is quite extensive, dominated by commercial gallery exhibitions and interspersed with a few European museum exhibitions that focused primarily on individual series. The catalogues associated with these exhibitions include: *Andy Warhol: Shadow Paintings* (New York: Gagosian Gallery 1989); *Warhol/Basquiat Collaborations* (Paris: Didier Lambert Fine Arts, 1989); Charles Stuckey, *Andy Warhol: Heaven and Hell Are Just One Breath Away! Late Paintings and Related Works, 1984–1986* (New York: Gagosian Gallery, 1992);

Thomas Kellein, *Andy Warhol: Abstrakt* (Basel: Kunsthalle Basel, 1993); Tilman Osterwold, *Collaborations: Warhol—Basquiat—Clemente* (Kassel: Museum Fridericianum; Munich: Museum Villa Stuck, 1996); *Andy Warhol: Rorschach Paintings* (New York: Gagosian Gallery, 1996); *Andy Warhol $* (New York: Gagosian Gallery, 1997); *Andy Warhol: Fifteen Abstract Paintings* (New York: Anton Kern Gallery, 1998); *Andy Warhol: Oxidation Paintings, Piss Paintings* (Munich: Galerie Daniel Blau, 1998); Carla Schultz-Hoffmann, ed., *Andy Warhol: The Last Supper* (Munich: Bayerische Staatsgemäldesammlungen/Staatsgalerie Moderner Kunst, 1998); *Andy Warhol: Camouflage* (New York: Gagosian Gallery, 1998); *Andy Warhol: Diamond Dust Shoes* (New York: Gagosian Gallery, 1999); *Andy Warhol: Diamond Dust Shadow Paintings* (New York: Gagosian Gallery, 2000); *Andy Warhol Jean-Michel Basquiat: Collaboration Paintings* (Los Angeles: Gagosian Gallery, 2002); *Andy Warhol: Piss & Sex Paintings and Drawings* (New York: Gagosian Gallery, 2002); *Andy Warhol B&W Paintings: Ads and Illustrations, 1985–1986* (New York: Gagosian Gallery, 2002); *Andy Warhol: The Late Work* (Düsseldorf: Museum Kunst Palast, 2004); *Andy Warhol: Dollar Signs* (New York: Van de Weghe Fine Art, 2004); and *Cast a Cold Eye: The Late Work of Andy Warhol* (New York: Gagosian Gallery, 2006).

16. Trevor Fairbrother, "Skulls," in Gary Garrels, ed., *The Work of Andy Warhol*, Dia Art Foundation, Discussions in Contemporary Culture, no. 3 (Seattle: Bay Press, 1989), pp. 93–114; and Jane Daggett Dillenberger. *The Religious Art of Andy Warhol* (New York: The Continuum Publishing Company, 1998), p. 36.

17. In various interviews with Warhol at this time, he repeatedly insisted, when asked, that he was the only person who did the painting, including on the portraits. See Phyllis Tuchman, "Pop! Interviews with George Segal, Andy Warhol, Roy Lichtenstein, James Rosenquist, and Robert Indiana," *Art News,* 73 (May 1974), p. 26; and Barry Blinderman, "Modern Myths: An Interview with Andy Warhol," *Arts Magazine,* 56 (Oct. 1981), p. 146.

18. Ivan Karp paraphrasing Andy Warhol in an interview conducted in the fall of 1978 by Patrick Smith, in Smith, *Warhol: Conversations*, pp. 217–18.

19. Andy Warhol, entry for Nov. 16, 1978, in Hackett, *The Andy Warhol Diaries*, p. 182.

20. McShine, *Andy Warhol*, p. 20.

21. Emile de Antonio quoted in Smith, *Warhol: Conversations*, p. 187. Ivan Karp recounts a similar story in ibid., pp. 211–12.

22. Buchloh, "An Interview with Andy Warhol," in Michelson, *Andy Warhol*, p. 123.

23. Ronnie Cutrone quoted in Smith, *Warhol: Conversations*, p. 353, discussing this period of work in Warhol's studio. These paintings were casually called "piss paintings" in the studio and given the more formal title *Oxidation Paintings* when they were exhibited at Documenta 7 in 1982.

24. Cutrone elaborates on this series of paintings in the interview published in *Andy Warhol: Oxidation Paintings, Piss Paintings*. After the exhibition of the *Oxidations* at Documenta 7 in 1982 and at Gagosian Gallery in the fall of 1986, they were not exhibited again until the above-referenced 1998 exhibition at Galerie Daniel Blau, whose catalogue includes excellent interviews with Cutrone, Vincent Fremont, and Diana Brill. Four years later the Gagosian Gallery in New York hosted its second exhibition of these paintings, *Andy Warhol: Piss & Sex Paintings and Drawings*, and published a catalogue with a racy essay by Bruce Hainley, who discusses the work from the perspective of queer theory.

25. Buchloh, "An Interview with Andy Warhol," in Michelson, *Andy Warhol*, p. 125. Warhol's idea of "invisible painting" was first manifested in Warhol's *Silver Clouds* (1966), which he also described as floating sculptures.

26. *Warhol*, exh. cat. (London: Tate Gallery, 1971), p. 8.

27. Both Charles Stuckey and Jay Shriver have remarked on the reference to Duchamp as self-evident: Stuckey, "Warhol in Context," in Garrels, *The Work of Andy Warhol*, p. 8; and Shriver, interview with the author.

28. Ronnie Cutrone paraphrasing Fred Hughes, quoted in Bob Colacello's essay, "Andy Warhol, Abstraction, and the Camouflage Paintings," in *Andy Warhol: Camouflage*, p. 7. Cutrone repeated this story in a number of his interviews. Jay Shriver clearly recognized Warhol's ambitions to be an abstract artist: "By that point, abstraction was part of the vocabulary. . . . he always liked abstraction." And, "It was made very clear to me that abstraction was an important element"; interview with the author. In an interview about his *Rorschach* paintings, Robert Nickas asked Warhol, "Does all this mean you're going to be an abstract painter now?" And Warhol answered, "Well, maybe . . . yeah." See Robert Nickas, "Andy Warhol's Rorschach Tests," *Arts Magazine*, 60 (Oct. 1986), p. 32. See also the interview with Cutrone in *Andy Warhol: Oxidation Paintings, Piss Paintings*.

29. Ronnie Cutrone described this process in considerable detail at the time they were being created (fall 1978) in Smith, *Warhol: Conversations*, pp. 349–50.

30. Fairbrother, "Skulls," in Garrels, *The Work of Andy Warhol*.

31. Andy Warhol, entries for January 23 and 27, 1979, in Hackett, *The Andy Warhol Diaries*, pp. 198, 200; and Warhol, "Painter Hangs His Own Paintings." The Lone Star Foundation (which merged with Dia Art Foundation in 1980) commissioned the *Shadows*, showing them at Heiner Friedrich, Inc., in 1979. (The gallery could accommodate only 66 of the 102 paintings.) They were next displayed at the inaugural exhibition opening of the Menil Collection, Houston, beginning June 7, 1987. Dia installed 60 of the paintings in its Chelsea location from December 1998 through June 1999, and 72 paintings were installed in 2003 when Dia opened its museum Dia:Beacon in Beacon, New York. The second body of the *Shadows* was exhibited at

the Gagosian Gallery in 1989, complete with a catalogue that included the essay by Julian Schnabel reprinted in this book.
32. Thomas Lawson, "Andy Warhol/Heiner Friedrich," *Flash Art*, nos. 88–89 (Mar–Apr. 1979), p. 23.
33. Charles Stuckey, "Warhol Backwards and Forwards," *Flash Art*, no. 101 (Jan.–Feb. 1981), p. 13.
34. Warhol was very impressed with the sudden rush of celebrity that surrounded the new generation of artists. In his 1985 interview Benjamin Buchloh attempted to draw Warhol into criticizing the Neo-Expressionists, to which Warhol responded, "I'm just really excited about all the kids coming up, like Keith Haring and Jean-Michel [Basquiat] and Kenny Scharf"; "An Interview with Andy Warhol," in Michelson, *Andy Warhol*, p. 128. Yet, he was also concerned, challenged, and even threatened by their tremendous productivity and the then-exorbitant prices that they were receiving for their work: "Keith Haring is so big. . . . These kids are selling everything. Jean-Michel Basquiat's show sold out in Los Angeles." Or, in the case of Clemente, "He produces a lot. So many paintings. . . . Then they wanted to see my 'studio' so we went to the office, and there was just nothing there. The contrast was so—evident. We've gotten so involved with fashion. . . . I didn't have any art to show them." And, he dictated in his diary, "I got so nervous thinking about all these new kids painting away and me just going to parties, I figured I'd better get cracking"; Hackett, *The Andy Warhol Diaries,* pp. 434–35, 493, 532. This feeling also applied to his peers such as Roy Lichtenstein, whose 1981 retrospective at the Whitney, according to Warhol, "was great, I was so jealous"; ibid., p. 416. Warhol's paranoia was exacerbated by the success of others.
35. Robert Rosenblum, "Andy Warhol: Court Painter to the Seventies," in David Whitney, ed., *Andy Warhol: Portraits of the Seventies*, exh. cat. (New York: Whitney Museum of American Art, 1979), pp. 9, 18.
36. Thomas McGonigal, "Andy Warhol," *Arts Magazine,* 54 (Jan. 1980), p. 17; and Stuart Morgan, "Andy Warhol: Whitney Museum," *Artforum*, 18 (Feb. 1980), p. 96.
37. Andy Warhol, entries for Dec. 20, 1979, and May 1, 1980, in Hackett, *The Andy Warhol Diaries*, pp. 249, 285.
38. Andy Warhol, entry for Thursday, July 24, 1980, in ibid., p. 306.
39. Thomas Lawson, "Andy Warhol," *Artforum*, 20 (Apr. 1982), p. 75. Cutrone recounted this incident in John O. O'Connor and Benjamin Liu, *Unseen Warhol* (New York: Rizzoli, 1996), p. 70. Because of this Cutrone surmised that Warhol had yielded to business interests, succumbed to the criticism, and given up on the art world. Cutrone felt it was time to leave the studio. From this point forward Jay Shriver, who began in 1980, became the principal assistant in the studio.
40. Andy Warhol, entry for Nov. 20, 1981, in Hackett, *The Andy Warhol Diaries*, p. 416.
41. In an interview at this time, Warhol casually remarked, "I'm doing knives and guns. Just making abstract shapes out of them." See Blinderman, "Modern Myths," p. 147. In a diary entry for July 16, 1980, Warhol expressed concern about the impending election of Ronald Reagan, writing, "it does look scary"; Hackett, *The Andy Warhol Diaries*, p. 304).
42. Andy Warhol quoted in "New Talent USA," *Art in America,* 50, no. 1 (1962), p. 42.
43. Andy Warhol, entry for Oct. 8, 1984, in Hackett, *The Andy Warhol Diaries*, p. 606.
44. John Richardson revealed Warhol's devout Catholicism to the public in his eulogy at Warhol's funeral. Previously, only his closest confidants were aware of his religious beliefs. Charles Stuckey has noted that Warhol had wanted to make religious imagery since 1980. Stuckey's assumption is probably based on the interview in which Warhol confesses to beginning a "Madonna and Child" series in 1980; Blinderman, "Modern Myths," p. 147. These factors suggest the importance of religious iconography to Warhol, despite Jay Shriver's claim that these were "just another button to push"; interview with the author.
45. Warhol's Carnegie classmate and roommate in New York City, Joseph Groell, remarked, "He was always sending out postcards. They would have these little ovals—Easter Eggs—pasted on them"; quoted in Smith, *Warhol: Conversations*, p. 32). Jay Shriver also confirmed this, saying that the *Eggs* "began as Easter presents. . . . Those little gift-giving occasions were important to Andy"; interview with the author.
46. These paintings were first exhibited by Anton Kern Gallery, New York, in 1998. The essay by James Hofmaier in the accompanying catalogue provides the only published information on the paintings; see *Andy Warhol: Fifteen Abstract Paintings*. The exhibition was reviewed by Richard Kalina, "Andy Warhol at Anton Kern—New York, New York," *Art in America*, 86 (Nov. 1998), p. 130.
47. Thomas Kellein explains the circumstances surrounding this commission in his landmark publication *Andy Warhol: Abstrakt,* p. 45. Jay Shriver described the process of creating the *Yarn* painting. "It's just yarn that was taken off its . . . skein and draped on a white paper background where we could photograph it. We tried doing a picture of a roll of yarn as well, and that wasn't very persuasive as a painting. It was blah, and Rupert even tried a rainbow roll. That was Rupert's solution to just about everything was 'Let's do a rainbow roll' and that will make it more fantasy. . . . With a 'rainbow roll' you get all the colors of the rainbow in the silkscreen. In the screen the ink that's applied with one screen has a gradation of color across it. So you might start at one edge of the screen with red and you might end up on the other end of the screen with green. And all the different colors of the rainbow in between being screened across one screen. And that's called a 'rainbow roll.' . . . They might bring to mind kind of a silkscreened Pollock."

48. At this time Warhol had purchased a larger building on 33rd Street. Over the summer *Interview* magazine moved out of the Union Square building and for the first time in his career, Warhol had a large space in which to work. The result was a dramatic increase in the scale of his paintings, which continued after he moved his studio into the ballroom on 33rd Street in November 1984. See Hackett, *The Andy Warhol Diaries*, pp. 501, 538, 619.

49. In an interview with the author, Jay Shriver elaborated on the circumstances surrounding the creation of the *Rorschachs*: "The other big thing that happened was *Interview* moved from 860 Broadway to the new building on 33rd Street in 1984. By then 860 was basically just an empty 14,000-square-foot loft, left for Andy to paint in. That's when the paintings get really huge. We could back up the overhead projector the length of a football field from the wall. He could get any scale he wanted. And nobody was there to bother him. That's what enabled the *Rorschachs*. Andy said, 'We need a new idea.' And, by that time it had been made very clear to me that abstraction was an important element that he wanted to pursue and abstractions weren't being commissioned. So, I thought of the *Rorschachs* because it was primitive printmaking. I thought we would be printing the images or somehow incorporating the screening of the images onto the canvas. I didn't think we would physically be making them until after I made the first maquettes for the idea. The question was, how could we get a similar image repeated by using this very rudimentary printing procedure of folding a paper in half?

"As it turned out, we made huge ten-foot-by-eight-foot paintings in the same manner, by folding them in half and playing with the viscosity of the paint to get a more inky kind of texture. We would take the canvas (the little canvases were the size of a piece of paper), and then fold it in half, so you'd have your median and then on one half you have a shape. What I did is make one *Rorschach*, as a *Rorschach* would be made, folding the painting in half to get an image. With carbon paper, I traced half of the image from that painting and transferred that half onto the other canvases. Then I filled in that image of the half *Rorschach* with ink or Liquatex black paint. Then, I'd fold them over, hoping to get relatively the same image. But, of course, each one is going to be significantly different from the other ones. Any printing process is. Like all of Andy's work.

"Andy painted the big ones, and that's why he was having so much fun. We had since given up on reproducing the same image. So each painting was a new creation. We had these huge canvases that we had to fold over and press together so that the paint was evenly distributed on both halves of the canvas. We took some of the huge dowels, on which canvas was shipped, and Andy, Augusto [Bugarin], Benjamin [Liu], and myself would get on our hands and knees, rolling the dowels and patting the canvas to get an even pressure across the entire surface. Naturally, it ran out at one end. Later, Andy found out later that there is a standard set of *Rorschach* blots that I was unaware of. He would have been much happier finding those and just straight away printing those onto these large canvases. At least that's what he claims. But we had a lot of fun making these. It was truly a creative process that was being experienced. It was really kind of experimentation. Then at the end we were moving onto other things. It was kind of a step to other things. It didn't evolve any further. Nobody showed it. The only person that really showed any interest in them was Jasper Johns. He has a couple of really nice white ones—white on white. He traded for them. I remember being surprised that he had even heard that Andy was doing these."

50. Nickas, "Andy Warhol's Rorschach Tests," pp. 28–32.

51. Rosalind Krauss, "Carnal Knowledge," in *Andy Warhol: Rorschach Paintings*, p. 9.

52. Andy Warhol quoted in 1985 in Buchloh, "An Interview with Andy Warhol," in Michelson, *Andy Warhol,* p. 12[illegible]. He said nearly the same thing a year later: "I was trying to do these to actually read into them and write about them"; Nickas, "Andy Warhol's Rorschach Tests," p. 29.

53. Andy Warhol, entry for Oct. 4, 1982, in Hackett, *The Andy Warhol Diaries*, p. 462. See also the essay by Bruno Bischofberger in this volume. In an interview with the author, Jay Shriver related an interesting story about a trade that he had engineered for Warhol. "For the first trade I went to Jean-Michel's studio. I just kind of introduced myself off the street and I went up. He told me he thought I was Puerto Rican so he let me up, because I had some kind of hair on my face at the time, so when I screamed up at him on Crosby Street he let me in. And, because he'd always been a big Andy fan, we did a trade. We did a portrait of Jean-Michel and in return we would get to choose a couple paintings of his. I chose one particular painting that he said, 'But it's for Bruno. You can't take this.' Finally, he agreed, "Okay, you can take it, but you have to get it out of here soon." So, I took it right then. I was lugging this big painting up Lafayette Street trying to figure out how to get it to Warhol's studio. And, I actually convinced a plumber to give me a ride in his van from Crosby Street up to Union Square for five bucks. It's a turquoise painting that's hinged and has liberty and Indian-head nickels attached to it. So, that was the first painting of Jean's that Andy traded for. And, I got it up to the studio and Andy was thrilled. He loved the painting. It's big, it has bright colors, and we had it in the front room. That was a big day in my Warhol years.

"Andy was getting back into hand-painted imagery on his own. Jean-Michel and Andy just kind of happened upon working on the *Collaborations* together. Jean-Michel started to come up to the studio regularly, and Andy said, 'Well you can paint on this,' and handed him a painting. Without hesitation Jean-Michel started painting on these little paintings. Andy thought that was great, so he kept on handing him small paintings. And then he said, 'Well, you'll have to come by tomorrow. We'll do bigger paintings.' And so after Jean-Michel left,

I remember Andy working on many big paintings, so that when Jean-Michel came back the next day there would be bigger surfaces for him to work on. At that time I did quite a bit of painting on the hand-painted stuff. Just to get a beginning. By the time Bruno commissioned the *Collaborations*, Andy and Jean-Michel had made around one hundred paintings."

54. Over the period of his involvement with Jean-Michel Basquiat, from October 4, 1982, to approximately January 1986, Warhol repeatedly remarked on the liveliness of the art scene and how it reminded him of the vitality of the 1960s: "[T]he Whitney, the Biennial . . . is just like the sixties," and "I'm going around with Jean Michel and we're getting so much art work done, and then his party with Schnabel and Wim Wenders and Jim Jarmusch. . . . I mean, being with a creative crowd, you really notice the difference." Entries for Mar. 23, 1983, and Nov. 14, 1984, in Hackett, *The Andy Warhol Diaries*, pp. 493, 615.

55. See the Bischofberger essay in this volume.

56. Max Wechsler described the exhibition as "disappointing" and said he "expected more" of this "illustrious group." See Wechsler, "Reviews: Collaborations, Gallery Bruno Bischofberger," *Artforum*, 23 (Jan. 1985), p. 99.

57. Andy Warhol, entry for Apr. 16, 1984, in Hackett, *The Andy Warhol Diaries*, p. 566.

58. Andy Warhol, entry for May 29, 1984, in ibid., p. 579. He states, "We painted an African masterpiece together. One hundred feet long. He's better than I am, though."

59. Andy Warhol, entries for Sept. 14, Sept. 19, and Nov. 24, 1985, in ibid., pp. 677, 680, and 695. See also Vivian Raynor, "A Basquiat–Warhol Pas de Deux," *The New York Times,* Sept. 20, 1985, p. 85.

60. Andy Warhol, entry for Sept. 17, 1984, in Hackett, *The Andy Warhol Diaries*, p. 600.

61. Smith, *Warhol: Conversations*, p. 184.

62. Jay Shriver, interview with the author.

63. In these personal works Warhol clarifies his stance on the left of the political barometer. Describing Warhol's late work as "his most corrupted and debased moments," Benjamin Buchloh argues that by rejecting the primacy of the mechanical image, returning to painting, and seeming to champion such figures as Nancy Reagan and Imelda Marcos on the cover of *Interview* magazine, Warhol positions himself as an aesthetic neo-conservative who contributes to fetishizing the commercial art object; Buchloh, "The Andy Warhol Line, in Garrels, *The Work of Andy Warhol*, pp. 60–65.

64. Pat Hackett wrote, "[T]oward the end of the seventies he started to mellow," and "The personal and emotional problems he himself went through during the years covered by the diaries left him looking for comfort, not drama, in his friendships. By the last year of his life, he was kinder and easier to be around than at any time since I'd met him"; Hackett, "Introduction," *The Andy Warhol Diaries*, pp. xix, xx.

65. Andy Warhol, entry for Mar. 21, 1986, in ibid., p. 715. By this time Warhol realized that his partner, Jon Gould, would succumb to AIDS (he died in Sept. 1986), and he increasingly experienced health problems. As he had done when his mother died in 1972, he remained silent, telling no one.

66. Andy Warhol, entry for May 21, 1986, in ibid., p. 734. See also entry for July 13, 1986, p. 742, where Warhol described the opening: "D'Offay 'art-directed' the whole show—he'd tell me he wanted a certain picture, and then I'd think he'd never remember, so I'd do the one I liked instead, and when he'd come back to New York he'd say that wasn't the one he'd picked."

67. Anthony d'Offay quoted by Dietmar Elger in "The Best American Invention—To Be Able to Disappear," in Elger, ed., *Andy Warhol: Selbsportraits/Self-Portraits*, exh. cat. (Ostfildern-Ruit, Germany: Hatje Cantz, 2004), p. 127.

68. In an interview with the author, Jay Shriver discussed the genesis and the proposed purpose of the *Camouflage* paintings:
"For the *Camouflage* paintings I brought in the piece of netting that I had been using in my painting, which was left over, and he says, 'Great. Trace it. This will be great. We'll make a painting.' And, for the first painting, we actually took a photograph of the net and screened the netting as a half tone over the image. He decided it was too literal. Andy did little handwork on the *Camouflage* paintings. He didn't specifically choose colors. But they weren't commissions, and that's what makes them personal. The whole notion of the print was accepted as a means for creating an image. The intention with the *Camouflage* was, I think, an event, much like the *Silver Clouds* or the wallpaper.
"He had an idea for an installation of *Camouflage* paintings that was expressed to me from a very early point, but was never acted on. The idea was to hang smaller paintings onto a backdrop of big *Camouflage* paintings. How to accomplish that feat, other than by making wallpaper, I don't know. But, wallpaper can't be sold for the same price as a painting. There are vast rolls of screened *Camouflage* on cloth. Stephen Sprouse loved the camouflage. He thought that was the greatest. And, Stephen asked Andy if he could, in fact, use this to make fabric for his clothing. Stephen Sprouse has a camouflage line, thanks to Andy. And, those bolts of fabric printed with camouflage imagery come from the maquette that Stephen wound up using for his fabrics. It was the same maquette that was printed up to use as tablecloths at the party following Andy's memorial service."

69. Brenda Richardson develops this idea in her essay, "Hiding in Plain Sight: Warhol's Camouflage," published in the 1998 catalogue for the first exhibition of the *Camouflage* paintings, *Andy Warhol: Camouflage*, pp. 11–31.

70. Jane Daggett Dillenberger asserts that this is the most important series of religious art in the United States since John Singer Sargent's murals *The Triumph of Religion* (1890–1919) in the Boston Public Library; Dillenberger, *The Religious Art of Andy Warhol*, p. 41).

71. Andy Warhol quoted in Paul Taylor, "The Last Interview: Andy

Warhol," *Flash Art*, no. 133 (Apr. 1987), p. 42. In several interviews, including this one, Warhol deflected questions about his personal beliefs, claiming he accepted the commission because "It's a good picture," or "It's something that you see all the time. You don't think about it." Ibid., 41.

72. In an interview with the author, Jay Shriver described the problems in selecting a good source for *The Last Supper* paintings: "Andy liked the idea, and we started doing it. The *Last Suppers* took over a year for the work to be done. We started out with the da Vinci original, but I think there was some issue about appropriating that image. And then Andy wanted to do it from some other source. I mentioned that I had seen some porcelain copies when I would walk to my bank over on 40th Street, and we bought one. I took Polaroids of it with a special camera with close-up lenses, given to Andy by Polaroid. That was such a pain that we ended up going back to the chromo of the original. So we were doing lots of these big paintings. They were printed. They weren't painted." Rupert Smith gave a slightly different version of the story in an interview published in Jörg Schellmann, ed., *Andy Warhol: Art from Art* (Cologne and New York: Edition Schellmann, 1994), p. 77.

73. Schultz-Hofmann, *Andy Warhol: The Last Supper*, p. 32.

74. Donna de Salvo shared this observation in a conversation with the author, Oct. 17, 2008.

75. Schultz-Hofmann, *Andy Warhol: The Last Supper*, p. 29.

76. This source also carries allusions to AIDS, which was, at the time, known as the gay cancer, and relates to Warhol's partner, who had been diagnosed with AIDS at about this time. Source material in the Warhol Archives, The Andy Warhol Museum, Pittsburgh.

77. John Coplans, *Andy Warhol* (New York: New York Graphic Society, 1970), p. 52; Andy Warhol quoted in "New Talent USA," 42.

78. Buchloh, "An Interview with Andy Warhol," in Michelson, *Andy Warhol*, p. 124.

79. Robert Pincus-Witten, "Entries: Big History, Little History," *Arts Magazine*, 54 (Apr. 1980), p. 184.

Andy Warhol: Abstraction

Keith Hartley

Andy Warhol was ambivalent about abstraction. On the one hand he was fascinated by it—especially Abstract Expressionism—captivated by the almost religious reverence and hero worship accorded to its chief American practitioners, especially Jackson Pollock. In New York during the 1950s it would have been hard for the ambitious young commercial artist not to envy (and secretly admire?) the enormous success of Pollock. And yet, at the same time, Warhol was as much repelled as attracted by the macho, hard-drinking lifestyle of artists such as Pollock. Even though he had a high regard for Pollock's art, Warhol must have known that his own deeply ironic approach to life was incapable of the unquestioning self-assurance needed to produce the self-sustaining monologue of Abstract Expressionist painting. Warhol needed images of real life, with their own stories and their own resonances, with which to react and set up a dialogue. Nevertheless, throughout his career, Warhol seems to have revered the purity and raw energy of Abstract Expressionism, and again and again he came up with strategies to allow him to compete with it. Whether these strategies were straight homage or attempts at collapsing the heroics and sublime individualism of Abstract Expressionist painting is a moot point. This essay argues that the artist's approach to abstraction is a mixture of both and that Warhol remained ambivalent on the question.

Before Andy Warhol arrived in New York from Pittsburgh in June 1949, it is doubtful he was much aware of the Abstract Expressionist painters then beginning to make a name for themselves in the city.[1] He had set his sights, initially at least, on a career in commercial art, and in this he was very successful, getting work straight away with a magazine in the Condé Nast empire. Commercial artwork was an area in which Carnegie Tech, Warhol's school in Pittsburgh, had specialized. He had received training in Bauhaus-derived design, which saw no principled difference between so-called commercial art and fine art, and one of the artists who had a strong influence on his drawing at that time was Paul Klee.[2] A large percentage of the drawings that Warhol made in the late 1940s and 1950s was connected with his commercial work: book illustrations and advertisments in magazines and newspapers. Much has been made of the sparseness and elegance of the line in these drawings, as well as the use of the blotted-line technique to obtain a lightness and discontinuity of touch. Many have commented on the whimsy and lighthearted humor of these drawings. But just as significant and perhaps more seminal for Warhol's future

Fig. 34. *Sprite Heads Playing Violins*, 1948. Ink, graphite, and tempera on Manila paper, 10⅝ x 9¼ in. (27 x 23.5 cm). The Andy Warhol Museum, Pittsburgh; Founding Collection, Contribution The Andy Warhol Foundation for the Visual Arts, Inc.

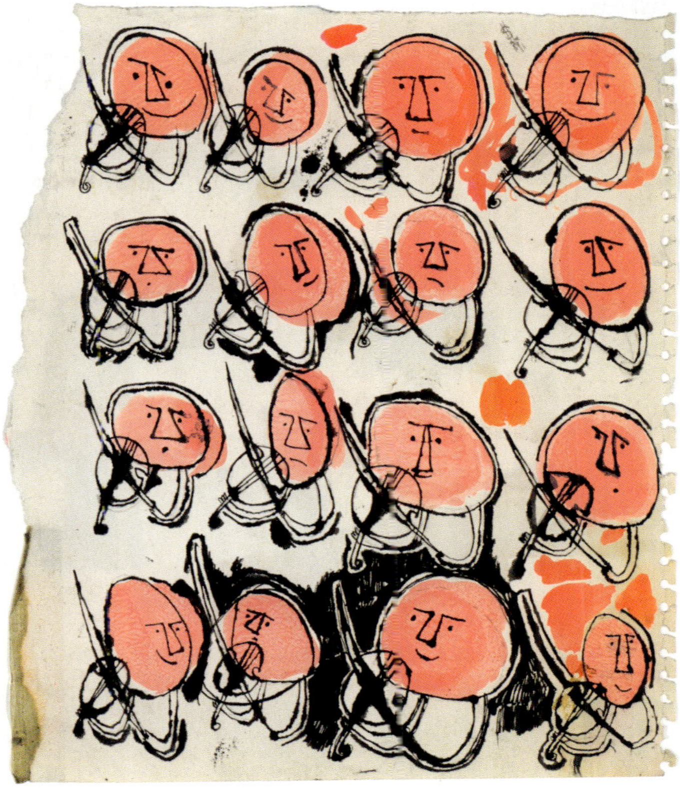

development were the various ways in which he abstracted from reality and emphasized the abstract qualities of the drawing. Very often Warhol would reduce objects and body parts to simple geometric forms, and instead of representing a scene, he would simply repeat these simplified shapes to create patterns. Sometimes he would vary the shapes very slightly, but at other times he would repeat them exactly, either by tracing or by blotting—the technique of pressing a still-wet ink drawing on to another piece of paper. In some works he would use rubber stamps to print the same image again and again.

Examples of such repetitive pattern-making go back to Warhol's days at Carnegie Tech. *Sprite Heads Playing Violins* (1948, fig. 34) is a drawing that he did for the school magazine, *Cano*. Each violinist is reduced to two spindly arms holding a violin and a bow and, above all, a large head, which is little more than a roughly drawn circle or oval and a highly schematized set of eyes, nose, and mouth. The humor of the drawing lies in the variety of emotions concisely adumbrated on each face. But what is most remarkable is that even at art school Warhol was working with grids and repetitive elements. The differing characterization of each head is effective precisely because the heads are so similar and line up in rows. Difference becomes readily apparent in a context of similarity. That is surely why Warhol not only accepted but positively welcomed misprintings, misalignments, and over- and underinkings in his screenprinted, multiple portraits of the 1960s. For example, the overinking of one vertical line of heads in his *Marilyn Diptych* (1962) stands out against the homogeneity of most of the other images, and the error serves to convey a tragic overtone.

Back at art school, and even in the early 1950s, it is unlikely that Warhol was thinking about commodification, the effects of industrial production, or mass media. The most likely influences on his thinking at this stage in his career were Paul Klee's ideas about rhythm and movement and the highly structured, gridlike works Klee made at the Bauhaus in the mid-1920s. In a painting such as *Wandbild (Mural)* (1924, fig. 35), which was shown in the Klee exhibition at the Museum of Modern Art, New York, in early 1950,[3] the repetition and alternation of various geometric, architectural structures, such as semicircular arches, pointed arches, windows and roofs, are typical of what Klee meant by the rhythms that could be set up between "dividual" and "individual" forms in a work of art.[4]

In addition to the linear repetition of pictorial elements, another feature Warhol seems to have taken from Klee is

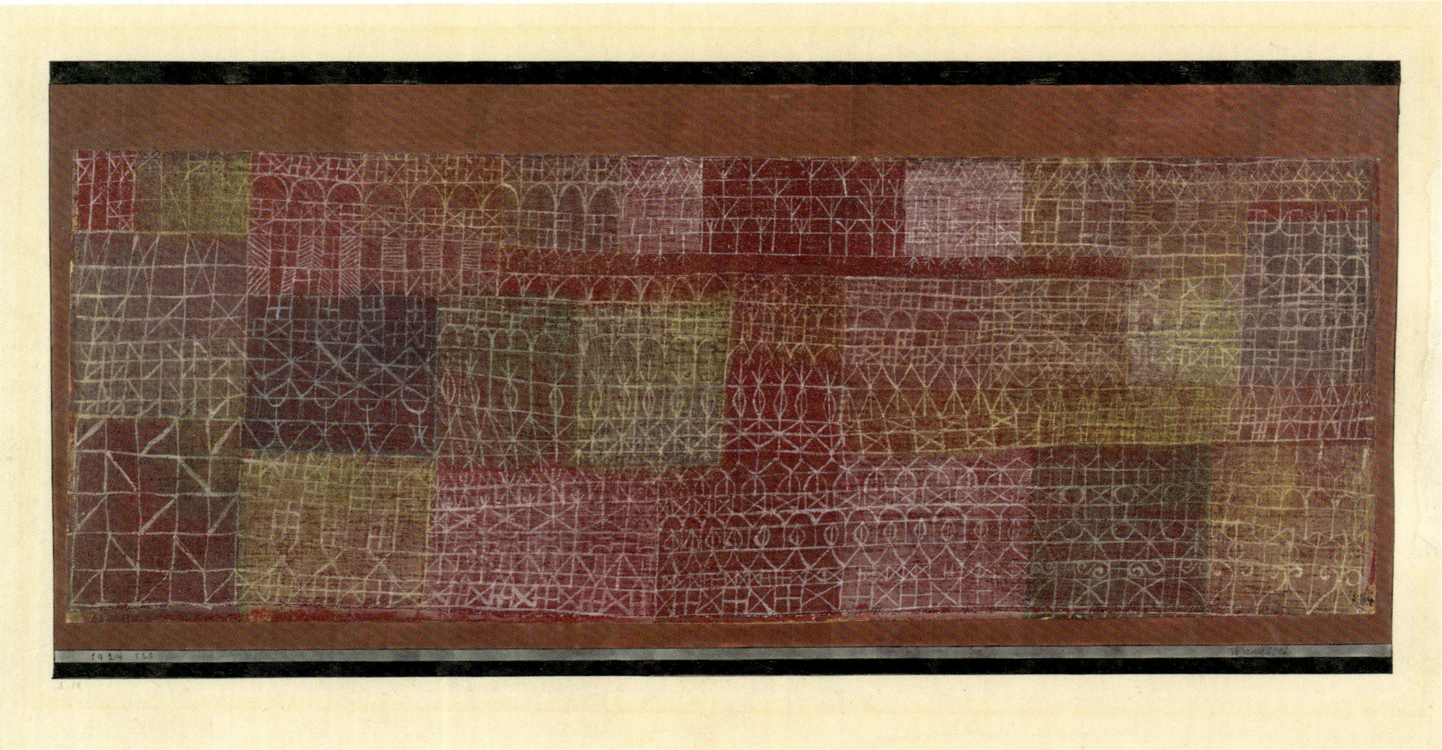

Fig. 35. Paul Klee, *Wandbild (Mural)*, 1924 (128). Watercolor on primed muslin on paper on cardboard, 10 x 21⅝ in. (25.4 x 55 cm). Zentrum Paul Klee, Bern

the all-over composition or lack of compositional focus (or foci). This was, of course, one of the chief characteristics of Pollock's drip paintings of the late 1940s and early 1950s; but even before Warhol felt the full impact of Pollock's work, Klee's example was crucial. Throughout the 1950s Warhol continued to make frequent use of linear repetition and all-over compositions. In a drawing such as *NYC Street Map (Uptown)* (1950s, fig. 36) the grid structure of Upper Manhattan provides the basis for the repetitive pattern of horizontals and verticals, but the schematized houses, with their pitched roofs, and the rows of trees in Central Park are what really create the rhythm—the element that Klee felt was so important. In *Untitled (Four Rows of Eyes)* (c. 1952, fig. 37), simply by abstracting single eyes from their facial context and placing them in horizontal and vertical lines, Warhol emphasizes not only their generic and their individual qualities but also their ability to metamorphose into fish, complete with fins (eyelashes) and their

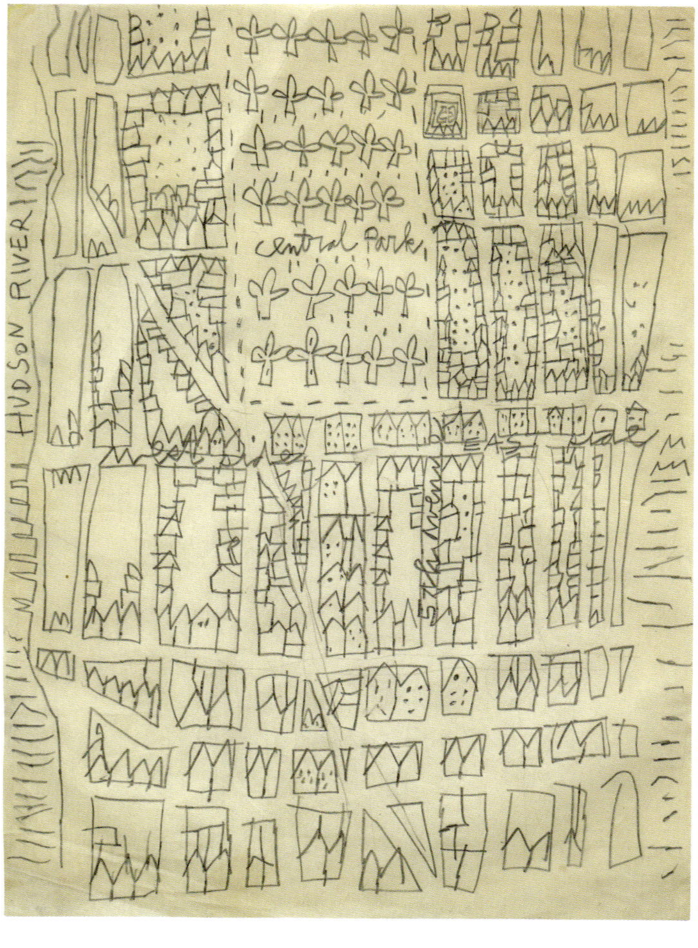

Fig. 36. *NYC Street Map (Uptown)*, 1950s. Graphite on off-white bond paper, 11⅞ x 9 in. (30.2 x 22.9 cm). The Andy Warhol Museum, Pittsburgh; Founding Collection, Contribution The Andy Warhol Foundation for the Visual Arts, Inc.

own eyes (eyeballs and pupils), swimming in a disciplined shoal from left to right. The wit and formal playfulness are again reminiscent of Klee, as can be seen, for example, in his *Migrating Fish* (1926),[5] but the abstraction of a key facial feature is typical of Warhol and anticipates the way he highlighted the eyes, lips, and hair in his early 1960s screenprint paintings, particularly the *Marilyns* and, above all, *Marilyn Monroe's Lips* (1962, fig. 38).

During the 1950s, when Warhol was earning his living drawing advertisements for commercial products, his art (both personal and professional) was affected increasingly by the very nature of mass production. The items he was promoting were not unique but made to be as alike as possible. Warhol understood the profound impact that this was having on society, its culture, and especially its art. In his book *POPism: The Warhol '60s* he tells the story of how his friend Emile de Antonio (at that time—about 1961–62—an artist's agent) praised Warhol's no-frills, no-drips, no-smears painting of a Coke bottle (fig. 8, page 20): "[I]t's our society, it's who we are, it's absolutely beautiful and

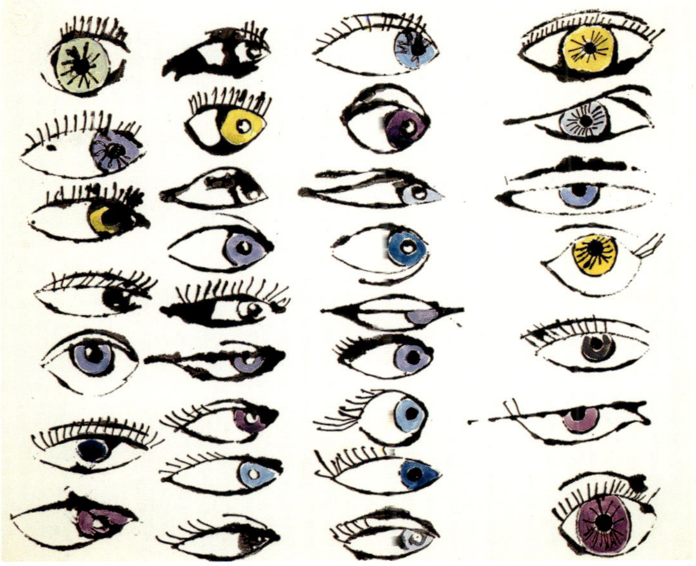

Fig. 37. *Untitled (Four Rows of Eyes)*, c. 1952. Ink and aniline paint on paper, 13 x 15¾ in. (33 x 40 cm). Kunstmuseum Basel, Kupferstichkabinett

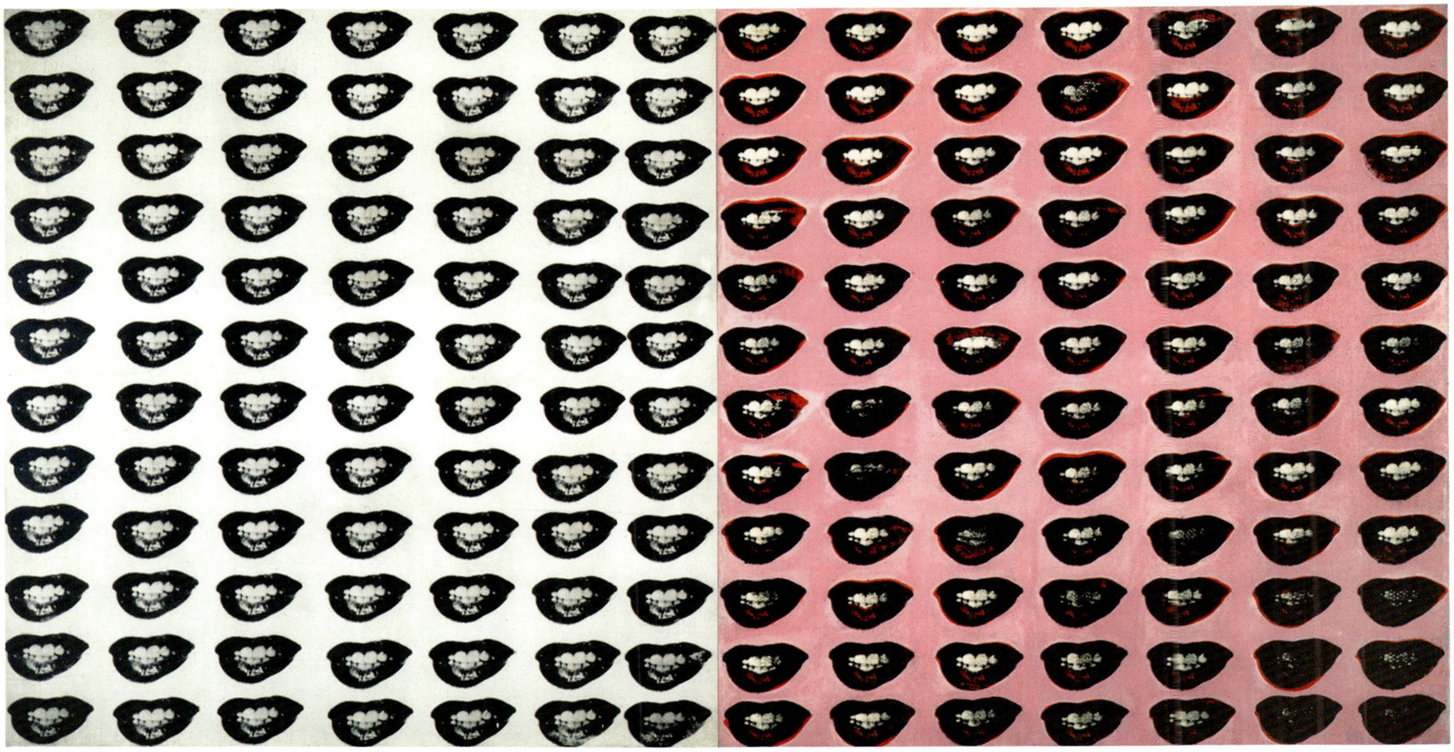

Fig. 38. *Marilyn Monroe's Lips*, 1962. Acrylic, silkscreen ink, and pencil on canvas, two parts, 82¾ x 80 in. (210.7 x 204.9 cm), 82¾ x 80⅜ in. (210.7 x 209.7 cm). Hirshhorn Museum and Sculpture Garden, Smithsonian Institution, Gift of Joseph H. Hirshhorn, 1972

naked."[6] This story is often quoted; however, a sentence earlier in the book is cited less frequently: "De [Antonio] was the first person I know of to see commercial art as real art and real art as commercial art and he made the whole New York art world see it in that way too."[7]

Warhol was persuaded that the time had come for art to reflect the everyday culture of commercial products (such as Coke bottles) and that snobbish distinctions between fine and commercial (so-called high and low) art were no longer valid. But he needed confirmation of his feelings from someone who knew the New York art scene and was highly respected by the potentially hostile (true, as it turned out) Abstract Expressionist artists, who then held the high cultural ground. Warhol was forthright and pithy in his defense of low (democratic) culture, as this statement in *The Philosophy of Andy Warhol* (1975) demonstrates: "A Coke is a Coke and no amount of money can get you a better Coke than the one the bum on the corner is drinking. All the Cokes are the same and all the Cokes are good. Liz Taylor knows it, the President knows it, the bum knows it, and you know it."[8] However, at the same time, he was in awe of the Abstract Expressionist painters, of Jackson Pollock in particular, and one gets the impression that he always felt they somehow provided a benchmark against which his own and other art had to be measured. The question is, was the benchmark simply a result of the fame and prestige that Abstract Expressionism attained in the 1950s or evidence of Warhol's genuine admiration for its artistic values? The answer is complex. It has as much to do with Warhol's feelings of being an outsider (sexual, as much as anything else) as with his desperate need to feel part of a group. If he could not be part of the Establishment group, then he would create his own alternative group and beat the Establishment at its own game.

It is not accidental that Warhol begins his book *POPism* by looking at the origins of Pop art in the context of and in opposition to Abstract Expressionism. This was the beast he had to slay before a new era, the Warhol 1960s, could begin. The 1950s was Jackson Pollock's decade. It began, symbolically, in August 1949, two months after Warhol arrived in New York from Pittsburgh, with a major article in *Life* magazine, entitled "Jackson Pollock: Is He the Greatest Living Painter in the United States?" (fig. 39).[9] Although Pollock's drip paintings had received publicity the year

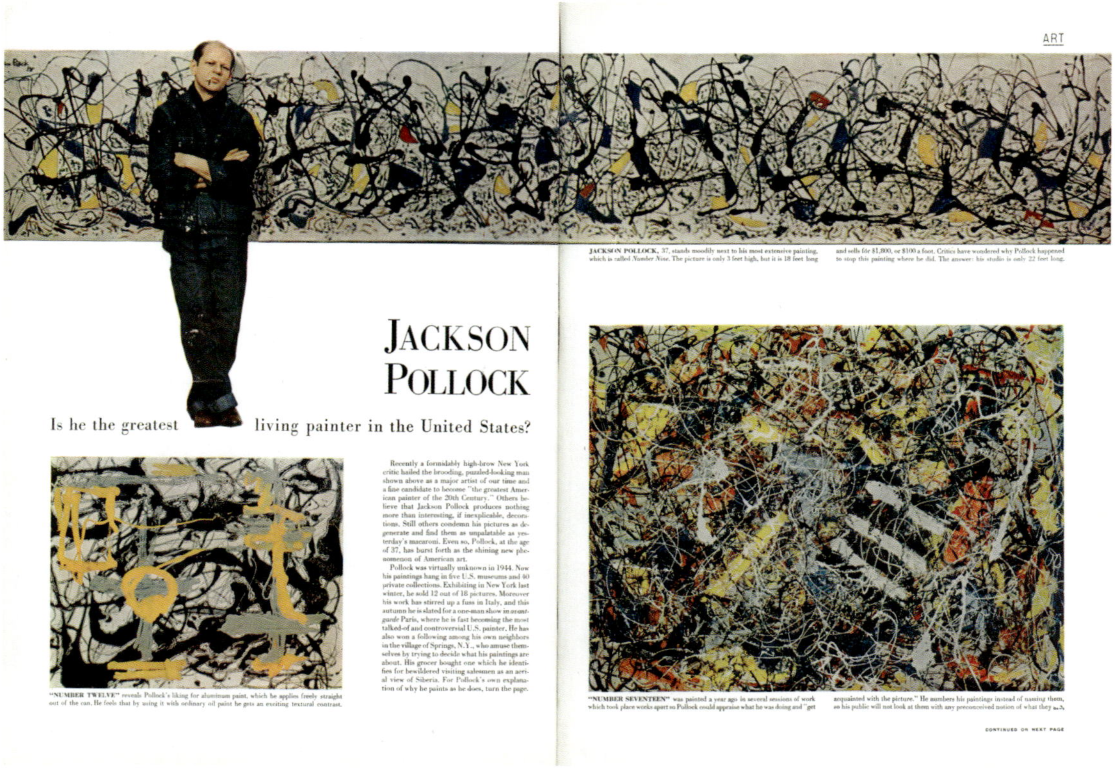
ART

JACKSON POLLOCK, 37, stands moodily next to his most extensive painting, which is called *Number Nine*. The picture is only 3 feet high, but it is 18 feet long and sells for $1,800, or $100 a foot. Critics have wondered why Pollock happened to stop this painting where he did. The answer: his studio is only 22 feet long.

JACKSON POLLOCK

Is he the greatest living painter in the United States?

Recently a formidably high-brow New York critic hailed the brooding, puzzled-looking man shown above as a major artist of our time and a fine candidate to become "the greatest American painter of the 20th Century." Others believe that Jackson Pollock produces nothing more than interesting, if inexplicable, decorations. Still others condemn his pictures as degenerate and find them as unpalatable as yesterday's macaroni. Even so, Pollock, at the age of 37, has burst forth as the shining new phenomenon of American art.

Pollock was virtually unknown in 1944. Now his paintings hang in five U.S. museums and 40 private collections. Exhibiting in New York last winter, he sold 12 out of 18 pictures. Moreover his work has stirred up a fuss in Italy, and this autumn he is slated for a one-man show in *avant-garde* Paris, where he is fast becoming the most talked-of and controversial U.S. painter. He has also won a following among his own neighbors in the village of Springs, N.Y., who amuse themselves by trying to decide what his paintings are about. His grocer bought one which he identifies for bewildered visiting salesmen as an aerial view of Siberia. For Pollock's own explanation of why he paints as he does, turn the page.

"NUMBER TWELVE" reveals Pollock's liking for aluminum paint, which he applies freely straight out of the can. He feels that by using it with ordinary oil paint he gets an exciting textural contrast.

"NUMBER SEVENTEEN" was painted a year ago in several sessions of work which took place weeks apart so Pollock could appraise what he was doing and "get acquainted with the picture." He numbers his paintings instead of naming them, so his public will not look at them with any preconceived notion of what they are.

CONTINUED ON NEXT PAGE

Fig. 39. "Jackson Pollock: Is He the Greatest Living Painter in the United States?" *Life*, August 8, 1949 before in connection with his show at the Betty Parsons Gallery[10] and in a roundtable discussion published in *Life*, in which Pollock's *Cathedral* (1947) was illustrated, it was the 1949 *Life* article that really drew general attention to his work. To an ambitious young artist like Warhol, although intent on a career in commercial art, Pollock must have seemed like a distant hero, occupying a position in the art world that Warhol could only dream of, but a hero nonetheless. Pollock was, after all, a native-born American who had taken on the Europeans at their own game and won. Abstract art had been largely a European phenomenon before World War II, but Pollock had made it American by developing it on a completely new scale and with a new virile energy. Sexual epithets comparing the masculinity of American Abstract Expressionism with the perceived effeteness of European abstract art became commonplace. Much of this was owed to the article in *Life*. Arnold Newman's famous photograph of Jackson Pollock seeming to lean against his friezelike painting *Summertime: Number 9A* (1948) became the archetypal image of the macho artist. Wearing a denim jacket and jeans, he appears with his arms folded in aggressive self-protection, his head tipped to the side with half-closed eyes as if he were sizing up the opposition, a cigarette hanging out the corner of his mouth in almost slovenly informality, and his legs crossed with self-conscious nonchalance.[11]

The stark Coke bottle painting that Emile de Antonio liked so much was not the only painting Warhol showed his friend. He also showed him another painting of a Coke bottle, which Warhol described in *POPism* as having "Abstract Expressionist hash marks halfway up the side."[12] De Antonio rejected it as "a piece of shit, simply a little bit of everything"[13] Another friend, Ivan Karp, who then worked for the dealer Leo Castelli, was asked for his opinion about the two modes of painting. According to Warhol's later testimony in *POPism*, Karp was even more specific about the references to Abstract Expressionism: "[The] blunt, straightforward works are the only ones of any consequence. The others are all homage to Abstract Expressionism and are not."[14] In evaluating these remarks, it should be remembered that *POPism* was published in 1980 and that Warhol had quite a capacity to both invent and deliberately forget things. However, Pat Hackett, who collaborated with Warhol on *POPism*, did a huge amount of research in the form of interviews, which she incorporated into the book. According to Bob Colacello (another Warhol employee): "Pat Hackett was struggling with Andy's version of the sixties. The most credible portions of that book, *POPism*, were based on her interviews with Henry Geldzahler, Emile de Antonio, and other sixties players, not Andy."[15] Therefore, it seems Warhol not only wished to play up the fact that his early Pop paintings were influenced by Abstract Expressionism but also that his friends saw it this way as well.

Friends such as de Antonio and Larry Rivers (both quoted at length in *POPism*) also sought to highlight one of the reasons why Warhol did not fit in with New York's Abstract Expressionist painters: Warhol was gay and showed it in his camp behavior, whereas Pollock and the Abstract Expressionist painters were (or had the reputation for being) aggressively macho. According to Warhol, "The world of Abstract Expressionists was very macho. The painters used to hang around the Cedar Bar on University Place were all hard-driving, two-fisted types who'd grab each other and say things like 'I'll knock your fucking teeth out' and 'I'll steal your girl.' . . . The toughness was part of a tradition, it went with their agonized, anguished art. They were always exploding and having fistfights about their work and their love lives. This went on all through the fifties when I was new in town, doing whatever jobs I could get in advertising and spending my nights at home drawing to meet deadlines."[16] One wonders if Warhol were in some way envious of Pollock and his friends raising hell at the Cedar Tavern while he had to stay at home and work. Warhol's friends did not call him Drella—a combination of Cinderella and Dracula—for nothing. But Warhol knew he could never fit in with such macho artists and instead went out of his way to play up his camp, gay mannerisms. "And as for the 'swish' thing, I'd always had a lot of fun with that—just watching the expressions on people's faces. You'd have to have seen the way all the Abstract Expressionist painters carried themselves and the kinds of images they cultivated, to understand how shocked people were to see a painter coming on swish. I certainly wasn't a butch kind of guy by nature, but I must admit, I went out of my way to play up the other extreme."[17]

Reading *POPism,* it almost seems as if the course Warhol's art took from 1961–62 onward was part of this "playing up the other extreme." The Abstract Expressionists disliked having anything to do with commercial art; Warhol made commercial-product and media branding central to

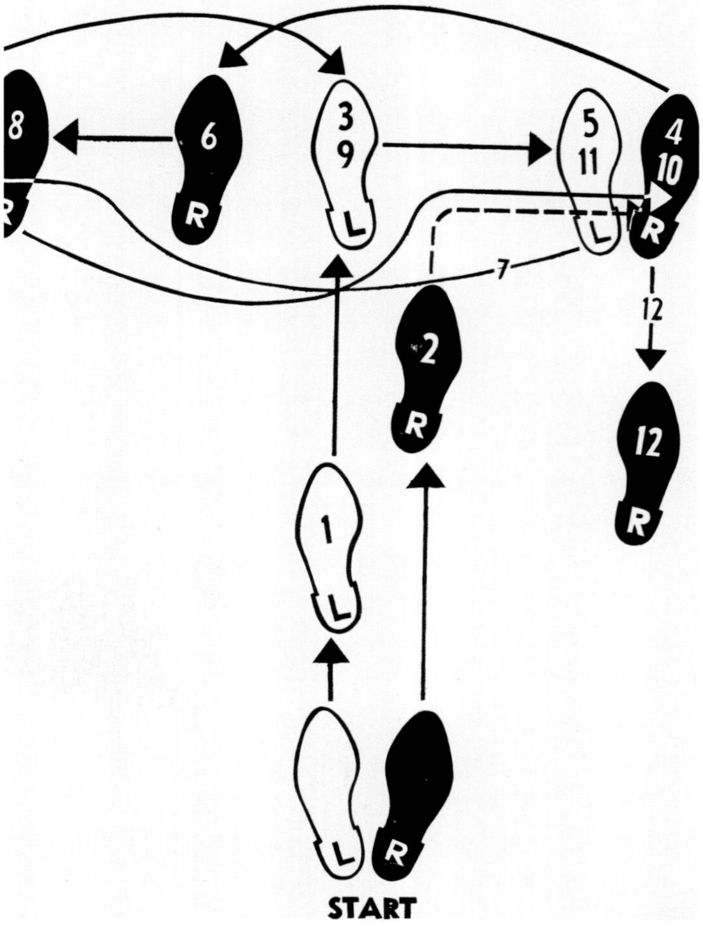

Fig. 40. *Dance Diagram [2]* [Fox Trot: "The Double Twinkle-Man"], 1962. Casein and graphite on linen, 71½ x 51¾ in. (181.6 x 131.4 cm). The Andy Warhol Museum, Pittsburgh; Founding Collection, Contribution The Andy Warhol Foundation for the Visual Arts, Inc.

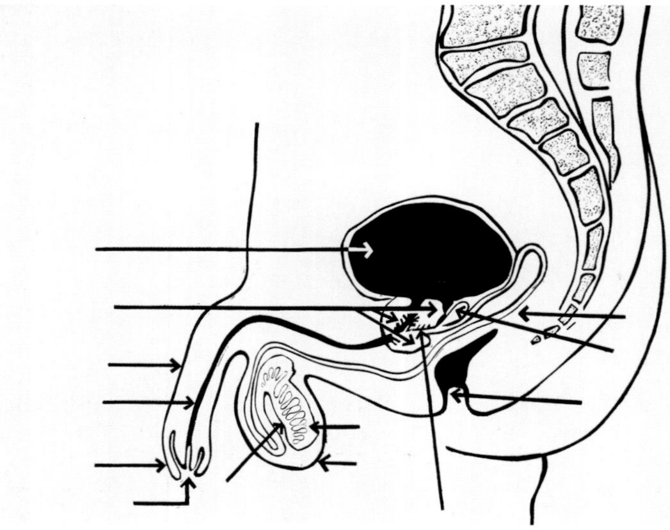

Fig. 41. *Male Genital Diagram*, 1962. Casein and pencil on linen, 54 x 72 in. (137.2 x 182.9 cm). The Andy Warhol Museum, Pittsburgh; Founding Collection, Contribution The Andy Warhol Foundation for the Visual Arts, Inc.

his art, provocatively calling business art the best type of art. His detractors thought Warhol wanted to kill art and do away with personal expression; Warhol said he wanted to be a machine. But one could argue that Warhol "played up" so much, adopted seemingly opposed tendencies, because deep down he was attracted to the heroic scale of Abstract Expressionism and, in the case of Jackson Pollock, the constant, repetitive action in his drip paintings. Put bluntly, he wanted on one level to like (and be liked by) Pollock and the other macho artists, but because he was rejected by them, he adopted a contrary stance. Nowhere does this mixture of fascination with and simultaneous rejection of Pollock find a more iconic expression than in Warhol's *Dance Diagram* (and the related *Male Genital Diagram*, figs. 40, 41) of early 1962. The *Diagram* paintings not only invite bodily movement across the canvas; Warhol even facilitates this possibility by displaying them on the floor in their first showing at the Stable Gallery in New York in November 1962.[18] As Benjamin H. D. Buchloh and Rosalind Krauss have pointed out, certain aspects of the paintings seem to refer to Pollock's drip paintings: their "participatory aesthetics," their invitation to repeat the rhythmic gestures made by the artist, and their record of the artist walking over the canvases laid out on the floor. That Warhol should choose to paint diagrams of dance steps suggests the extent to which he understood the dancelike movements that Pollock performed to paint his drip paintings. He may even have seen some of Hans Namuth's famous photographs of Pollock at work, several of which were published in *Time* magazine. Warhol knew that the action of successive bodily movements was a key element in the work of Pollock and other Abstract Expressionists, but he chose to reduce this activity, described and analyzed in lofty, even sublime, terms by contemporary critics such as Harold Rosenberg, to its mechanical basics—and to imply, with a dose of irony, that this is how you, the viewer, can do it as well.

It has been pointed out that Robert Rauschenberg had already used a dance diagram in a collage of about 1951 (*Should Love Come First?*) and that a similar dance diagram had appeared in a Fluxus "newspaper" (*Yam Festival "Newspaper,"* edited by George Brecht and Robert Watts, n.d.),[19] found in Warhol's papers. But another potential source for Warhol's paintings were contemporary advertisements in the daily newspapers for the Arthur

Murray Dance Studio, which used similar dance diagrams.[20] What seems to have attracted Warhol to the diagrams is what attracted Rauschenberg and the Fluxus artists, namely, their absurdist, Dadaist quality. The Dadaists frequently used mechanical drawings and illustrations of machine parts to reduce the high-flown rhetoric of high art to the basic mechanics of movement and bodily functions. In their eyes the industrialized killing machines of World War I had rendered humans little more than automatons. Warhol is known to have been interested in Marcel Duchamp's work. He went to the opening of Duchamp's retrospective exhibition at the Pasadena Art Museum in 1962 and, according to Victor Bockris, "was so excited and thrilled by the show."[21] Although Duchamp supposedly said that Pop had "nothing to do with Dadaism," he did acknowledge that Pop and Warhol's work, in particular, resembled Dada (and his own art) in being more concerned with the concept behind an image than its retinal quality.[22] In a famous interview that Warhol gave to G. R. Swenson in 1963, he said: "Dada must have something to do with Pop—it's so funny, the names are really synonyms," both being terms for *father*.[23] He went on to talk about Jasper Johns and Robert Rauschenberg in connection with Neo-Dada. This makes quite explicit that Warhol was aware of the importance that Dada and Neo-Dada held for Pop art in general and his own art in particular.

One event that may have had an impact on Warhol's use of the dance diagrams was the Max Ernst exhibition at the Museum of Modern Art in New York in 1961. Ernst's use of advertisements in his early collages and especially diagrammatic line drawing in his suite of lithographs *Fiat modes pereat ars* (c. 1919, fig. 42) could well have been a catalyst for Warhol's development at this crucial juncture.[24] *Fiat modes pereat ars,* with its lines of projected movement between manikins and figure numbers, as well as its title, which means "Let there be fashion, let art perish," is very relevant to what Warhol was to do in the subsequent months. When asked by his friend the poet John Giorno in 1963 what he thought about Abstract Expressionism, Warhol replied: "Art is Dead." And, when asked why, he opined: "Nobody thinks. Nobody uses imagination anymore. Imagination is finished."[25] The fact that Warhol referred to the death of art in relation to Abstract Expressionism is highly significant. Warhol identified Pollock and the other Abstract Expressionists with high art, but this development,

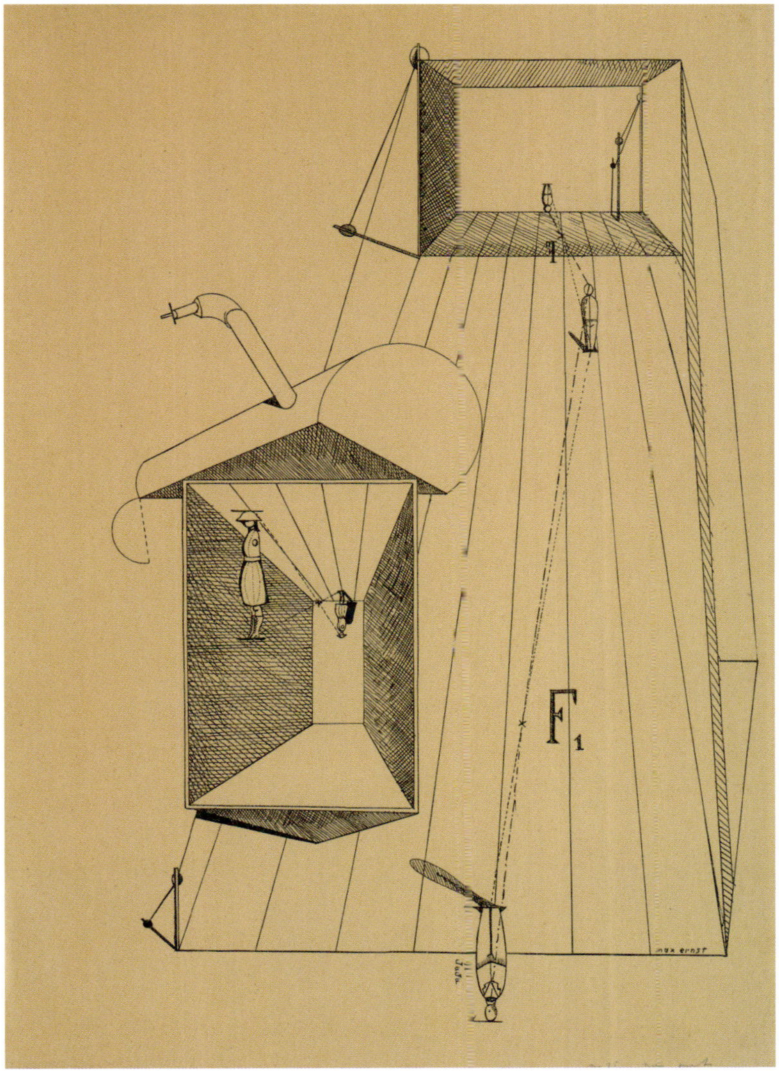

Fig. 42. Max Ernst, *Untitled*, plate VI from *Fiat modes pereat ars (Let There Be Fashion, Down with Art)*, c. 1919. One from a portfolio of eight lithographs, composition (irreg.): 15¾ x 10½ in. (40 x 26.6 cm); sheet: 17³⁄₁₆ x 12⁹⁄₁₆ in. (43 x 31.9 cm). Purchase (9239.1935.1), The Museum of Modern Art, New York

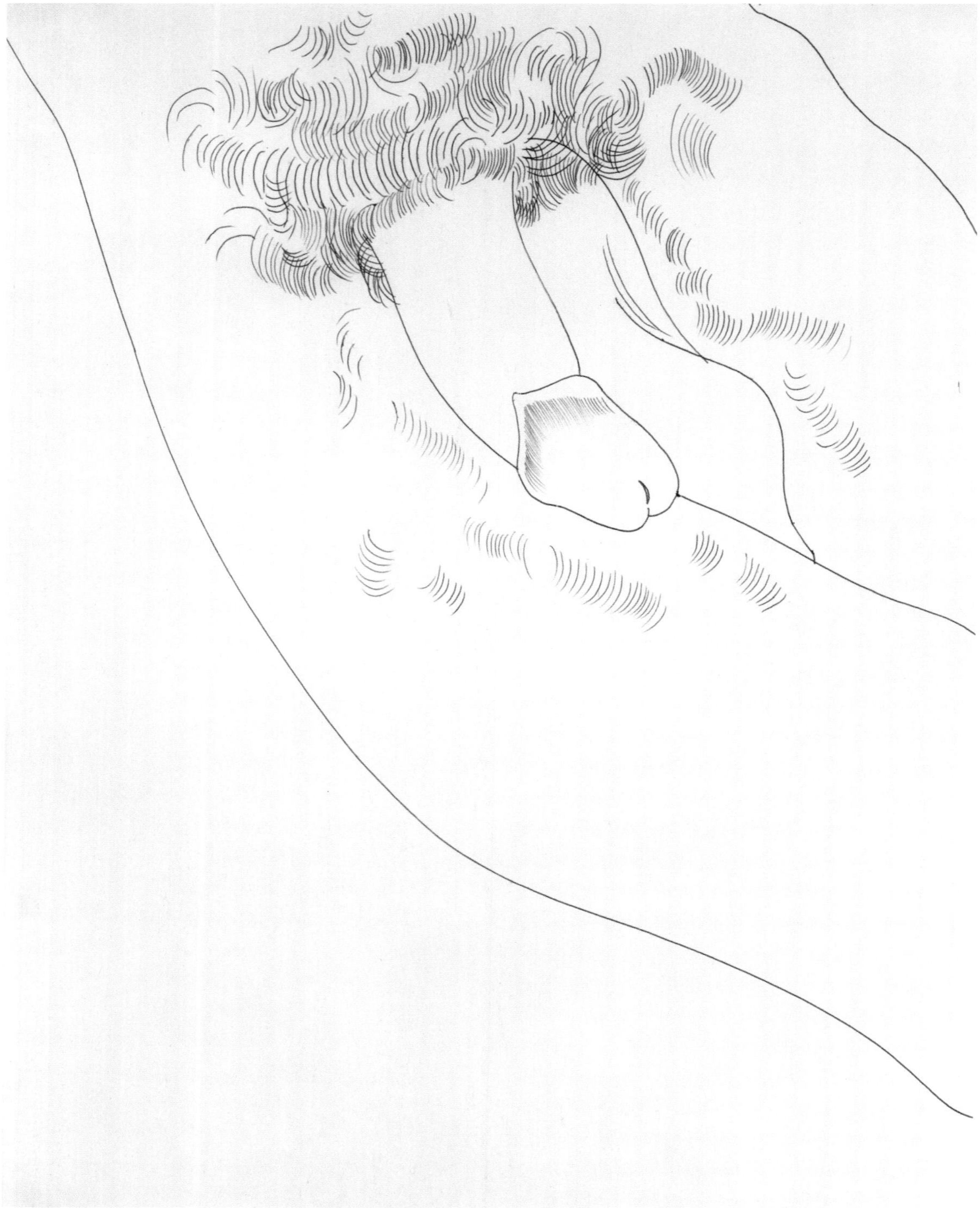

Fig. 43. *Reclining Male Nude Torso*, 1950s. Ballpoint pen on paper, 17⅛ x 14 in. (43.5 x 35.6 cm). The Andy Warhol Museum, Pittsburgh; Founding Collection, Contribution The Andy Warhol Foundation for the Visual Arts, Inc.

he felt, had come to an end. Duchamp, Ernst, and the Dadaists had helped lead him to this conclusion.

One significant cognate work that Warhol probably painted about the same time as the *Dance Diagram* paintings is *Male Genital Diagram* (fig. 41). This work can also be interpreted in relation to both Warhol's ambivalent attitude toward Jackson Pollock and his fascination with Dada, especially the work of Marcel Duchamp. It also anticipates Warhol's *Oxidation* and *Cum Paintings* of 1977–78 and the related *Torso* and *Sex Part* works (fig. 44), as well as recalls the stylized line drawings of male genitalia that he made in the 1950s (fig. 43). Concerning Pollock, Warhol relates (in *POPism*) what Larry Rivers had told him about Pollock's homophobic behavior: "I'll tell you what kind of guy he was . . . he'd ask a homosexual, 'sucked any cocks lately?'"[26] There were also several well-known stories about Pollock urinating on paintings before releasing them to clients he did not like or relieving himself into Peggy Guggenheim's fireplace. It is hard to know if, at this stage in Warhol's career, he was equating urinating with drip painting (as he was to do in relation to his *Oxidation Paintings*), although as early as 1961 he did a number of "piss paintings," which have since disappeared.[27] It is important to not read too much into this one work, *Male Genital Diagram*. All one can say is that because of its typological similarity with the *Dance Diagrams*, it suggests that Warhol wanted to reduce human activities and behavior, whether elevated or uncouth, to mechanical functions of the body. As has been pointed out,[28] Duchamp's *Fountain* (1917) and his *Large Glass* (1912–23), with their use of plumbing and machine analogies for human activities, also may have inspired Warhol.

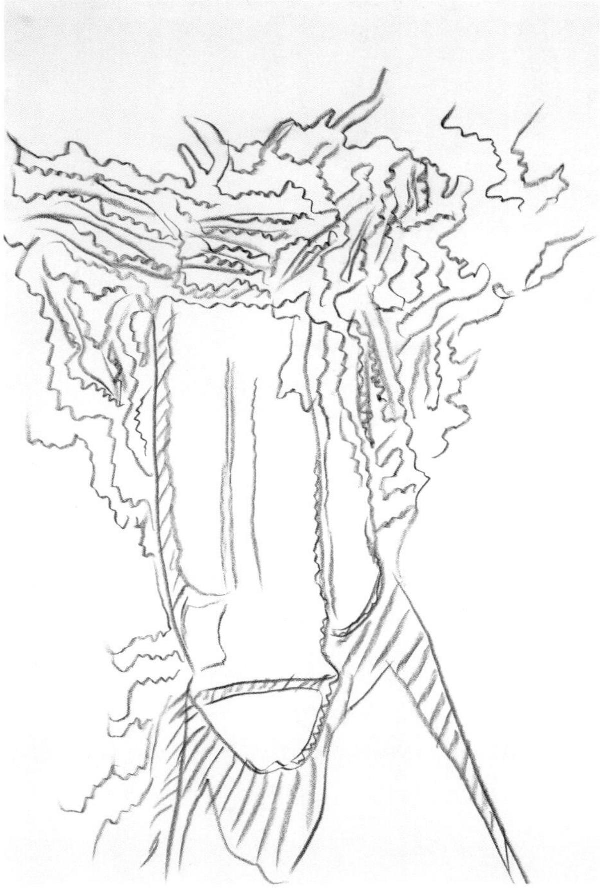

Fig. 44. *Male Genitals*, c. 1978. Graphite on J. Green paper, 41 x 28 in. (104.1 x 71.1 cm). The Andy Warhol Museum, Pittsburgh; Founding Collection, Contribution The Andy Warhol Foundation for the Visual Arts, Inc.

In the 1960s and beyond, Pollock seems to have represented for Warhol the most important and charismatic abstract painter, but Ellsworth Kelly and Color Field painting also influenced his practice. This was part and parcel of Warhol's aversion (in the 1960s, at least) to painterliness and the gestural nature of certain types of Abstract Expressionism. In an interview with David Bourdon about 1962–63, he said why he liked the hard-edged, clean-cut machine aesthetic: "I'm for mechanical art."[29] He also admitted his admiration for Ellsworth Kelly in a 1981 interview: "I always liked Ellsworth's work, and that's why I always painted a blank canvas. I loved that blank canvas thing" (figs. 45, 46).[30] Again and again in the 1960s Warhol would paint a blank, monochrome canvas the same size and color as a canvas with screenprinted images on it.[31] In part, this was simply an extension of his practice of creating two opposing halves to a composition. In the 1950s he had done this by mounting side by side a drawing and its monotyped (smudged) copy as mirror images of each other (fig. 47). In his ad paintings of the mid-1980s he would create similar oppositions by painting negative, black-and-white versions of the same white-and-black images (pls. 51–56). In addition to repetition and monotonous rhythms, Warhol liked oppositions and mirroring. Not for nothing had he studied the basic design lessons of the Bauhaus (as taught by Klee and László Moholy-Nagy, especially) back in Pittsburgh. In other paintings of the 1960s Warhol created the oppositions and monochrome areas on the same canvas, and in a small group of *Match-Book Cover* paintings of 1962 the monochrome areas are part of the found images (fig. 48). There is, perhaps, more than a hint of ironic referencing in these last works.

On a more profound level, Warhol's use of "empty," blank space in opposition to rows of repeated images was perhaps a suggestion that they were, in fact, two sides of the same coin. Repeated often enough an image can become abstract, just as a monotonously recited mantra can empty the mind and lead to a meditative state. Warhol

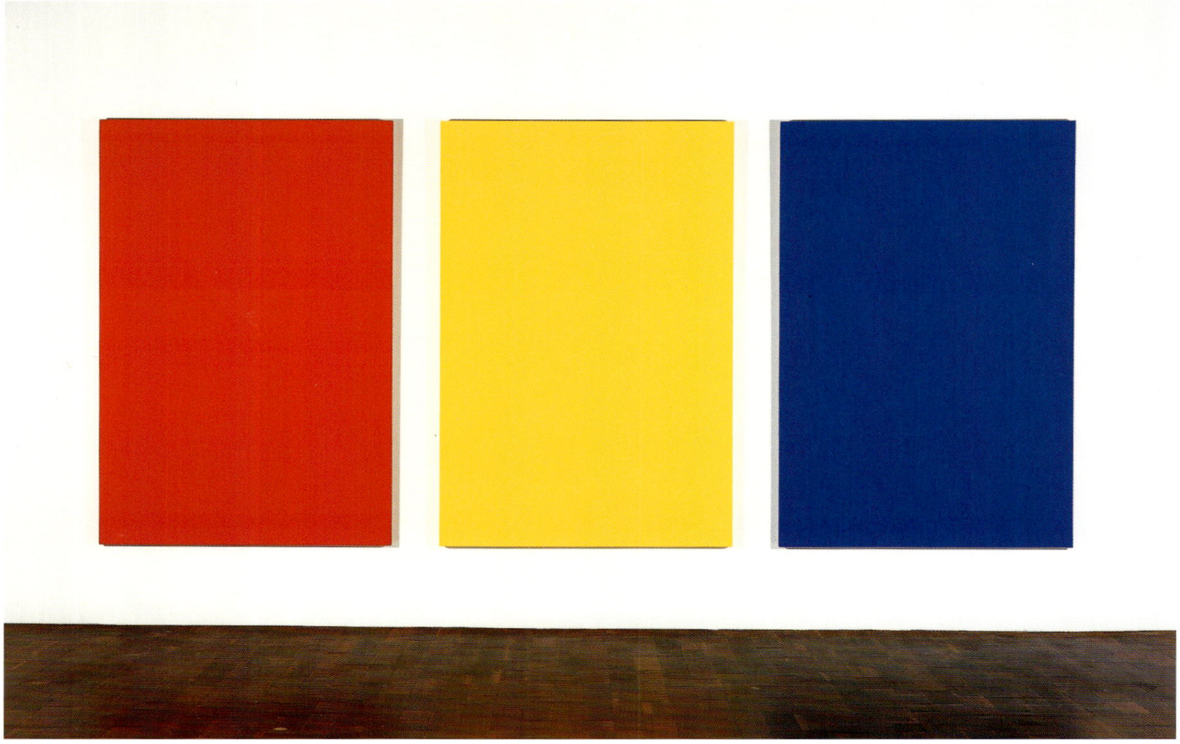

Fig. 45. Ellsworth Kelly, *Red, Yellow, Blue II*, 1965. Acrylic on canvas, three separated panels, 82 x 57 in. (208.3 x 144.8 cm) each; 82 x 189 in. (208.3 x 480.1 cm) overall. Milwaukee Art Museum, Gift of Mrs. Harry Lynde Bradley

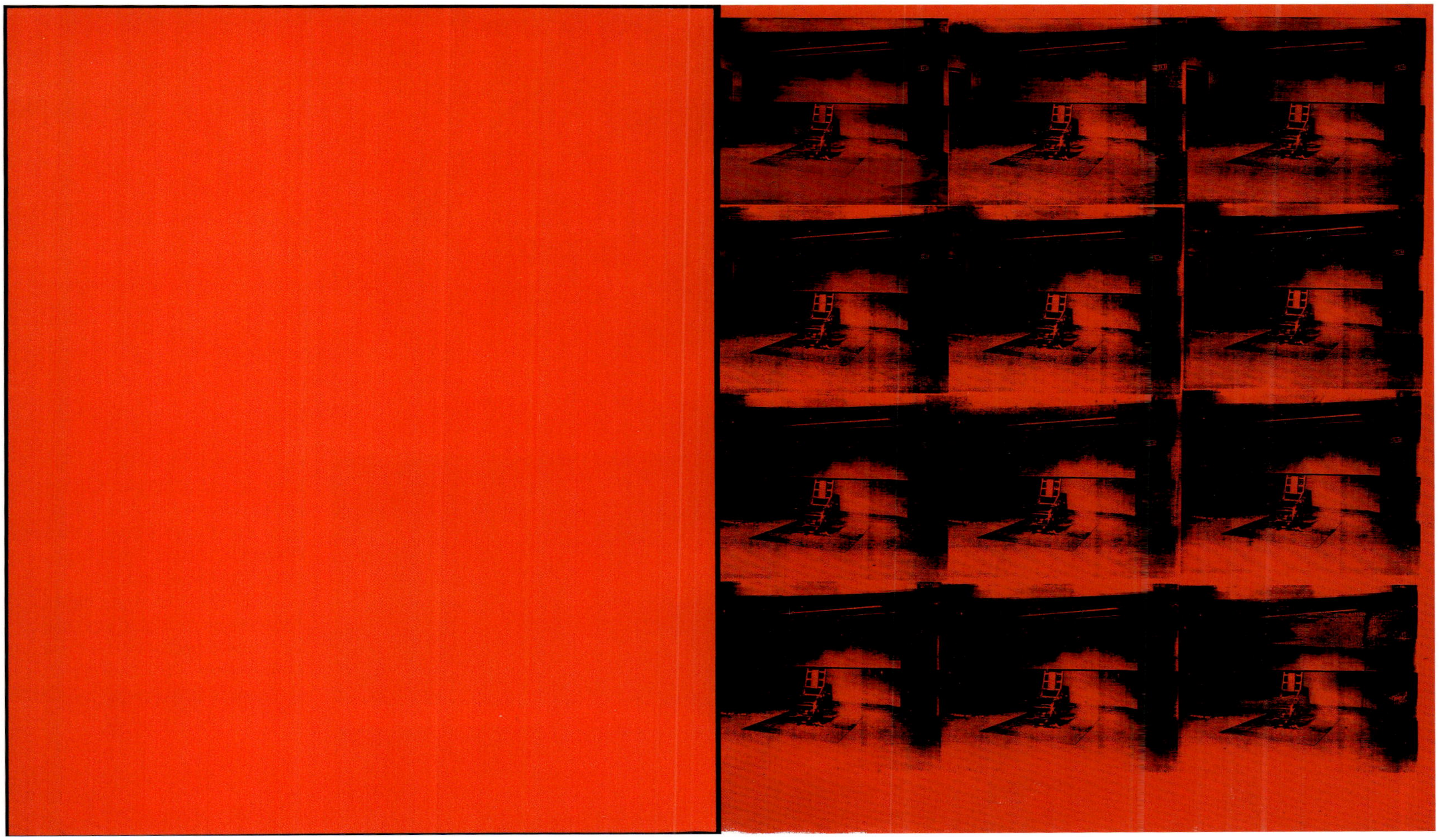

Fig. 46. *Red Disaster*, 1963, 1985. Acrylic and silkscreen ink on canvas, two panels, 93 x 80¼ in. (236.2 x 203.8 cm) each. Museum of Fine Arts, Boston, Charles H. Bayley Picture and Painting Fund

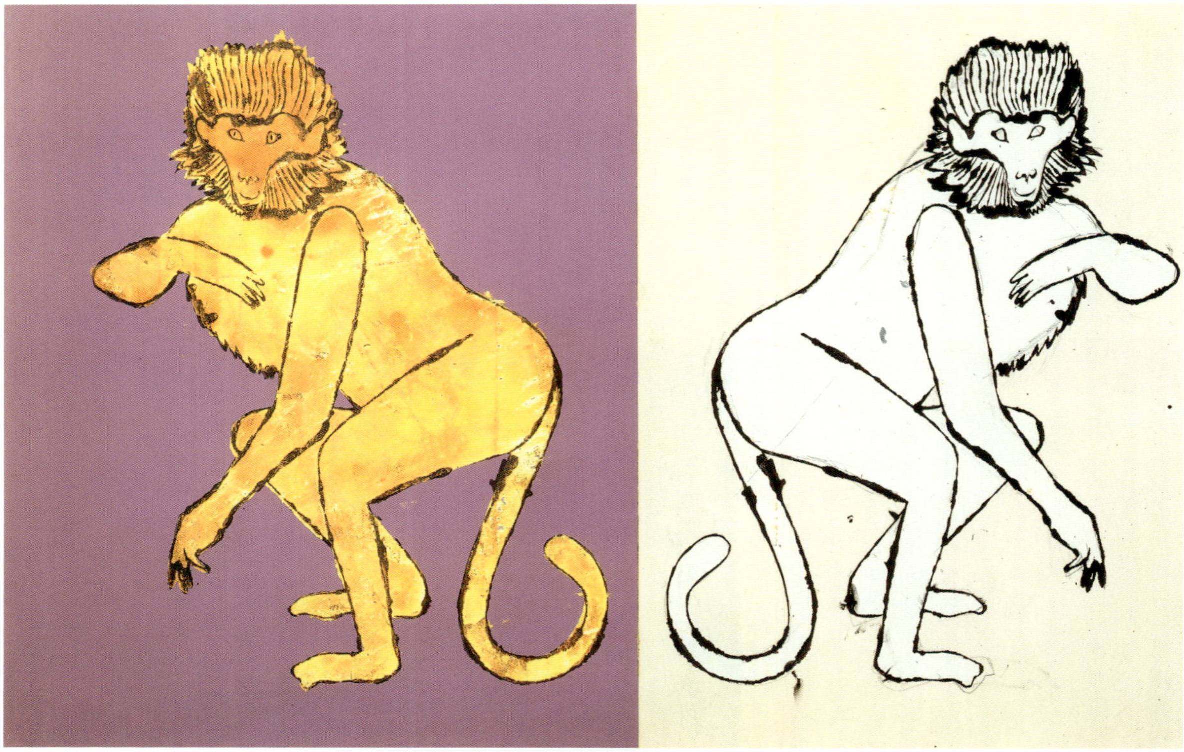

Fig. 47. *Baboon*, 1957. Pen and ink and gold leaf on paper, 24 x 18 in. (45 x 71.1 cm). ARTIST ROOMS. Tate and National Galleries of Scotland. Acquired jointly through The d'Offay Donation with assistance from the National Heritage Memorial Fund and The Art Fund 2008

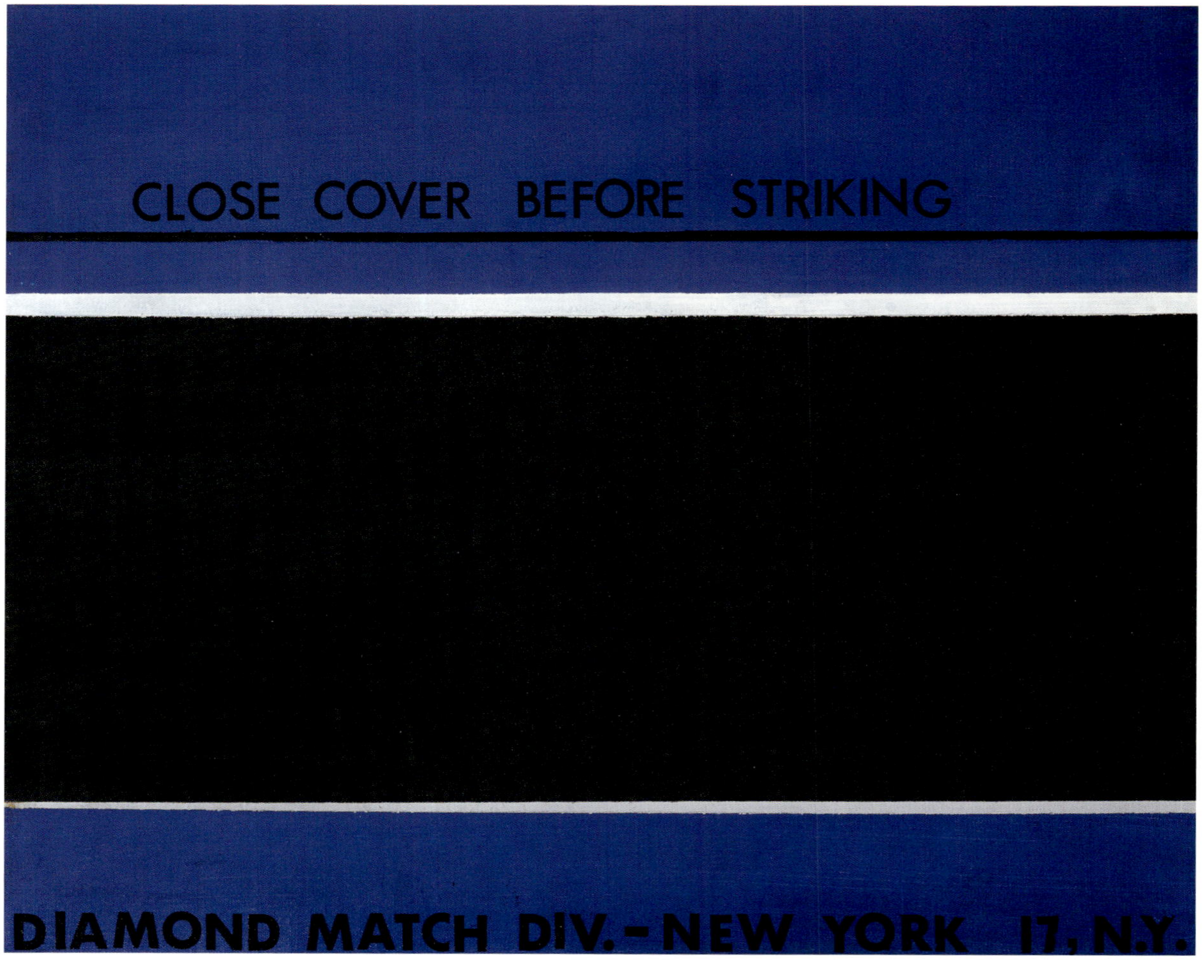

Fig. 48. *Blue Close Cover Before Striking*, 1962. Acrylic, Letraset®, and sandpaper on linen, 16 x 20 in. (40.6 x 50.8 cm). The Andy Warhol Museum, Pittsburgh; Founding Collection, Contribution The Andy Warhol Foundation for the Visual Arts, Inc. in celebration of the First Anniversary of the Directorship of Thomas Sokolowski

often spoke of staring at the same scene for long periods of time—most famously, watching John Giorno sleep, which led to Warhol's film *Sleep* (1963). He was obsessed by the seeming opposites of existence and nothingness, of objects and empty space. In his book *The Philosophy of Andy Warhol* he muses about this age-old conundrum: "Some critic called me the Nothingness Himself and that didn't help my sense of existence any. Then I realized that existence itself is nothing and I felt better. But I'm still obsessed with the mirror and seeing no-one, nothing."[32] In the same book he says: "When I look at things, I always see the space they occupy. I always want the space to reappear, to make a comeback, because it's lost space when there's something in it. If I see a chair in a beautiful space, no matter how beautiful the chair is, it can never be as beautiful to me as the plain space."[33] These statements, made in 1975, are a reflection of the time when Zen and meditation were becoming popular within the avant-garde scene, when John Cage's work valued silence as much as sound.

Warhol went even further in his investigation of the existence/nothingness duality. In 1964, in response to being told to replace or remove the mural painting *The Thirteen Most Wanted Men* on the facade of the American pavilion at the New York World's Fair because it might cause offense, Warhol decided to simply paint over it with silver paint (fig. 49). Although usually seen as either a fit of pique or a Dadaist gesture of defiance, the act and its result can also be seen as a precursor to Warhol's *Silver Clouds* (1966, fig. 50), which likewise mirror their surroundings. Warhol saw his *Silver Clouds* floating freely in Leo Castelli's gallery as moving paintings that could float away into the sky—an ideal farewell to painting, as announced by Warhol in Paris in 1965. As he explained to Gretchen Berg in 1966: "I didn't want to paint any more so I thought that the way to finish off painting for me would be to have a painting that floats, so I invented the floating silver rectangles that you fill up with helium, and let out of your window."[34]

When Warhol returned to painting with an exhibition of his *Mao* series in Paris in 1974, it was plain that he had rethought his "anti-smudge" views (fig. 3, page 16). Mao's impassive features were screenprinted (in black) on a ground of colorful, gesturally expressive paint. This

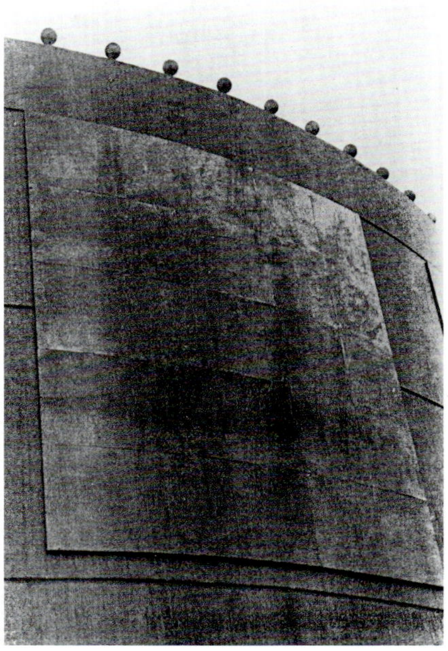

Fig. 49. *Thirteen Most Wanted Men* mural, painted over, New York State Pavilion, New York World's Fair, 1964

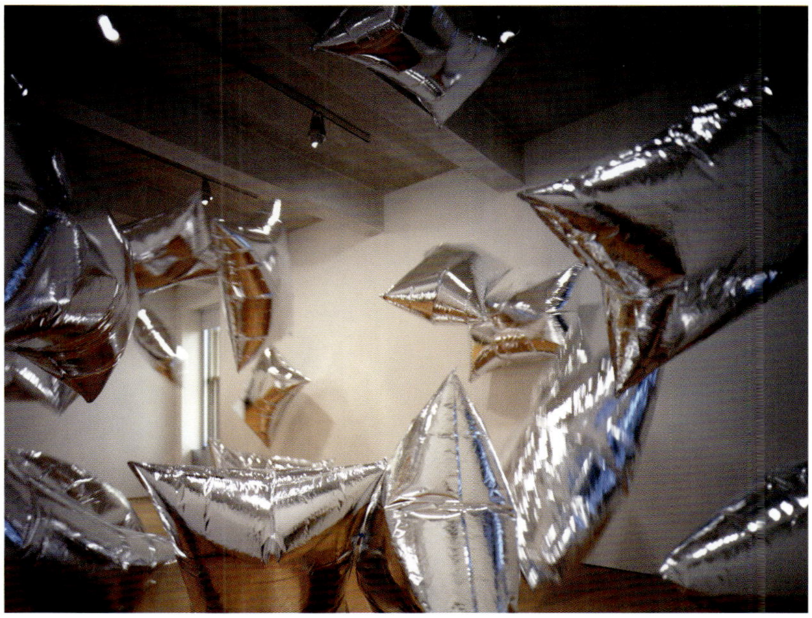

Fig. 50. Andy Warhol, Billy Kluver (contributor), *Silver Clouds* [Warhol Museum Series], 1994 (Refabricated for The Andy Warhol Museum in cooperation with The Andy Warhol Foundation for the Visual Arts, Inc., and Billy Kluver, 1994). Helium-filled metallized plastic film (Scotchpak), 36 x 51 in. (91.4 x 129.5 cm). Manufactured by CTI Industries Corp., Barrington, Illinois. The Andy Warhol Museum, Pittsburgh

was quite a volte-face. In a way it represented a shift in allegiances, away from the hard-edged color fields of artists such as Ellsworth Kelly toward the swirls and skeins of paint of Jackson Pollock, or, more pointedly, the colorful expressiveness of Picasso's late works, particularly the figure paintings (such as the *Musketeers)* of the late 1960s (fig. 51). Picasso had died in 1973. It is noticeable how much more gestural and colorful Warhol's *Mao* paintings became between 1972 and 1973.[35] Warhol was a great admirer of Picasso and always wanted to know if Picasso had heard of him. He admitted that his 1975 series of paintings of drag queens, *Ladies and Gentlemen* (fig. 52), was influenced by Picasso. "Since the transvestite portraits, I've tried to work more into the paintings. I may have been thinking of Picasso at the time."[36] Warhol maintained that this new painterliness was in demand to popular pressure. "I really would still rather do just a silkscreen of the face without all the rest, but people expect just a little bit more. That's why I put in all the drawings."[37] But the fact that he would soon do a series of works that consisted of nothing but "drawing," with no screenprinted images (or only rarely), shows that a deeper process was underway in his art.

Warhol's series of *Oxidation* (or *Piss*) *Paintings* (1977–78, pls. 10–15) looks back, as previously mentioned, to a few experimental "piss paintings" made in 1961, which were probably Neo-Dadaist in inspiration. It is important to note that there were two types of *Piss Paintings*. The first type was made by urinating on canvases that had been painted with copper or bronze metallic paint. Because the copper paint was still wet, it reacted with the uric acid and oxidized, turning varying shades of green in the process. On June 28, 1977, Warhol recorded in his diary: "I was painting with the sponge mop in the back [his studio]. I haven't peed on any canvases this week. This is for the *Piss* paintings. I told Ronnie [Cutrone, his assistant] not to pee when he gets up in the morning—to try to hold it until he gets to the office, because he takes a lot of vitamin B so the canvas turns a really pretty color when it's his piss."[38] This and other diary entries (as well as testimony from others) show that Warhol was not the only person to direct his urine onto the canvases, although he was always the director of the proceedings, pressing coworkers and friends (women included) into action. The second type of *Piss Paintings* had a gessoed white surface instead of a ground of copper paint. Paper was also used. These "paintings"

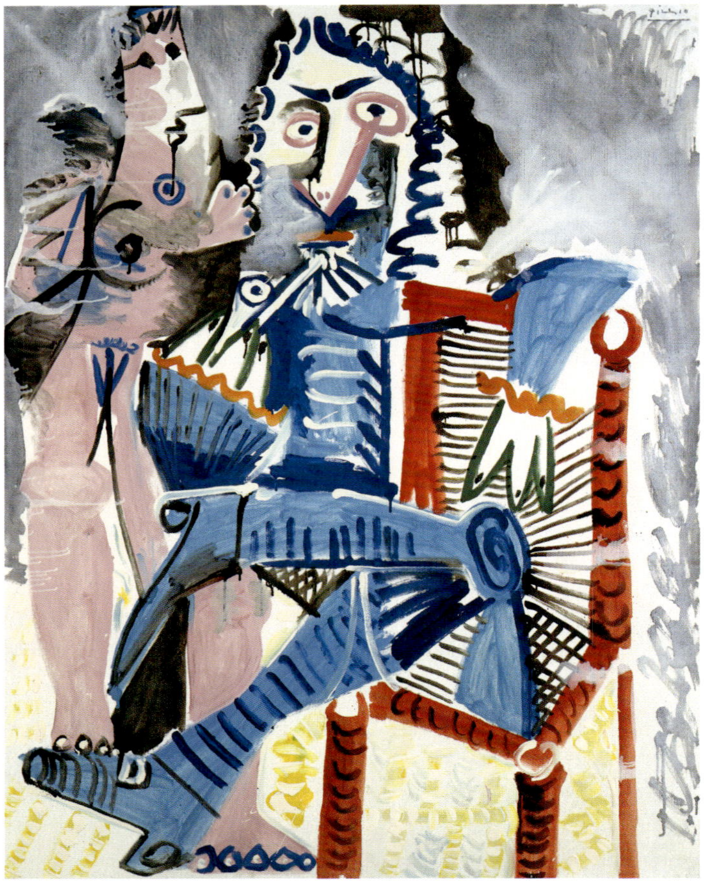

Fig. 51. Pablo Picasso, *Standing Female Nude and Seated Musketeer*, 1968. Oil on canvas, 63¾ x 51 in. (161.9 x 129.5 cm). The Metropolitan Museum of Art, Gift of A. L. and Blanche Levine, 1981

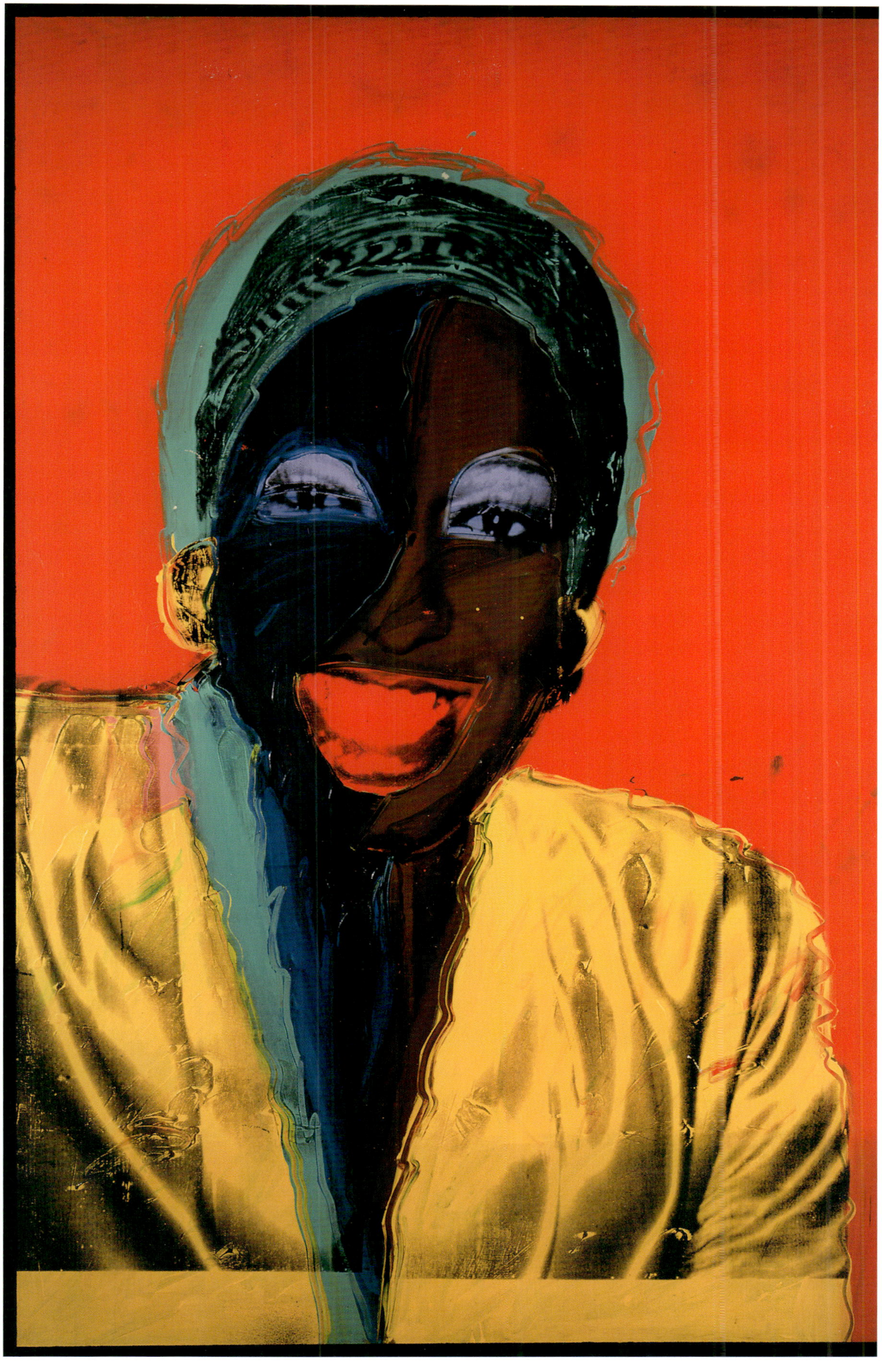

Fig. 52. *Ladies and Gentlemen*, 1983. Acrylic and silkscreen ink on canvas, 120 x 80 in. (304.8 x 203.2 cm). Mugrabi Collection

(and "drawings") did not change color and so retained a more "natural," if discolored, stainlike look. In addition to the *Piss Paintings* Warhol also made a number of *Cum Paintings*. Whether Warhol masturbated to produce the semen or left this to someone else is unclear.

The *Piss Paintings* vary in their form, from very linear compositions with rhythmic arcs moving across large horizontal canvases; to concentrated circular puddles of color, green against copper, on small portrait-format canvases; to stains of indeterminate shape on multiple rows of canvases. The more linear works bear a certain resemblance to Pollock's drip paintings (fig. 39, page 52), a comparison that was noted by critics (along with reference to Pollock urinating in Peggy Guggenheim's fireplace) when the works were shown in Europe in 1979. But, in fact, several commentators, such as Buchloh and Krauss, have pointed out a number of references other than Pollock.[39] Principal among these are works that form part of the Dadaist and Neo-Dadaist traditions, such as Duchamp's *Fountain* (1917), Francis Picabia's infamous inkblot "portrait" of the *Holy Virgin* (1920), and Piero Manzoni's *Artist's Shit* (1961). References also extend to infamous theatrical performances that included urinating in public, such as those given by the arch-exhibitionist and enfant terrible Arthur Cravan (1887–1918) and Charles Ludlam's camp melodrama *Stage Blood,* based on *Hamlet* and staged in New York in 1975.[40] Bob Colacello, who worked with Warhol for many years, remembers various things that may have given Warhol the idea of doing his *Piss Paintings*: "I'm pretty sure that the Piss Paintings ideas came from friends telling him about what went on at the Toilet, reinforced perhaps by the punks peeing at his Paris opening. He was also aware of the scene in the 1968 Pasolini movie *Teorema*, where an aspiring artist pisses on his paintings. 'It's a parody of Jackson Pollock,' he told me, referring to rumors that Pollock would urinate on a canvas before delivering it to a client he didn't like. Andy liked his work to have art-historical references, though if you brought it up, he would pretend he didn't know what you were talking about."[41]

If Warhol wanted the *Piss Paintings* to resonate in some way with allusions to Pollock's drip paintings, the Dada tradition of irreverence, and sexual shock tactics, he surely also wanted them to speak for themselves directly and positively. Perhaps the most important thing that they convey is an unashamed affirmation of life at its most basic. Everyone urinates; it is essential to the cycle that keeps us alive. Urine may be a waste product that has to be expelled from the body, but it is not to be despised and hidden away as unmentionable. Warhol wanted to turn this equivalent of base metal into gold. By using copper metallic paint that oxidized in contact with the urine, he made an alchemical metamorphosis visible in a spectacular way. He also showed how the body could express itself directly, without having to use paint and brushes—in a manner analogous to the way the Turin Shroud was created. As a devout Catholic, Warhol was aware of the religious connotations of artistic transformations. The circular, puddlelike stains on the portrait-format canvases even seem to assume the form of human heads.

In one case Warhol screenprinted a particular head, that of the artist Jean-Michel Basquiat, onto a *Piss* painting (fig. 24, page 32). Warhol not only collaborated with Basquiat on a number of paintings but also hung out with him socially. Although there was no more than friendship between Warhol and the young artist, Warhol was certainly very fond of him. Setting his portrait on a coppery gold background and showering it with green oxidation, Warhol indirectly declared his affection for Basquiat in an intimate manner.

The *Piss Paintings* are typical of Warhol's so-called abstract paintings in that they may not depict anything but they are very far from being non-objective. Warhol always uses forms or substances from the real world. The urine is real urine, the semen is real semen. And such substances have powerful connotations, not the least of which are sexually charged. In Warhol's case they amount to a veritable celebration of (his) homosexuality. At the same time as he was making his *Piss Paintings*, he was also making his *Sex Part* and *Torso* paintings, which he coyly called his "landscapes." He, or rather his helper in such matters, Victor Hugo, would hire or invite men to undress so that Warhol could photograph their bodies, especially their genitals, and on occasion the men having sex with each other. Warhol would then make paintings and drawings based on a careful selection of the photographs. Pushing the boundaries of what was considered acceptable, he was reflecting the sexual revolution of the 1970s (specifically, the gay and women's liberation movements), which was particularly strong in New York.[42] This is one context in which one should see the *Piss Paintings*. Another is the continued focus on experimentation, performance, and process in the New York art world of the 1970s. Warhol had faced considerable criticism during this decade for his commissioned portraits, which were widely considered a sellout after his radical 1960s work. The *Piss Paintings* were part of Warhol's bid to regain critical credibility within the artistic community. The use of chance, the relishing of uncontrollability (or, at least, of limited controllability), the emphasis on natural processes, the implied critique of established artistic models as well as of unquestioning masculinity, the sexual politics: these aspects of the *Piss Paintings* chimed well with contemporary developments in the New York art world. It is, therefore, ironic that Warhol chose not to show them in New York but in Europe. Perhaps he felt more likely to receive unbiased—and favorable—reviews in Europe. In this he was probably correct.

Warhol's next incursion into abstraction followed directly from, and, in a sense, came out of the *Piss* and *Sex Part* paintings. The *Shadows* series (pls. 16–21) began as early as 1977. In his diary for November 7 of that year he noted: "Jed [Johnson, Warhol's long-suffering partner] came by the office and was in the back in my working area when he saw the stacks of Polaroids of all the 'landscapes' I photographed for the Shadow paintings—all the close-ups of cocks and things—he began screaming that I had degenerated so low."[43] Warhol's assistant at the time, Ronnie Cutrone, in an interview with Patrick Smith in December 1978, confirms that Warhol was interested in the abstract shapes of the shadows in the Polaroids taken for the *Sex Parts* and *Torso* paintings: "[I]t was a way of cutting-up the body, and getting nice shapes and shadows again."[44] The word *again* refers to Warhol's predilection for photographing shadows and incorporating their forms in his paintings. Shadows had assumed an important role, concerning not only composition but also subject matter, in the *Skulls* series (fig. 4, page 17) and the *Hammer and Sickle* paintings of 1976. Just at the time when he was creating his *Piss Paintings*, he began looking for others ways to paint abstract works. Ronnie Cutrone again explains: "Well, Andy wanted to do something abstract, and he didn't know what. I sort of felt that it wouldn't be too healthy for him to do something abstract, unless it was really something. I mean a Shadow *is* something, and it isn't, which is sort of what Andy is noted for in a way. Something, you know, whether it is a definition of an image or an opinion on an image. There's always a double edge to it. So, I thought we should try a shadow because it was actually something physically."[45] That Warhol, in fact, used the shadows cast by body parts, such as male genitals, for his *Shadows* is doubtful. Cutrone remembers making cardboard shapes whose cast shadows he photographed.[46] He described the whole process from beginning to end in detail:

> In the case of the *Shadows* I just got matte boards and pieces of cardboard . . . arranged them and tone them up and photograph them. And, then, we get the photographs back, pick the photographs that we like the best, usually more than we're actually going to do so we have a choice. Then, they're matted . . . onto acetates or positives. Depending on what size we see the images at . . . if it's a print, the photograph will be blown up on acetate approximately . . . 30 x 40 . . . if it's a painting, larger. And then we just lay it down on white paper and see how it looks blown up. . . . Then, in the case of a painting, it would be mopped out on to the canvas. . . . Just the loose outline of the image, and, then, contrary to popular belief, it's painted *first*, not after the screen is put on . . . the photograph is always intact and it lays on top of the painting.[47]

Whatever is throwing the shadows the resulting paintings do not disclose the source. Ambiguity and mystery are central to their very power. Warhol assembled a large group of paintings of the same "subject" and size, but differently colored, for a show at Heiner Friedrich, Inc., in New York in January 1979 (fig. 53). The paintings were hung butted up to each other, forming what was, in effect, a continuous mural around the gallery. Warhol had returned to an earlier formula of repeating certain formal elements to create an overall rhythm but varied the colors to provide breaks and competing rhythms. Warhol had learned this formula from Klee and found it corroborated on a mural scale by Pollock. Works such as Pollock's eight-by-twenty-foot *Mural* of 1943 (commissioned by Peggy Guggenheim, fig. 54), *Summertime: Number 9A* of 1948 (illustrated in the famous 1949 *Life* magazine article, fig. 39, page 52), or *Blue Poles* of 1952 (shown from July 1959 for a time in the Four Seasons restaurant in New York, before being sold in 1973 for a record sum to the National Gallery of Australia)

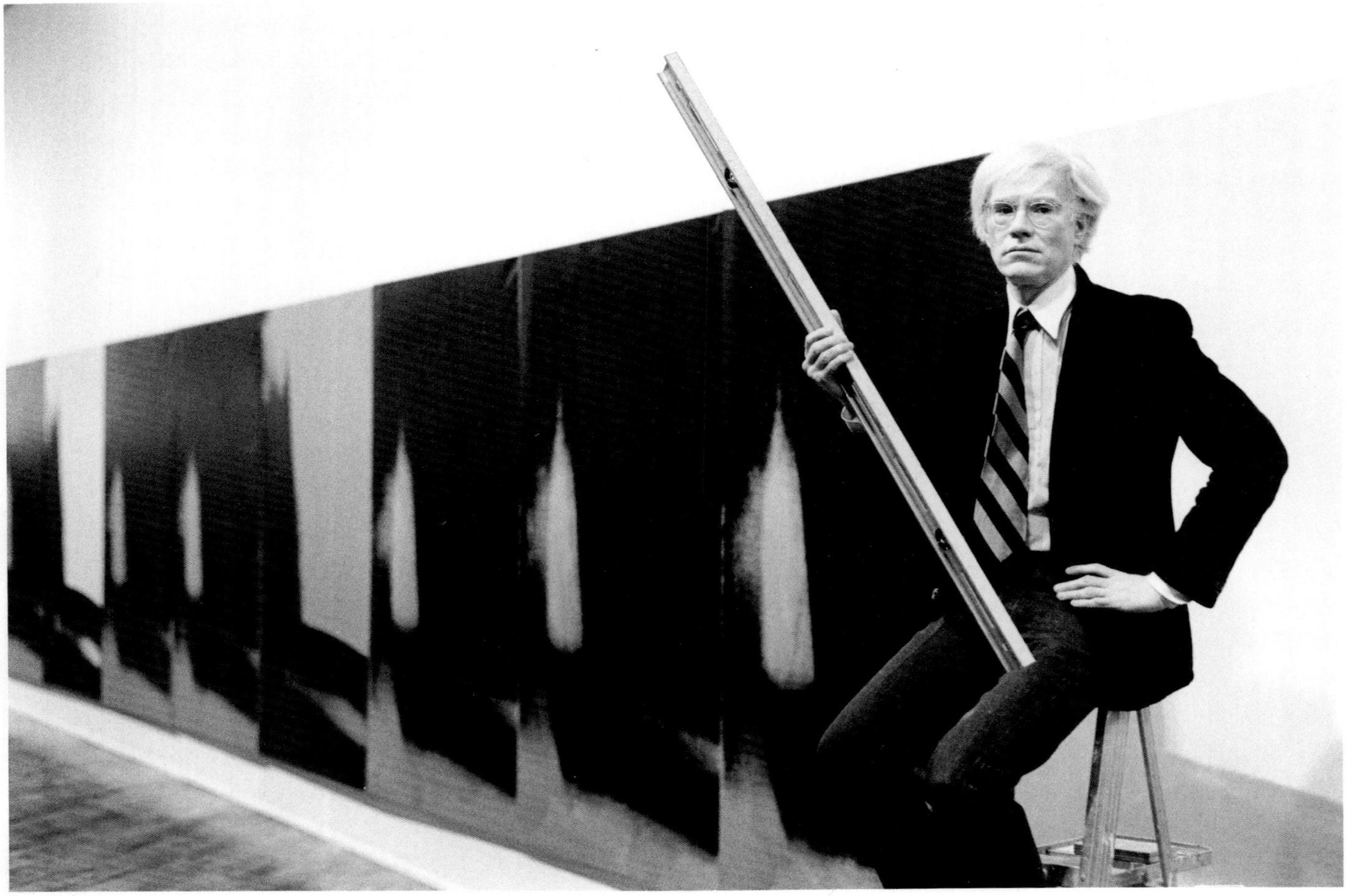

Fig. 53. Arthur Tress, *Andy Warhol*, 1979. Gelatin silver print, 8 x 10 in. (20.3 x 25.4 cm). The Andy Warhol Museum, Pittsburgh; Founding Collection, Contribution The Andy Warhol Foundation for the Visual Arts, Inc.

could have provided Warhol with models against which to measure himself.

Typically, Warhol was self-deprecating and offhand in describing the *Shadows* paintings—and, in particular, their installation at the Heiner Friedrich gallery—as "disco decor." But as is so often the case with Warhol's seemingly throwaway remarks, there is perhaps a kernel of revelation in this description. *Decor* can refer to decorative wall painting, which is one type of mural art. The late 1970s was also the heyday of discos in New York, and Warhol was almost a nightly feature at Studio 54, mixing with the rich, the famous, and the beautiful. Discos were the new temples of pleasure and decadence. What could be more fitting than paintings of ambiguous shadows in a dark, shadowy environment, where an indeterminate sexuality held sway?

But if the shadows in Warhol's paintings were ambiguous, their mystery could also be dark and questioning. By reversing the usual relationship between shadows and background and creating the odd painting where the shadow becomes the light element and the surroundings dark, Warhol questions (as he had done in his meditations on existence and nothingness in *POPism*) the

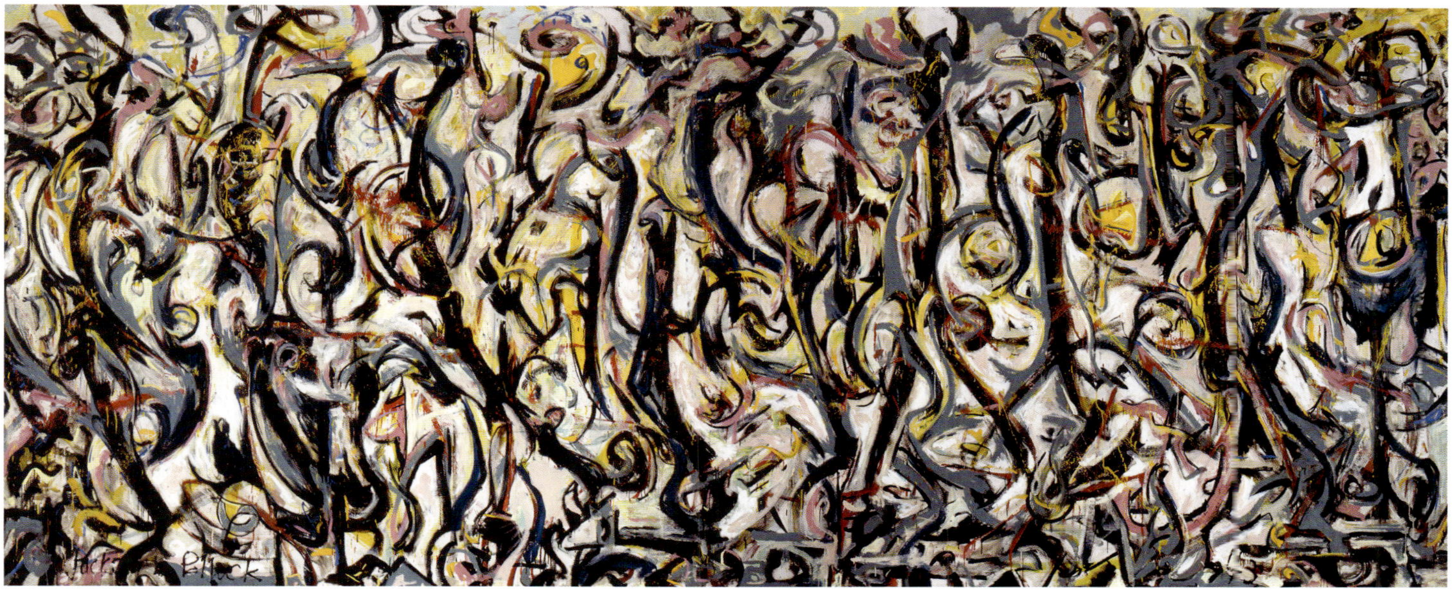

Fig. 54. Jackson Pollock, *Mural*, 1943. Oil on canvas, 96 x 238 in. (247 x 605 cm). Gift of Peggy Guggenheim, University of Iowa Museum of Art, Iowa City, 1959.6

very notion of what reality is. How can we distinguish between shadow and reality? Had not Plato likened our perception of reality to seeing shadows on the wall of a cave? Reality lies outside the cave in the sun, but we are forever condemned to look backward from the entrance of the cave and watch the dancing shadows. Traditionally, shadows have been linked to transience and ultimately to death. Warhol had chosen to emphasize the cast shadows in his *Skulls* of 1976. In his later *Shadows* it is impossible to overlook the threat of death as one interpretation of the ambiguous shapes. In view of the impending (but not yet known) impact of HIV/AIDS on the sexual promiscuity of New York disco culture, one is tempted to read a more somber element in the shadow theme. Even if HIV/AIDS had not yet been identified as the cause of the growing number of deaths in the gay community, sexually transmitted diseases were still seen as an ever-present danger.

In November 1980 Warhol noted in his diary that he had met Julian Schnabel in his New York loft: "[He] does sort of bad paintings. . . . [T]here's this whole group of kids doing this bad art."[48] Over the next couple of years Warhol got to know several of this new generation of painters, in particular Jean-Michel Basquiat. Gestural, expressive painting was back in fashion, and Warhol was reenergized by it. The lines between abstract and figurative painting were blurred, as were those between original expression and quotation. This climate suited Warhol's constant slippage between categories. From 1982 to 1984 Warhol worked on three separate series of abstract paintings, two of which were based (like the *Shadows*) on photographs: the *Eggs* (1982, figs. 19, 20; page 28) and *Yarn* (1983, pls. 25–30) series.[49] The *Eggs* look back vaguely to *art concret* in Europe before World War II, whereas the *Yarn* paintings make a very direct and obvious reference to Pollock's classic drip paintings.[50] In the spring of 1983 Warhol began his series of *Rorschach* paintings (pls. 31–35), which question the very notions of abstraction and figuration and what forms might actually mean.[51] To create the abstract shapes in the *Rorschach* paintings, Warhol poured paint onto one side of a canvas, folded the canvas vertically down the middle, and then pressed the empty side against the side with the wet paint on it. A mirror image of the first side was created on the second or, in other words, a symmetrical pattern was created on the whole canvas. In the 1950s Warhol had used this so-called blotting technique regularly to create drawings, and in many cases he retained the "original" drawing and placed it next to the "copied" drawing.

Already in the 1950s, therefore, Warhol was interested in questions of symmetry, mirroring, doubling, and the meaning of "original" versus "copy." He acknowledged this in an interview in 1986: "When I used to draw, to get a new kind of line—I just hated my lines—I used to draw that way. All my shoe drawings are done that way, with a blotted line. You could blot them together and get a repeat on the other side. It [the way the *Rorschach* paintings were made] might have something to do with that."[52] The *Rorschach* paintings are, in effect, a combination of Pollock-esque abstraction and formal copying, an approach Warhol had not only used in the 1950s but also made central to his Pop aesthetic in the 1960s (even if the technical means were then different). One could argue that Warhol was attempting to dismantle the very edifice of Abstract Expressionism by denying its uniqueness. There is certainly a strong ironic quality to the *Rorschach* paintings, but one could also see them differently. The "copied" side is not an exact copy; it is a mirror image, just as the right hemisphere of the brain mirrors the left. Perhaps Warhol was more interested in trying to read meaning into abstraction than is generally assumed. Could there be underlying figurative forms in the abstract patterns, just as some critics had maintained about Pollock? They had argued for hidden imagery buried beneath the webs and swirls of paint, similar to subconscious desires suppressed by the conscious mind. Rorschach tests were invented precisely to try and bring to the surface some of those subconscious desires. The images read into the Rorschach test cards might give a clue to the hidden world of the libido.

Warhol feigned not knowing that the Swiss psychiatrist Hermann Rorschach had devised a set of ten abstract shapes, saying that he thought that the patient was supposed to make his or her own. He deliberately mixed up the idea that one could analyze someone's handwriting (as well as squiggles and marks) with the much more highly structured Rorschach tests. He remarked: "I was trying to do these to actually read into them and write about them, but I never really had the time to do that. So I was going to hire somebody to read into them, to pretend that it was me, so that they'd be a little more . . . interesting. Because all I would see would be a dog's face or something like a tree or a bird or a flower. Somebody else could see a lot more. But maybe they shouldn't have any reading into them at all. None at all."[53] So Warhol leaves open the question of whether anything significant can be read into the *Rorschach* paintings and, by extension, into abstract painting in general.

One of the most striking features of several of the *Rorschach* paintings is their large size—almost fourteen feet in height. Warhol commented, "[A]ll I was trying to do, because everyone had done them smaller, was to make them big and see if they could work really big."[54] Did he mean by this, that even Pollock and the Abstract Expressionists painted on a smaller scale? Indeed, Warhol's huge *Rorschach* paintings dwarf some of their large abstractions. The size also turns the paintings into large wall decorations; their symmetry, after all, makes them into patterns. Warhol obviously relished the irony of making what is in essence a private, personal window into his soul a very public billboard.

Irony was also a key ingredient in Warhol's last abstract series, his *Camouflage* paintings (pls. 69–73). The very idea of painting works with a pattern that was devised to make things disappear is a paradox that Warhol enjoyed—particularly when he used the camouflage pattern on top of portraits, such as those of Joseph Beuys and of himself (pl. 68). There was the added irony that camouflage was invented for the military and was heavily used in the Vietnam War. Anyone less militaristic than Warhol is hard to imagine.

The notion of using camouflage may have come to Warhol early in the 1980s. In a diary entry for May 4, 1981, he noted: "I had a death threat. . . . So . . . I went to Sporting World to buy a hat to disguise myself. I got a camouflage hunter's hat."[55] Warhol had always tried to disguise himself—wearing a wig that was obviously a wig, talking dumb to the press and people he did not know, rarely showing his real feelings. One of his earliest self-portraits is a drawing in which he covers most of his face with his fingers. According to Bob Colacello: "The Camouflage Paintings began with an idea from Jay Shriver, Warhol's art assistant in the 1980s, who had been experimenting with pushing paint through camouflage-printed mesh. As usual, Warhol took someone else's idea and made it his by reducing it to its essence and then pushing it to its limit. He threw out the mesh and focused on the camouflage pattern itself, playing with both its meaning and form."[56] This may well have been the impetus for Warhol's using camouflage patterns, but the background was broader. Warhol was interested in anything having to do with war and the military. In his diary of January 4, 1986, he noted:

"Looked through some *Soldier of Fortune* magazines, because I want to do war pictures."[57] On January 15 he noted further: "I'm working on the War pictures and they're so hard, I don't know what they should look like. I'm doing Guns, but I've done guns before."[58]

The war paintings that Warhol was working on are probably those known as the *Ad* paintings, which deal not only with war but more generally with death and religion. The mid-1980s, with Ronald Reagan as president, was a period marked by renewed Cold War tension between the United States and the Soviet Union, the Strategic Defense Initiative (so-called Star Wars), and the ascendance of the evangelical Right. Warhol, ever attuned to changes in political and social conditions, reflected this new situation in his work. The camouflage patterns allowed Warhol to deal with these same issues but in a subtle and indirect way. Also, by using a wide range of colors not normally associated with camouflage, such as pinks, reds, oranges, yellows and blues; varying the size of the pattern (for example, enlarging it to emphasize individual shapes); and stretching the format to fit whole walls, Warhol could modify the connotations and emotional timbre of the paintings. Associations include Claude Monet's giant water lily paintings, Henri Matisse's cutouts, Pollock's mural-size paintings, and the contemporary abstractions of the so-called Neo-Geo artists, such as Philip Taaffe. One intriguing possibility that Warhol considered but failed to carry out was to make camouflage paintings so large that he could hang smaller camouflage paintings on them, effectively turning the super-size paintings into the equivalent of wallpaper, similar to the wallpapers Warhol had made earlier in his career. The repeating patterns in the camouflage paintings are, in fact, the logical outcome of not only Warhol's wallpapers but also his Pop paintings (and of many of his pre-Pop drawings). They also realize in space what his early films, such as *Sleep* (1963) and *Empire* (1964), had done in time: given a taste of infinity. Warhol understood that what people usually call boredom could be, under certain circumstances, an early stage on the road to a Zen-like consciousness.

Warhol's use of camouflage patterning to cover several figurative paintings—self-portraits, portraits of others, images of the Statue of Liberty and *The Last Supper*—shows that he made no hard-and-fast distinctions between abstraction and figuration. Both were ultimately subject to the artist's manipulation of the formal means at his disposal. Just as the repetition of images could lead to a loss of meaning, so abstract forms had connotations and significance that no amount of purification could eradicate. In one of his last great works, the vast *Camouflage Last Supper* (1986, pl. 76), Warhol not only covers Leonardo's famous image with green camouflage patterning but doubles it as well. Because of the enormous size of the painting, the effect is to suggest an endless repeat of image and pattern. The specifics of Leonardo's image begin to fade away—the camouflage makes it difficult to take in the composition anyway—and we are left focusing on its central idea, both formal and iconographic: the figure of Christ. Warhol deliberately made a white part of the camouflage pattern serve as a background to Christ's head. At the same time, the camouflaging does not just blur the images behind it; it also foregrounds the constant presence of military conflict and the threat of war. By bringing these two ideas—Christ and War—into such close proximity, Warhol uses abstraction to give new and powerful meaning to an image made hackneyed by overexposure.

For Warhol, non-objective abstraction was at once an unattainable ideal and a formal means to an end. It was unattainable not only personally, because he knew that he needed real life as the raw material for his art, but also in some way theoretically, because deep down he did not believe anyone could ever leave behind the facts of their bodily circumstances, least of all Pollock with his drip paintings. Nevertheless, many of his coworkers over the years attested to the fact that he was in some ways mesmerized by abstraction. The Abstract Expressionists, who came to international fame just as Warhol arrived in New York to start his career, represented this ideal. But Warhol knew this was an ideal and, as his references to Pollock's work show, he sought to deflate the notion that this ideal was a reality.

Notes

1. Victor Bockris quotes a contemporary of Warhol (Albert Goldman) at Carnegie Tech about the artists admired at the time: "The heroes of the age were Picasso, Michelangelo and Matisse. Looking back on it I can see that we were totally out of touch with reality. We didn't have any idea of what was really going on in the arts or the theatre. Who'd ever heard of Jackson Pollock?" Victor Bockris, *Warhol* (Harmondsworth, England: Penguin, 1990), p. 71.

2. One of Warhol's friends at Carnegie Tech, Arthur Elias, noted the main influences on Warhol's drawing style: "Andy was very influenced by Ben Shahn and Paul Klee." See ibid., p. 74.

3. *Paintings, Drawings and Prints by Paul Klee from the Klee Foundation, Berne, Switzerland with Additions from American Collections,* exh. cat. (New York: The Museum of Modern Art, 1949), no. 33. The exhibition was on view in New York from December 20, 1949, to February 19, 1950. It had already traveled to the San Francisco Museum of Art; the Portland Art Museum, Portland, Oregon; the Detroit Institute of Arts; and the City Art Museum, St. Louis. It continued on to The Phillips Gallery, Washington D.C., and the Cincinnati Art Museum.

4. See Robert Kudielka, *Paul Klee: The Nature of Creation, Works 1914–1940*, exh. cat. (London: Hayward Gallery, 2002), p. 138, who quotes Klee's *The Nature of Nature*: "In order to perceive something as rhythm, a balance has to be set up between a regular element and irregularities, or as Klee says, between 'norm' and 'a-norm,' between a 'major' dominant and a 'minor' variants. Only through this tension can a repetitive structure be perceived as rhythmic 'when the eye brushes past line after line.'"

5. Paul Klee's drawing *Migrating Fish* (1926) was illustrated in *Paul Klee on Modern Art,* introduction Herbert Read (London: Faber and Faber, 1948), p. 36.

6. Andy Warhol and Pat Hackett, *POPism: The Warhol '60s* (New York and London: Harcourt Brace Jovanovich, 1980), p. 6.

7. Ibid., p. 4.

8. Andy Warhol, *The Philosophy of Andy Warhol (from A to B and Back Again)* (New York: Harcourt Brace Jovanovich, 1975), p. 101.

9. "Jackson Pollock: Is He the Greatest Living Painter in the United States?" *Life*, Aug. 8, 1949.

10. Betty Parsons Gallery, New York, Jan. 5–23, 1948.

11. Pollock's macho pose and denim jeans were echoed in the famous poster image of James Dean for *Rebel Without a Cause* in 1955. Warhol was to play with this image in *A Gold Book* (1957) and his film *Blow Job* (1964), both a far cry from the androgynous image of Truman Capote, captured in Harold Halma's famous photograph and used on the back of the dust jacket of Capote's *Other Voices, Other Rooms* (1948), which had obsessed Warhol back in Pittsburgh.

12. Warhol and Hackett, *POPism*, p. 6.

13. Ibid.

14. Ibid., p. 7.

15. Bob Colacello, *Holy Terror: Andy Warhol Close Up* (New York: Harper Collins, 1990), p. 419.

16. Warhol and Hackett, *POPism*, p. 13.

17. Ibid., pp. 12–13.

18. See illustration in *Time*, Nov. 16, 1962, reproduced in Georg Frei and Neil Printz, eds., *The Andy Warhol Catalogue Raisonné: Paintings and Sculpture*, vol. 1: 1961–63, (London and New York: Phaidon, 2002), p. 85.

19. See ibid.

20. I am indebted to Dennis Adrian for this and other pieces of information in this essay.

21. Bockris, *Warhol*, p. 208.

22. Ibid., p. 185.

23. G. R. Swenson, "What Is Pop Art? Answers from 8 Painters, Part 1," in *Art News*, 62 (Nov. 1963); reprinted in Kenneth Goldsmith, ed., *I'll Be Your Mirror: The Selected Andy Warhol Interviews, 1962–1987* (New York: Carroll & Graf Publishers, 2004), p. 19.

24. *Max Ernst*, exh. cat. (New York: The Museum of Modern Art, 1961), cat. 234.

25. John Giorno, "Andy Warhol Interviewed by a Poet," 1963, previously unpublished manuscript from the Andy Warhol Archives, Pittsburgh, in Goldsmith, *I'll Be Your Mirror*, p. 23.

26. Larry Rivers quoted in Warhol and Hackett, *POPism*, p. 14.

27. A reproduction of one of these 1961 "piss paintings" appeared in an interview with Warhol in *The Unmuzzled Ox*, 4, no. 2 (1976), p. 46; the same image was reproduced in Rosalind E. Krauss, *The Optical Unconscious* (Cambridge, Mass.: MIT Press, 1993 [1994]), p. 272.

28. See ibid., pp. 169–277, and Benjamin H. D. Buchloh, "A Primer for Urochrome Painting," in *Andy Warhol: The Late Work*, exh. cat. (Düsseldorf: Museum Kunst Palast: Munich: Prestel, 2004), pp. 88–97.

29. David Bourdon, "Warhol Interviews Bourdon," 1962–63, previously unpublished manuscript in the Andy Warhol Archives, Pittsburgh, in Goldsmith, *I'll Be Your Mirror*, p. 9.

30. Barry Blinderman, "Modern Myths: An Interview with Andy Warhol," *Arts Magazine*, 56 (Oct. 1981); reprinted in Goldsmith, *I'll Be Your Mirror*, p. 293.

31. According to Frei and Printz, *Andy Warhol Catalogue Raisonné*, p. 331, the first documented time that Warhol added what he called a "blank" to a figurative canvas was with *Blue Electric Chair* (1963) for the exhibition of his work at the Sonnabend Gallery in Paris in 1964. A photograph of the work taken in Warhol's studio in May 1963 shows the painting without a monochrome canvas. It is perhaps no coincidence that Ellsworth Kelly's two-panel painting *Blue Tablet* (1962) was shown in the important exhibition *Towards a New Abstraction* at The Jewish Museum, New York, from May to September 1963.

32. Warhol, *The Philosophy of Andy Warhol*, p. 7.

33. Ibid., p. 144.

34. Gretchen Berg, "Andy Warhol: My True Story," *The East Village*

Other, Nov. 1, 1966; reprinted in Goldsmith, *I'll Be Your Mirror*, p. 96.
35. Picasso's death on April 8, 1973, inspired huge international press coverage. Previously, *Life* had devoted a special double issue to Picasso on December 27, 1968, and there had been many articles and features in newspapers and magazines on the occasion of his ninetieth birthday (Oct. 25, 1971). Both *Life* and *Time* devoted major articles to him. Writing in *Time* (Monday, Nov. 1, 1971), however, Robert Hughes chose to say that Duchamp was more influential on living artists than Picasso.
36. Blinderman, "Modern Myths," p. 296.
37. Ibid., p. 294.
38. Andy Warhol, entry for June 28, 1977, in Pat Hackett, ed., *The Andy Warhol Diaries* (New York: Warner Books, 1989), p. 55.
39. Buchloch, "A Primer for Urochrome Painting," and Krauss, *The Optical Unconscious.*
40. Charles Ludlam (1943–1987) founded the Ridiculous Theatrical Company in New York in 1967.
41. Colacello, *Holy Terror*, p. 342.
42. The works of Lynda Benglis and Vito Acconci seem particularly relevant with respect to Warhol's *Piss Paintings*. Consider Benglis's *Contraland* (1969) made of latex poured directly onto the floor and Acconci's notorious performance, *Seedbed* (1972), in which he masturbated underneath a wooden ramp in the Sonnabend Gallery while talking with visitors directly above him. See Donna de Salvo, "New York 1969–1974," in *Century City: Art and Culture in the Modern Metropolis*, exh. cat. (London: Tate Modern, 2001), pp. 124–45.
43. Andy Warhol, entry for Nov. 7, 1977, in Hackett, *The Andy Warhol Diaries*, p. 86.
44. Patrick S. Smith, "Interview with Ronnie Cutrone, New York, 13 December 1978," *Andy Warhol's Art and Films* (Ann Arbor, Mich.: UMI Research Press, 1981, 1986), pp. 274–92.
45. Ibid.
46. Some of these photographs are reproduced in *Cast a Cold Eye: The Late Work of Andy Warhol*, exh. cat. (New York: Gagosian Gallery, 2006), p. 108.
47. Smith, "Interview with Ronnie Cutrone."
48. Andy Warhol, entry for Nov. 1980, in Hackett, *The Andy Warhol Diaries*, p. 343.
49. The *Yarn* paintings were commissioned by the Italian textile company Filpucci. See Thomas Kellein, *Andy Warhol: Abstrakt*, exh. cat. (Basel: Kunsthalle Basel; Munich: Prestel, 1993), p. 45.
50. There may also be a less obvious reference to Duchamp's *Three Standard Stoppages* (1913–14), made by dropping thread onto the floor.
51. Andy Warhol, entry for May 14, 1983: "Did two big Rorschachs and they looked kind of good"; in Hackett, *The Andy Warhol Diaries*, p. 501.
52. Andy Warhol quoted in Robert Nickas, "Andy Warhol's Rorschach Tests," *Arts Magazine*, 60 (Oct. 1985), pp. 28–32; reprinted in *Andy Warhol: The Late Work*, pp. 98–101.
53. Andy Warhol quoted in ibid., p. 98.
54. Andy Warhol quoted in ibid., p. 100.
55. Andy Warhol, entry for May 4, 1981, in Hackett, *The Andy Warhol Diaries*, p. 377.
56. Bob Colacello, "Andy Warhol, Abstraction and the Camouflage Paintings," in *Andy Warhol: Camouflage*, exh. cat. (New York: Gagosian Gallery, 1998), p. 8.
57. Andy Warhol, entry for Jan. 4, 1986, in Hackett, *The Andy Warhol Diaries*, p. 706.
58. Andy Warhol, entry for Jan. 15, 1986, in ibid., p. 709.

The Late, Great Andy Warhol

Gregory Volk

1.

"Buying is much more American than thinking and I'm as American as they come," Andy Warhol wrote in *The Philosophy of Andy Warhol*.[1] On one level, like many of Warhol's pronouncements, this one seems pithy, funny, plainspoken, and readily understandable: he was an acquisitive guy living in and enamored of the most consumerist society that the world has yet known, and he was making no bones about it. However, the more time one spends considering this quotation in light of Warhol's prodigious work, the more open-ended and suggestive it seems, especially that bit about "I'm as American as they come." In fact, Warhol's Americanness may be far greater, more complex, and more thoughtful than questions of shopping and buying, even though such matters are certainly important, and may be characterized by issues of religiosity, democracy, utopianism and its breakdown, and selfhood exalted to a mythic scale, among others. Warhol is a consummate artist of the second half of the twentieth century, but there is a great deal in his sprawling oeuvre (and outsize life) that suggests a profound affinity with certain nineteenth-century figures: the Transcendentalist poet/philosopher Ralph Waldo Emerson and poet Walt Whitman; the showman, huckster, and impresario extraordinaire P. T. Barnum; and even the Hudson River School painters and painters of the American West like Albert Bierstadt, Frederic Church, Thomas Cole, and Thomas Moran, whose works were colorful, spectacular, and spiritually charged. When Church unveiled his masterpiece *The Heart of the Andes* in 1859, at the Tenth Street Studio Building in New York City, it was an immediate popular sensation, for which the public was charged admission and provided with opera glasses (the hype drove up the eventual purchase price of the painting to $10,000, at the time a whopping figure). This conflation of art, spectacle, celebrity, notoriety, entertainment, and frank commercialism anticipates what Warhol was up to in the same city a hundred or so years later, including his April 1966 multimedia parties/extravaganzas called the *Exploding Plastic Inevitable*, held at a Polish club on St. Mark's Place, which, incidentally, was just a few blocks away from the building where Church's 1859 blockbuster event occurred.

Before delving a bit further into these nineteenth-century associations, I would first like to consider one of Warhol's relatively early works and one late series. Warhol's iconic *Self-Portraits* (1986, pls. 60–68) were accomplished during a period of renewed and intense commitment to painting, and also one year before his untimely death. These works do not seem to portray someone identified with an American absorption with buying. In one version (pl. 64), a reddish-orange Warhol with fierce, piercing eyes, a slightly open mouth, and gaunt cheeks appears against a black background. His famous faux hair is unruly, giving him a wild, freakish appearance. He looks right at you, staring you down, which makes the work seem both intimate and unnerving, but he also seems implacably remote, completely ensconced in the private, unfathomable world behind his riveting eyeballs.

It is impossible to know if this is Warhol feigning intensity or a more intense Warhol disclosed, if this was Andy as he really (perhaps secretly) was or Andy on a lark presenting himself as a demented horror-movie fiend or a zombie. There is a fiery, even apocalyptic, look to the work: a bright orange glow with blackness behind it. That this blazing self-portrait was made very shortly before his death is not only uncanny but also startling and mysterious because, in a peculiar way, the Warhol in this portrait already seems to have one foot in the hereafter. This is a portrait made in the studio, but the studio seems to be at the cusp between heaven and earth. The work is enthralling, and you find yourself captivated by the image and what it might evince. In fact, there is a great deal of humanity in this portrait, ranging from impassioned intensity and unflinching self-scrutiny to palpable sadness and fragility. At the same time, it brings to mind the illuminated villains and demons who pop up in theme-park tunnel rides to scare the children out of their wits, and freak-show denizens who are at once repulsive and attractive. The painting posits, but by no means pins down, an extreme psyche and keyed-up inner life, but it does so with an aura of spectacle and raucous theatricality that is enhanced by the circuslike, carnivalesque elements of garish makeup and an outrageous costume. For those who think that they have Warhol pegged as a sardonic Pop artist cannily mirroring a shopping-addicted, televisionized, tabloidized America, this is a very good painting to study indeed.

Speaking of circuses and carnivals, for his 1966 exhibition at the Leo Castelli Gallery in New York City Warhol presented *Silver Clouds*, featuring pillow-shaped balloons made of metallized plastic film filled with helium, which is now installed at the Andy Warhol Museum (fig. 50, page 61). The balloons slowly bounce off the walls, float up to the ceiling, drift down to the floor, and envelop the viewer. It is a wonderful work, at once goofy and enchanting, festive and meditative. As has often been noted, it is a send-up and subversion of Minimalist aesthetics—instead of weighty, identical, static forms on the floor made of wood, metal, or stone, which are presented in a particular way and no other, these weightless, silvery balloons slowly cavort about the room with an aerial exuberance. But perhaps even more pertinent are the work's suggestions of party decorations, joyful parades, and childhood excursions to street festivals, carnivals, or amusement parks. You think of children with shiny balloons held aloft atop thin wooden sticks or jam-packed boardwalk souvenir shops. You think of religious festivals (perhaps like those in Warhol's working-class Pittsburgh), which easily segue into street fairs and cheesy carnivals. Ushering all of this pop-culture stuff into art, into the gallery and the museum was, of course, exactly the kind of thing at which Warhol excelled, but in this work something surprising also happens: it becomes an oddly sublime (although ultramediated) skyscape, suggesting a beatific moment watching the clouds drift across the sky. In another, very different American era, commenting on such enraptured moments, Emerson, in one of his special conflations of the Bible and nature, wrote in his journal, "The sky is the daily bread of the eyes."[2] This is the kind of sentiment that affected the Hudson River School landscape painters, but even more so Luminist painters like Fitz Henry Lane and Martin Johnson Heade, who lavished attention on the vast, ever-changing sky precisely because it elicited such psychological upsweep, because it was a permeable membrane between the earthly and the divine, and because it allowed them to concentrate acutely on light. Warhol's shiny, ersatz clouds, with their entertaining connotations and willful campiness, nevertheless have a dreaminess and an effervescent loveliness that are loosely suggestive of sublime experiences with nature.

2.

Emerson and Barnum, two of the most visionary, enduringly influential, and seemingly antithetical nineteenth-century Americans, were, in fact, contemporaries: Emerson, largely living just outside Boston in Concord, Massachusetts, was born in 1803 and died in 1882, and Barnum, largely living in New York, was born in 1810 and died in 1891. Both responded to a country in profound transition, a country moving from a religious past to an increasingly secular and commercial present, growing more urbanized as it absorbed waves of immigrants, and morphing from its agrarian roots to become a freewheeling behemoth with a booming popular culture and an appetite for entertainment and spectacle. Both men, in some measure, also inherited and radically updated a utopianism that had been part of the culture since an intrepid band of early seventeenth-century Puritans attempted to establish their heaven on earth in coastal Massachusetts: Barnum with his logic-warping sensations (which turned out to be hoaxes), mind-bending emporiums filled with sundry curios and attractions, and traveling circuses; and Emerson, the former Unitarian minister who gravitated to poetry and art for his spiritual inquiry, with the enormous claims he made on art, seeing it as inseparable from questions of individual character, psychological growth, revelation, and redemption. Emerson was typically dismissive of art that did not arise from the galvanic inspiration that he wanted, and he advocated instead a kind of untrammeled wildness, an organic fusion of art and the total person, and a thorough willingness to take risks. He believed that formalism itself would solve nothing; however, "the instant dependence of form upon soul," as he wrote in his 1844 essay "The Poet" (incidentally the first great statement in the United States about radical and experimental art-making strategies), could offer a great many possibilities—artistic forms that would elastically take the shape of the artist's own psyche and also respond to the constantly changing character of the country itself.[3]

Where the spiritually inclined Emerson and the commercially obsessed Barnum really met was in a realm of available wonder. Barnum wanted to bedazzle your town with his rollicking circus, bring famous European performers (like Swedish opera singer–international superstar Jenny Lind) to your city, and lure you (whether you were wealthy or poor, a blueblood or an immigrant) over and over to his idiosyncratic New York City museum filled with animals and oddities, artworks and skeletons, natural history specimens and cultural artifacts. Moreover, he wanted these experiences to be enthralling, cathartic, memorable, instructive, and, of course, profitable, which they most definitely were. For Emerson, who was much more focused on inner life and on fraught encounters with nature, which he understood to be suffused with divinity, routine acts like walking, looking, and breathing had potentially ecstatic possibilities. "Every touch should thrill," Emerson wrote in "The Poet," which succinctly encapsulates what he was really (perhaps impossibly) most avid for, namely, an individual life, in this very place and time, to be filled with discovery and to resonate with cosmic importance.[4] In this sense, even the term "Transcendentalism" is somewhat misleading. Emerson (and the other members of the movement allied with him) did not, properly speaking, seek to transcend anything. He did not seek to go elsewhere, but to be *here*, more intensely, and to approach and absorb what is already here with a real freshness and openness.

I would hold that one part—perhaps even a big part—of Warhol's remarkable achievement was an ability to fuse his Pop sensibility with some of the attitudes, inclinations, religious impulses, and artistic riskiness of Emerson, as well as with the flamboyance, showmanship, theatricality, and go-for-broke vitality of Barnum, who was the instigator, after all, of "The Greatest Show on Earth." It makes no difference whether or not Warhol was conscious of these associations (and he probably was not) because both figures have long since permeated the culture in different ways and become part of the aesthetic and ideational vernacular. Barnum's exploits and business acumen very much anticipate the amusement parks, theme parks, television shows, Hollywood movies, and pervasive advertisements that define our entertainment-addicted culture and provided so much fodder for Warhol's work. Emerson directly influenced artists and writers around him in Concord like Henry David Thoreau, author of *Walden*; poet Walt Whitman; and both the Hudson River School and Luminist painters; as well as many later artists and writers, including Edward Hopper (who read Emerson extensively), Mark Rothko, and Barnett Newman (in 1936, the newlyweds Barnett and Annalee Newman traveled to Concord on their honeymoon, in order to visit sites associated with Emerson and Transcendentalism). Emersonian inclinations—such as a fluid, ever-cycling exchange between an artwork and its surroundings, an orientation toward vastness, a way of reaching out toward the ungraspable or ineffable, and a magical aspect emerging from what would otherwise be mundane circumstances or materials—have abided and flourished in American art since Transcendentalism's relatively brief heyday. What has certainly persisted is a core sense of personal mission, urgency, and discovery, which was picked up on by the major Abstract Expressionist

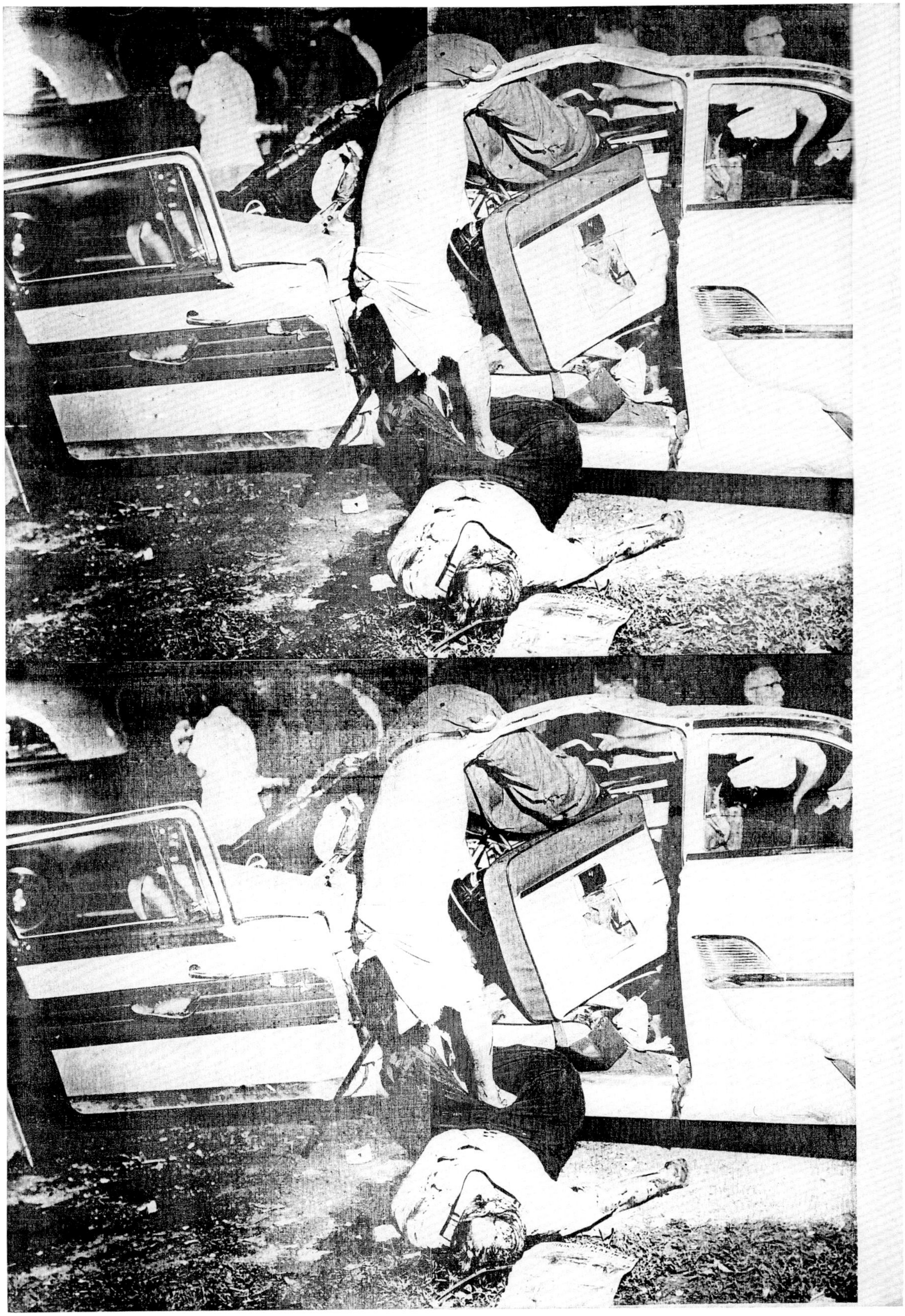

Fig. 55. *Saturday Disaster*, 1964. Acrylic and silkscreen enamel on canvas, 118⅞ x 81⅞ in. (302 x 208 cm). The Rose Art Museum, Brandeis University, Gevirtz-Mnuchin Purchase Fund, by exchange

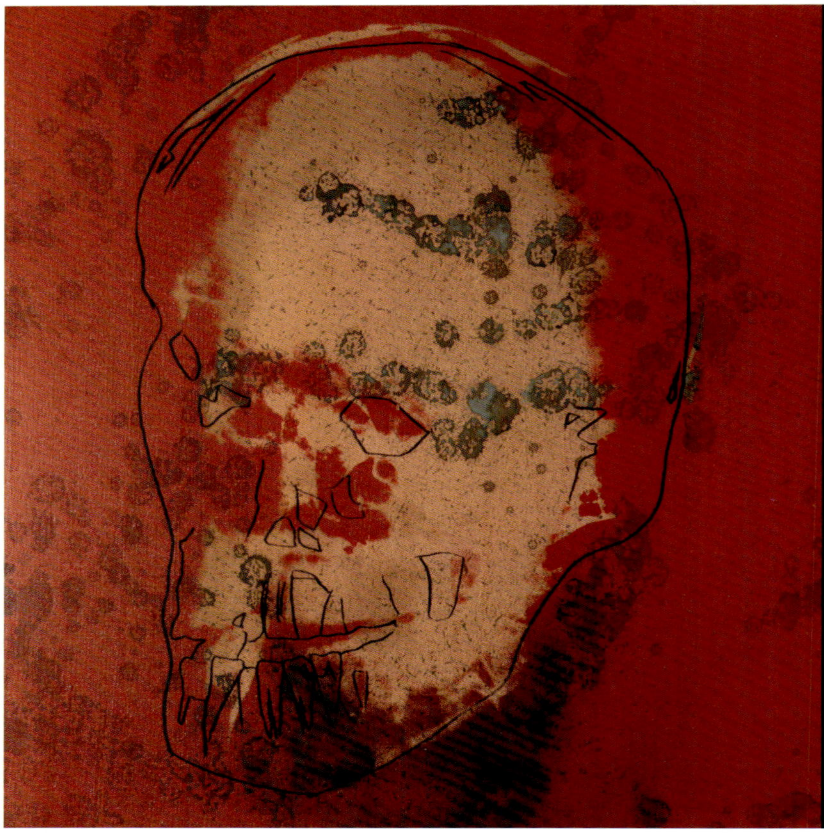

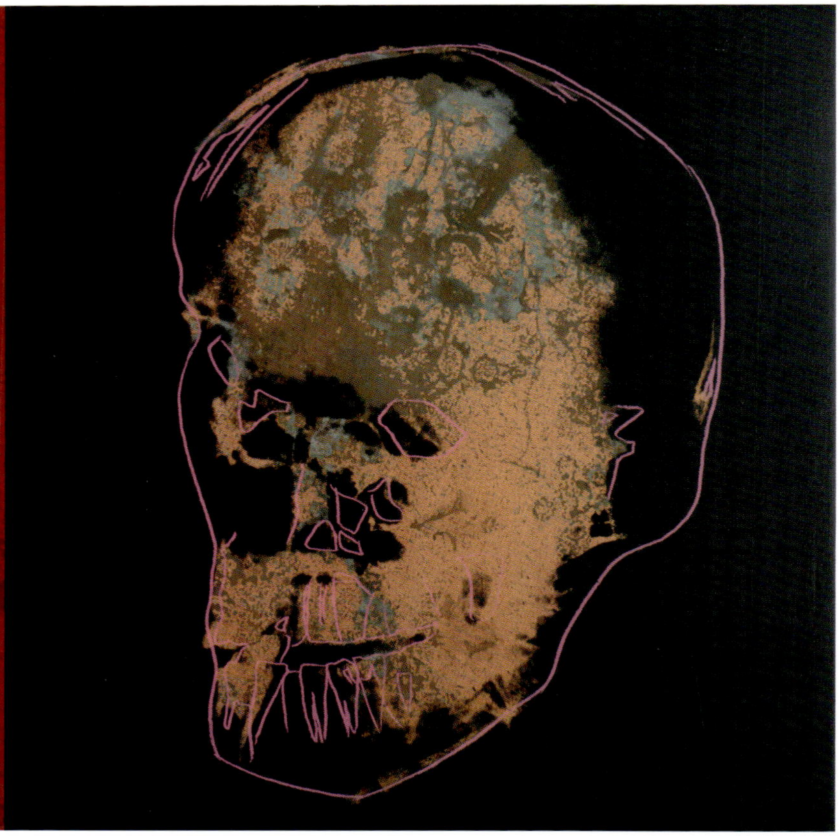

Fig. 56. *Philip's Skull (CAT Scan)*, c. 1985. Acrylic, silkscreen ink, and urine on canvas, 40 x 40 in. (101.6 x 101.6 cm). The Andy Warhol Museum, Pittsburgh; Founding Collection, Contribution The Andy Warhol Foundation for the Visual Arts, Inc.

Fig. 57. *Philip's Skull (CAT Scan)*, c. 1985. Acrylic, silkscreen ink, and urine on canvas, 40 x 40 in. (101.6 x 101.6 cm). The Andy Warhol Museum, Pittsburgh; Founding Collection, Contribution The Andy Warhol Foundation for the Visual Arts, Inc.

painters with their claims to revelation, exultation, purity, and great feeling. Indeed there are many places in his writing where Emerson seems to be directly addressing future artists of an especially questing bent, offering them not exactly advice but rather a profound sense of encouragement and legitimacy.

Warhol's affinity with Barnum is fairly obvious. Like Barnum, he had a knack for generating attention and for converting that attention into cash. He was interested in spectacles and celebrities, and he fully understood the hypnotic power that celebrity has on the culture. He knew how to strike while the iron was hot and to milk an idea for all it was worth. He knew the power of the media and publicity and how important it is to have one's name in print, on people's tongues, and talked up in high places. He knew the allure of bright colors and brazen images, and the power of advertising slogans. He understood the human fascination with death, revealed by his 1960s *Disaster* paintings (fig. 55), and the public's endless attraction to skeletons and skulls, revealed by his brightly colored *Skulls* of 1976 (fig. 4, page 17) and his *Philip's Skull* paintings of 1985 (figs. 56, 57), which feature screenprints made from CAT-scan films of the skull of the Greek shipping heir, art collector, and noted socialite Philip Niarchos. He also understood a fascination with animals, and there is something extremely Barnumesque about Warhol's 1983 *Endangered Species* series (fig. 58), in which screenprints of animals facing extinction are done up in brilliant, psychedelic colors and presented on wallpaper printed with the images of fish (fig. 59). You see a Black Rhinoceros with a green head, blue body, and pulsating red outlines; and a Grévy's Zebra with a red, yellow, purple, and blue body. You see a San Francisco Silverspot Butterly (commonly called Myrtle's Silverspot Butterly) in rainbow colors and white outlines, as if it had somehow absorbed the acid trips and tie-dyed clothing of counterculture San Francisco in the 1960s and 1970s; and a Giant Panda with a red body suggestive of China and Mao. The fact that these alluringly colored animals are really in peril and facing not only death but extinction only adds to their appeal. When P. T. Barnum acquired the faltering Scudder's American Museum in New York and set about transforming it into what would become the wildly popular Barnum's American Museum, one of his innovations was installing large oval paintings of animals on the facade between the windows of

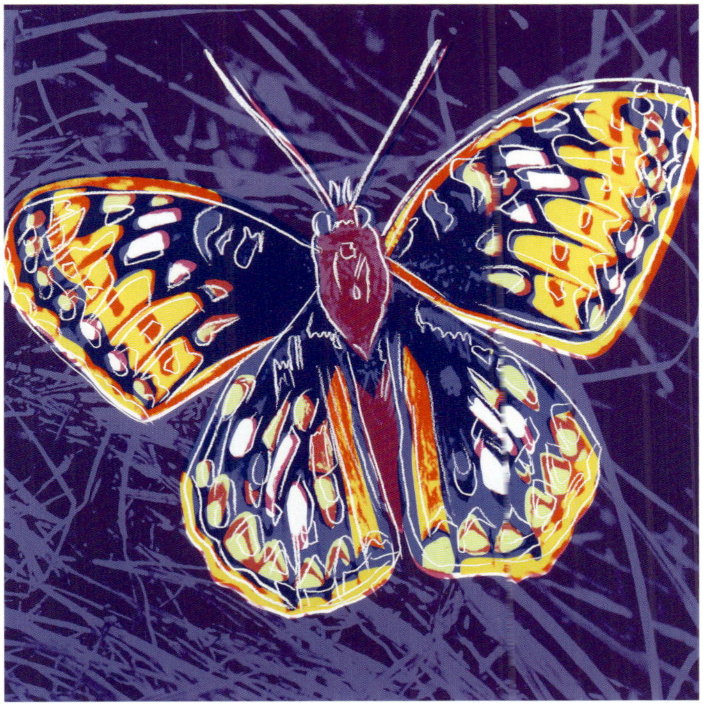

Fig. 58. *San Francisco Silverspot*, 1983. Screenprint, 38 x 38 in. (96.5 x 96.2 cm). Courtesy Ronald Feldman Fine Arts, New York

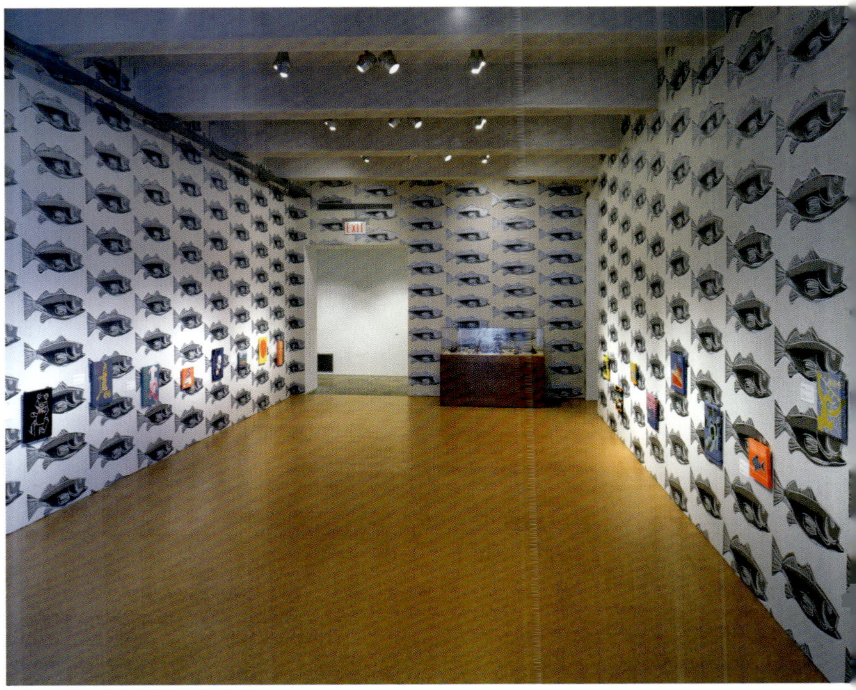

Fig. 59. *Paintings for Children* and *Fish Wallpaper* at The Andy Warhol Museum, Pittsburgh

the building's upper floors: passersby were attracted by paintings of an elephant, ostrich, giraffe, kangaroo, tapir, gnu, eagle, and pelican, among others.

Like Barnum (from humble origins in Bethel, Connecticut), Warhol (from humble origins in Pittsburgh) made a beeline to glamorous, action-packed New York, where he invented himself as a cutting-edge artist, entrepreneur, tastemaker, and leading man about town. Very much like Barnum, he knew the power of brand appeal and functioned as the attention-grabbing spokesman for his particular brand. The promotional poster for *Andy Warhol's Exploding Plastic Inevitable Show* (fig. 60), held at Poor Richard's in Chicago in June 1966, looks amazingly similar to the posters for *P. T. Barnum's Great Travelling Museum Menagerie* and *P. T. Barnum's Greatest Show on Earth—Season of 1878* (fig. 61).

Warhol's affinity with Emerson is much less obvious but just as profound, even though Warhol, with his paintings of soup cans, money, movie stars, disasters, camouflage patterns, and women's shoes, seems about as anti-Transcendentalist as one can get. For one thing, each inspired an eccentric and, in some ways, utopian social milieu. Emerson was at the center of, and catalyst for, a band of seekers, visionaries, poets, writers, and radical theologians who turned Concord into an epicenter of artistic experimentation in the 1830s and 1840s. Warhol was also at the center of, and a catalyst for, a similar hotbed of artistic ferment, including the artists, musicians, filmmakers, and so-called superstars whom he associated with at the Factory and elsewhere in New York. Religiosity, a consistent presence for Emerson, is occasionally pronounced in Warhol's work, and especially in his work from the 1980s. In *Heaven and Hell Are Just One Breath Away!* (1985–86, pls. 51, 52), what resembles a handwritten sign held by a religious fanatic is actually a surprisingly poignant painting that conjures the precariousness of existence and the great, whopping specter of eternity; it becomes all the more poignant when one realizes it was made just a couple of years before Warhol's death. Similarly prescient and haunting is *The Last Supper (Be a Somebody with a Body)* (1985–86, pl. 59), in which a graphic image of a young man accompanied by the injunction, "Be a Somebody with a BODY," resembling a Charles Atlas bodybuilding ad, is juxtaposed with an image of Jesus, excerpted from Warhol's

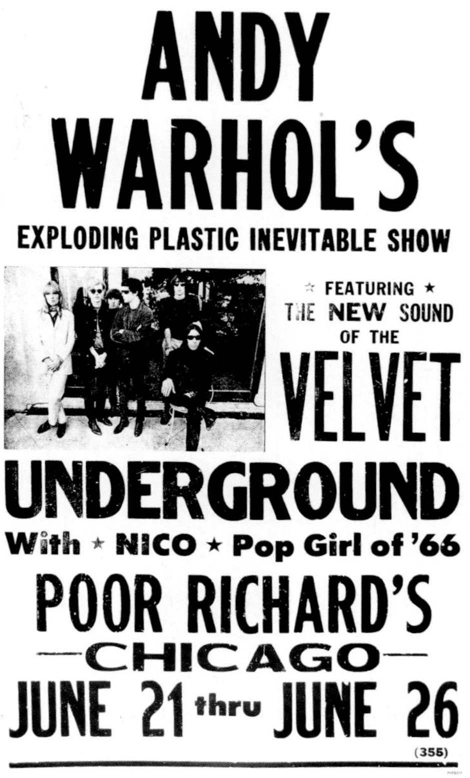

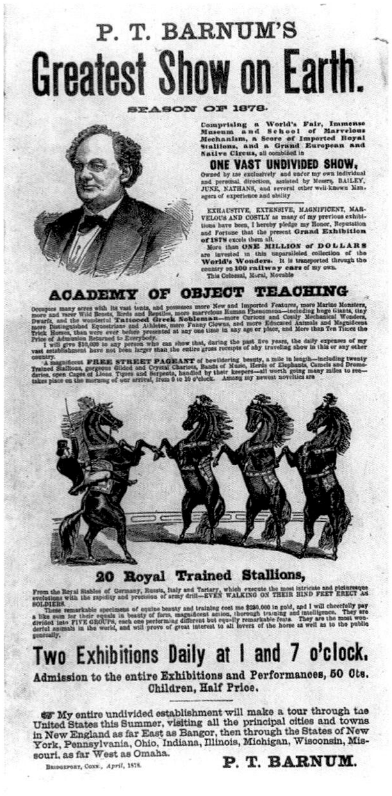

Fig. 60. *Andy Warhol's Exploding Plastic Inevitable Show*, 1966

Fig. 61. *P. T. Barnum's Greatest Show on Earth—Season of 1878*, 1878

The Last Supper series, who seems to be murmuring or whispering to the young man. Warhol's seemingly casual and perhaps irreverent image becomes a powerful meditation on corporeality and impermanence, life and mortality, earthliness and faith.

One thing you note about the otherwise cerebral Emerson is his interest in a radical openness to and fluid exchange with the world, really in an almost egoless merging of self with world. While he often theorized about such encounters, he rarely attempted to describe what they actually felt like. However, one famous passage in his essay "Nature" does so wonderfully. The passage begins, "Crossing a bare common, in snow puddles, at twilight, under a clouded sky, without having in my thoughts any occurrence of special good fortune, I have enjoyed a perfect exhilaration. I am glad to the brink of fear." Emerson then declares memorably, "I become a transparent eyeball; I am nothing; I see all; the currents of the Universal Being circulate through me; I am part and parcel of God."[5] It seems to me that Warhol—operating in a very different America, and in a very different cultural context—evinced a similar "transparent eyeball" quality, although his openness was not to a divinely suffused nature but instead to a complex and conflicted popular culture. His milieu, with all its tabloid photographs and supermarket foodstuffs, movie stars and art stars, entertainers and gruesome disasters, tedium and excitation, flowed into him, and he into it, seemingly without barriers. Just about anything could and did enter his art: cows, Lana Turner, women's shoes, electric chairs, hyacinths, automobile accidents, camouflage patterns, sundry advertisements, and Jacqueline Kennedy Onassis, to mention just a few examples. Moreover, Warhol's cultivated role as a willful naïf taking everything in, passing judgment on nothing, observing rather than opining on, and treating total banalities and important events with the same quizzical curiosity and innocent enthusiasm very much evokes Emerson's proto-Surrealist self-image as a transparent eyeball.

Throughout his career Warhol ceaselessly experimented with how to construct an image, moving freely among media and often combining painting (both representational and abstract), drawing, printmaking, sculpture, photography, and film. This fluidity squares with the kind of unfettered artistic voyaging Emerson counseled. In "The Poet," Emerson had this to say about poetry, although he could just as well have been describing any other art form, "For it is not metres, but a metre-making argument, that makes a poem,—a thought so passionate and alive, that, like the spirit of a plant or an animal, it has an architecture of its own, and adorns nature with a new thing."[6] At a time when there were strict conventions about what constituted poetic form, Emerson's notion of a "metre-making argument" was both liberating and incendiary. Essentially, Emerson declared himself for art that is cerebral, impassioned, risky, experimental, willing to find new forms (no matter how unorthodox), and capable of conveying driving ideas. The idiosyncratic artist who painted all thirty-two varieties of Campbell's soup (at a time when paintings of supermarket soup were not exactly in vogue) (figs. 1, 2; page 8), who made screenprint paintings of an electric chair, really excellent paintings of urine, and an eight-hour-and-five-minute film of the Empire State Building, was, in my opinion, advancing one heck of a "metre-making argument."

In the same essay, Emerson further addressed his eclectic approach to artistic materials and themes, announcing, "Thought makes every thing fit for use," and then adding a bit later, "Small and mean things serve as well as great symbols. . . . We are far from having exhausted the significance of the few symbols we use. We can come to use them yet with a terrible simplicity."[7] This is not exactly a nineteenth-century version of Pop but then again it is not all that far from one. Familiar things, things near at hand, things humble and seemingly inconsequential could easily be matters for art, as could the whole gamut of daily human activities. Ultimately, Emerson, who remained a buttoned-down Victorian gentleman and retained a sense of decorum, shied away from the full implications of his radical artistic notions. But one person who did not shy away was the journalist and then poet Walt Whitman, who once declared, "I was simmering, simmering, simmering; Emerson brought me to a boil." For the boiling Whitman, especially in the first (roughest, sexiest, most risky, and most frankly homoerotic) 1855 edition of *Leaves of Grass*, this meant a willingness to "sound my barbaric yawp over the roofs of the world." In "Song of Myself," for instance, he wrote this yawp: "The scent of these arm-pits aroma finer than prayer," which would have horrified many mid-nineteenth-century readers. It also meant a wildly democratic, nonhierarchical aptitude for just about anything that caught his eye and an impulse to scramble all distinc-

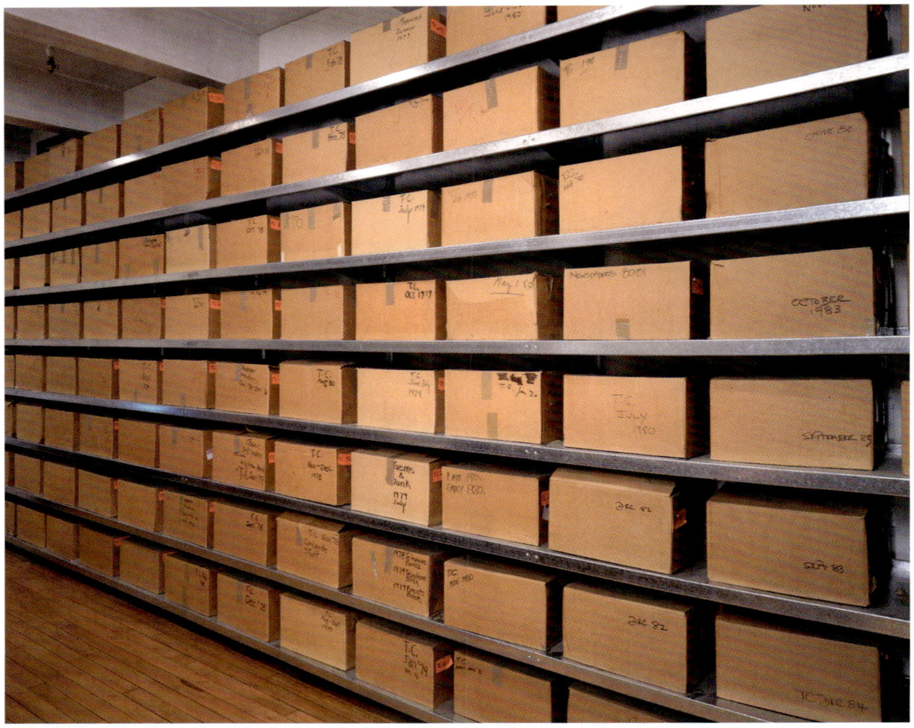

Fig. 62. 138 of Andy Warhol's 610 Time Capsules at The Andy Warhol Museum, Pittsburgh

tions between high and low, significant and insignificant, exalted and humble. This is something that you especially note in Whitman's elastic, sinewy lists, which are the verbal equivalent of cabinets crammed with objects, and which also, incidentally, prefigure Warhol's Time Capsules (fig. 62): 610 cardboard boxes that over the years he filled with the scraps and ephemera of his life, anything from personal letters and invitations to photographs, small artworks, newspaper clippings, and magazine ads. The great section 33 of "Song of Myself," for example, is a single sentence, stretching over four pages, that moves across a continent to encompass log huts, lumbermen, a panther, an alligator, a black bear and buckwheat, a quail and a bat, a hot-air balloon, a wrecked ship, a printing press, a shark fin, a copulating cock and hen, a Quaker woman, a moccasin print, and "a good game of base-ball," among other things. It seems to me that Whitman's expansive drive—an urge to locate and compile a democratic array of materials that subverts distinctions between valuable and valueless, evocative and banal—is another key to Warhol's work. And if you made a list of just some of the subjects that occupied Warhol from about 1977 until his death—like shadows, celebrities, urine, yarn, punching bags, weapons, advertisements, camouflage patterns, Jesus Christ and His disciples, Dolly Parton, motorcycles, African masks, and a good game of baseball—it might very well resemble one of Whitman's lists.

3.

Warhol's work from the late 1970s until his death—the period of his so-called late work, when he emphatically returned to painting and produced an astonishing array of important work that still has not been fully explored or received its just due—mixes his Pop sensibility with subtle, often partly obscured metaphysics and religiosity, as well as with a blatant Barnumesque interest in spectacle and razzle-dazzle entertainment. Warhol's *Shadows* (1978–79, pls. 16–21), which he blithely termed "disco decor" in their original form as 102 large panels arranged side by side around a room, and which were actually used at one point as the backdrop for a fashion shoot, have at their origins something banal and seemingly insignificant: photographs of shadows cast by small objects in the artist's studio. These shadowy forms are presented on lurid grounds, making for a dynamic interplay between deep black and brilliant colors such as bright purple, turquoise, and crimson. (Incidentally, this "disco decor," wrapping around the room, echoes nineteenth-century panoramas of landscapes, cityscapes, and battle scenes, which in the 1850s became a kind of pop-culture mania and remained significant until about 1900.)

In both his large panels in the series and his individual *Shadows*, Warhol combined screenprints of photographed shadows and pronounced brushwork, representation and abstraction. His amped-up small shadows, which otherwise convey a kind of ubiquitous nothingness, become tangible, palpable, richly alluring structures. It is intriguing that when Warhol returned to painting full on, he was drawn to subjects that, while not exactly abstract, because they always refer to familiar things in the world, certainly look abstract. His *Shadows* at once revisit, critique, poke fun at, and take in surprising new directions the works of some of the major abstract painters from the 1940s and 1950s, such as Franz Kline, Clyfford Still, and Ad Reinhardt. What Warhol accomplished in this series is a kind of reproducible abstraction, or rather a hybrid of representation and abstraction. Yet, on close observation, it becomes apparent that the paintings are wonderfully complex, revealing a great deal of surface intensity, variety, and individuality. In one example, chunky, sharply delineated black forms turn ragged and wispy at their borders where they intersect with a yellowish gold. Black forms on the left merge with and then yield to luminous white fields. In other works bare, shadowlike forms seem overwhelmed and subsumed by white fields. Sometimes the black forms are brazen and vivid; at other times they seem vaporous, drifting across the surface like dark mist. These paintings accentuate their status as artifices, or painting devices, and dispense with Abstract Expressionism's claims to originality and transcendent beauty. However, they still retain an aura of the sublime, in the term's common meaning as something of awe-inspiring beauty, but also in the sense put forth by Edmund Burke in *A Philosophical Enquiry into the Origin of Our Idea of the Sublime and Beautiful* (1756), of a beauty inextricably linked with terror. There is something vaguely menacing about Warhol's *Shadows*. His shadowy forms are enticing and luscious but also suggest, however obliquely and implicitly, encroaching blackness out there, and they may contain shuddering intimations of mortality and eternity. This becomes even more manifest in the several instances where he added glittering diamond dust into the mix, which not only introduces a note of ostentation and conjures nocturnal associations of sequined gowns, glittery makeup, and Las Vegas stage garb (like Liberace's suits) but also makes his quasi-abstractions loosely resemble vast and glinting interstellar expanses: shadows in one's own room suddenly correspond to universal dark matter and dark energy.

4.

On one level, Warhol's *Oxidation Paintings* (1977–78, pls. 10–15), which involved urinating on canvases that had been primed with copper-based paint, are a kind of "barbaric yawp" akin to Whitman's aromatic armpits. They are also hilarious, substituting the drips and splatters of urine for Abstract Expressionist freeform, energetic gestures, such as Jackson Pollock's famous drips and splatters made with paint. Aside from priming the canvases and setting the procedure in motion, Warhol did not control how these paintings would ultimately appear; their appearance arose solely from how the urine oxidized on the still-wet copper-based grounds. Nevertheless, these *Piss Paintings*, as they are also known, are strikingly gorgeous, and they have an intricate and varied visuality that one normally would not associate with Warhol. Light green, dark green, and at times near-black blobs, swirls, streaks, drops, and tendrils effloresce on reddish or gold metallic grounds. Colors blend in slight, captivating moments, and prominent shapes abut splays of tiny flecks and jots. If it is possible to be at once crusty and ethereal, that is exactly how these works seem. Throughout the series, the surfaces are incredibly active and reward sustained, patient viewing. For all their scatological daring (and humor), these paintings are also surprisingly nuanced and evocative. Some suggest the delicacy and solemnity of exquisite thousand-year-old Chinese ink landscapes, for instance, those by Song Dynasty scroll painter Xia Gui (c. 1195–1224); others are much more rugged and rough, as if the urine acted as a corrosive acid. Even though one "reads" these paintings as abstractions, they suggest many associations and connotations, ranging from microscopic structures (some photographs of stem cells are remarkably similar, fig. 63) to vast, cosmic forms like galaxy clusters, nebulae, and gas clouds. However,

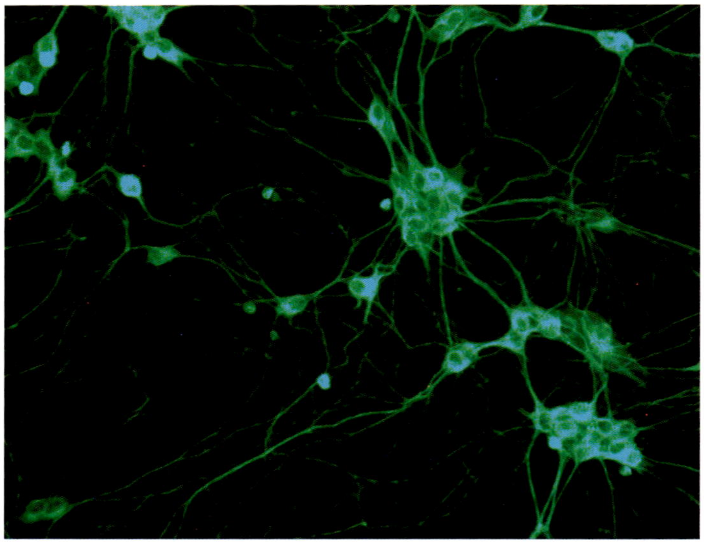

Fig. 63. Neural cells grown from a single neural crest stem cell taken from a fifteen-day-old rat. Photo by Genevieve Kruger, University of Michigan Medical School

because the works contain actual bodily traces, they also function as abstract portraits or self-portraits—made at a time when Warhol was increasingly occupied with questions of mortality and human ephemerality. Moreover, as a churchgoer (who frequented a Catholic church in New York) and the son of Carpatho-Rusyn parents from Slovakia who immigrated to the United States, Warhol would have been deeply aware of a long-standing tradition of icon paintings traditionally made with egg tempera and gold leaf. His *Oxidation Paintings*, with their coppery metallic grounds, have a distinct iconlike look, and they also almost effect a kind of alchemical miracle, turning base urine into something splendid, lustrous, and altogether beguiling.

5.

For both the *Shadows* and the *Oxidation Paintings*, Warhol settled on a blueprint and materials and then used this procedure to explore all sorts of possibilities and variations. He took a similar approach with his *Rorschach* paintings (1984, pls. 31–35), which are likewise a reeling mix of abstraction and representation. They take as their source the Rorschach inkblot test, invented by Swiss psychiatrist Hermann Rorschach in 1921. Patients are given ten standardized inkblots—including five that are black ink on white paper, two that are black and red ink on white paper, and three that are multicolored—and then tested and scored according to their responses. Warhol was probably attracted to the fact that the abstract shapes are standardized, impersonal, and repetitive, and that anyone can, theoretically, read into them what he or she will.

For his paintings, Warhol composed his own large, inkblotlike forms from acrylic paint, then folded the canvas over while the paint was still wet and pressed the two sides together to make a mirror image, thus mixing the processes of painting and printing. There are also many different versions of these works, some jet black on white grounds and some in various colors, some medium in size and some very large. Like the *Shadows* and *Oxidation Paintings*, these abstract works communicate nothing, at least overtly, about the artist's psyche, and therefore decisively undercut any of Abstract Expressionism's lingering mythology concerning heroism, vigor, fraught emotions, spiritual intensity, and self-revelation. Still, these works have a peculiar effect, which is much more humanly complex than it is breezy and irreverent. Warhol's paintings are intricate and seemingly ornate, like Baroque wallpaper and some Venetian chandeliers, but they are also scruffy and rough. Because of the way the paint's thickness and color tones fluctuate, the paintings can seem superpresent or fading and withdrawn—or sometimes both at the same time. Step up close, especially to the large ones, and they seem strictly abstract, but step back a bit and the recognizable pattern discloses all sorts of protean likenesses, or rather mere hints and slight suggestions of them, although—just like with actual Rorschach inkblot tests—every viewer comes up with her or his own interpretations. Rather than being expressive of personal meaning, these paintings provoke a plenitude of associations: human limbs, viscera, male genitalia, vertebrae, and spines; magical figures in flight and cartoonish creatures; things that ooze and things that grow; children's drawings and automatic doodles; scary aliens from comic books or science-fiction movies and gruesome medieval demons in hell; fanciful scenes that can seem lighthearted and whimsical or phantasmagorical scenes that can seem harrowing and violent. The complexity of these allegedly impersonal, neutral, and nonemotive paintings is not supplied by the artist but instead arises from a confluence between artist, artwork, and viewer. At one point Warhol, in his typically deadpan way, talked of hiring someone to discern what was in the paintings because he just was not up to the task.

6.

What all three of these series of paintings reveal (and the same could also be said of Warhol's *Camouflage* [1986, fig. 64, pls. 69–73] and *Yarn* [1983, pls. 25–30] paintings, as well as a great number of other works through the years) is that things so routine and familiar that you normally would not give them a second thought retain their mundane aspects, even a kind of excruciating banality, while they simultaneously enter into startling and transformative new conditions. The two contexts of the routine thing or action—as it normally is, and as it has been transformed and reinvented—coexist, and it is for the viewer to constantly shuttle between them. In the *Oxidation Paintings*, patterns of urine drops and splatters indicate a daily, bodily function but they are also iridescent and spectacular. Small Rorschach inkblots are made to be huge, eventful, and mysterious, towering over the viewer like holy frescoes on the walls of a cathedral. In the *Shadows* paintings, small, slight shadows like those one sees all the time (but very rarely thinks about) become looming forces at once enticing and frightening.

I have mentioned Warhol's myriad comparisons to the carnivalesque P. T. Barnum, yet here it is also worth recalling the great twentieth-century Russian literary critic Mikhail Bakhtin, and specifically his theory of the carnival, which he applied to literature but which could be applied equally to visual art and perhaps many other genres. According to Bakhtin, in a "carnivalized moment" or "carnivalized situation" the normal rules, hierarchies, values, and modes of apprehension are temporarily suspended in favor of a brand-new freedom, which can be simultaneously ungainly and spiritually elevated, at once confusing and substantially liberating. Excess, exaggeration, hyperbole, exuberance, and parody are intrinsic to these carnival situations, which also scramble distinctions between high and low, sacred and profane, human and animal, spirit and flesh. Importantly, for Bakhtin these carnivalized moments in no way seek to transcend or obliterate normal life; they are not revolutionary in the sense of wanting to substitute a new, improved consciousness for an exhausted, defunct one. Rather, both exist together, side by side, and one's primary experience is to move back and forth between the two, participating in the

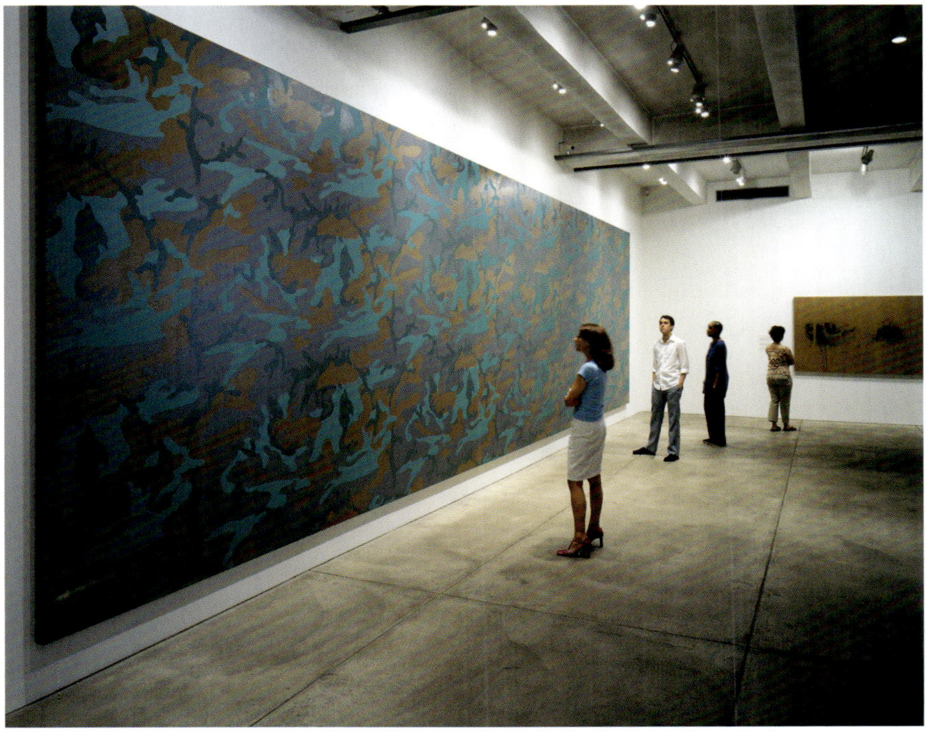

Fig. 64. *Camouflage* and *Oxidation* paintings at The Andy Warhol Museum, Pittsburgh

carnivalized situation in order to be tested and transformed and then returning to normal life with some of the wisdom that one gained.[8]

I do not mean to suggest that Bakhtin influenced Warhol, which is highly unlikely. But Warhol's works from this period and throughout his career exemplify what Bakhtin theorized as carnivalized situations. Things so known and normal that one would hardly give them a second thought take on surprising new characteristics, upending habits of thought and, while often willfully boring, inspiring a fresh response and orientation to one's culture and time. It is entirely normal to see a picture of Elvis Presley, but entirely carnivalesque and outlandish to see many huge, identical, silver pictures of Elvis side by side on a wall. It is entirely normal to see cardboard boxes in the supermarket containing Heinz ketchup bottles or Brillo soap pads, but jarring to see them in the gallery or museum as hand-painted boxes made out of wood. It is entirely normal (alas) to see a photograph of an electric chair, but entirely carnivalesque to encounter a massive, blue, eight-foot-by-six-foot screen-print image of an electric chair, along with an adjacent monochromatic blue painting of the same size. And it is interesting that all of these works were made by an artist who for years went about his daily life wearing a signature costume: those outlandish wigs, those cool sunglasses, those particular clothes.

7.

In America it is entirely normal that Leonardo da Vinci's masterpiece fresco *The Last Supper* (c. 1495–98), at Santa Maria delle Grazie in Milan, would be seen by most people in the form of a reproduction: as an illustration in a book, a poster, or a religious souvenir. It is, however, entirely unusual and completely carnivalesque that such derivations, reproductions, and knickknacks would be transformed back into compelling paintings (some of which are huge). According to Dia Art Foundation chief curator Lynne Cooke, in her insightful essay on *The Last Supper* paintings (1986, pls. 74–80), the Greek art dealer Alexandre Iolas invited Warhol to exhibit work in his new gallery, located across the street from the da Vinci fresco, and it was Iolas who suggested the theme for what would become Warhol's last great series of paintings. Warhol decided to base his paintings not on the da Vinci original but on reproductions and facsimiles. Although there remains some debate about which reproductions and facsimiles he ultimately used, Cooke convincingly identifies them as "a detailed black and white reproduction based on a nineteenth century copy of the rapidly deteriorating original, and a schematic outline drawing of the kind found in children's coloring books."[9]

Warhol's version was originally intended to be a parody or travesty of the da Vinci original right across the street. As Bakhtin points out, parody and travesty are essential components of a carnival sense of life, in which mighty things are temporarily cut down to size, sacred things are gleefully blasphemed, and revered things are lampooned and ridiculed, largely to suspend, if only for a brief while, the usual ubiquitous rules, restrictive categories, hierarchies, and stratification. According to Bakhtin, carnival life, involving free-spirited play and buffoonery, "combines the sacred with the profane, the lofty with the low, the great with the insignificant, the wise with the stupid." The same could be said for Warhol's *The Last Supper* paintings.

These paintings exist in several different versions, all of which are based on an outline rendition in acrylic or a screenprint image (often doubled), arrayed against colored grounds and sometimes overlaid with bands of colors, of the same scene depicted in the da Vinci work: Jesus and the aghast apostles at dinner as He announces that one of them will shortly betray Him. Just about everything that Warhol ever did in painting applies here: the doubling of an image and serial repetition; the combination of screen-printing and painting; celebrity portraits (Jesus being one of the most famous celebrities ever); the application of different color schemes to the same image in different works; the use of a found, widely known image and the juxtaposition of that image (or parts of it) with well-known cultural and commercial signifiers (for instance, in paintings where Jesus is excerpted and presented with logos for Dove soap and General Electric). It is as if Warhol was summing up much of his career, and emptying his whole bag of tricks, as he responded to one of the most powerful images in the history of Western art and also a scene fundamental to the Christian faith.

In the paintings involving outlines, Jesus and the apostles are clearly defined, although vaguely cartoonish or caricature-like, but also wavering, fragile, lovely, and precarious as they hover on white grounds. They are enveloped by blankness, by whiteness, and they are at once on and merging with, or dissolving into, all that whiteness. In the paintings involving screenprints, Warhol's use of color is masterful. In one painting, featuring two adjacent identical images, the whole scene is bathed in a red glow evocative of Times Square, blood, nightclubs, or police lights. In other examples foregrounded, differently colored rectangles and squares, reminiscent of both geometric abstraction and advertising graphics, at once meld with and occlude the underlying image. Although the figures of Jesus and the apostles are clearly visible, because of the way the silkscreen ink sits on the canvas they also seem to be fading or eroding in parts, which suggests the physical deterioration of the da Vinci fresco but also an interplay between faith and doubt, presence and absence, things that are held very dear and dear things that are inevitably lost. Throughout the series, Warhol's paintings are fractious—*The Last Supper* buffeted by carnival colors, stuccoed with company logos, almost overwhelmed by a camouflage pattern, and virulently infected by 1980s America—yet the famous scene retains its gravity, solemnity, and enduring humanity. It may be the case that *The Last Supper* paintings involve a questioning of religiosity and the deep pull of religious iconography in the midst of an overwhelming popular culture of rampant advertising, commercialism, and entertainment. It may also be the case (although this is hardly obvious) that *The Last Supper* paintings, for all their manipulation of a familiar image, involve a profound questioning of and reckoning with personal faith, which occurred very late, as it turns out, in Warhol's life.

Andy Warhol's work from the late 1970s until his death—and I've touched on only a fraction of this work—invites new appraisals of his overall achievement, including how this "King of Pop" (as he has often been called) made deeply engaging abstract paintings, how this purveyor of banalities was often steeped in religiosity and religious iconography, and how this icon of 1960s American art shares a kinship with the nineteenth-century icons Barnum and Emerson, who wrote, "[T]he quality of the imagination is to flow, and not to freeze."[10] As Warhol emerged from the 1970s and flourished in the 1980s with renewed vigor and experimentation, inspired in part by his friendship and occasional collaboration with younger artists like Jean-Michel Basquiat, Julian Schnabel, and Francesco Clemente, what one very much detects is a flowing and innovative imagination that yielded a host of works worthy of sustained attention and acclaim.

Notes

1. This quotation is prominently displayed at the Andy Warhol Museum in Pittsburgh.
2. Ralph Waldo Emerson, entry for May 25, 1843, in *The Journals and Miscellaneous Notebooks of Ralph Waldo Emerson*, eds. William H. Gilman and J. E. Parsons, vol. 8, 1841–43 (Cambridge, Mass.: The Belknap Press of Harvard University Press, 1970), p. 403.
3. Ralph Waldo Emerson, "The Poet" (1844), in *The Portable Emerson*, ed. Carl Bode, in collaboration with Malcolm Cowley (New York: Penguin Books, 1981), p. 242.
4. Ibid., p. 243.
5. Ralph Waldo Emerson, "Nature" (1844), in *The Portable Emerson*, ed. Carl Bode, in collaboration with Malcolm Cowley (New York: Penguin Books, 1981), pp. 10–11.
6. Emerson, "The Poet," p. 245.
7. Ibid., p. 250.
8. All quotations from and references to Mikhail Bakhtin are from his *Problems of Dostoevsky's Poetics*, ed. and trans. Caryl Emersson (Minneapolis: University of Minnesota Press, 1984), pp. 122–24.
9. All quotations from and references to Lynne Cooke are from her essay for the 1994–95 exhibition at Dia Center for the Arts, New York, "Andy Warhol: *The Last Supper Portraits,*" at www.diabeacon.org/exhibs/warhol/lastsupper/essay.html.
10. Emerson, "The Poet," p. 260.

PLATES

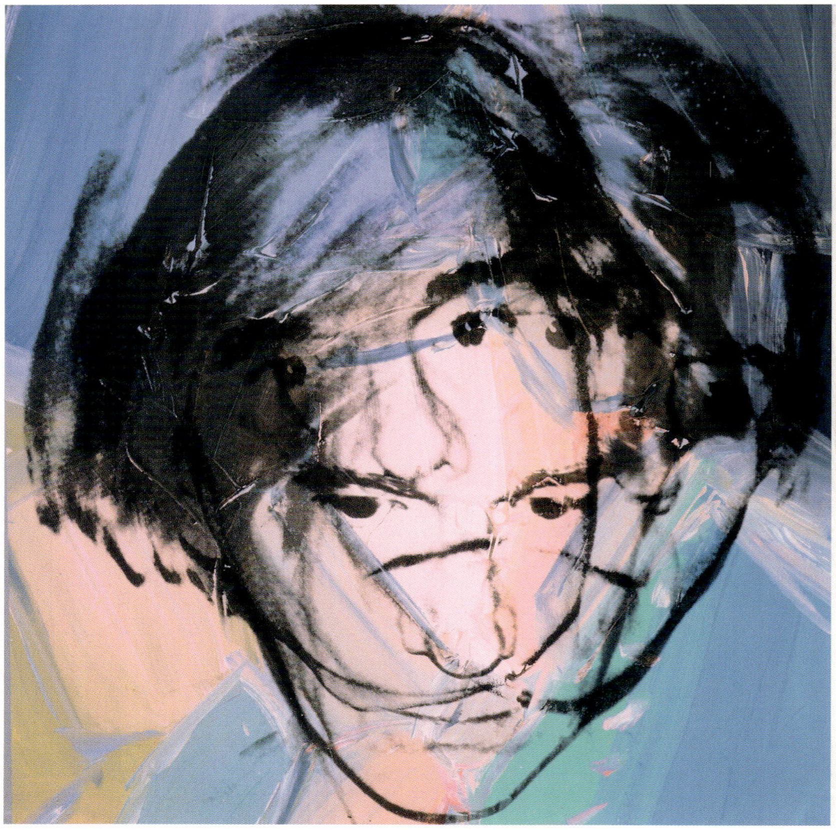

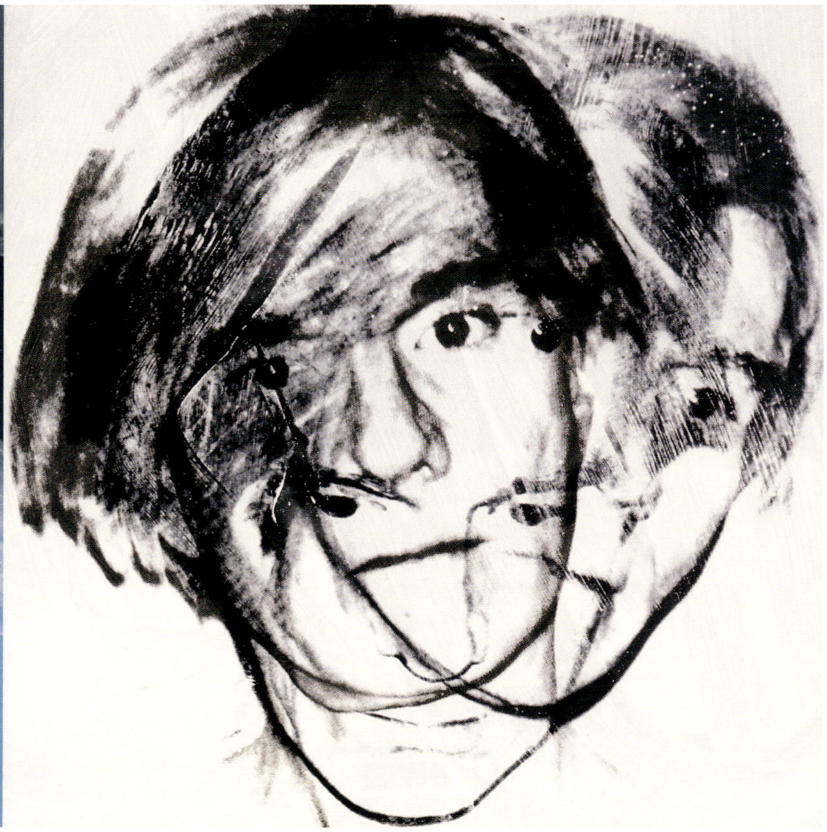

1. *Self-Portrait*, 1978. Acrylic and silkscreen ink on canvas, 40 x 40 in. (101.6 x 101.6 cm). The Andy Warhol Museum, Pittsburgh; Founding Collection, Contribution The Andy Warhol Foundation for the Visual Arts, Inc.

2. *Self-Portrait*, 1978. Acrylic and silkscreen ink on canvas, 40 x 40 in. (101.6 x 101.6 cm). The Andy Warhol Museum, Pittsburgh; Founding Collection, Contribution The Andy Warhol Foundation for the Visual Arts, Inc.

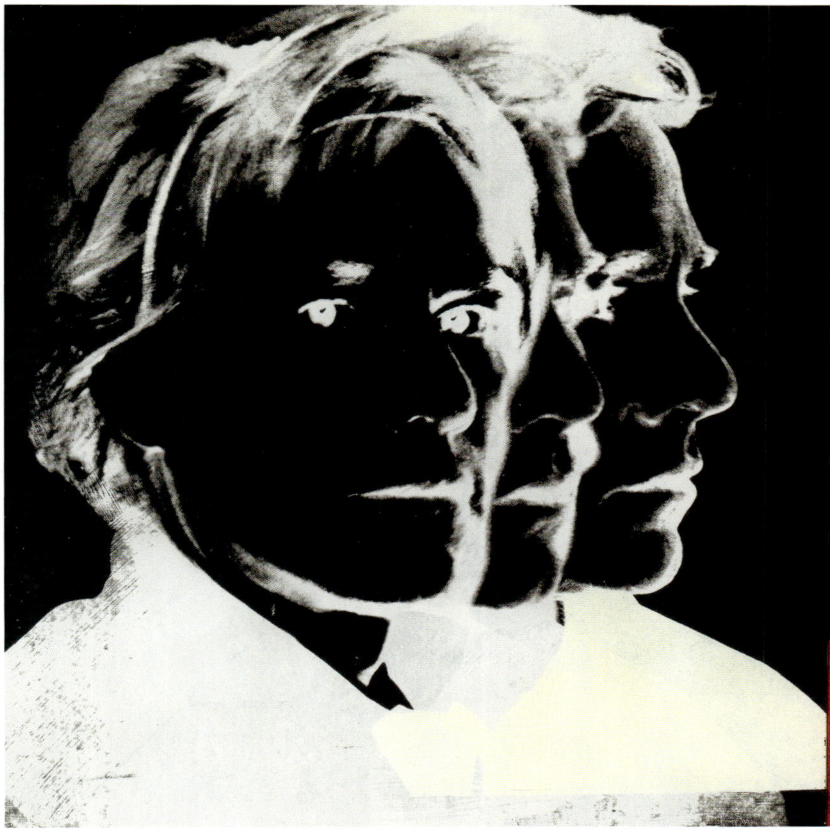

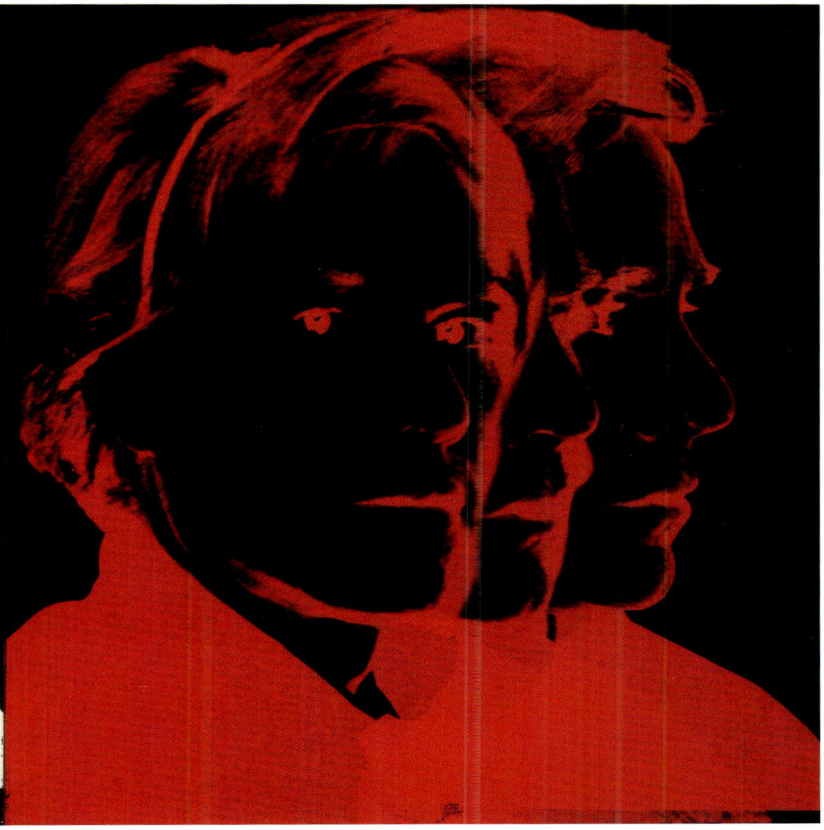

3. *Self-Portrait*, 1978. Acrylic and silkscreen ink on canvas, $40\frac{3}{8} \times 40\frac{3}{8}$ in. (102.6 x 102.6 cm). The Andy Warhol Museum, Pittsburgh; Founding Collection, Contribution The Andy Warhol Foundation for the Visual Arts, Inc.

4. *Self-Portrait*, 1978. Acrylic and silkscreen ink on canvas, $40\frac{3}{8} \times 40\frac{3}{8}$ in. (102.6 x 102.6 cm). The Andy Warhol Museum, Pittsburgh; Founding Collection, Contribution The Andy Warhol Foundation for the Visual Arts, Inc.

5. *Self-Portrait with Skull*, 1978. Acrylic and silkscreen ink on canvas, two parts, 16 x 13 in. (40.6 x 33 cm) each. Collection of Anthony d'Offay

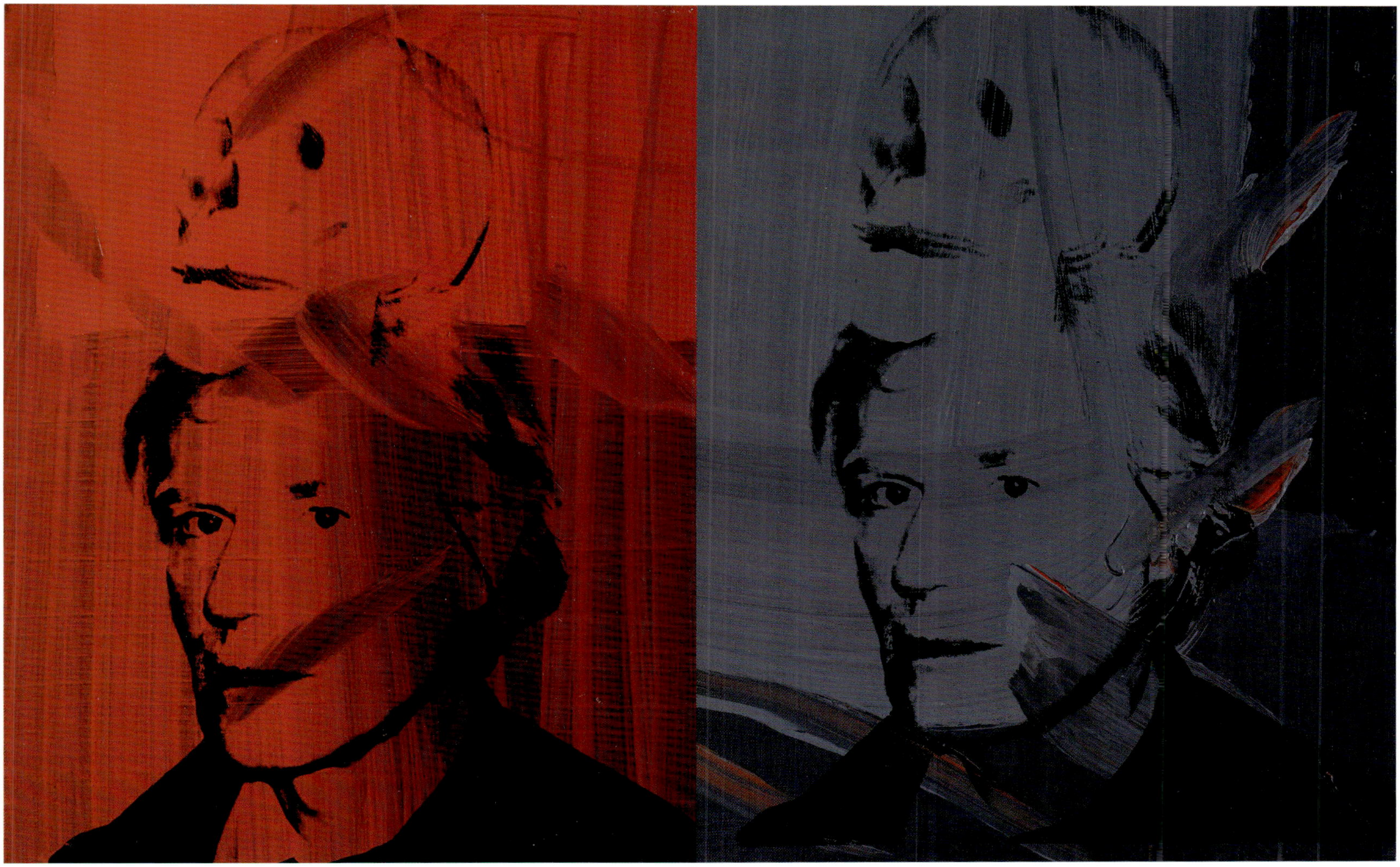

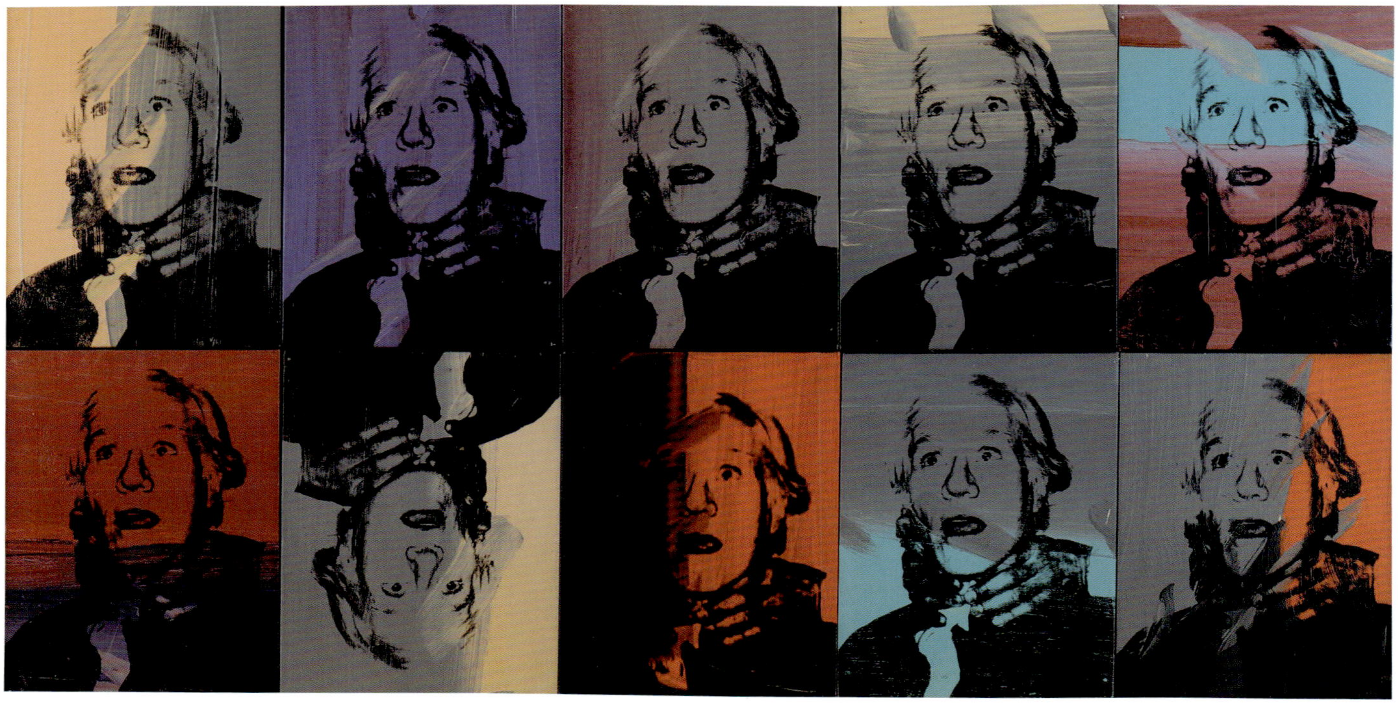

6. *Self-Portrait (Strangulation)*, 1978. Acrylic and silkscreen ink on canvas, ten parts, 16 x 13 in. (40.6 x 33 cm) each. Collection of Anthony d'Offay

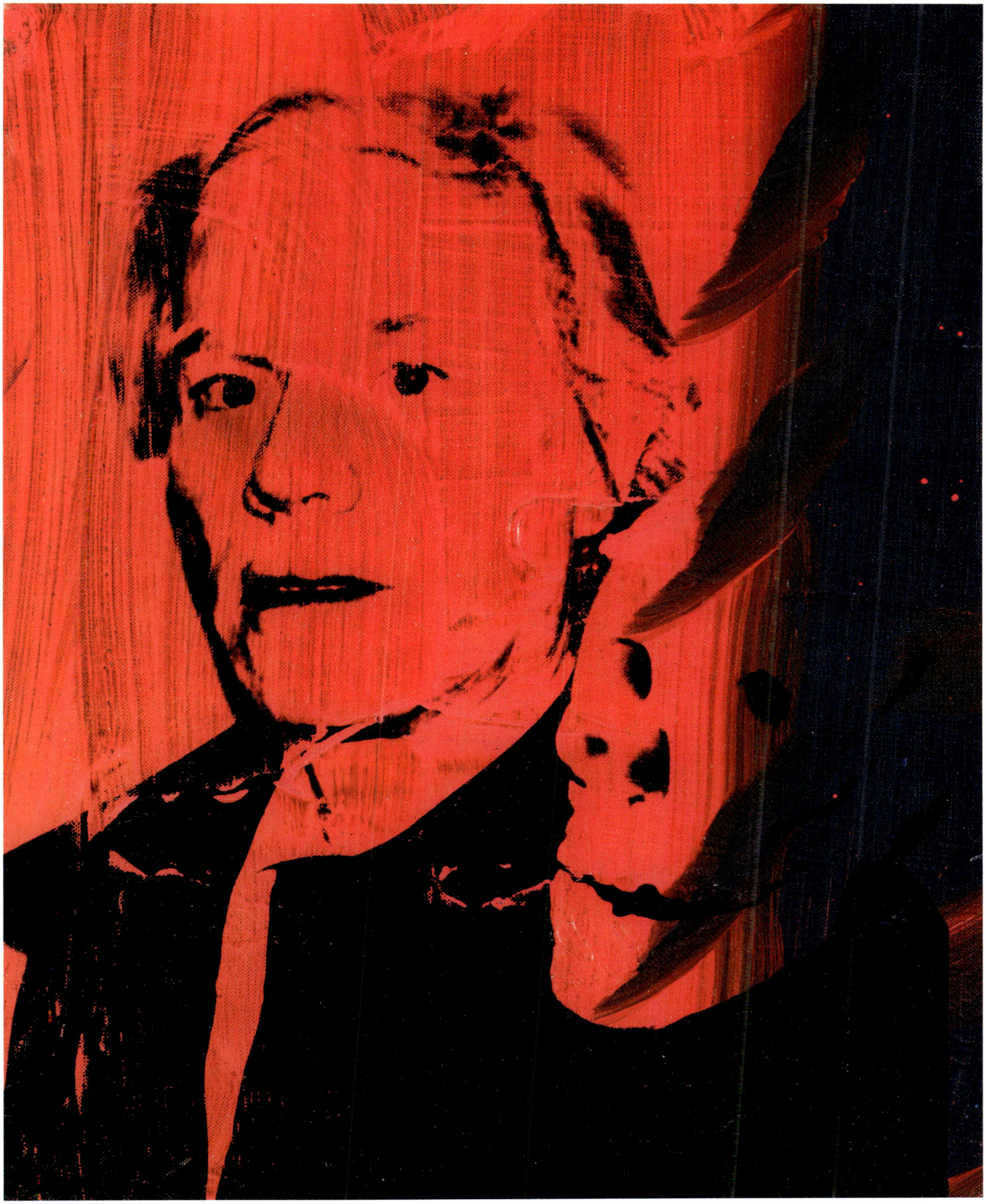

7. *Self-Portrait with Skull*, 1978. Acrylic and silkscreen ink on canvas, two parts, 16 x 13 in. (40.6 x 33 cm) each. ARTIST ROOMS, Tate and National Galleries of Scotland. Acquired jointly through The d'Offay Donation with assistance from the National Heritage Memorial Fund and The Art Fund 2008

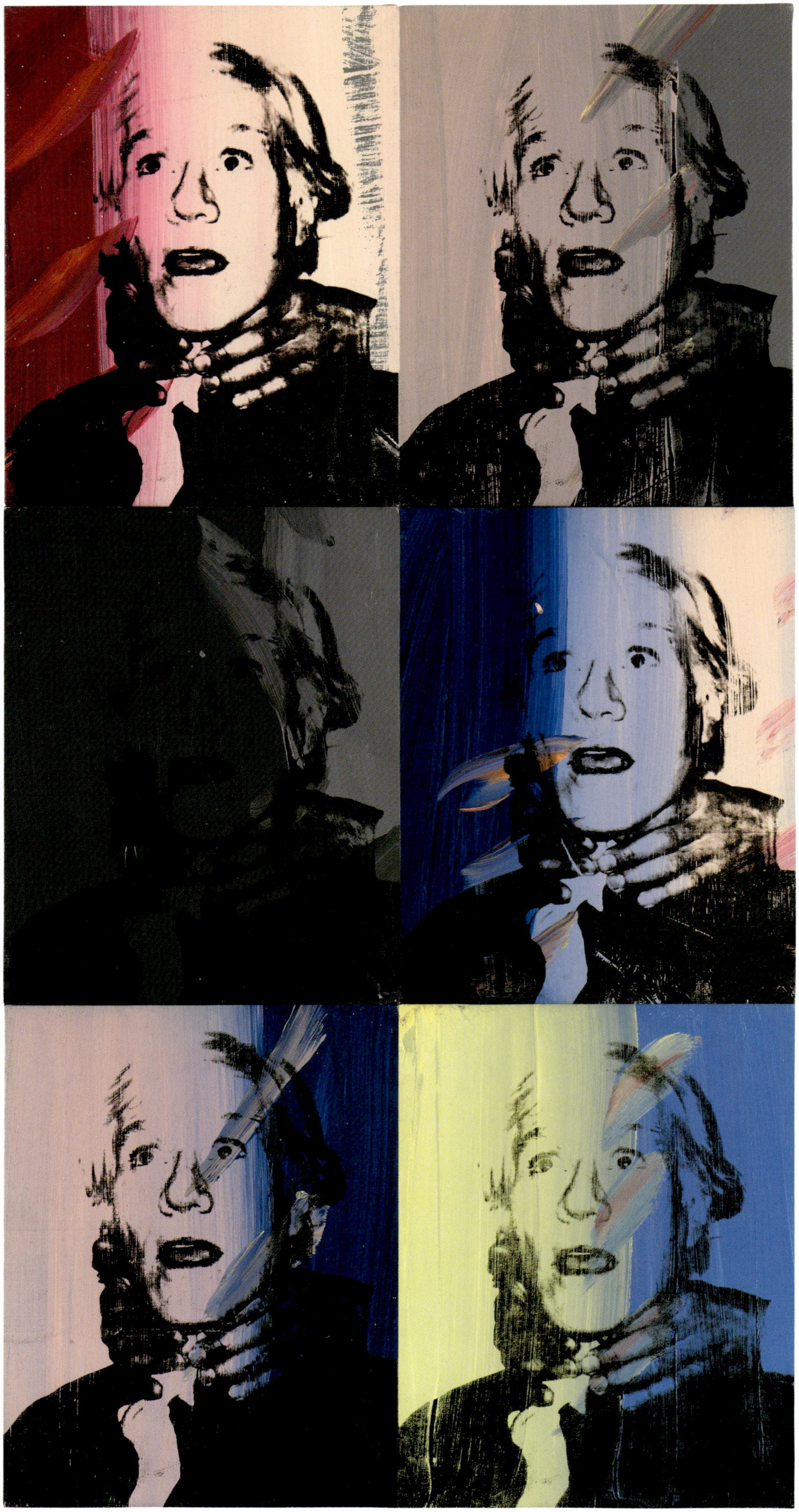

8. *Self-Portrait (Strangulation)*, 1978.
Acrylic and silkscreen ink on canvas, six parts, 16 x 13 in. (40.6 x 33 cm) each. ARTIST ROOMS. Tate and National Galleries of Scotland. Acquired jointly through The d'Offay Donation with assistance from the National Heritage Memorial Fund and The Art Fund 2008

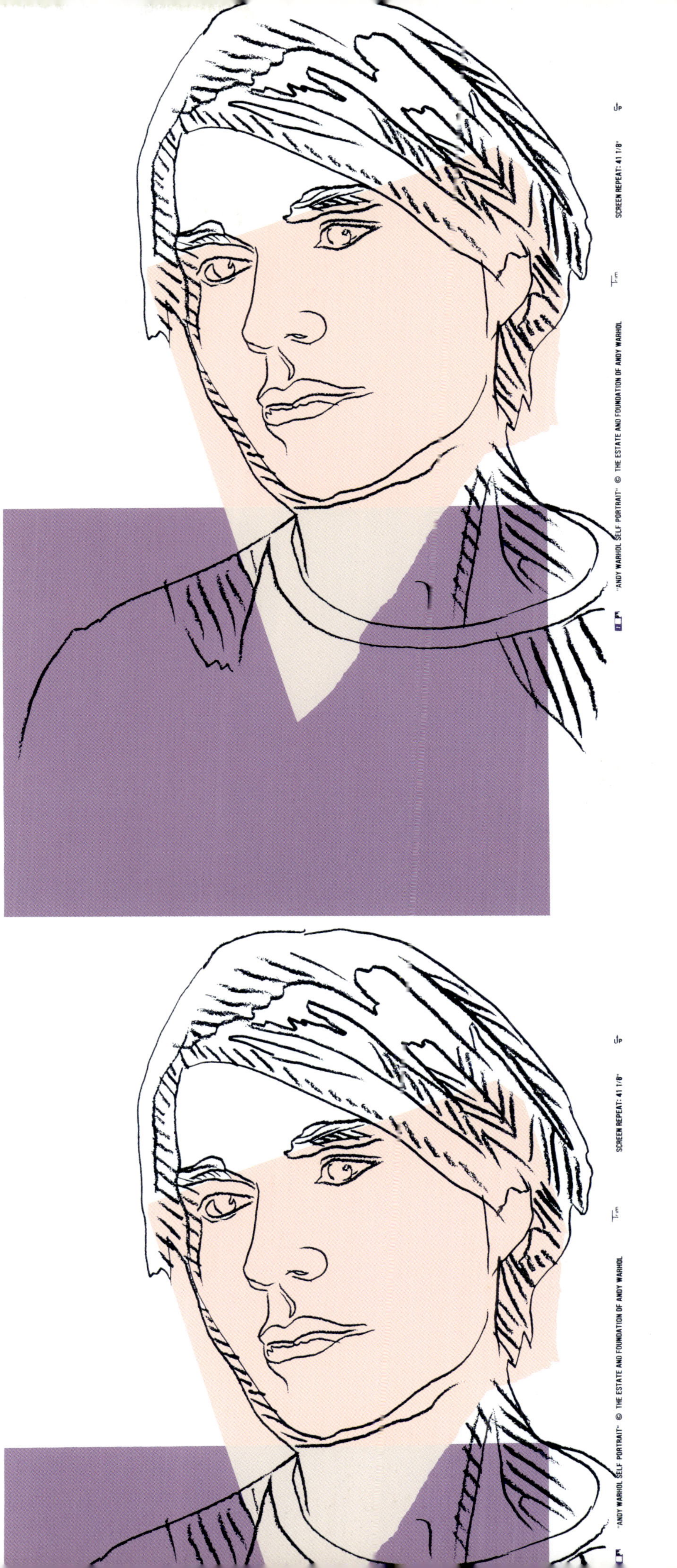

9. *Self-Portrait Wallpaper*, 1978. Screenprint on wallpaper, 180 x 28 in. (457.2 x 71.1 cm) each roll. The Andy Warhol Museum, Pittsburgh

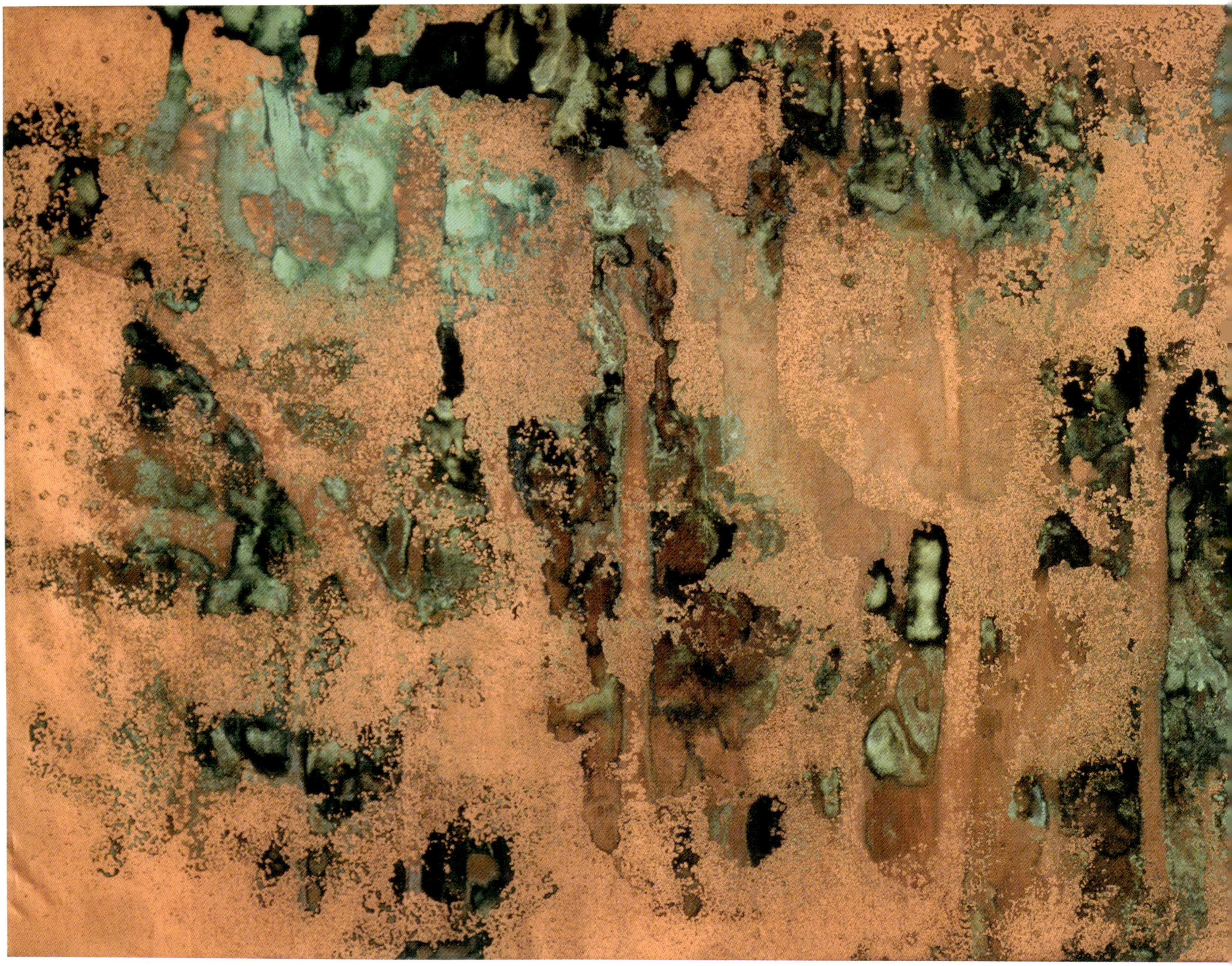

10. *Oxidation Painting*, 1978. Copper paint and urine on canvas, 78 x 208 in. (198 x 528 cm). Bischofberger Collection, Switzerland

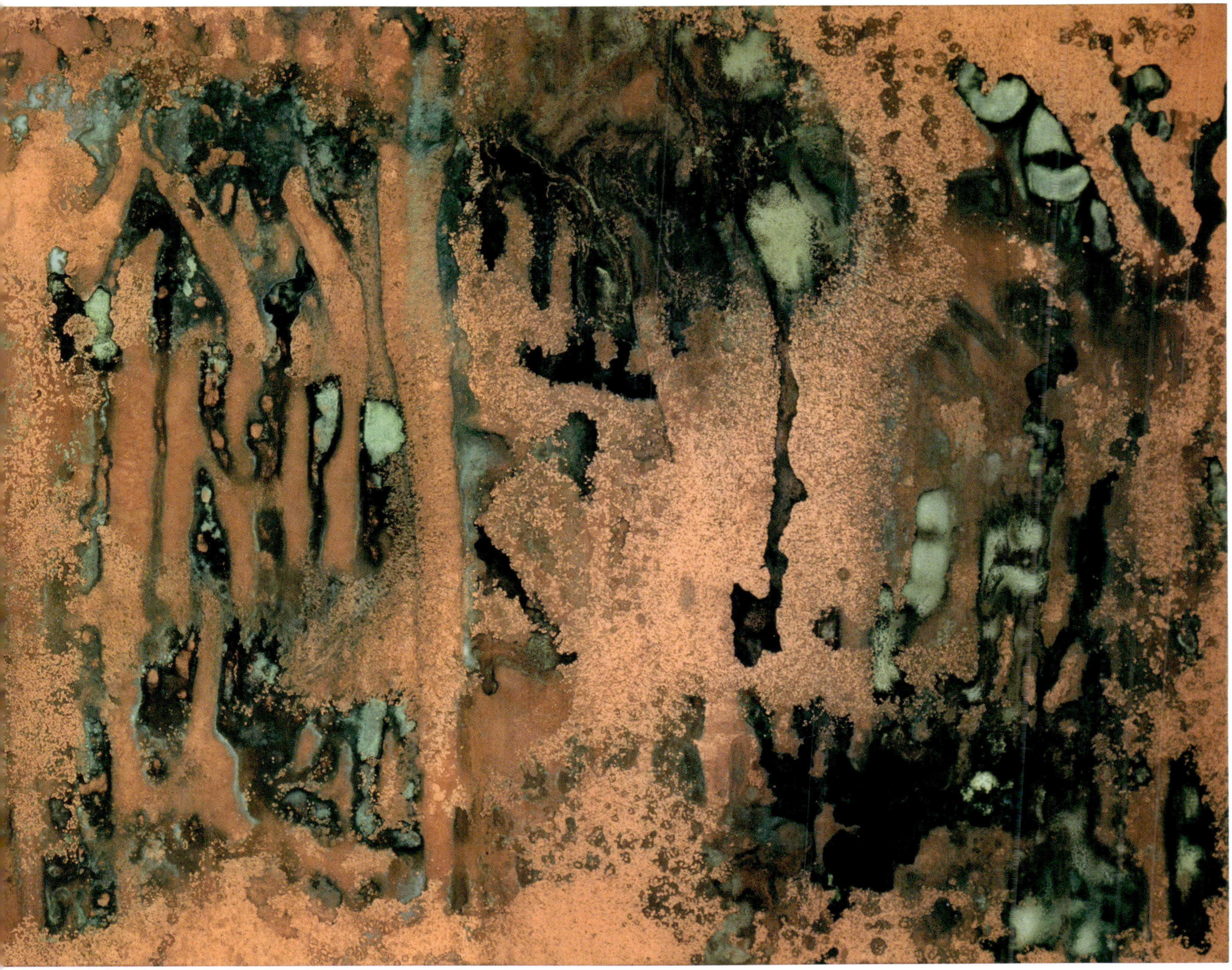

11. *Oxidation Painting* (in 12 parts), 1978. Acrylic and urine on linen, 48 x 49 in. (121.9 x 124.5 cm). The Andy Warhol Museum, Pittsburgh; Founding Collection, Contribution The Andy Warhol Foundation for the Visual Arts, Inc.

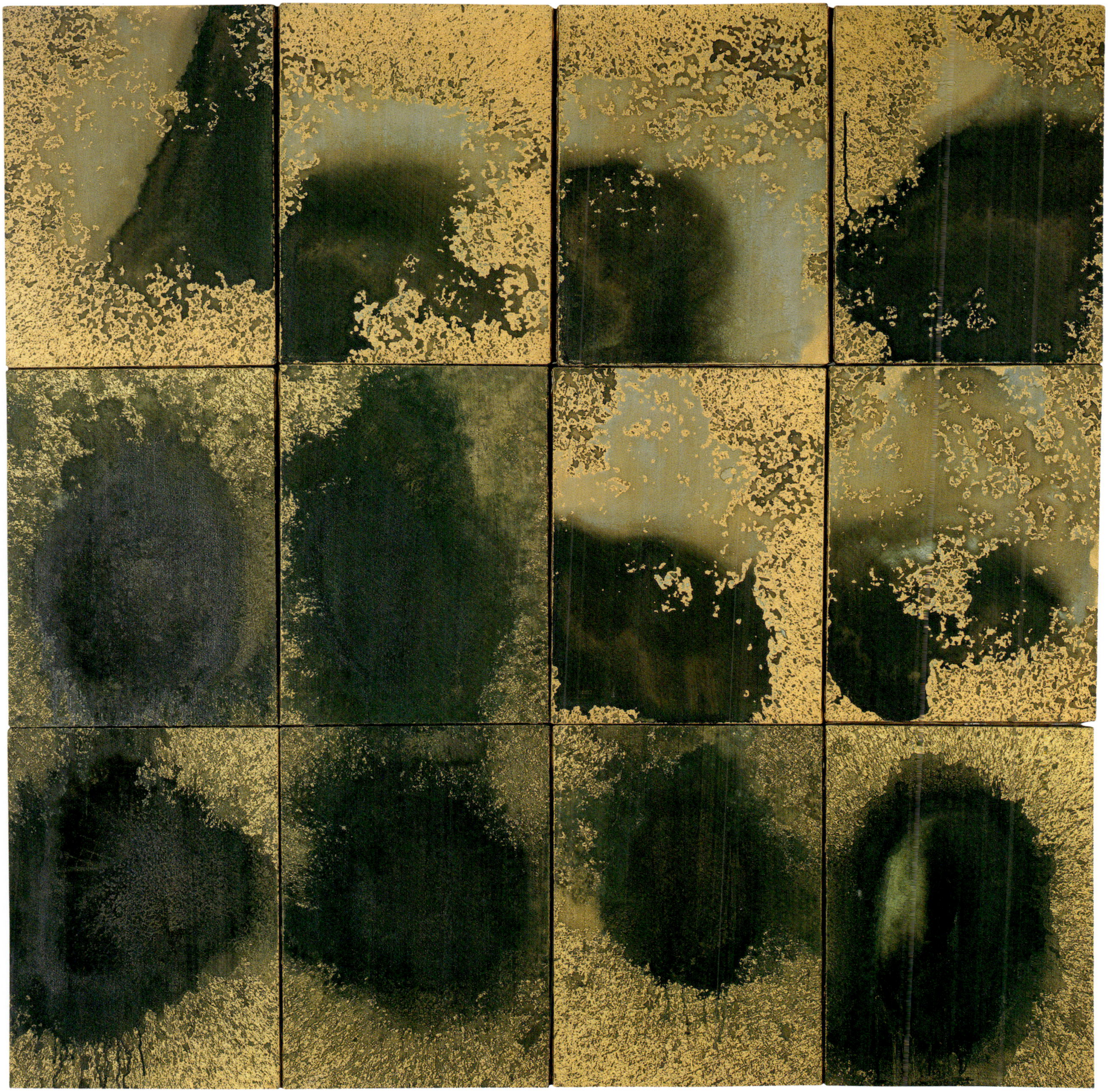

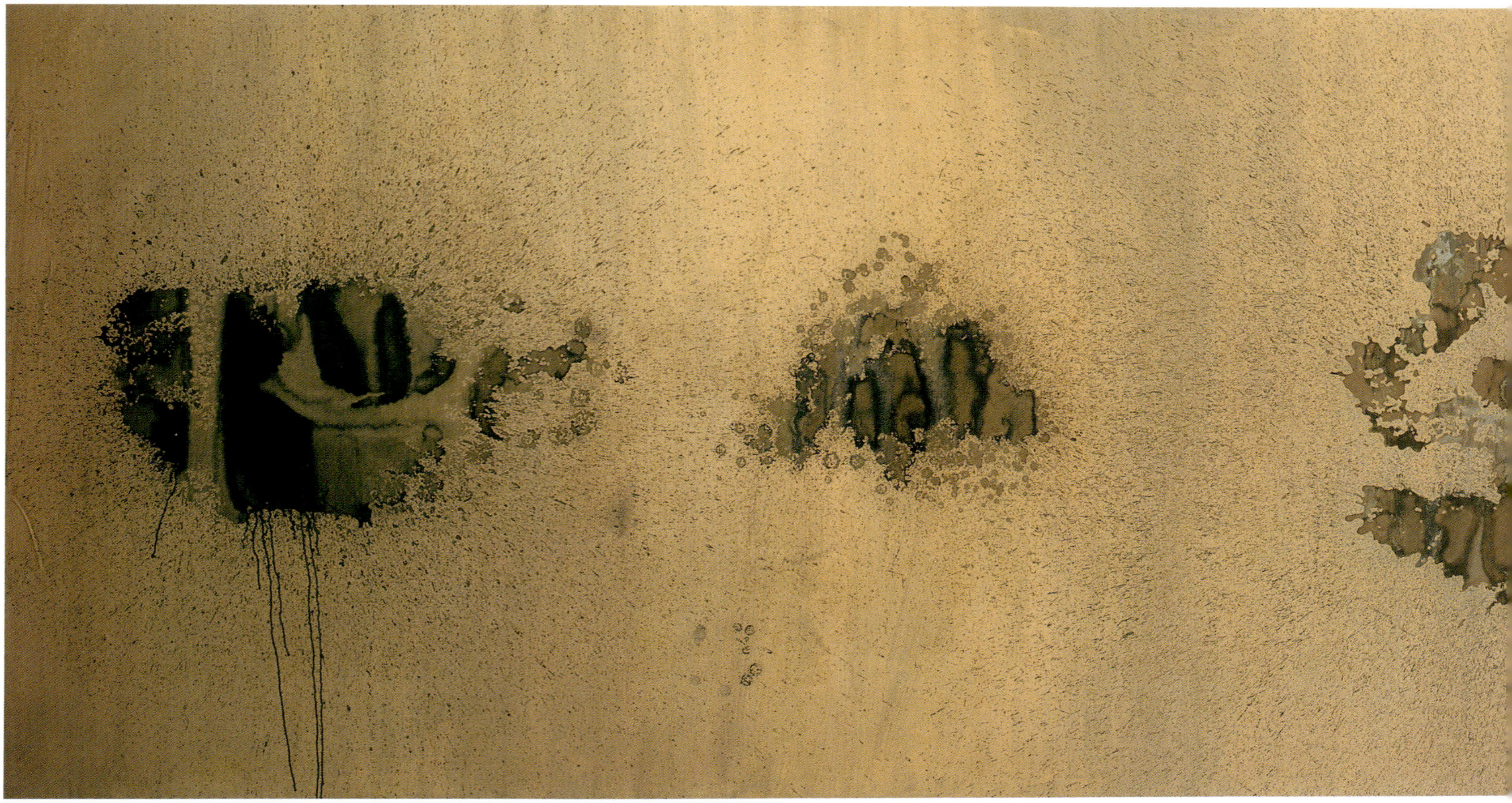

12. *Oxidation Painting*, 1978. Metallic pigment in acrylic medium and urine on canvas, 50 x 200 x 2 in. (127 x 508 x 5.1 cm). The Andy Warhol Museum, Pittsburgh; Founding Collection, Contribution The Andy Warhol Foundation for the Visual Arts, Inc.

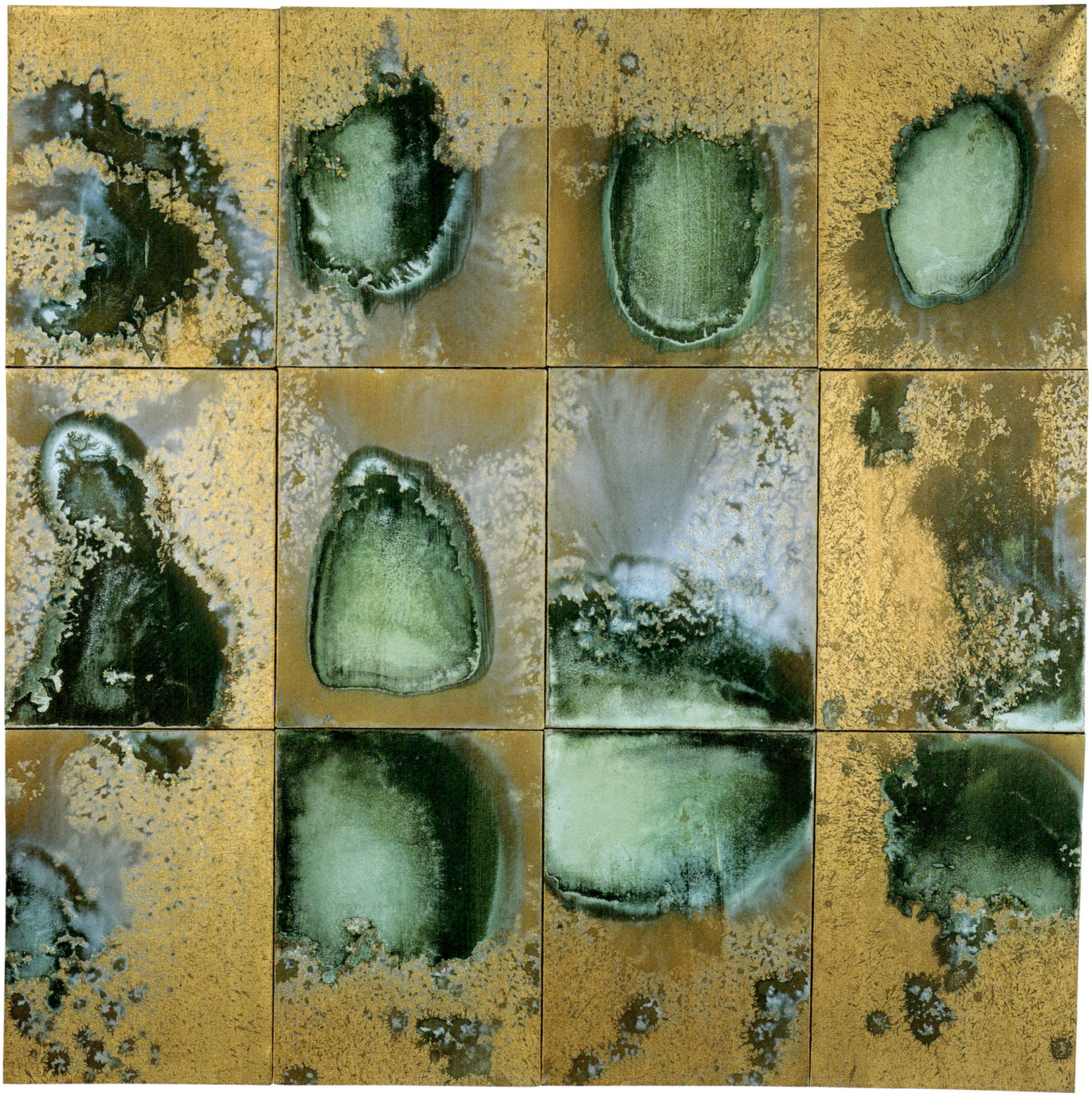

13. *Oxidation Painting* (in 12 parts), 1978. Copper metallic pigment and mixed media on canvas, 48 x 49½ in. (121.9 x 125.7 cm). Mugrabi Collection

14. *Oxidation Painting*, 1978. Urine and metallic pigment in acrylic medium on canvas, 76 x 52 in. (193 x 132 cm). The Baltimore Museum of Art: Purchase with funds provided by Esther and Richard Pearlstone through the Pearlstone Family Fund; and partial gift of The Andy Warhol Foundation for the Visual Arts, Inc.

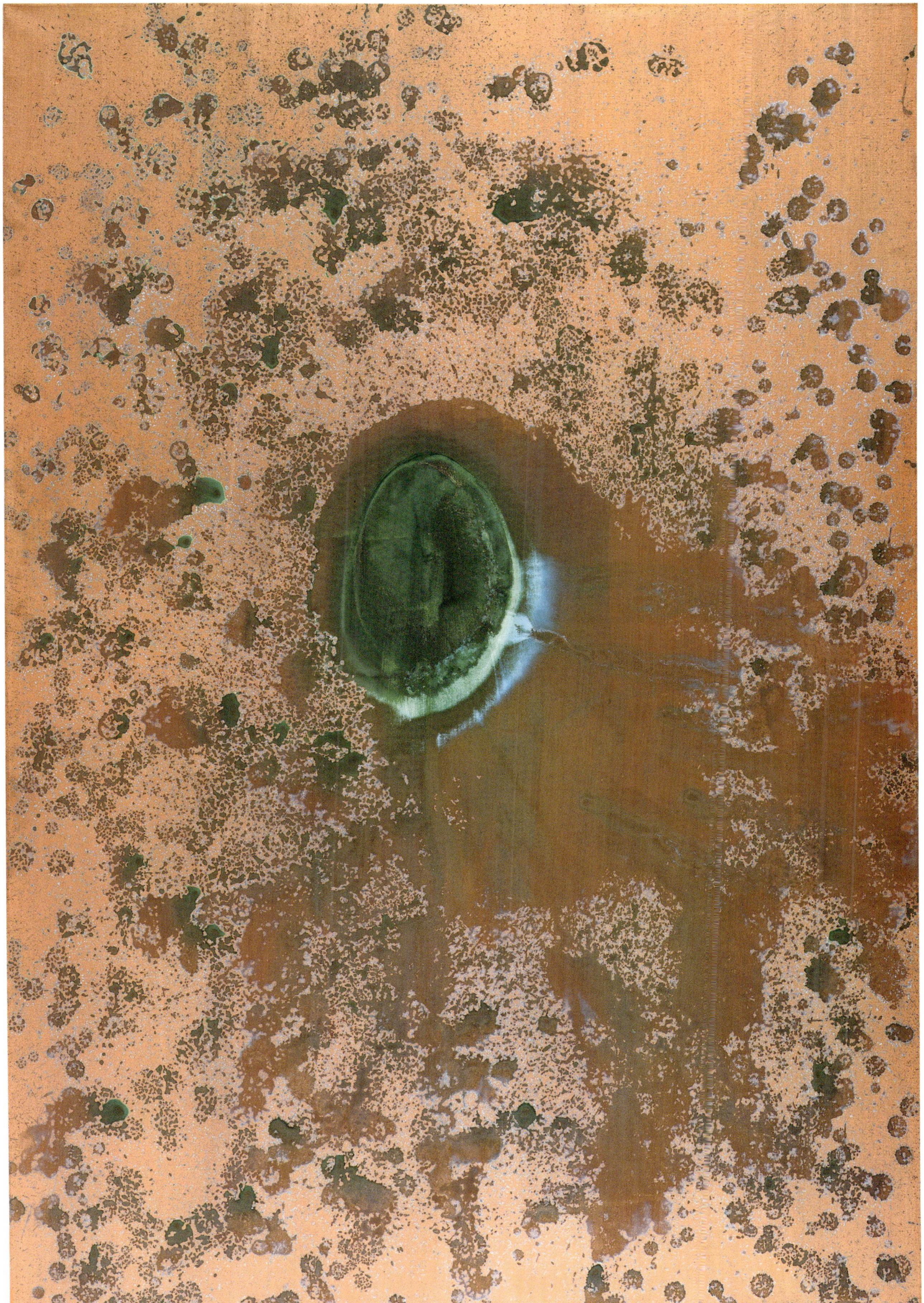

15. *Oxidation Painting*, 1978. Urine and metallic pigment in acrylic medium on canvas, 76 x 52 in. (193 x 132 cm). The Baltimore Museum of Art: Purchase with funds provided by Esther and Richard Pearlstone through the Pearlstone Family Fund; and partial gift of The Andy Warhol Foundation for the Visual Arts, Inc.

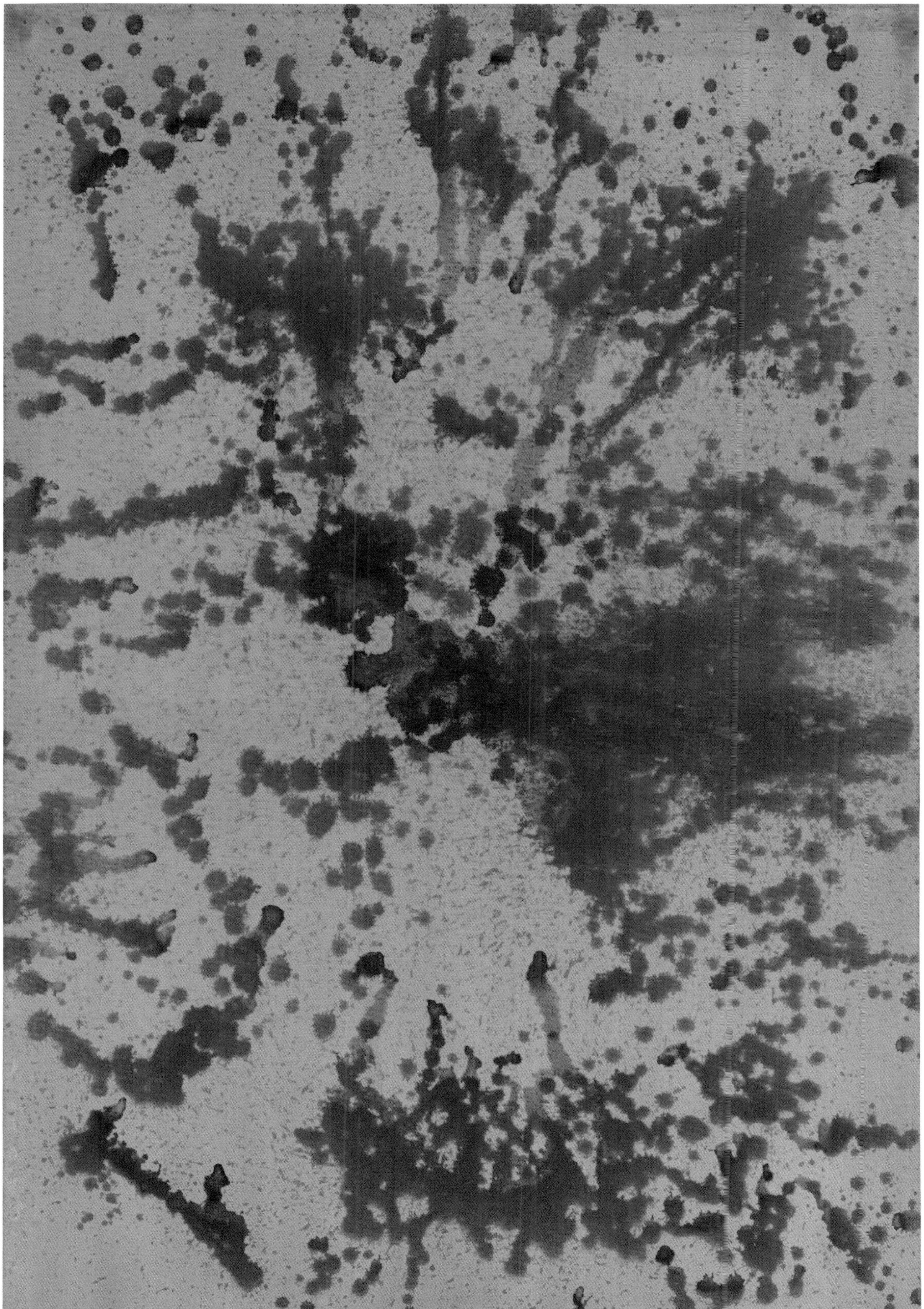

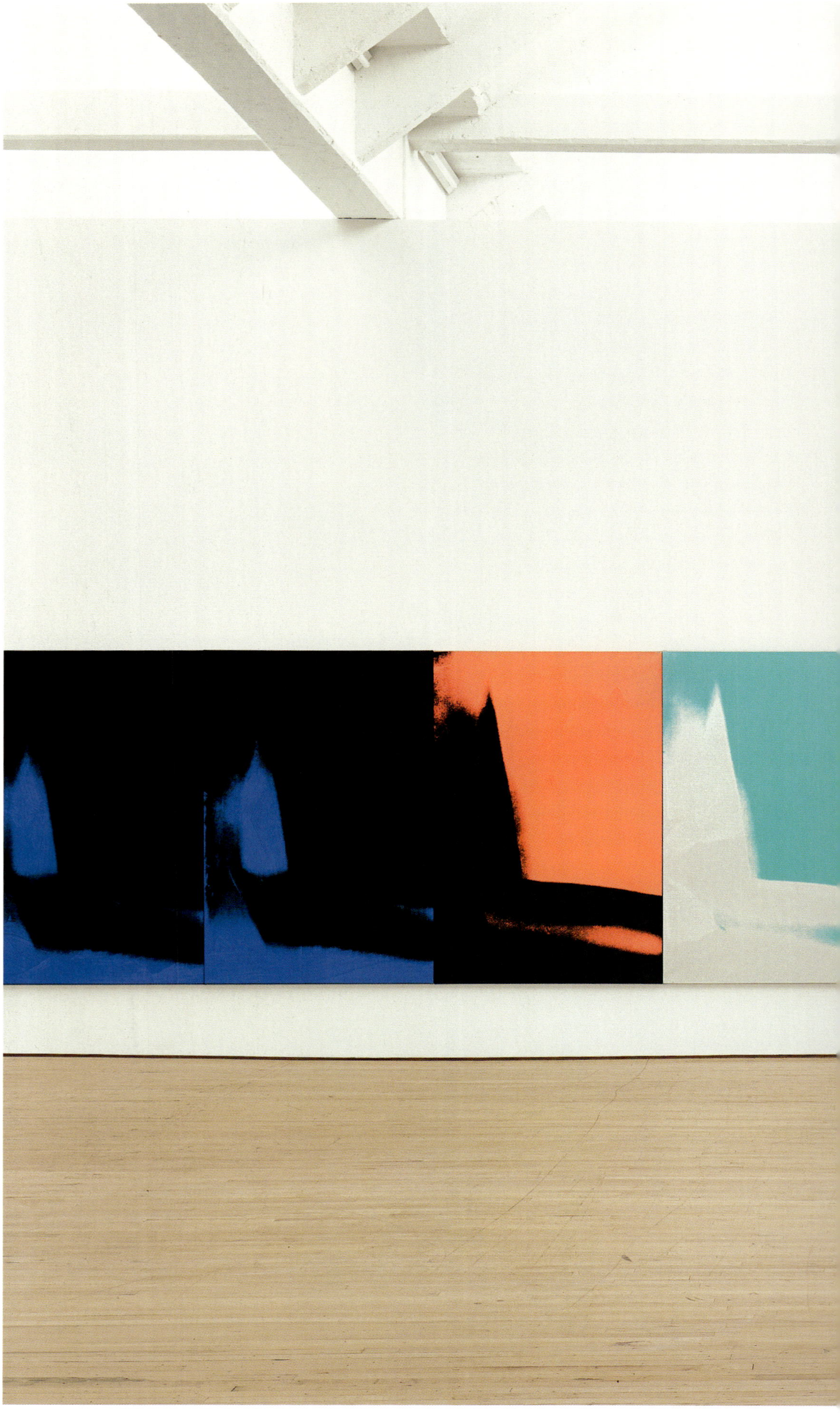

16. *Shadows*, 1978–79. Installation of 72 of 102 paintings. Acrylic, variously silkscreened and painted on canvas, 72 x 52 in. (193 x 132 cm) each. Dia Art Foundation

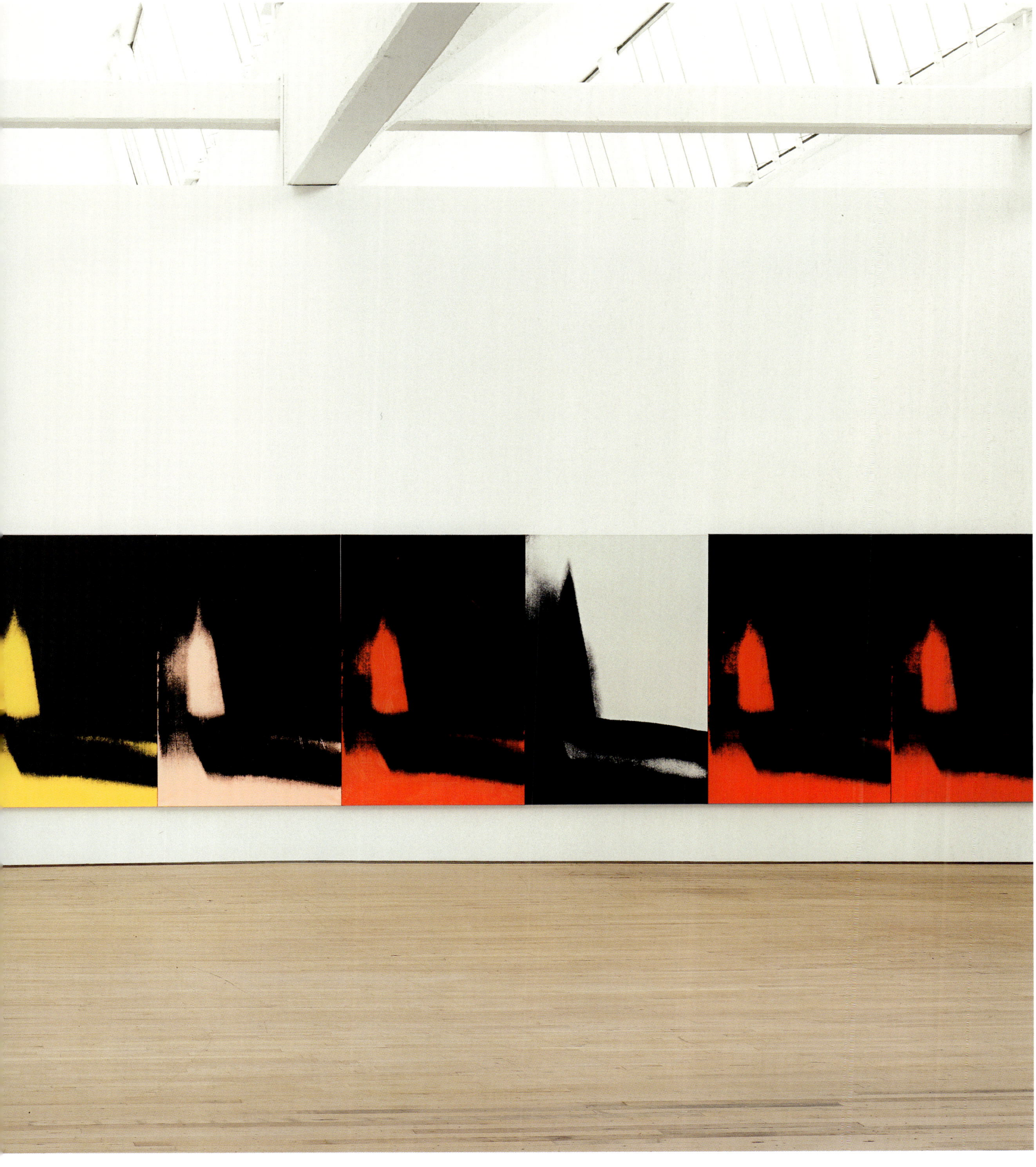

17. *Shadows*, 1978. Acrylic and silkscreen ink on canvas, 80 x 192 in. (203 x 488 cm). Private collection

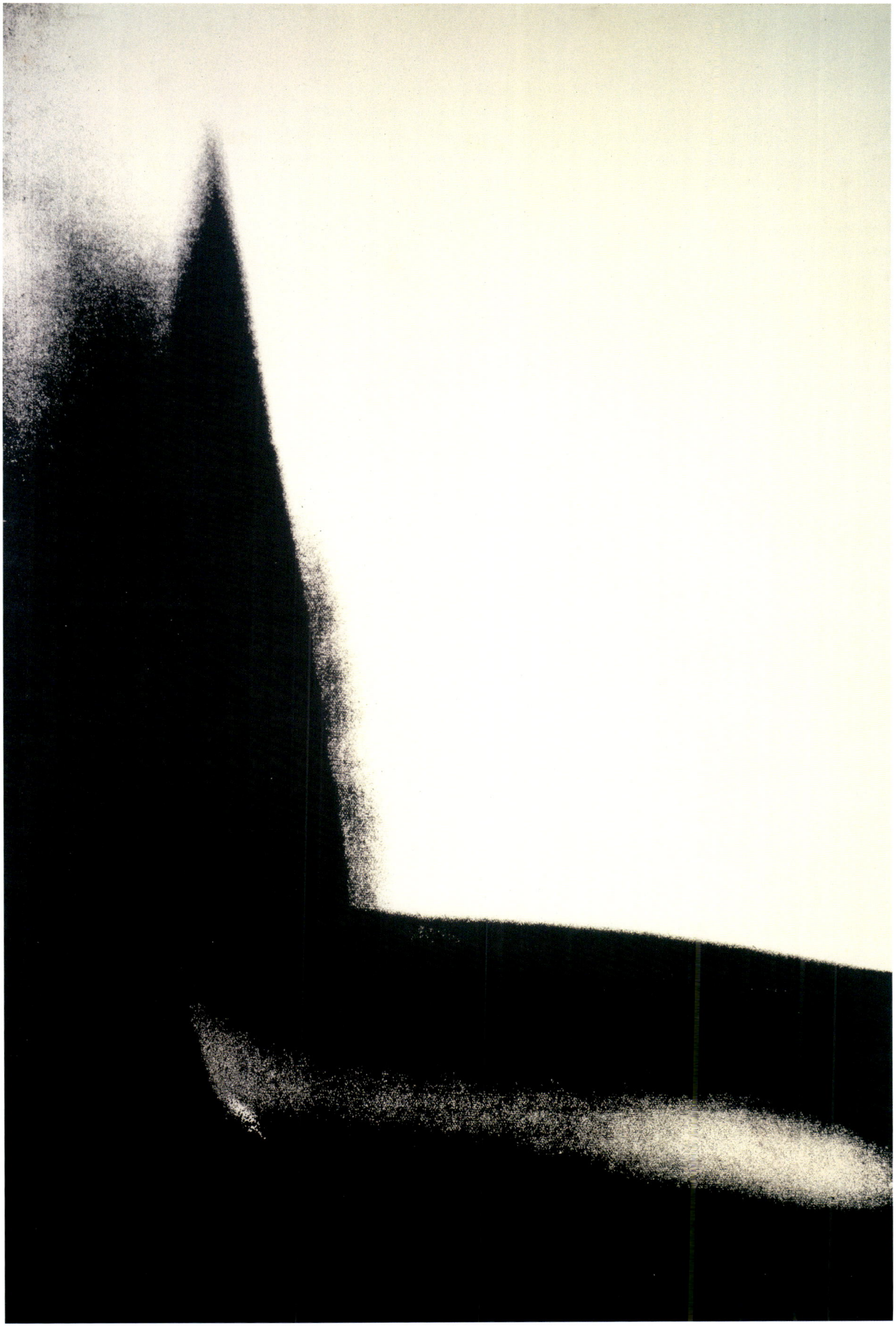

18. *Shadow*, 1978. Silkscreen ink on linen, 76 x 52 in. (193 x 132 cm). Private collection

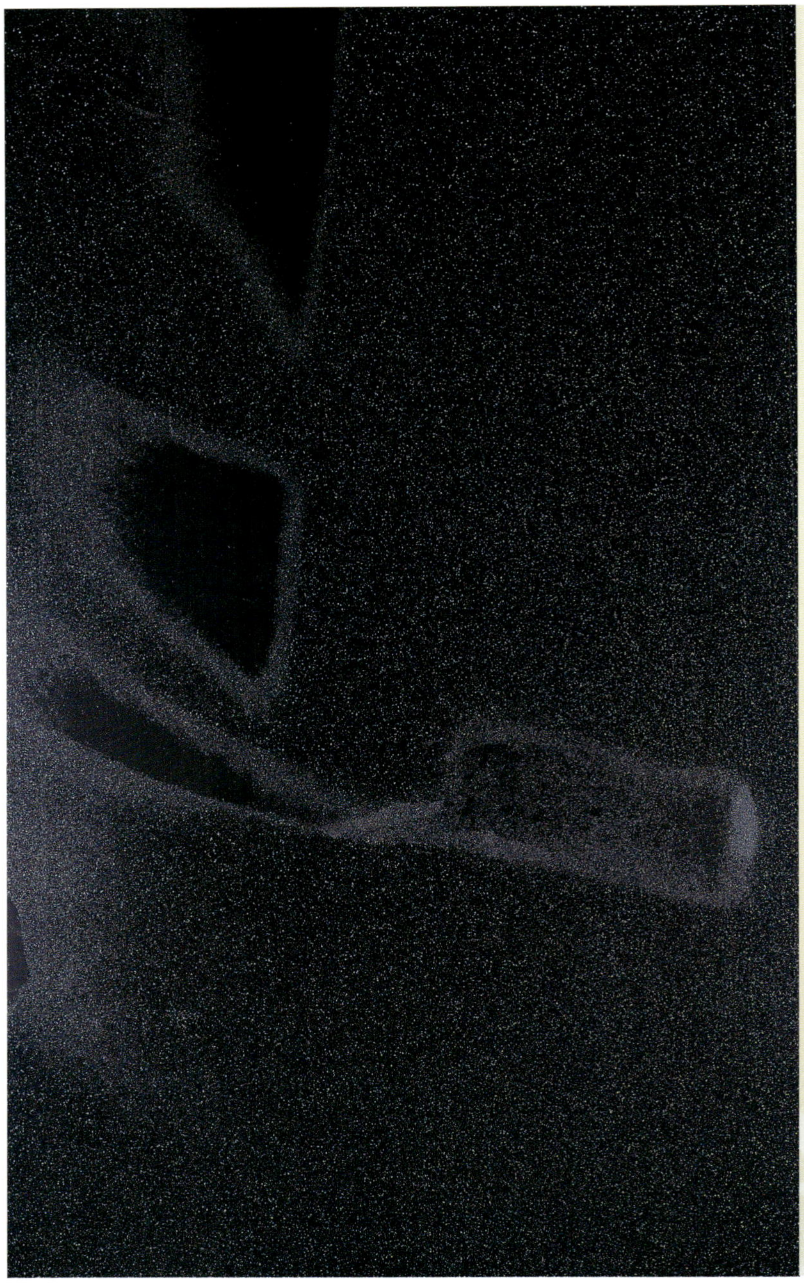

19. *Shadow*, 1978. Acrylic (black), diamond dust, and silkscreen ink on canvas, $78\frac{1}{16}$ x $50\frac{1}{16}$ in. (198.4 x 127.2 cm). The Baltimore Museum of Art: Purchased with funds provided by Laura R. Burrows-Jackson, Baltimore; and partial gift of The Andy Warhol Foundation for the Visual Arts, Inc.

20. *Shadow*, 1979. Acrylic, diamond dust, and silkscreen ink on canvas, $77\frac{3}{4}$ x 52 in. (197.6 x 132.1 cm). The Baltimore Museum of Art: Purchased with exchange funds from the Samuel and Tobie Miller Memorial Collection

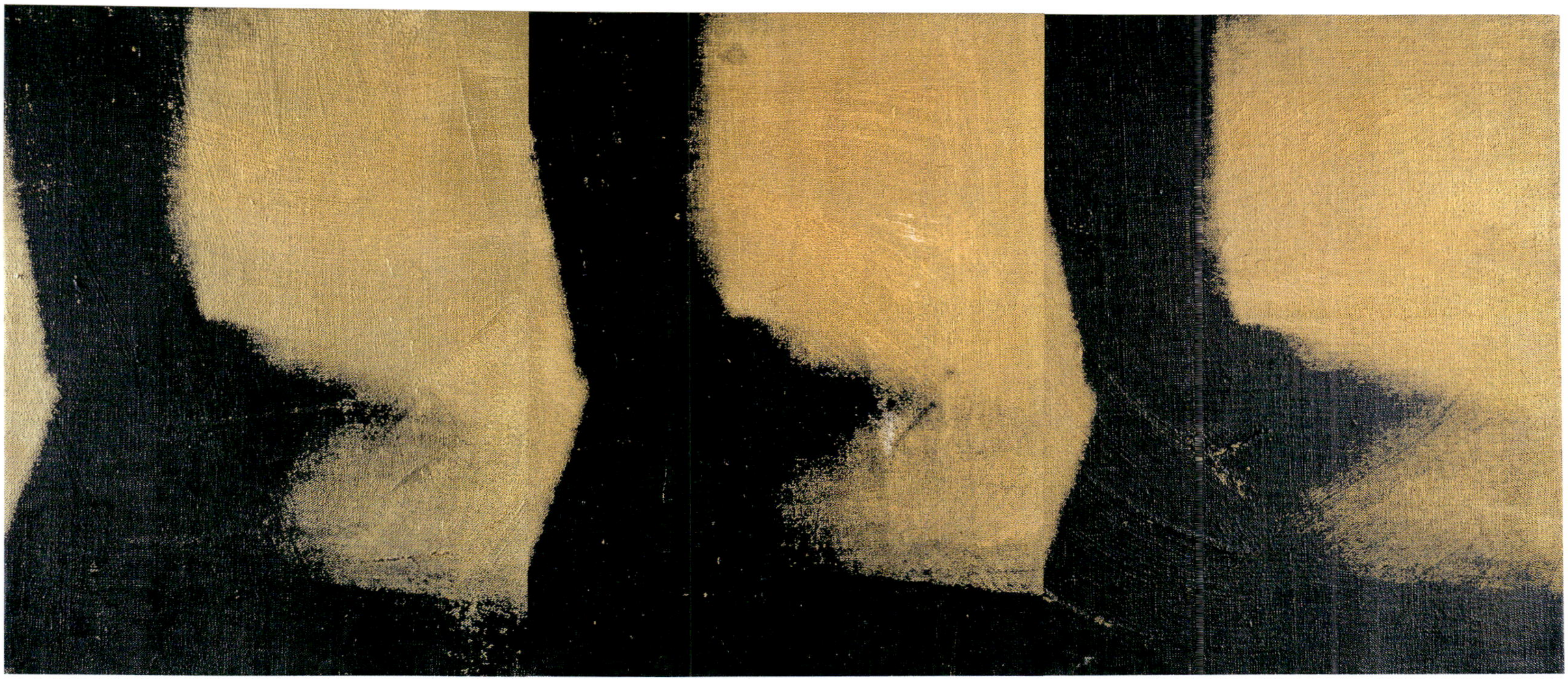

21. *Shadows*, 1980. Acrylic and silkscreen ink on canvas, three parts, 14 x 11 in. (35.6 x 27.9 cm) each. Mugrabi Collection

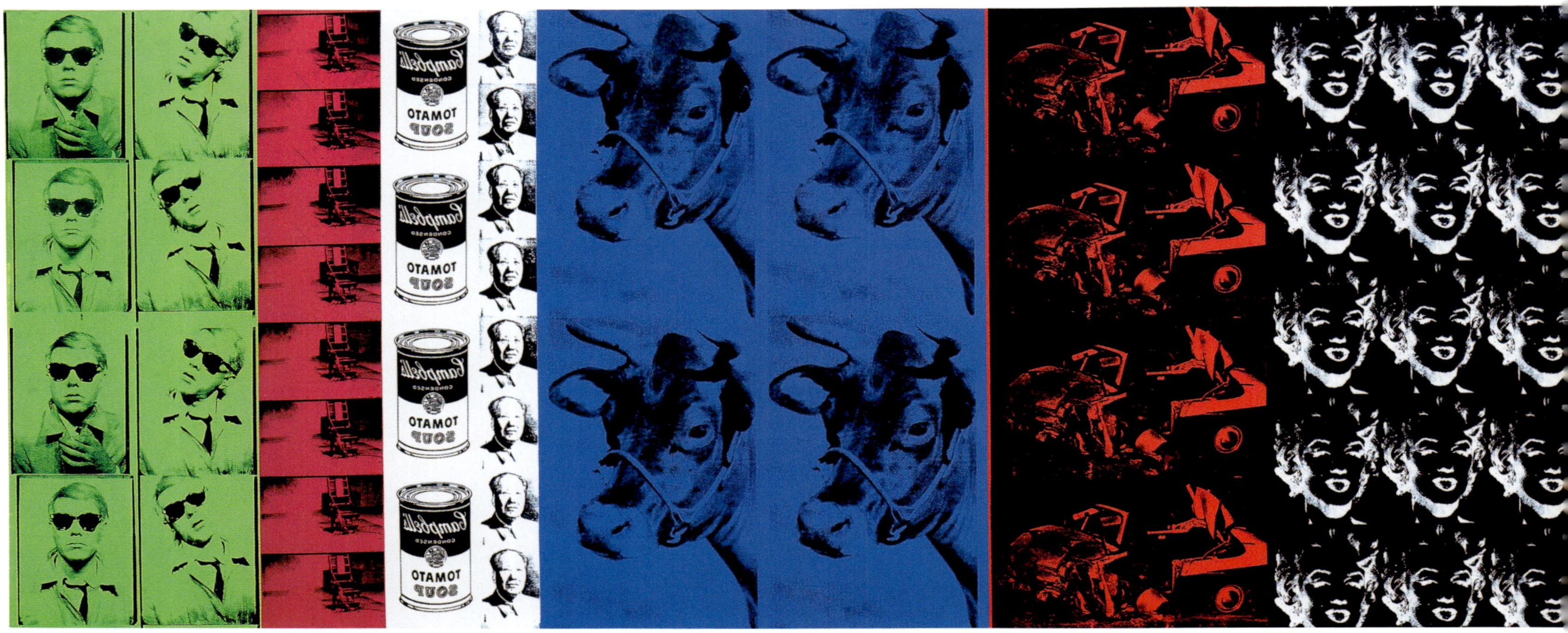

22. *Big Retrospective Painting*, 1979. Acrylic and silkscreen ink on canvas, 81½ x 425 in. (207 x 1080 cm). Private collection

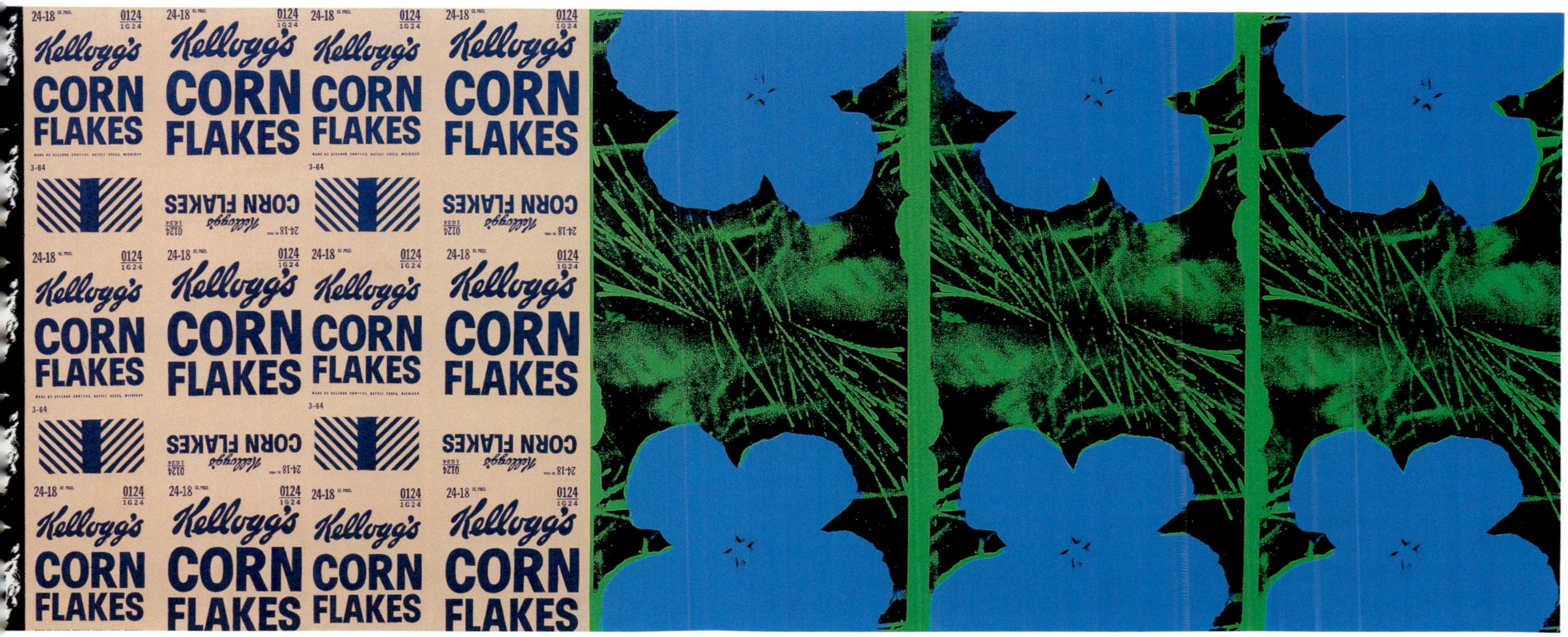
24-18
0124
1G24
Kellogg's
CORN
FLAKES
3-64
CORN FLAKES

23. *Marilyn (4)*, c. 1978. Acrylic and silkscreen ink on canvas, 36 x 28 in. (91.4 x 71.1 cm). The Andy Warhol Museum, Pittsburgh; Founding Collection, Contribution The Andy Warhol Foundation for the Visual Arts, Inc.

24. *Mona Lisa*, c. 1979. Acrylic and silkscreen ink on canvas, 80 x 100 x 1½ in. (203.2 x 254 x 3.8 cm). The Andy Warhol Museum, Pittsburgh; Founding Collection, Contribution The Andy Warhol Foundation for the Visual Arts, Inc.

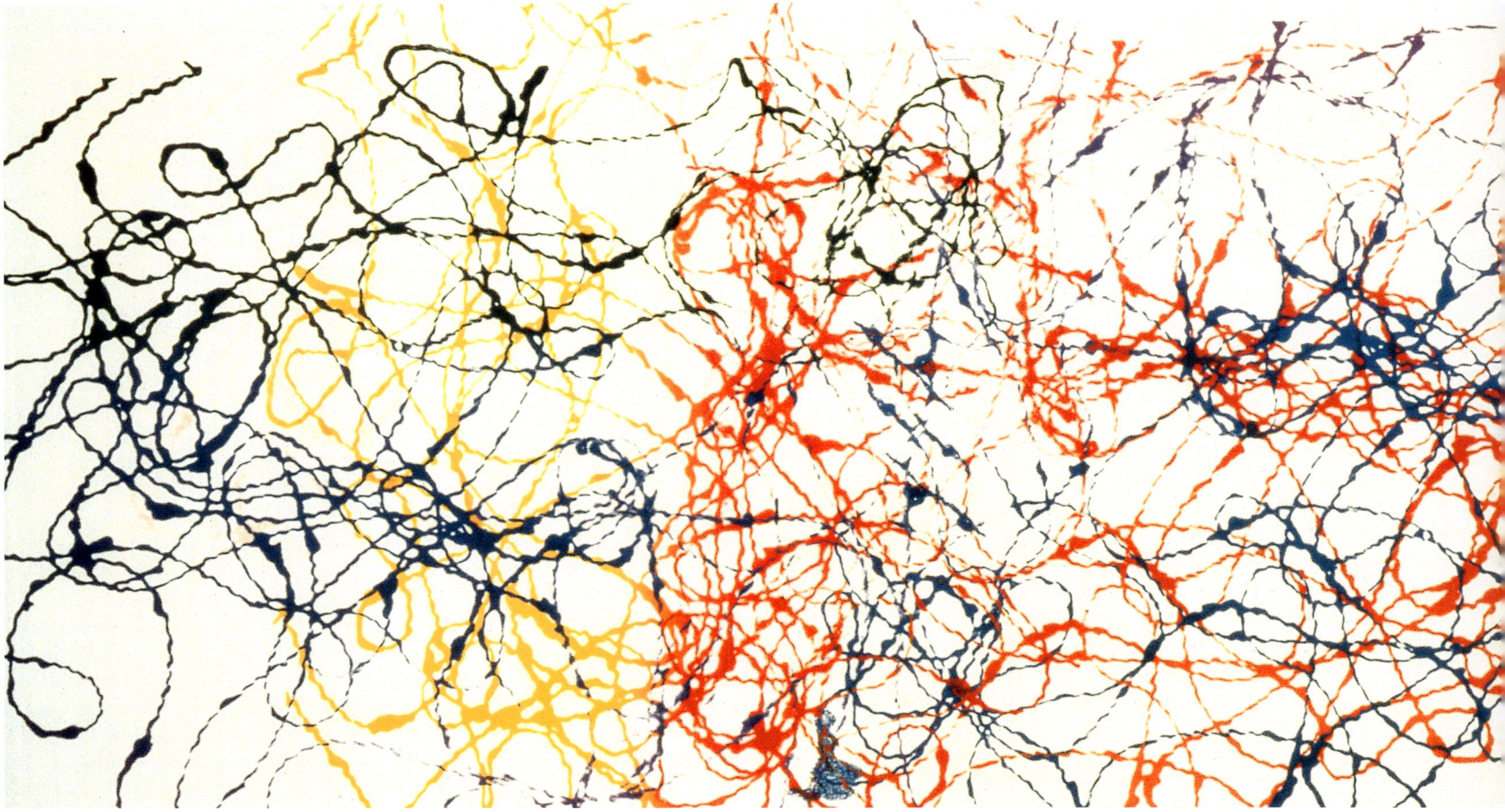

25. *Yarn*, 1983. Acrylic and silkscreen ink on canvas, 54 x 206 in. (137 x 523 cm). Staff Stiftung, Lemgo, permanent loan at Kunsthalle Bielefeld

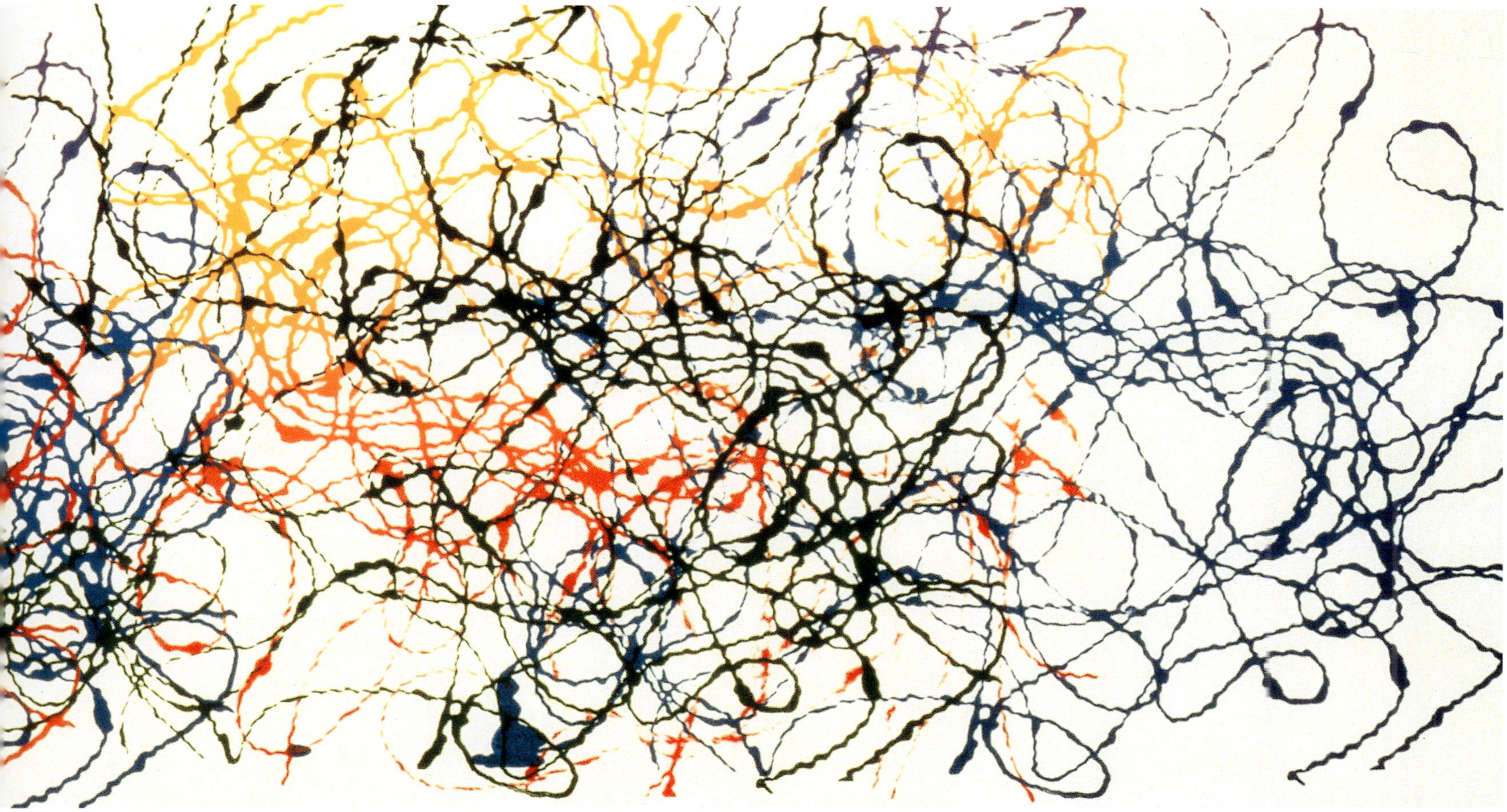

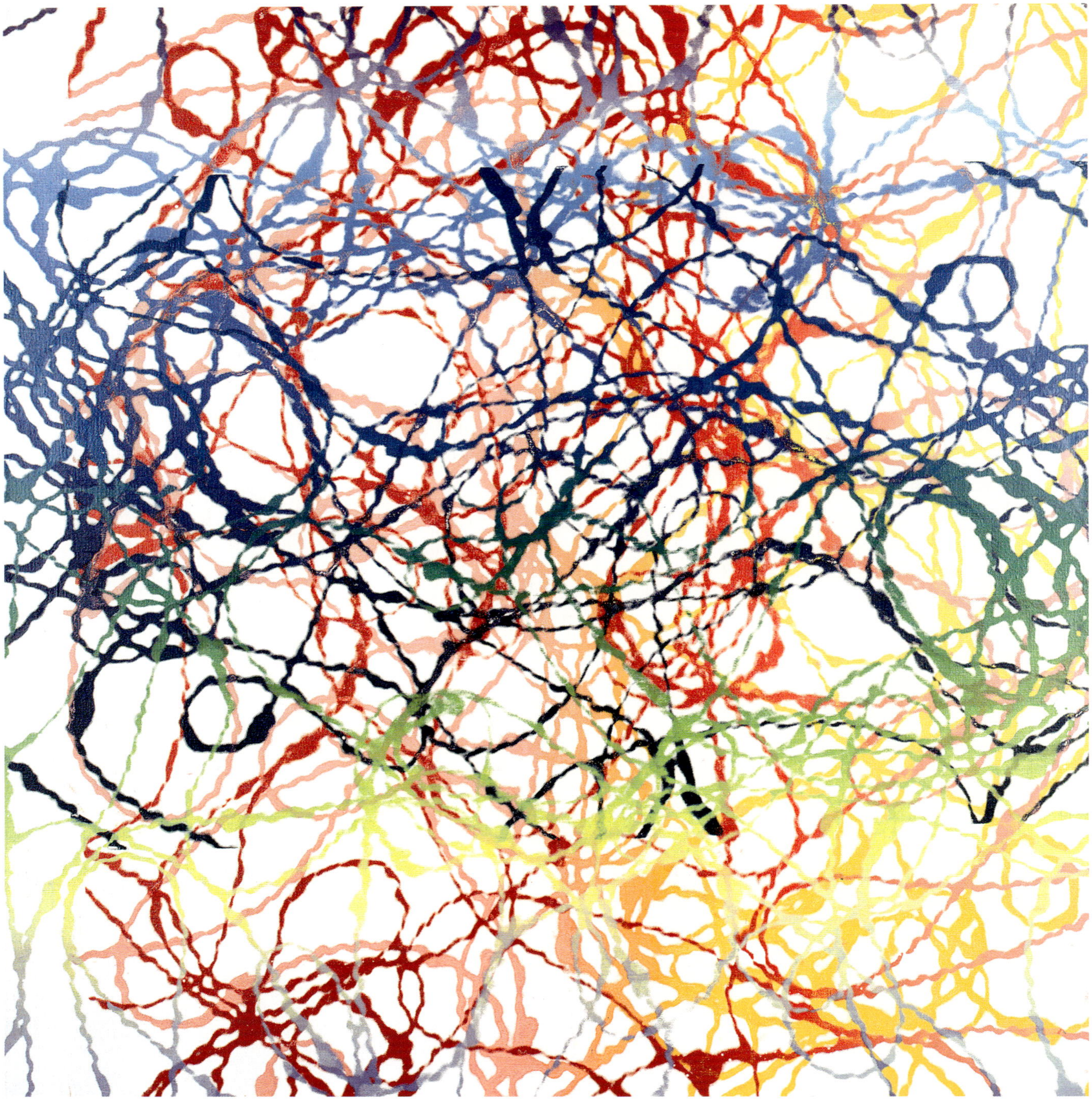

26. *Yarn*, 1983. Acrylic and silkscreen ink on canvas, 40 x 40 in. (101.6 x 101.6 cm). Staff Stiftung, Lemgo, permanent loan at Kunsthalle Bielefeld

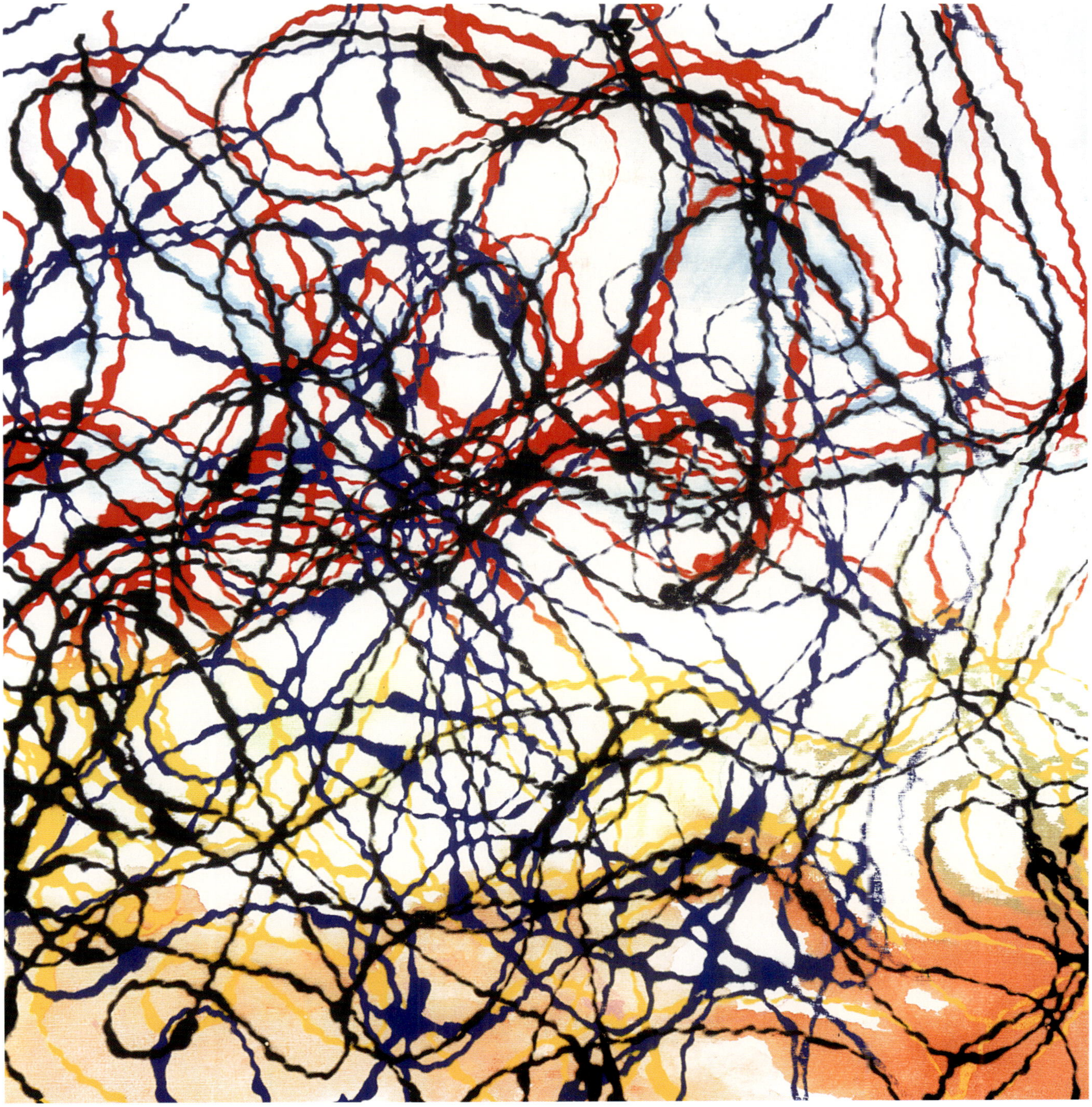

27. *Yarn*, 1983. Acrylic and silkscreen ink on linen, 40 x 40 in. (101.6 x 101.6 cm). The Andy Warhol Museum, Pittsburgh; Founding Collection, Contribution The Andy Warhol Foundation for the Visual Arts, Inc.

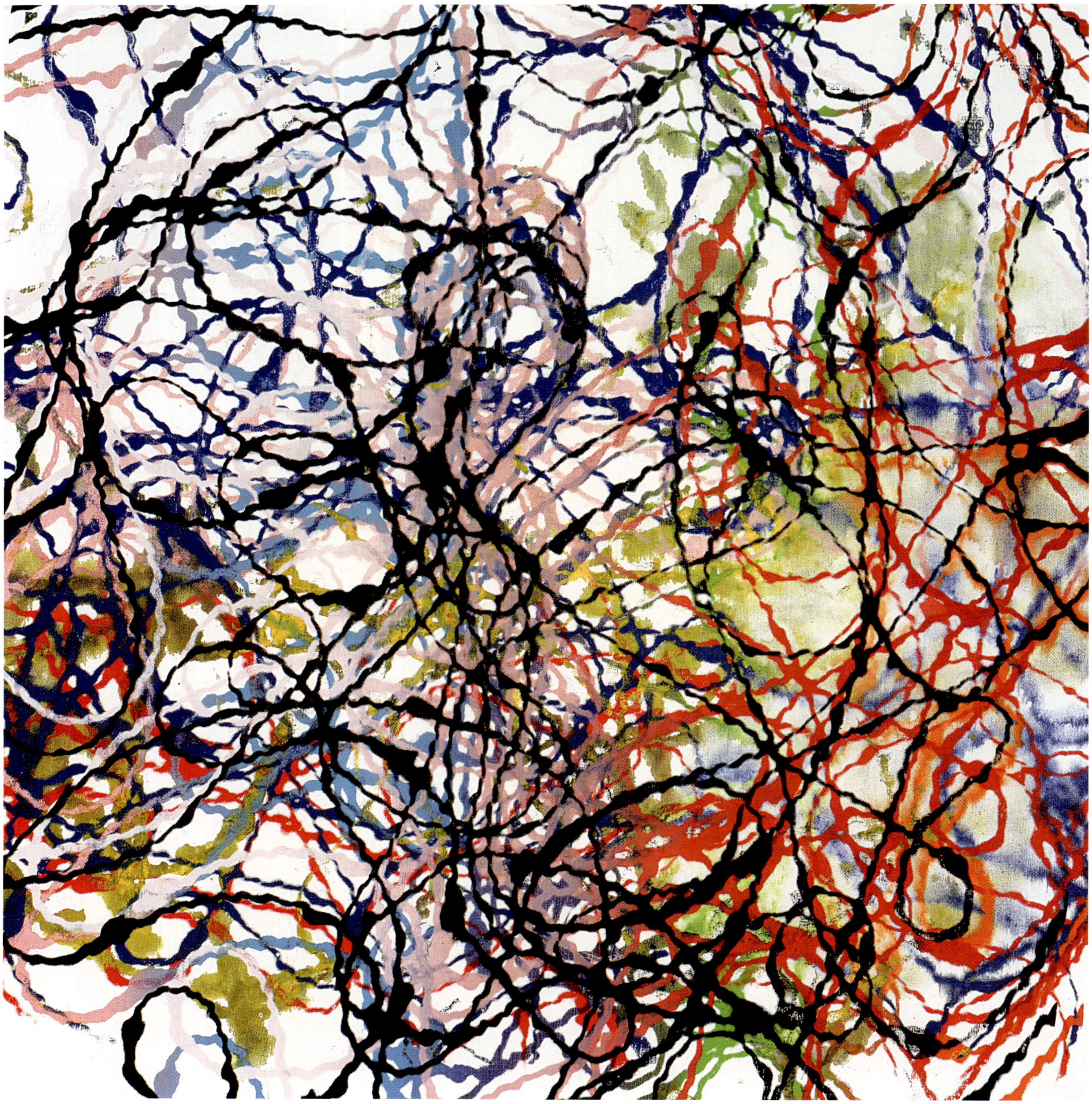

28. *Yarn*, 1983. Acrylic and silkscreen ink on linen, 40 x 40 in. (101.6 x 101.6 cm). The Andy Warhol Museum, Pittsburgh; Founding Collection, Contribution The Andy Warhol Foundation for the Visual Arts, Inc.

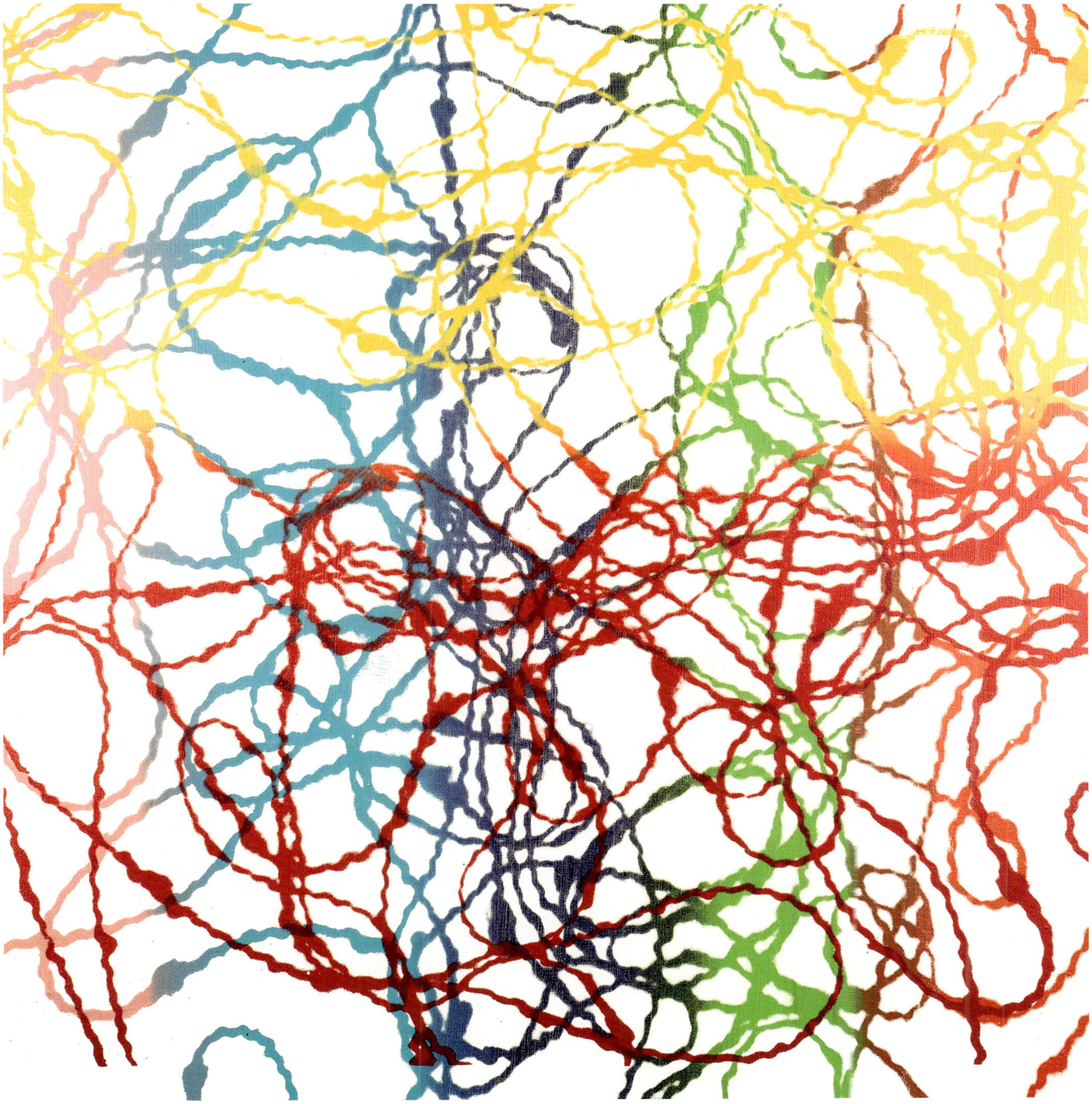

29. *Yarn*, 1983. Acrylic and silkscreen ink on canvas, 40 x 40 in. (101.6 x 101.6 cm). Staff Stiftung, Lemgo, permanent loan at Kunsthalle Bielefeld

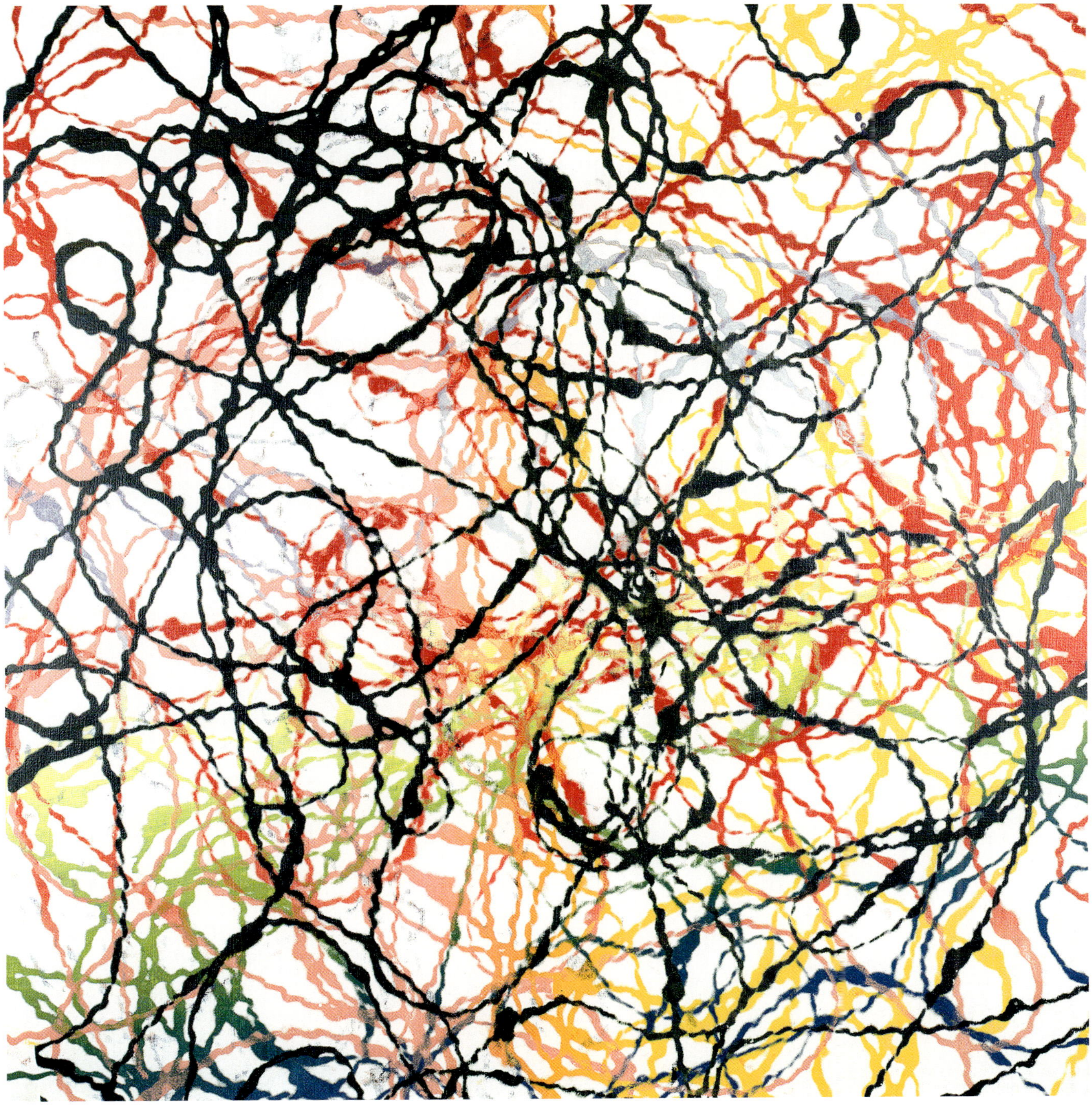

30. *Yarn*, 1983. Acrylic and silkscreen ink on canvas, 40 x 40 in. (101.6 x 101.6 cm). Staff Stiftung, Lemgo, permanent loan at Kunsthalle Bielefeld

31. *Rorschach*, 1984. Acrylic on linen, 164 x 115 x 2 in. (416.6 x 292.1 x 5.1 cm). The Andy Warhol Museum, Pittsburgh; Founding Collection, Contribution The Andy Warhol Foundation for the Visual Arts, Inc.

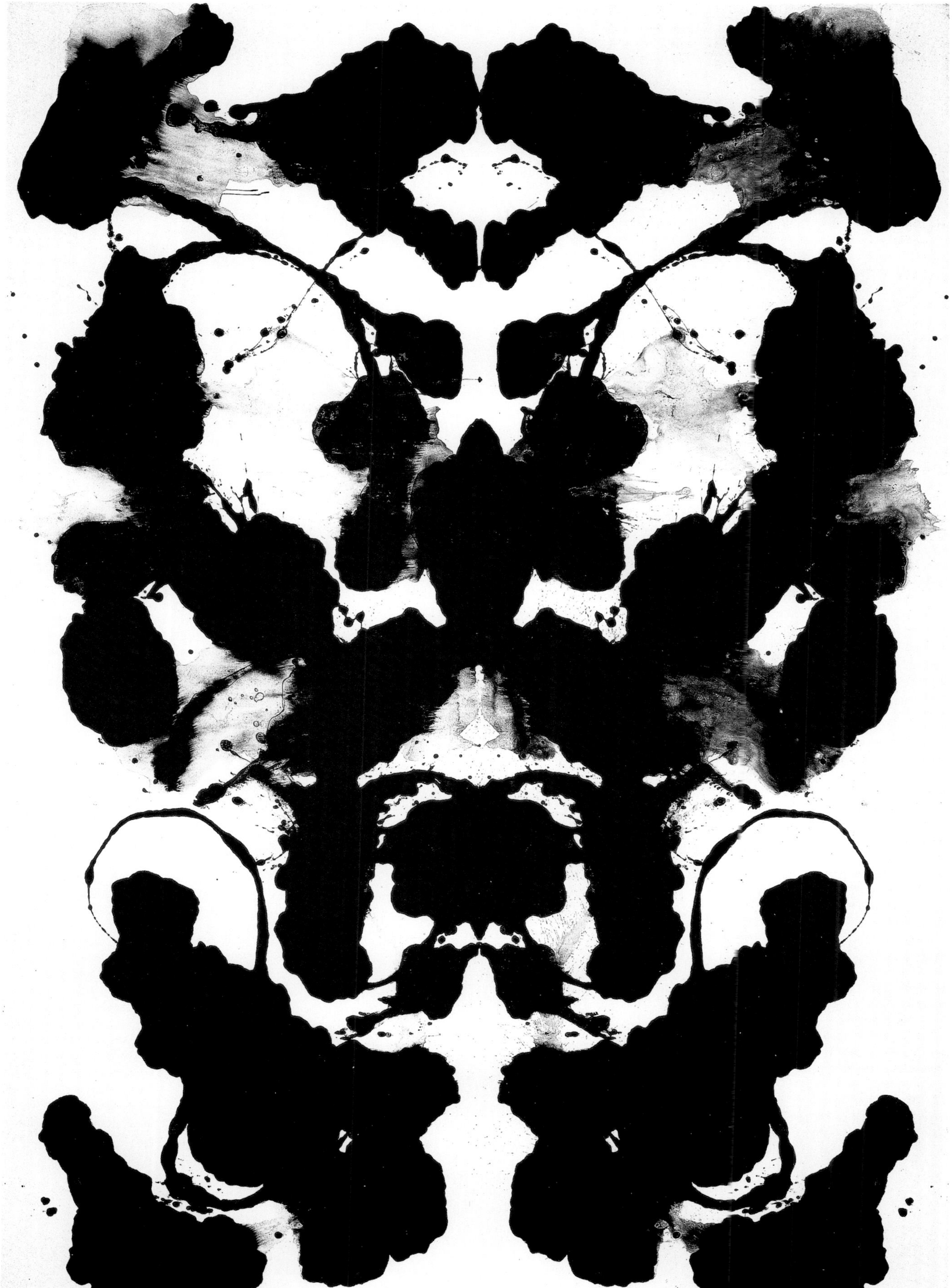

32. *Rorschach*, 1984. Acrylic on canvas, 164¼ x 115 in. (417 x 292 cm). Promised Gift of Virginia and Bagley Wright in honor of the 75th anniversary of the Seattle Art Museum

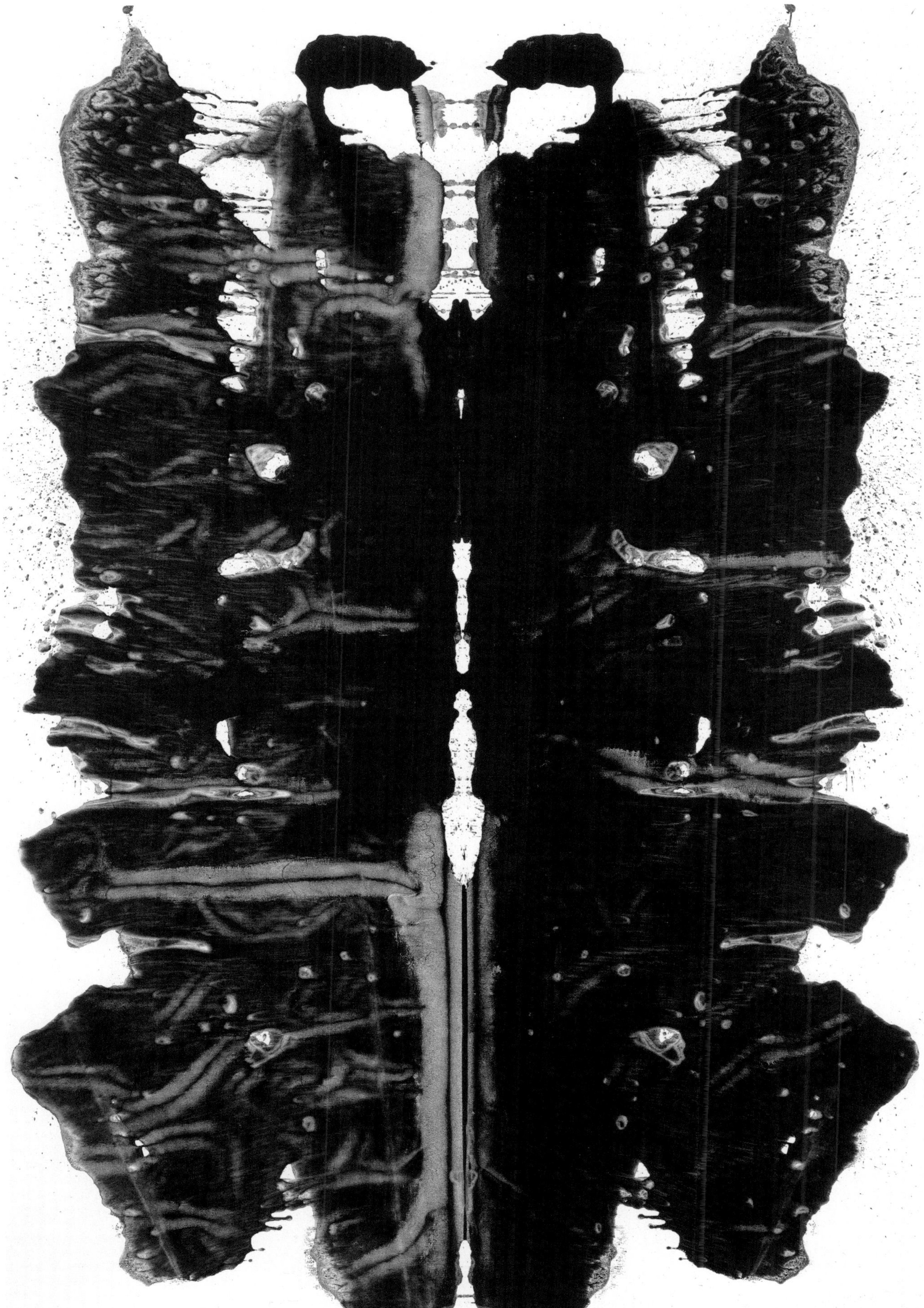

33. *Rorschach*, 1984. Acrylic on canvas, 158 x 110 in. (401 x 279.4 cm). The Baltimore Museum of Art: Purchase with funds provided by Laura R. Burrows-Jackson, Baltimore; and partial gift of The Andy Warhol Foundation of the Visual Arts, Inc.

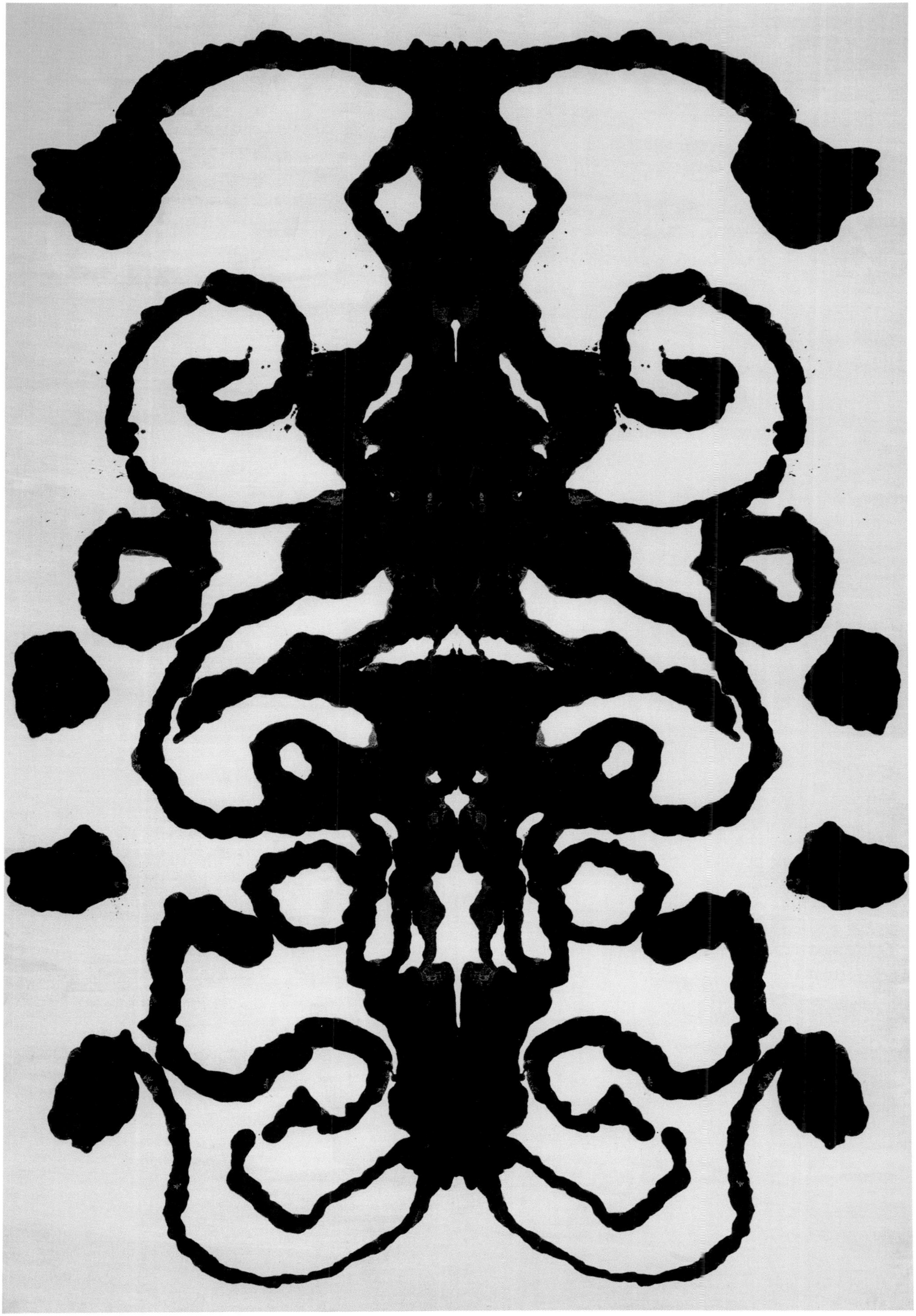

34. *Rorschach*, 1984. Acrylic on canvas, 164¼ x 115 in. (417.2 x 292.1 cm). Purchase, The Museum of Modern Art, New York

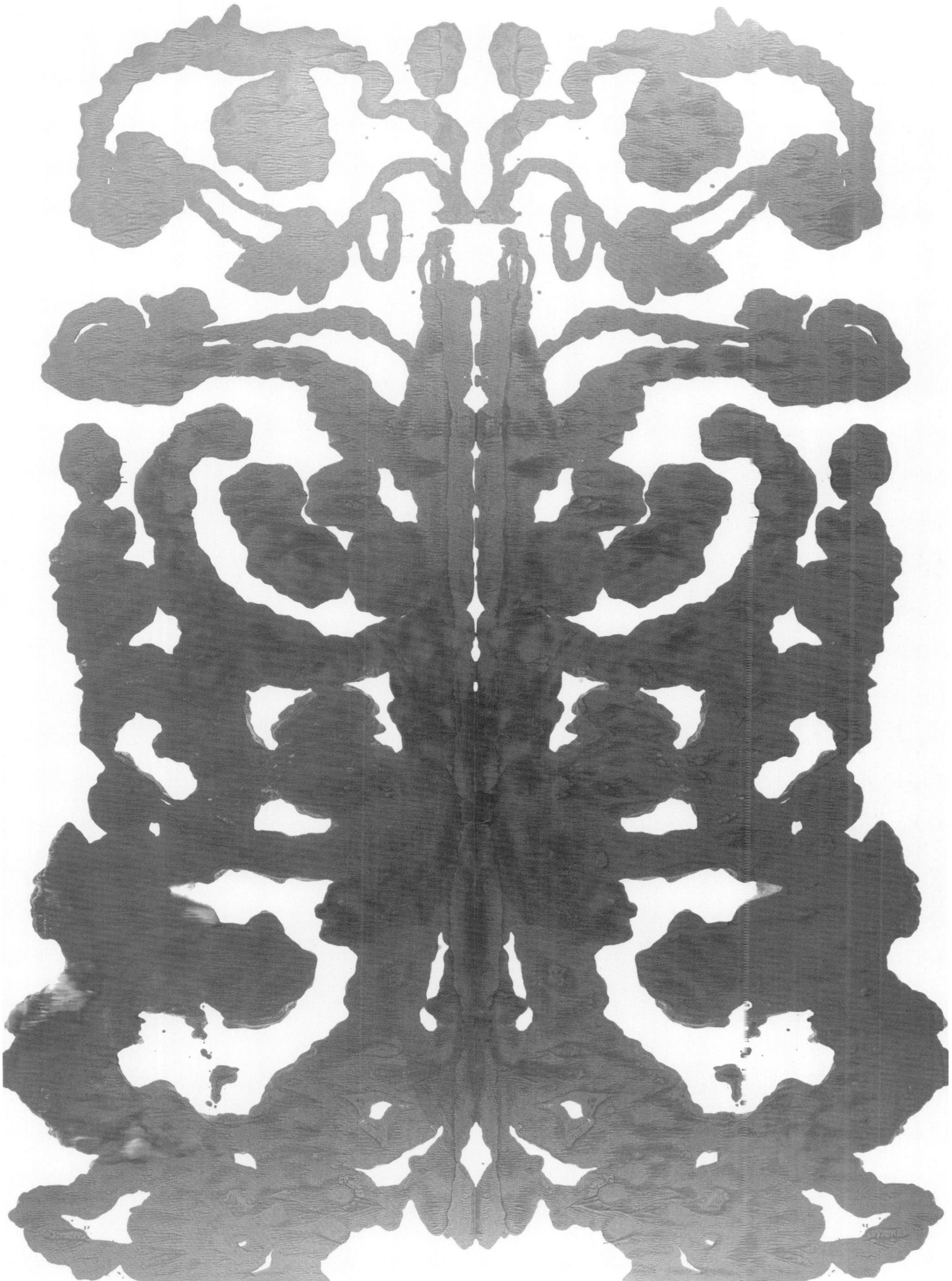

35. *Rorschach*, 1984. Acrylic on linen, 164 x 115 x 2 in. (416.6 x 292.1 x 5.1 cm). The Andy Warhol Museum, Pittsburgh; Founding Collection, Contribution The Andy Warhol Foundation for the Visual Arts, Inc.

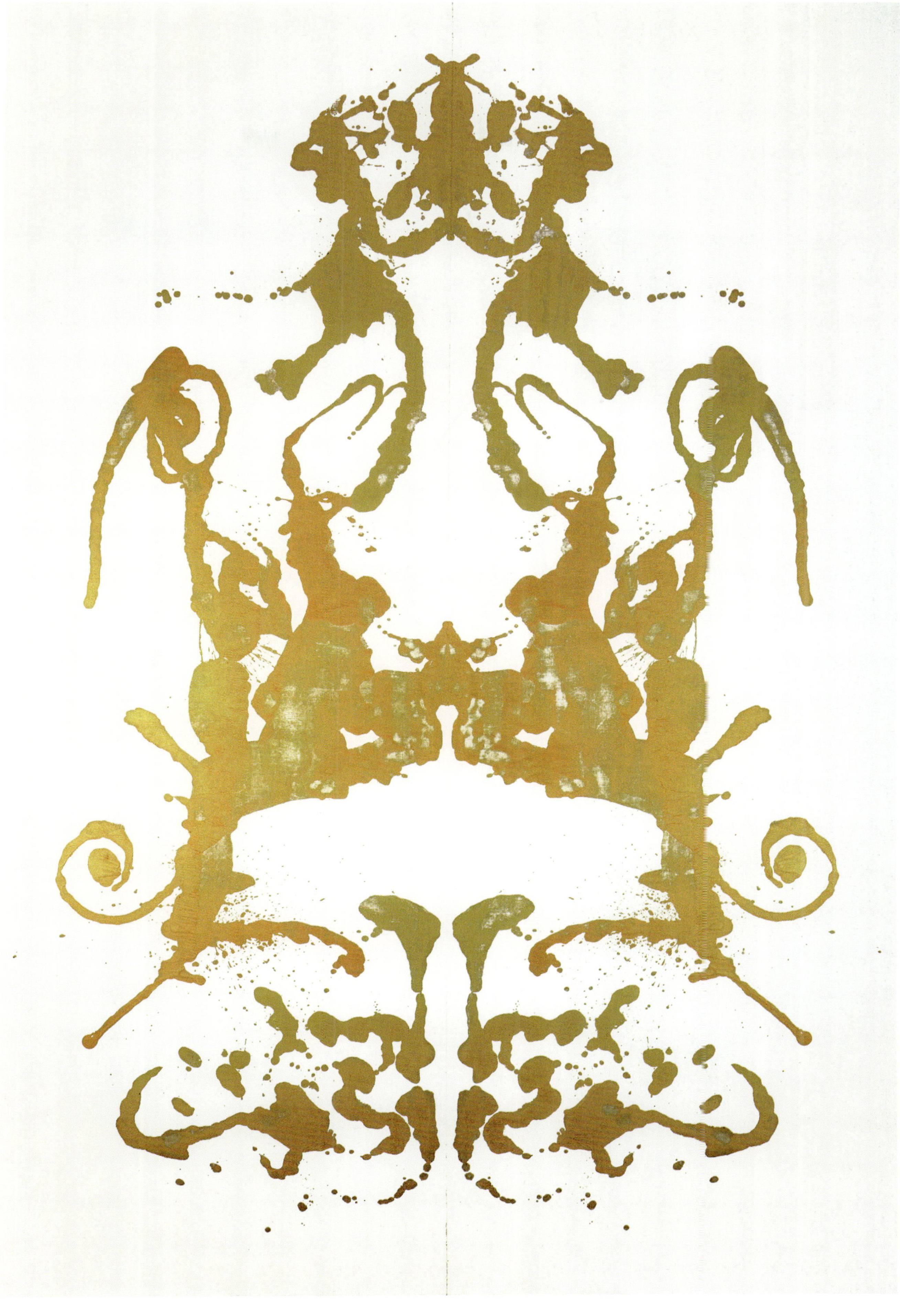

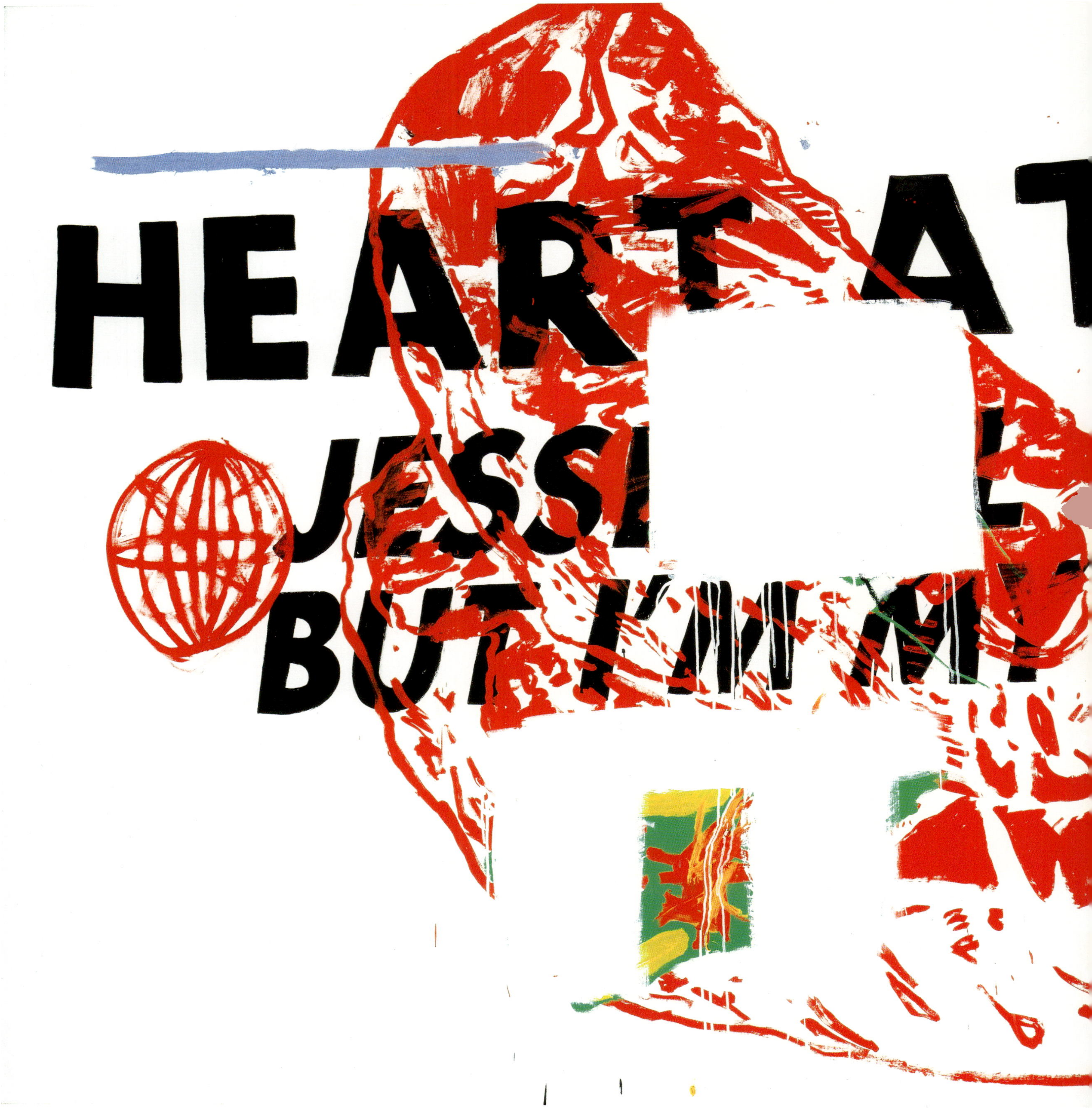

36. Andy Warhol and Jean-Michel Basquiat, *Untitled (Heart Attack)*, 1984. Acrylic on canvas, 76 x 156 in. (194 x 396 cm).
Mugrabi Collection

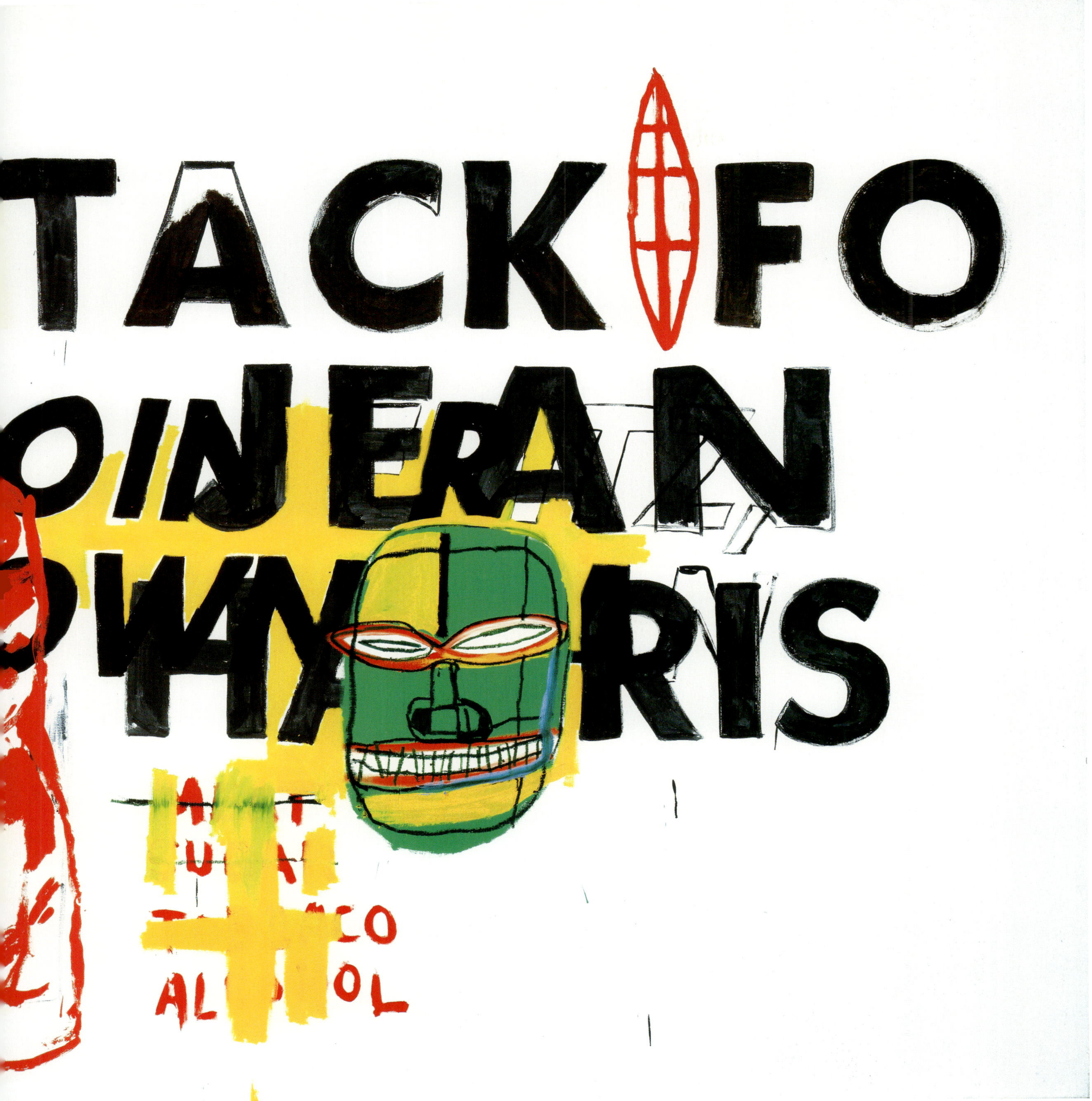
TACK FO
RIS

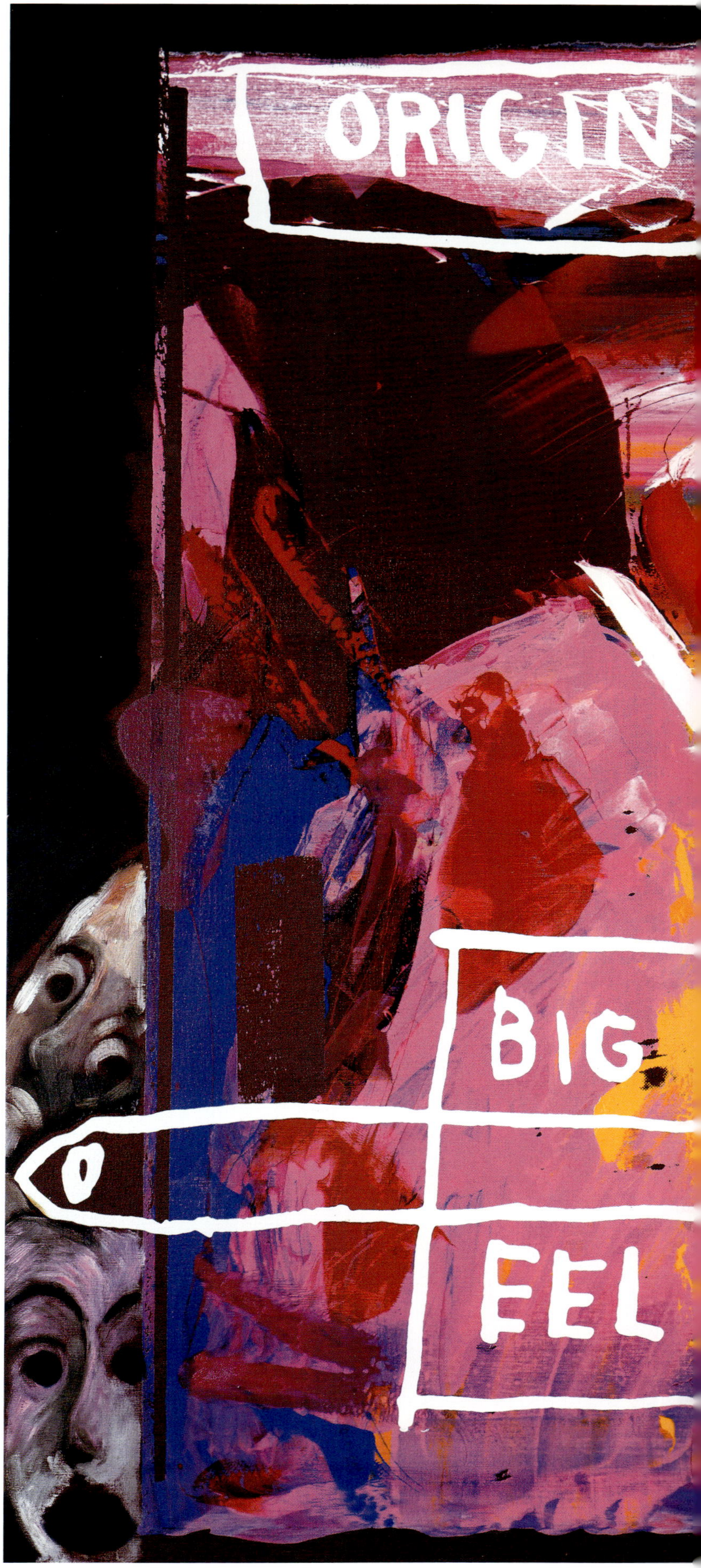

37. Andy Warhol, Jean-Michel Basquiat, and Francesco Clemente, *Origin of Cotton*, 1984. Mixed media on canvas, 48 x 66 in. (122 x 167.7 cm). Private collection

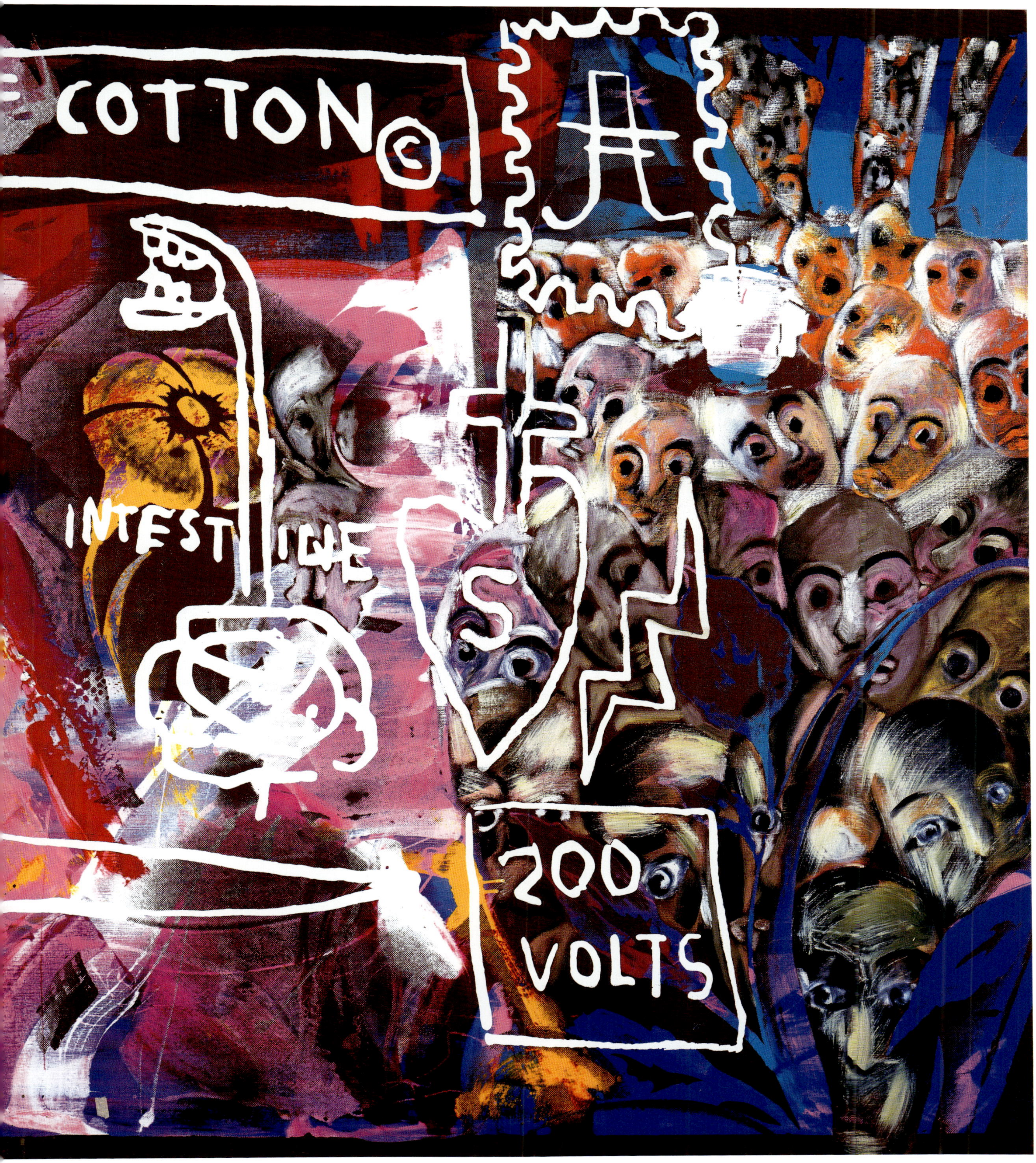
COTTON©
INTESTINE
200
VOLTS

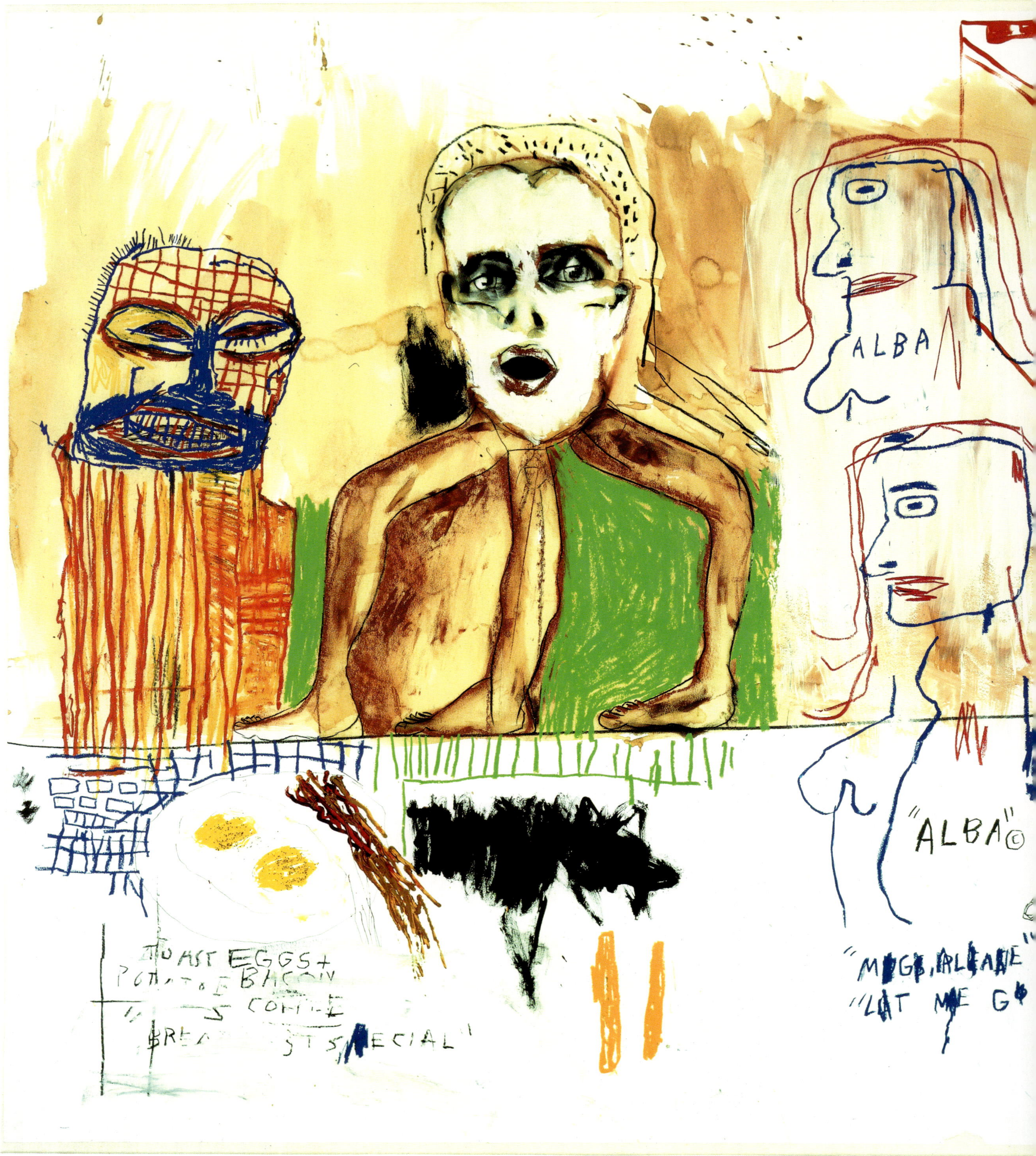
ALBA
"ALBA"©

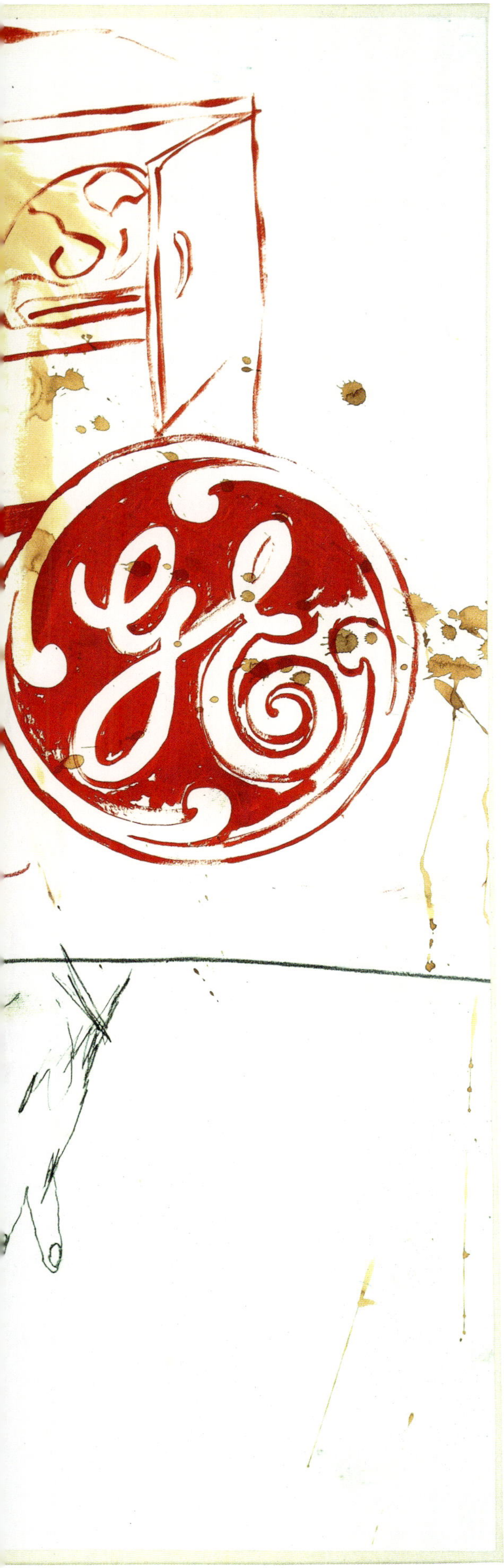

38. Andy Warhol, Jean-Michel Basquiat, and Francesco Clemente, *Alba's Breakfast*, 1984.
Mixed media on paper, mounted on canvas, 46 x 59 in. (117 x 150 cm).
Bischofberger Collection, Switzerland

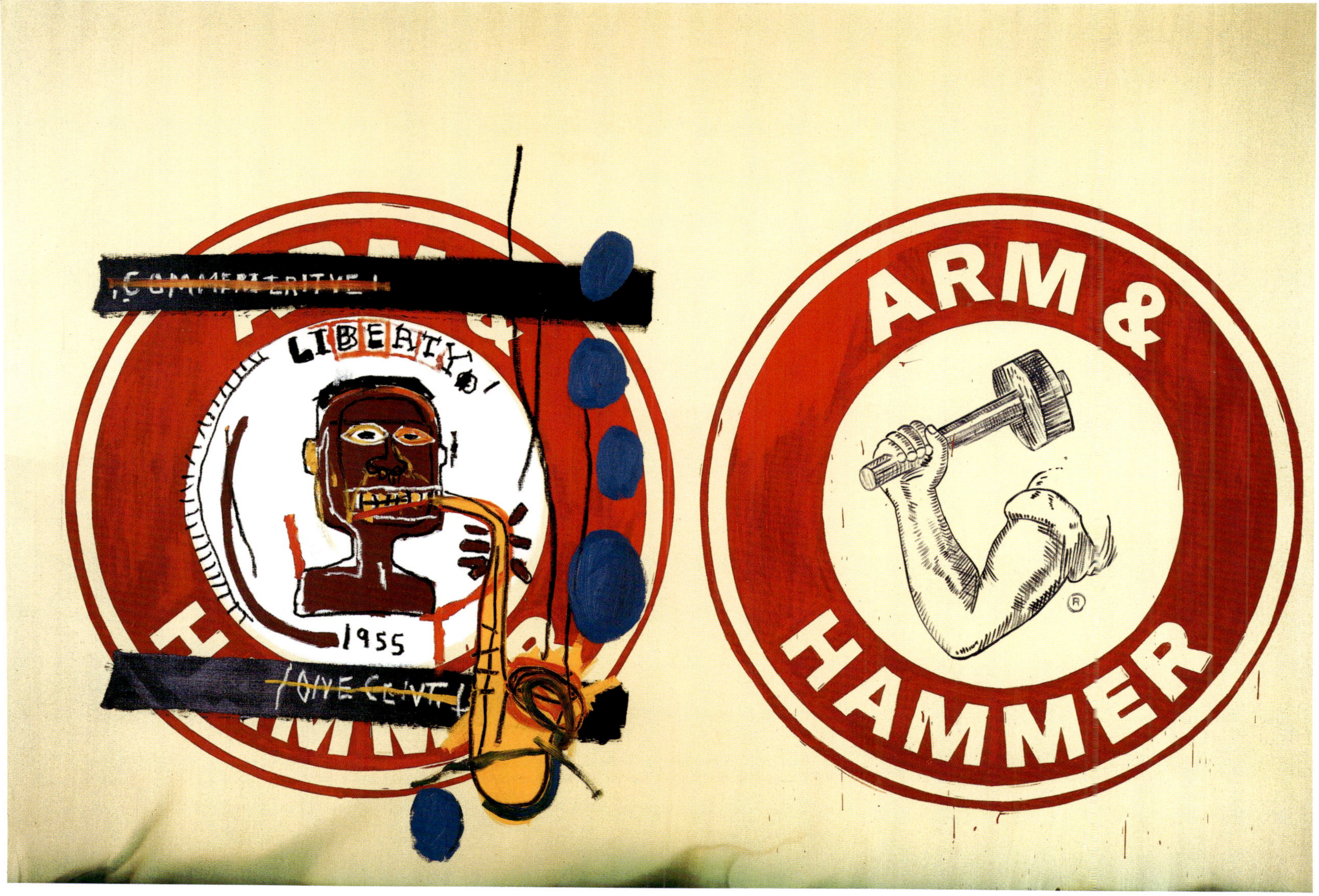

39. Andy Warhol and Jean-Michel Basquiat, *Arm and Hammer II*, 1985. Acrylic on canvas, 76 x 112 in. (193 x 285 cm). Galerie Bruno Bischofberger, Zurich

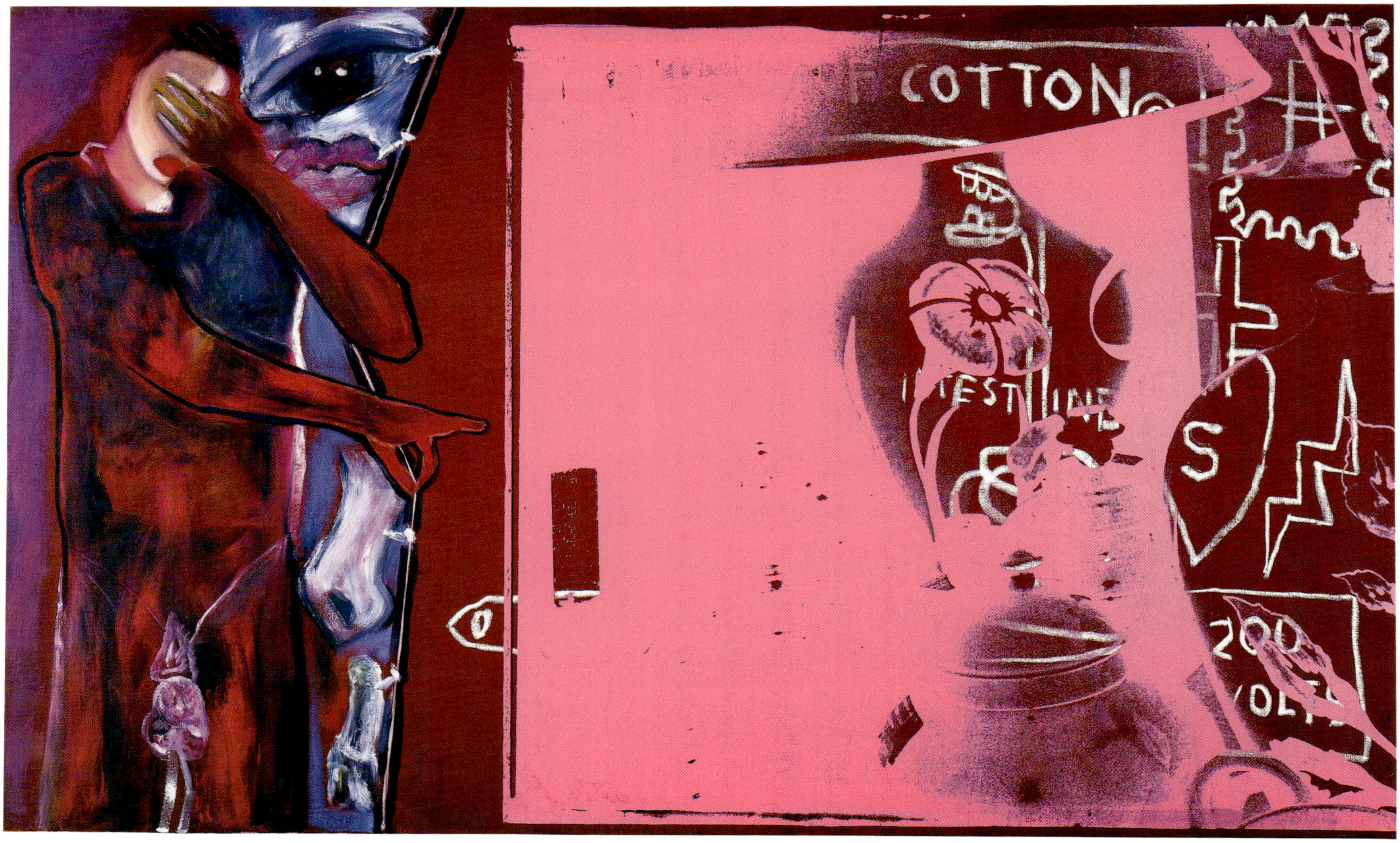

40. Andy Warhol, Jean-Michel Basquiat, and Francesco Clemente, *Casa del Popolo*, 1984. Mixed media on canvas, $50\frac{3}{8}$ x $84\frac{5}{8}$ in. (128 x 215 cm). Private collection

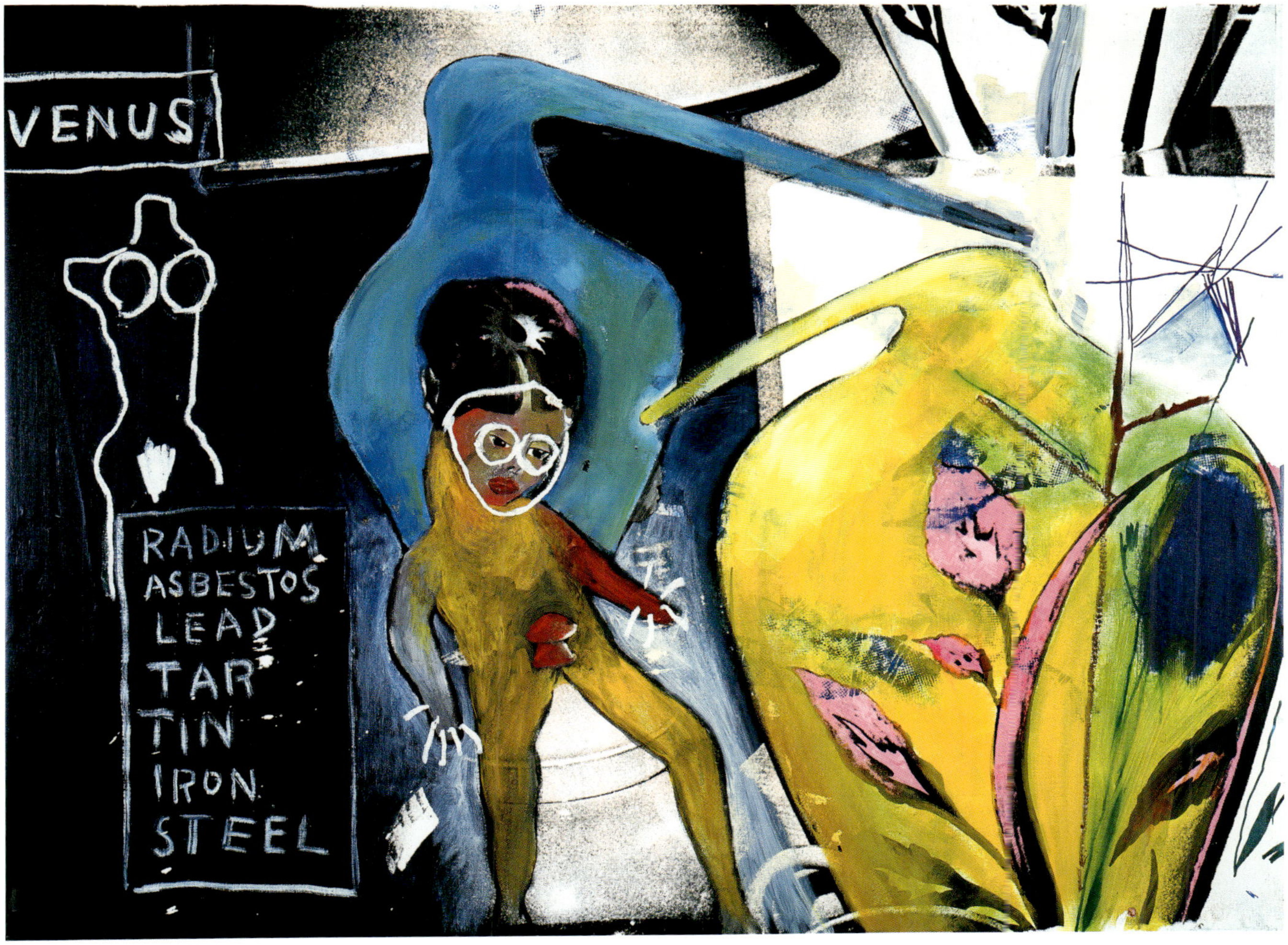

41. Andy Warhol, Jean-Michel Basquiat, and Francesco Clemente, *Ex-Ringeye*, 1984. Mixed media on canvas, 48 x 66 in. (122 x 167.5 cm). Private collection

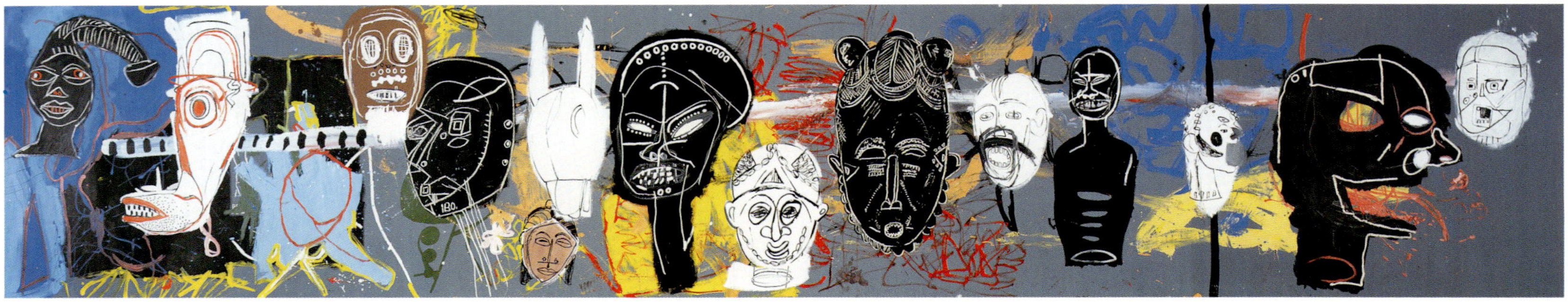

42. Andy Warhol and Jean-Michel Basquiat, *African Masks*, 1984. Acrylic and silkscreen ink on canvas, 84 x 420 in. (213.4 x 1066.8 cm). Private collection

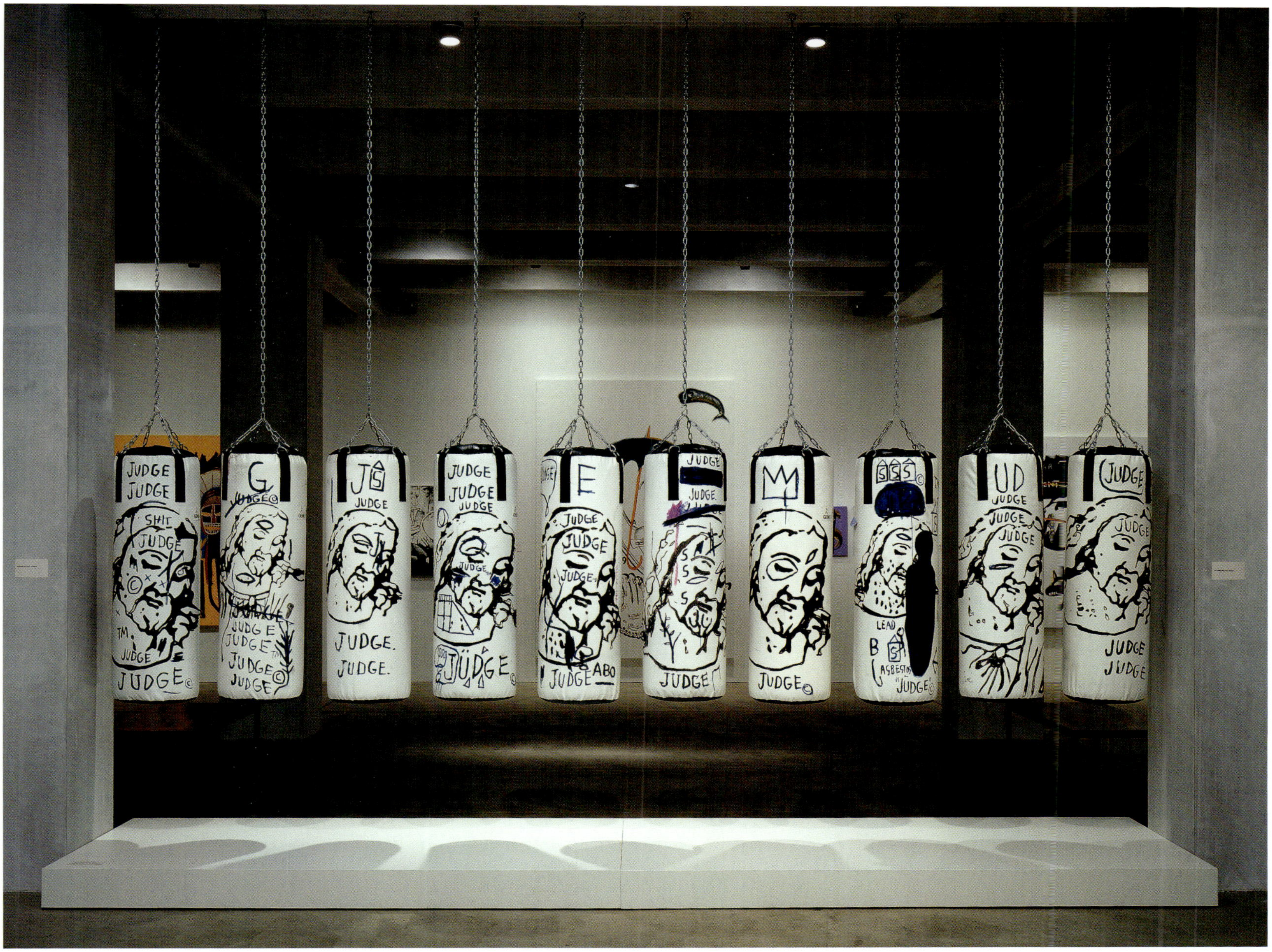

43. Andy Warhol and Jean-Michel Basquiat, *Ten Punching Bags (Last Supper)*, 1985–86. Acrylic and oil stick on punching bags, 42 x 14 x 14 in. (106.7 x 35.6 x 35.6 cm) each. The Andy Warhol Museum, Pittsburgh; Founding Collection, Contribution The Andy Warhol Foundation for the Visual Arts, Inc.

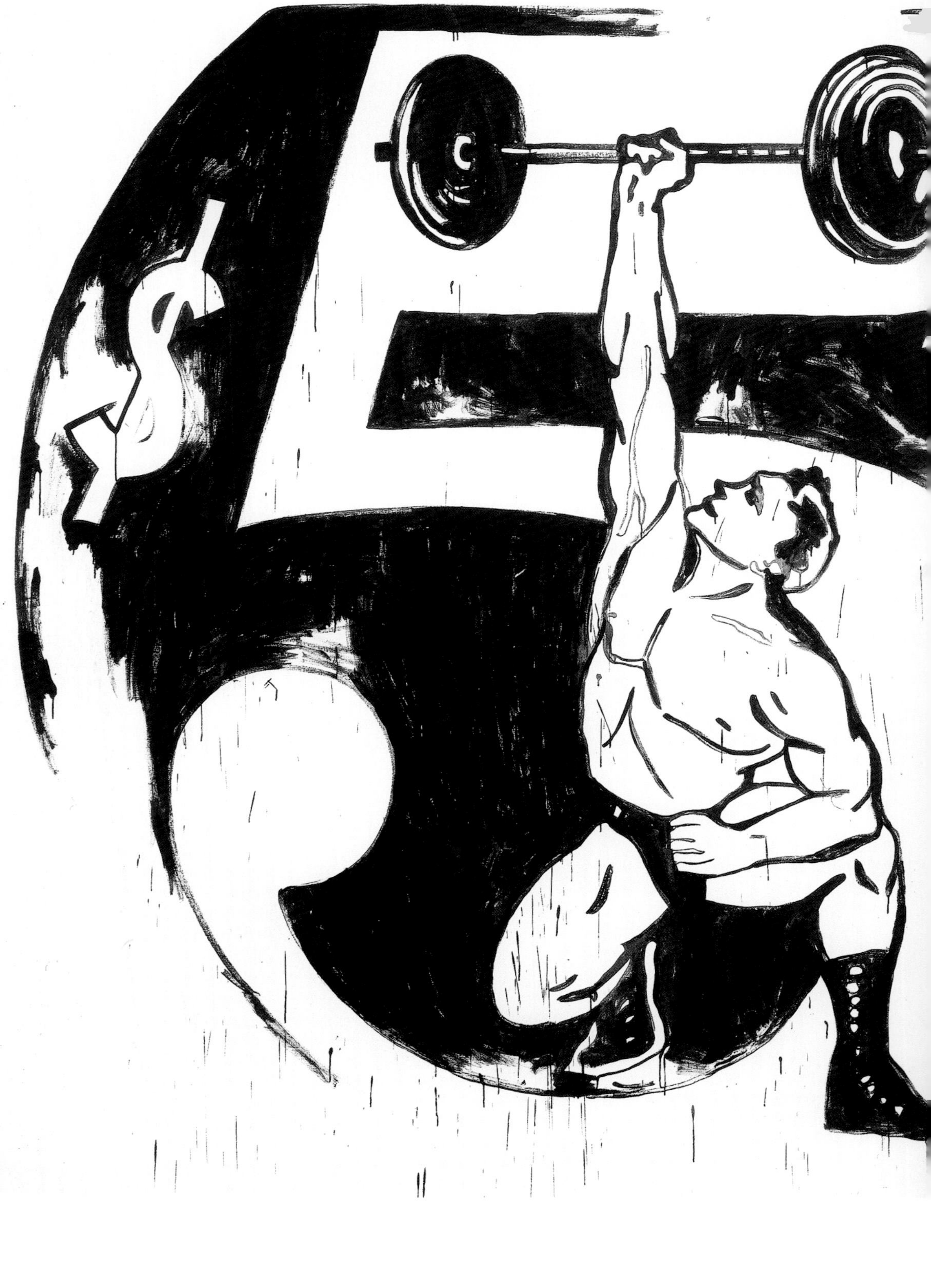

44. *Double $5/Weightlifter*, 1985–86. Acrylic on linen, 116 x 216½ in. (294.6 x 549.9 cm). The Andy Warhol Museum, Pittsburgh; Founding Collection, Contribution The Andy Warhol Foundation for the Visual Arts, Inc.

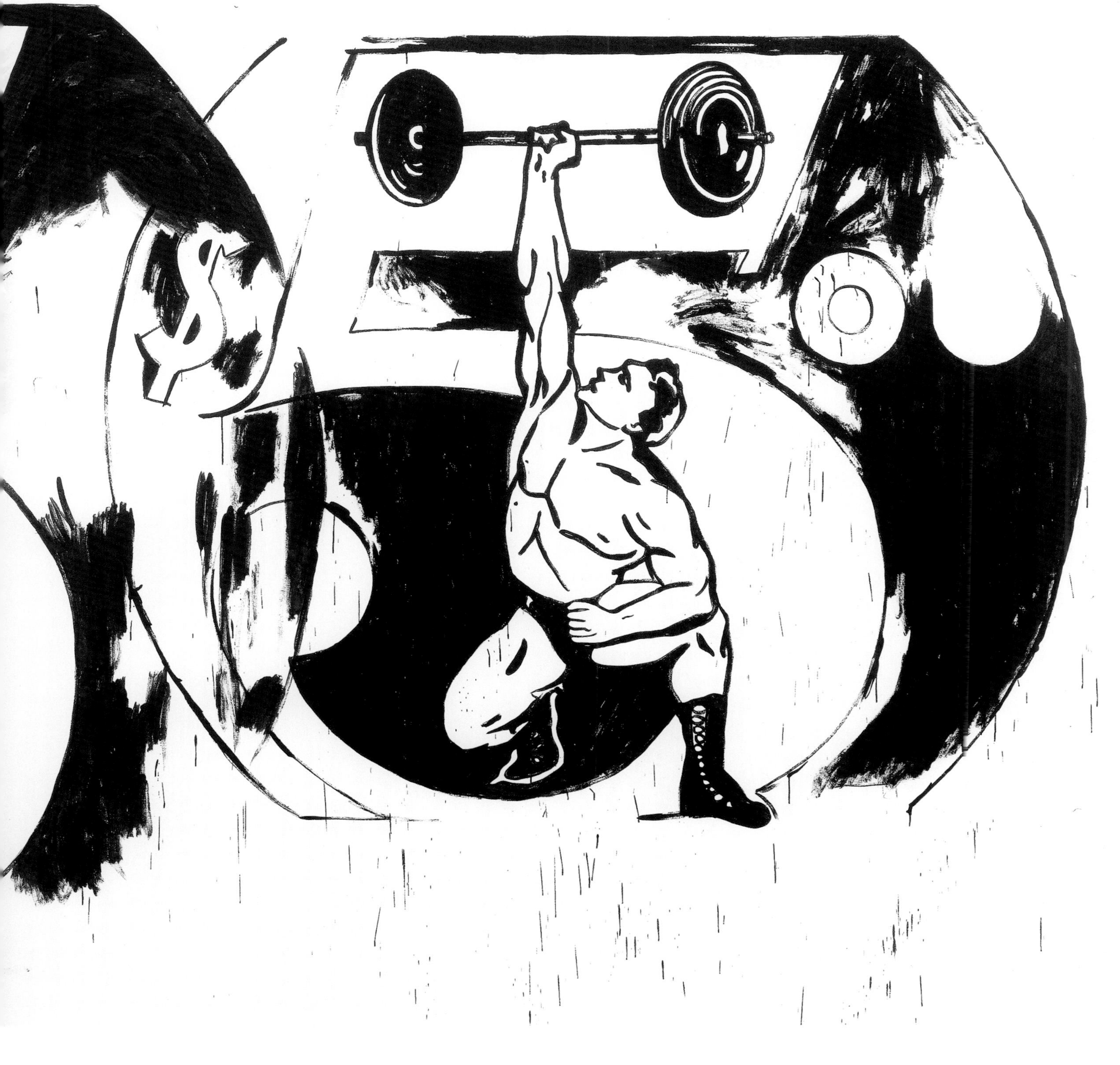

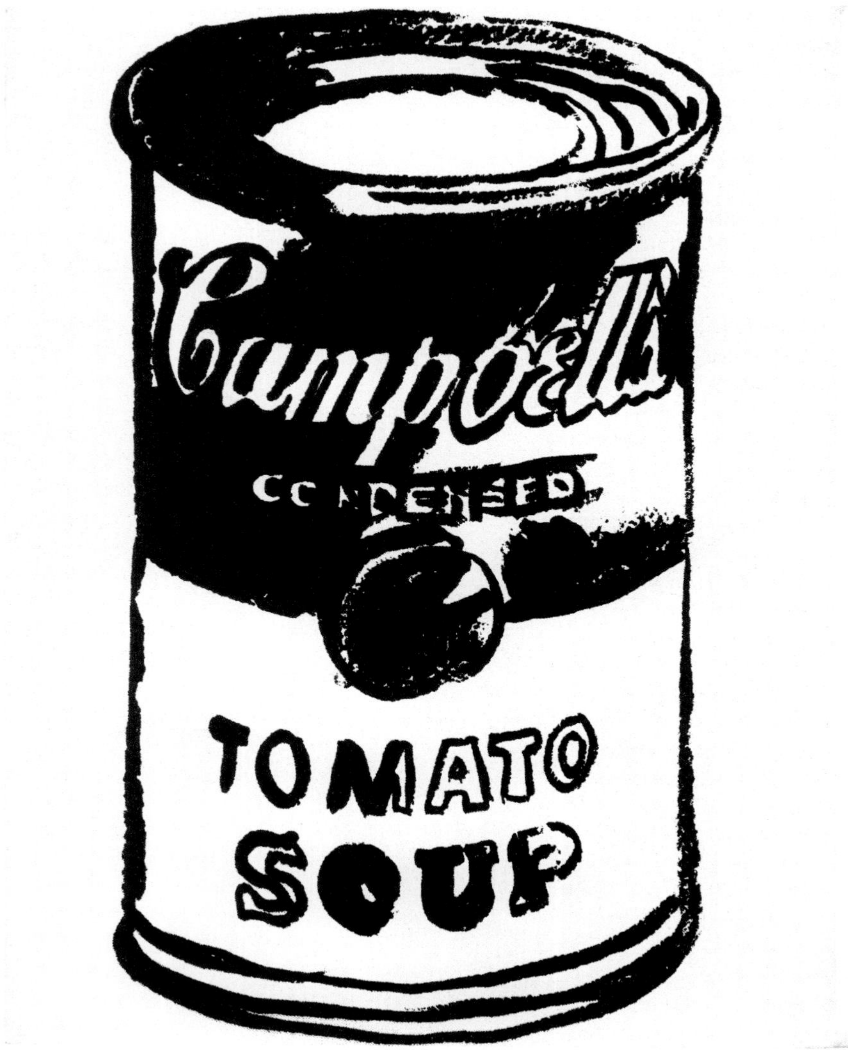

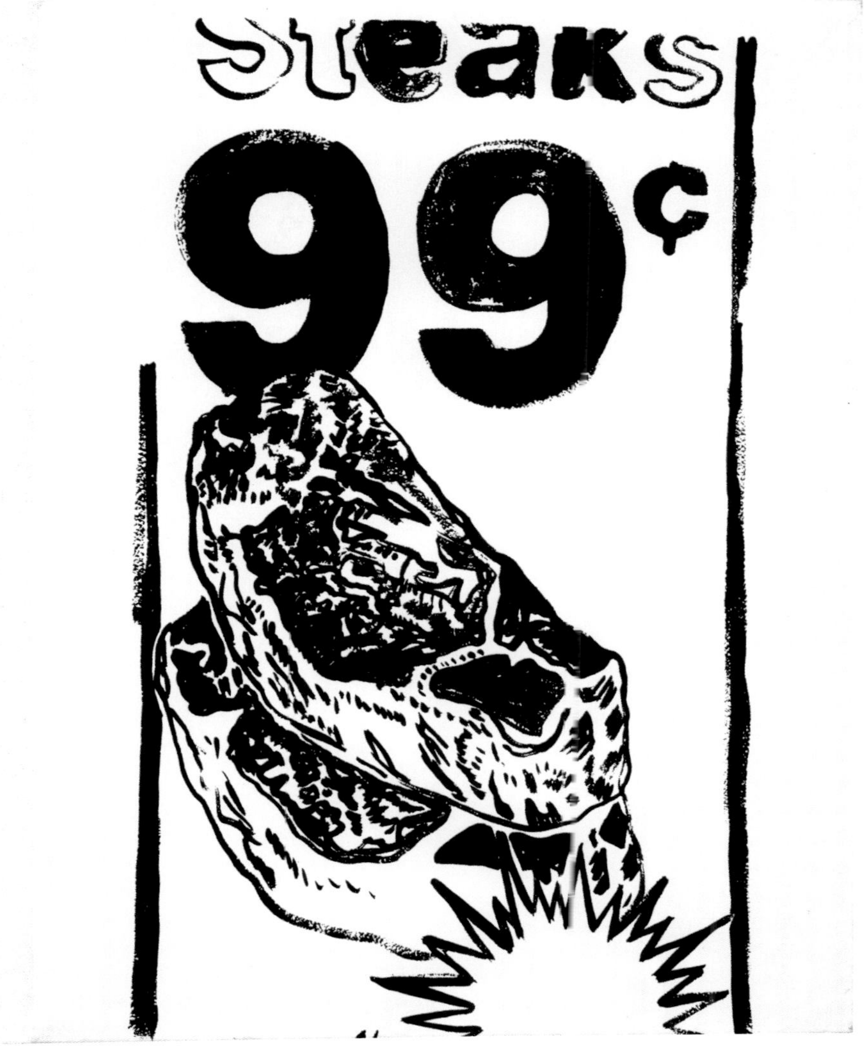

45. *Campbell's Soup (Tomato)*, 1985. Acrylic and silkscreen ink on canvas, 20 x 16 in. (50.8 x 40.6 cm). Collection of Debbie and Mark Attanasio

46. *Steaks 99 [cents]*, 1985–86. Acrylic and silkscreen ink on linen, 20 x 16 in. (50.8 x 40.6 cm). The Andy Warhol Museum, Pittsburgh; Founding Collection, Contribution The Andy Warhol Foundation for the Visual Arts, Inc.

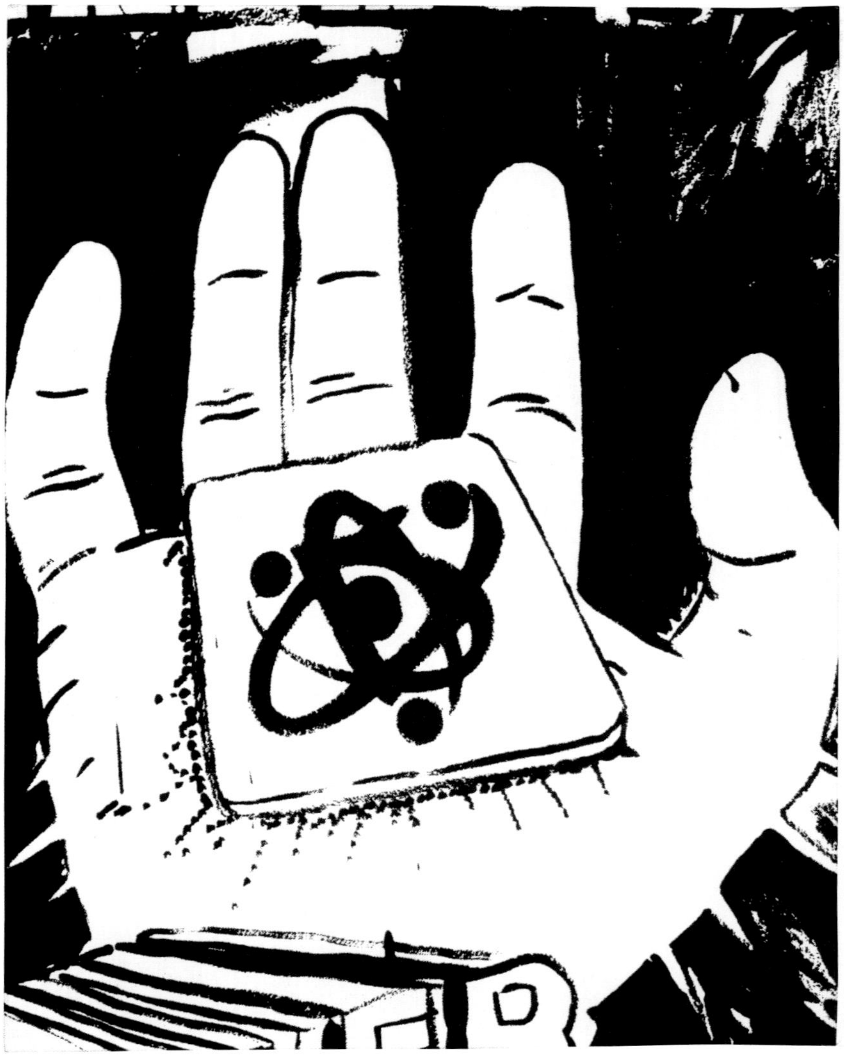

47. *Energy*, 1985–86. Acrylic and silkscreen ink on linen, 20 x 16 in. (50.8 x 40.6 cm). The Andy Warhol Museum, Pittsburgh; Founding Collection, Contribution The Andy Warhol Foundation for the Visual Arts, Inc.

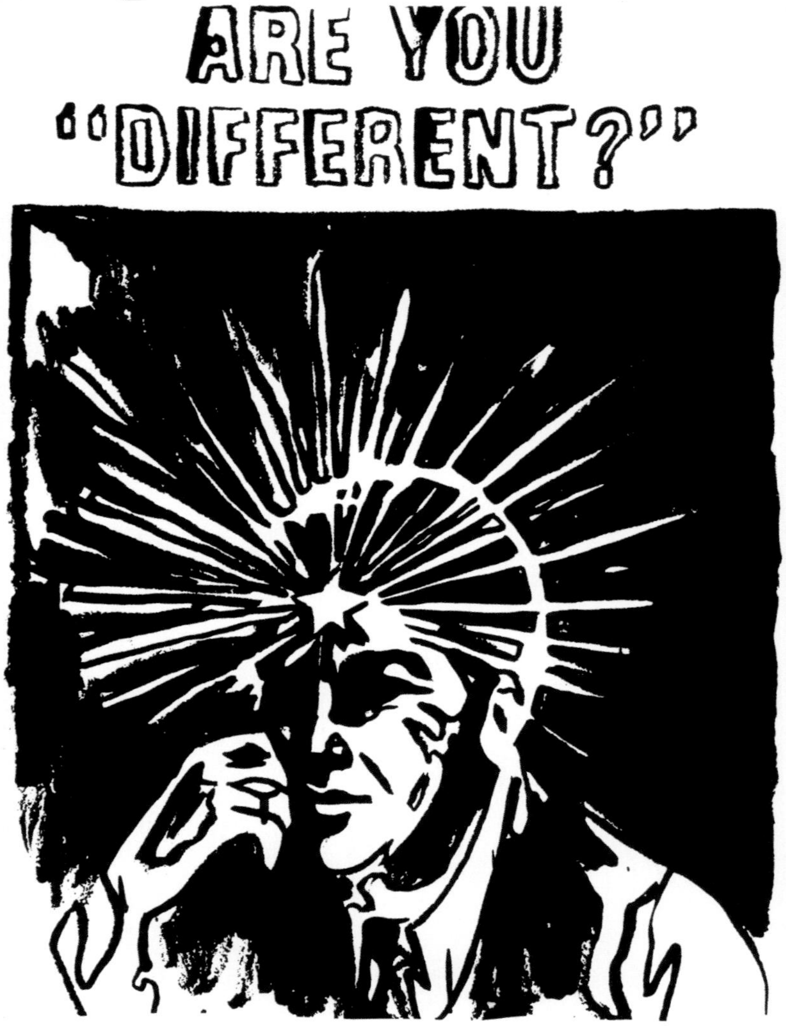

48. *Are You "Different"?*, 1985–86. Acrylic and silkscreen ink on linen, 20 x 16 in. (50.8 x 40.6 cm). The Andy Warhol Museum, Pittsburgh; Founding Collection, Contribution The Andy Warhol Foundation for the Visual Arts, Inc.

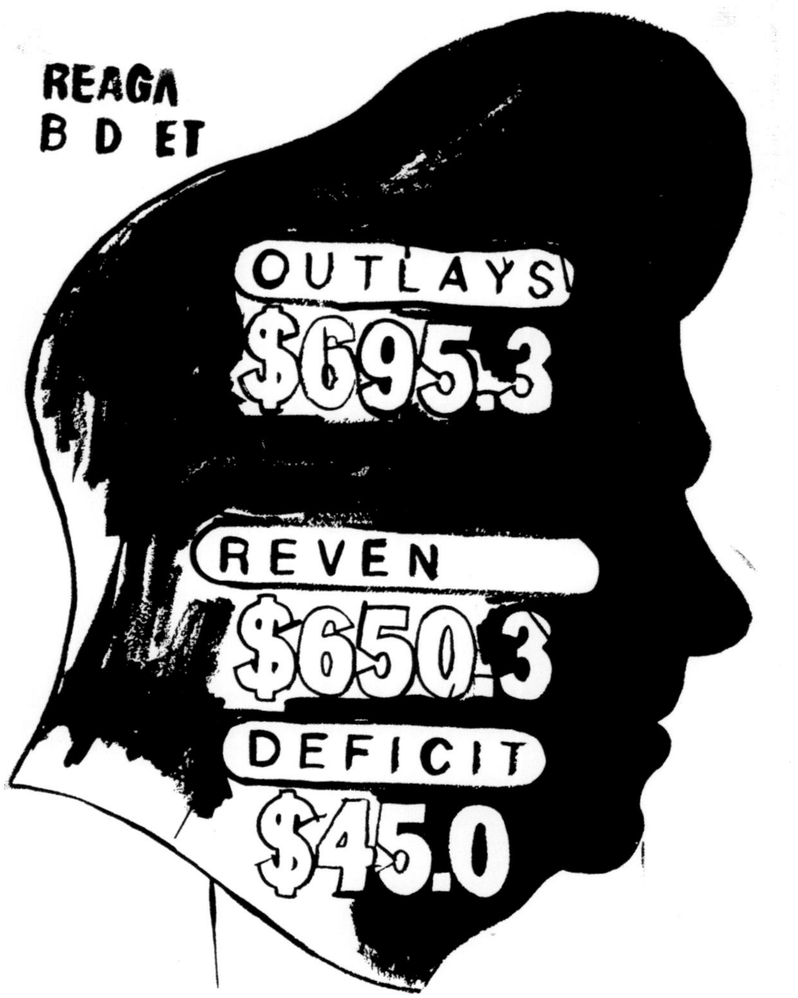

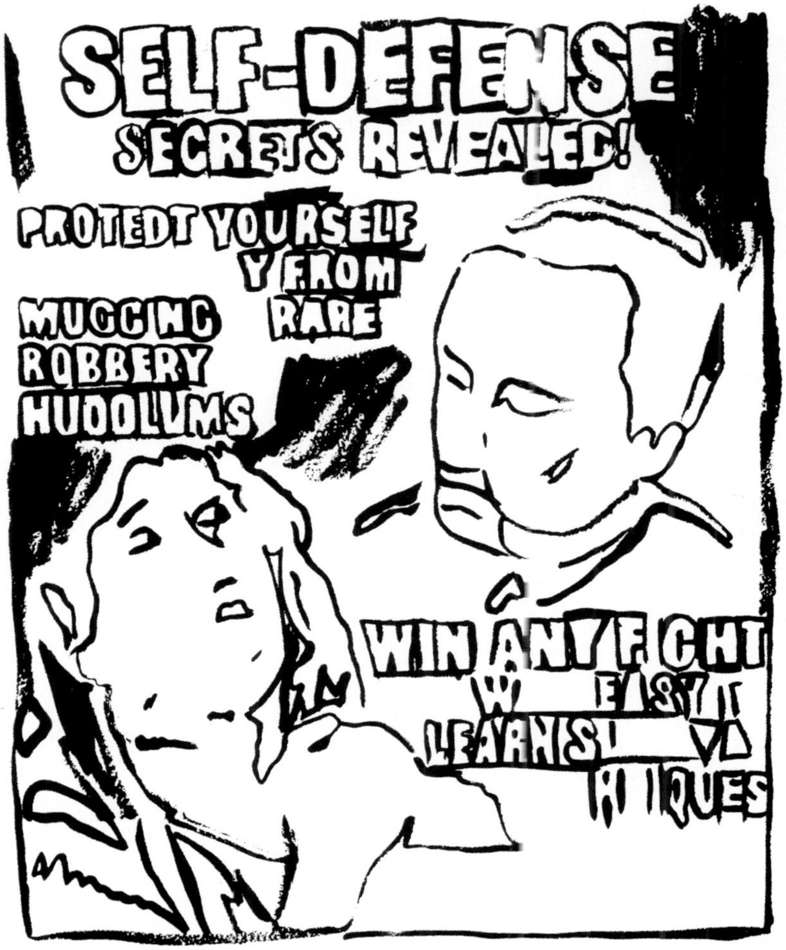

49. *Reagan Budget*, c. 1985–86. Acrylic and silkscreen ink on canvas, 20 x 16 in. (50.8 x 40.6 cm). The Andy Warhol Foundation for the Visual Arts, Inc.

50. *Self-Defense*, 1985–86. Acrylic and silkscreen ink on linen, 20 x 16 in. (50.8 x 40.6 cm). The Andy Warhol Museum, Pittsburgh; Founding Collection, Contribution The Andy Warhol Foundation for the Visual Arts, Inc.

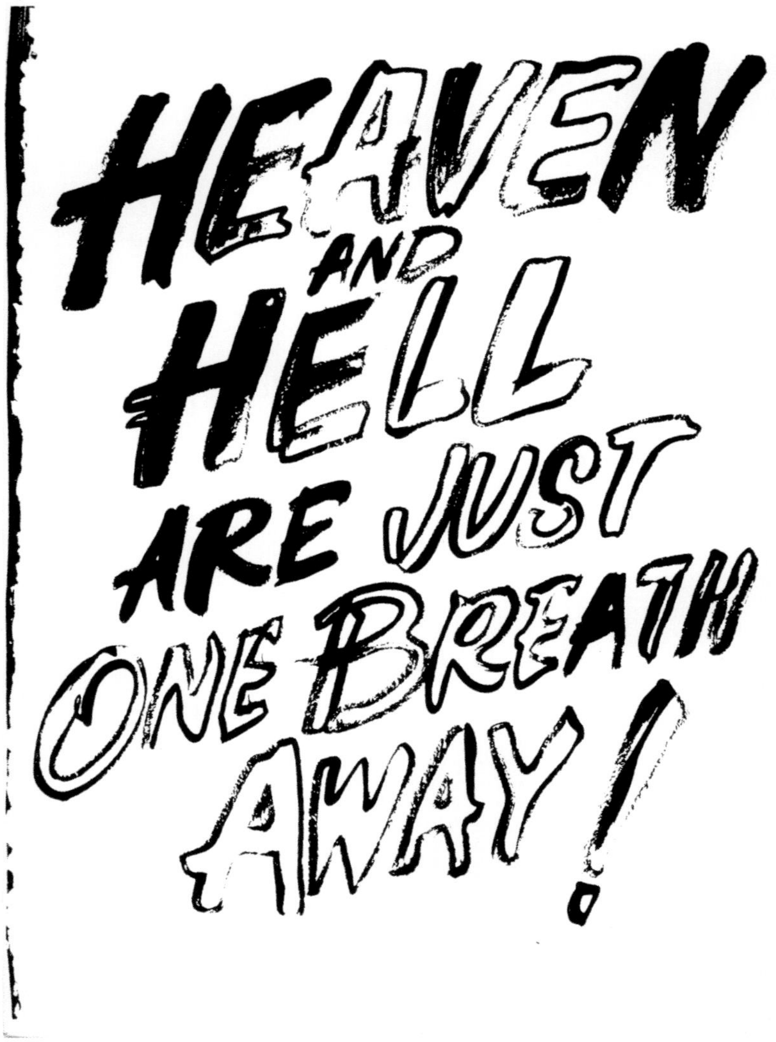

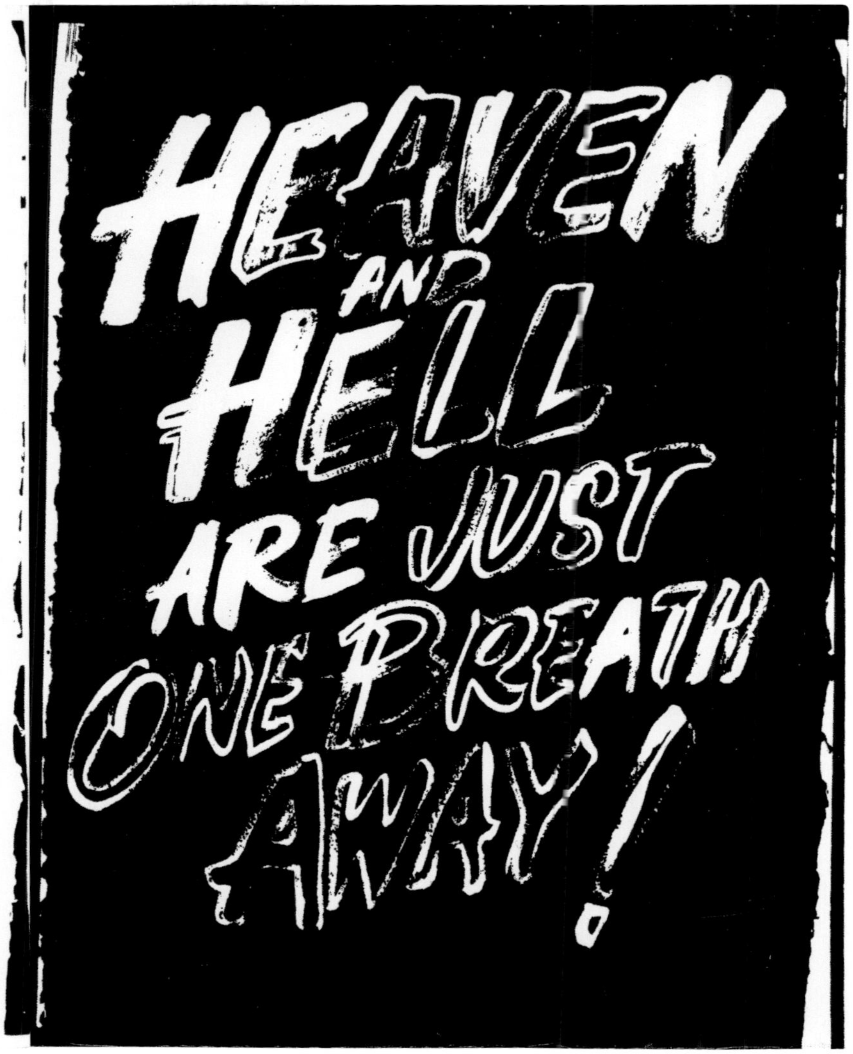

51. *Heaven and Hell Are Just One Breath Away!* 1985–86. Acrylic and silkscreen ink on linen, 20 x 16 in. (50.8 x 40.6 cm). The Andy Warhol Museum, Pittsburgh; Founding Collection, Contribution The Andy Warhol Foundation for the Visual Arts, Inc.

52. *Heaven and Hell Are Just One Breath Away!* 1985–86. Acrylic and silkscreen ink on linen, 20 x 16 in. (50.8 x 40.6 cm). Private collection

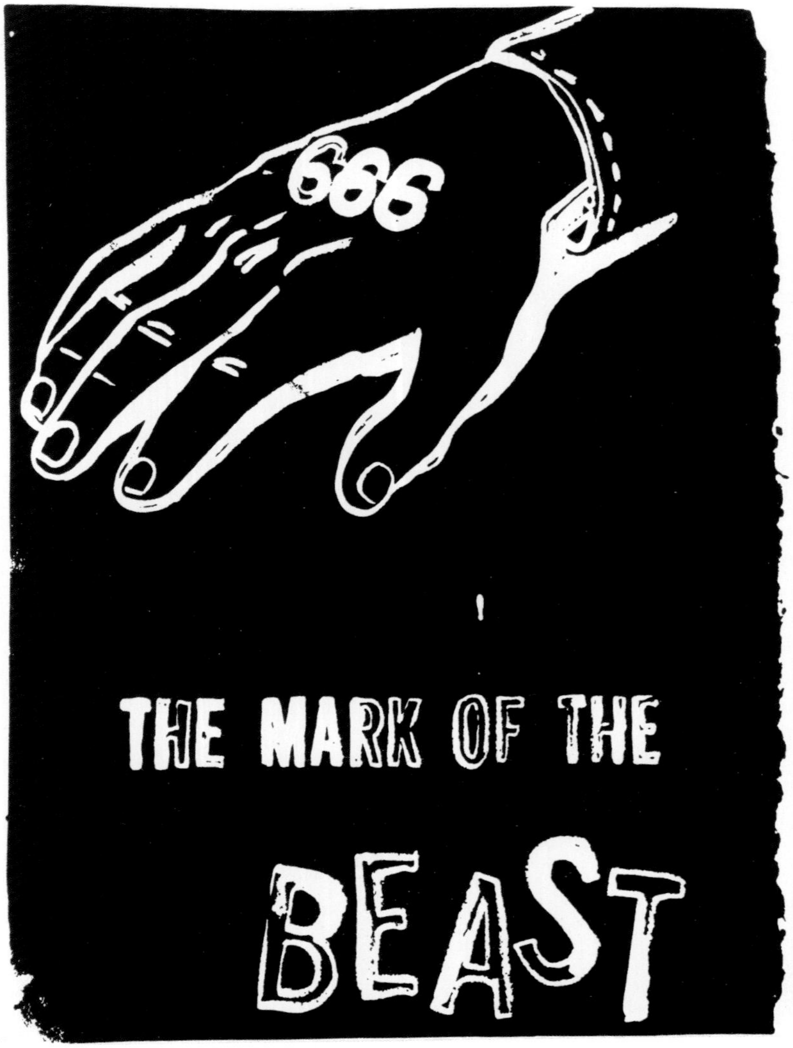

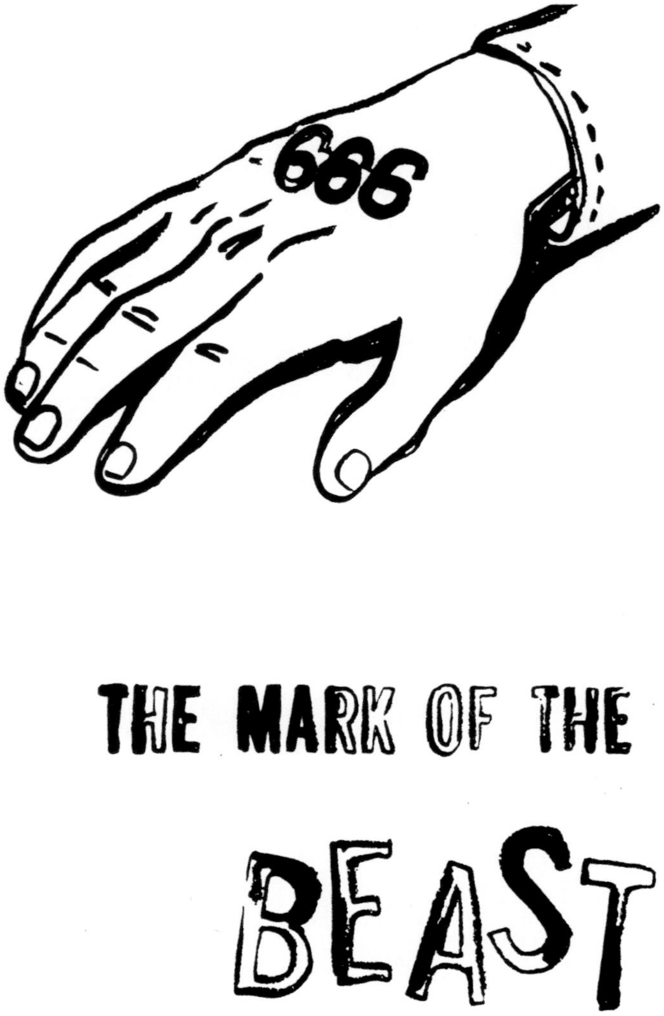

53. *The Mark of the Beast*, 1985–86. Acrylic and silkscreen ink on linen, 20 x 16 in. (50.8 x 40.6 cm). The Andy Warhol Museum, Pittsburgh; Founding Collection, Contribution The Andy Warhol Foundation for the Visual Arts, Inc.

54. *The Mark of the Beast*, 1985–86. Acrylic and silkscreen ink on linen, 20 x 16 in. (50.8 x 40.6 cm). DJT Fine Art, New York

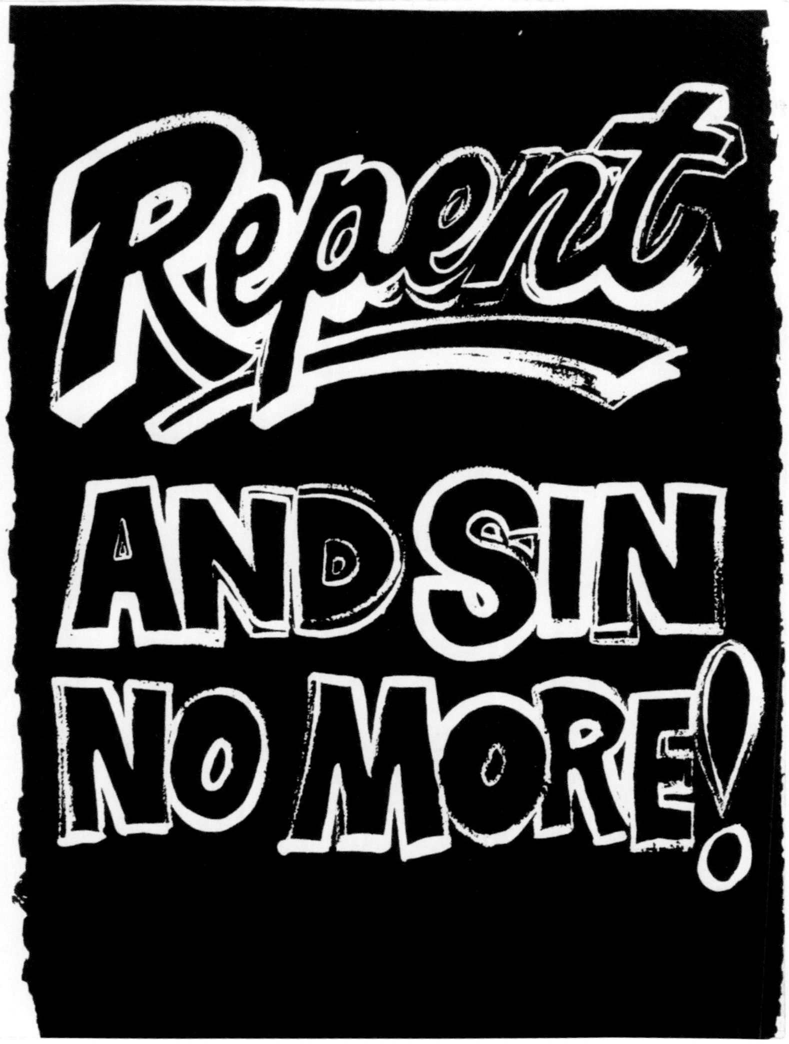

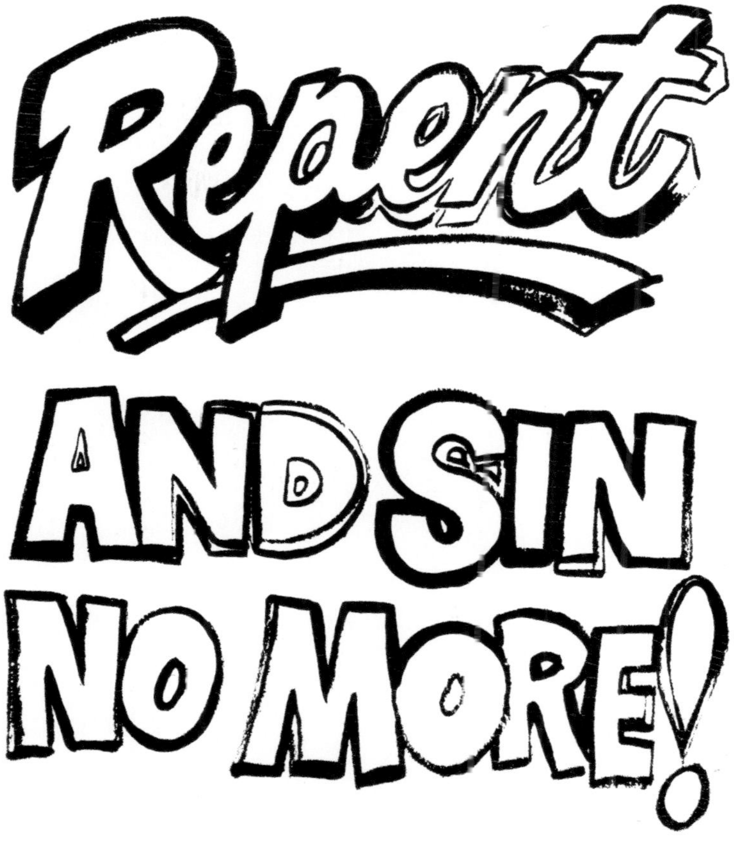

55. *Repent and Sin No More!* 1985–86. Acrylic and silkscreen ink on linen, 20 x 16 in. (50.8 x 40.6 cm). The Andy Warhol Museum, Pittsburgh; Founding Collection, Contribution The Andy Warhol Foundation for the Visual Arts, Inc.

56. *Repent and Sin No More!* 1985–86. Acrylic and silkscreen ink on canvas, 20 x 16 in. (50.8 x 40.6 cm). The Andy Warhol Foundation for the Visual Arts, Inc.

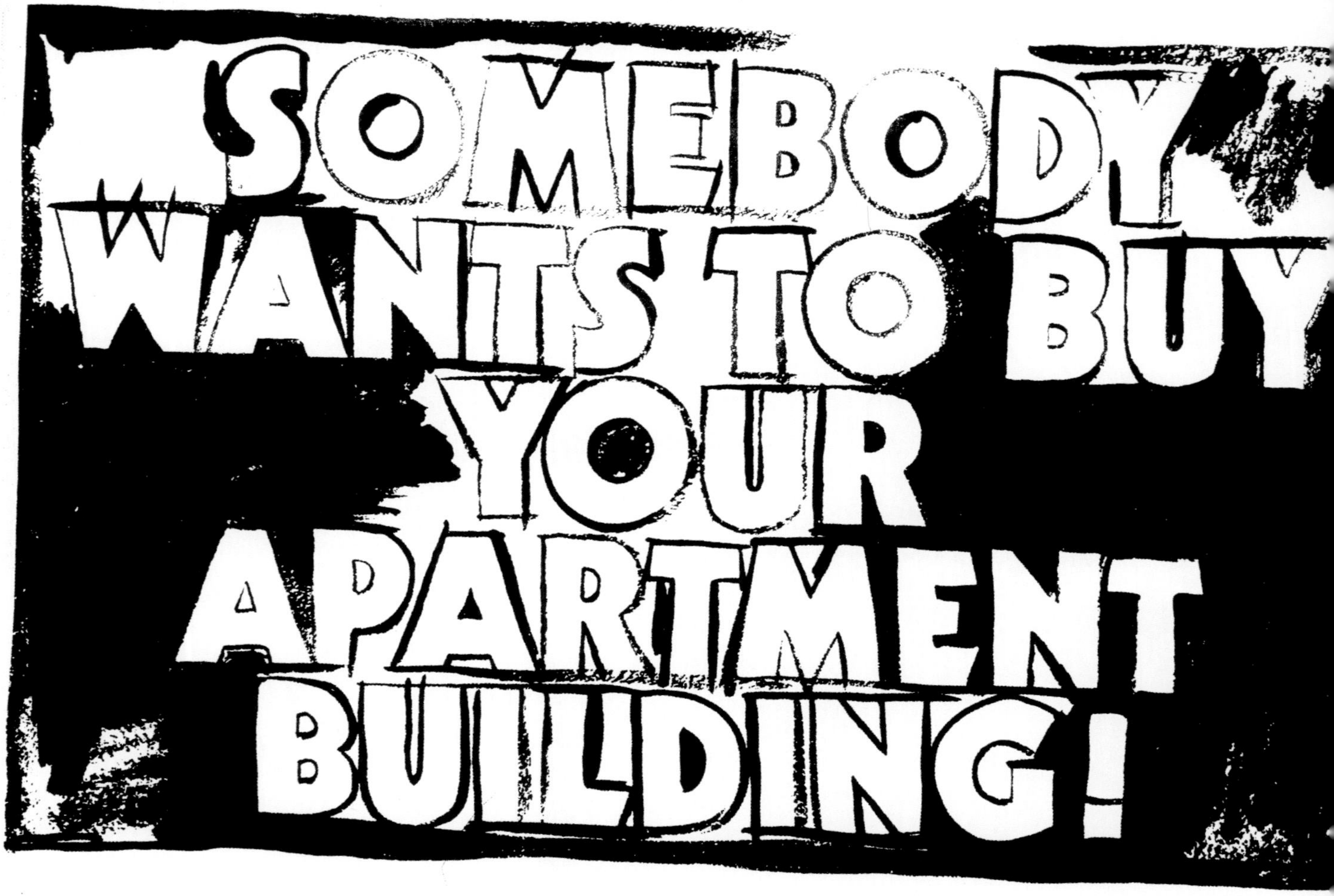

57. *Somebody Wants to Buy Your Apartment Building!* 1985–86. Acrylic and silkscreen ink on linen, 16 x 20 in. (40.6 x 50.8 cm). The Andy Warhol Museum, Pittsburgh; Founding Collection, Contribution The Andy Warhol Foundation for the Visual Arts, Inc.

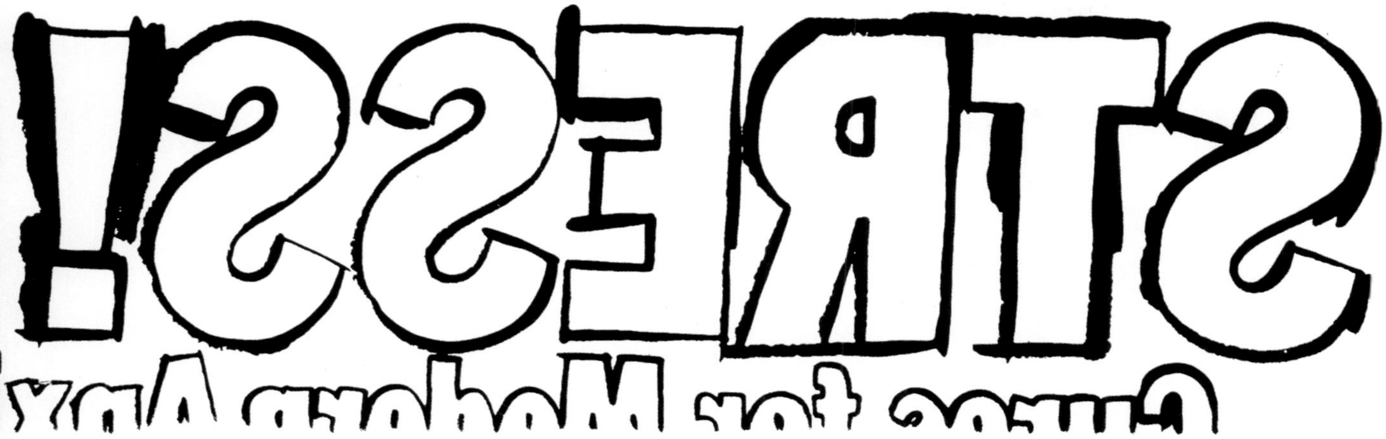

58. *Stress!* 1985–86. Acrylic and silkscreen ink on linen, 16 x 20 in. (40.6 x 50.8 cm). The Andy Warhol Museum, Pittsburgh; Founding Collection, Contribution The Andy Warhol Foundation for the Visual Arts, Inc.

59. *The Last Supper (Be a Somebody with a Body)* [detail], 1985–86. Acrylic on linen, 50 x 56 x 1½ in. (127 x 142.2 x 3.2 cm). The Andy Warhol Museum, Pittsburgh; Founding Collection, Contribution The Andy Warhol Foundation for the Visual Arts, Inc.

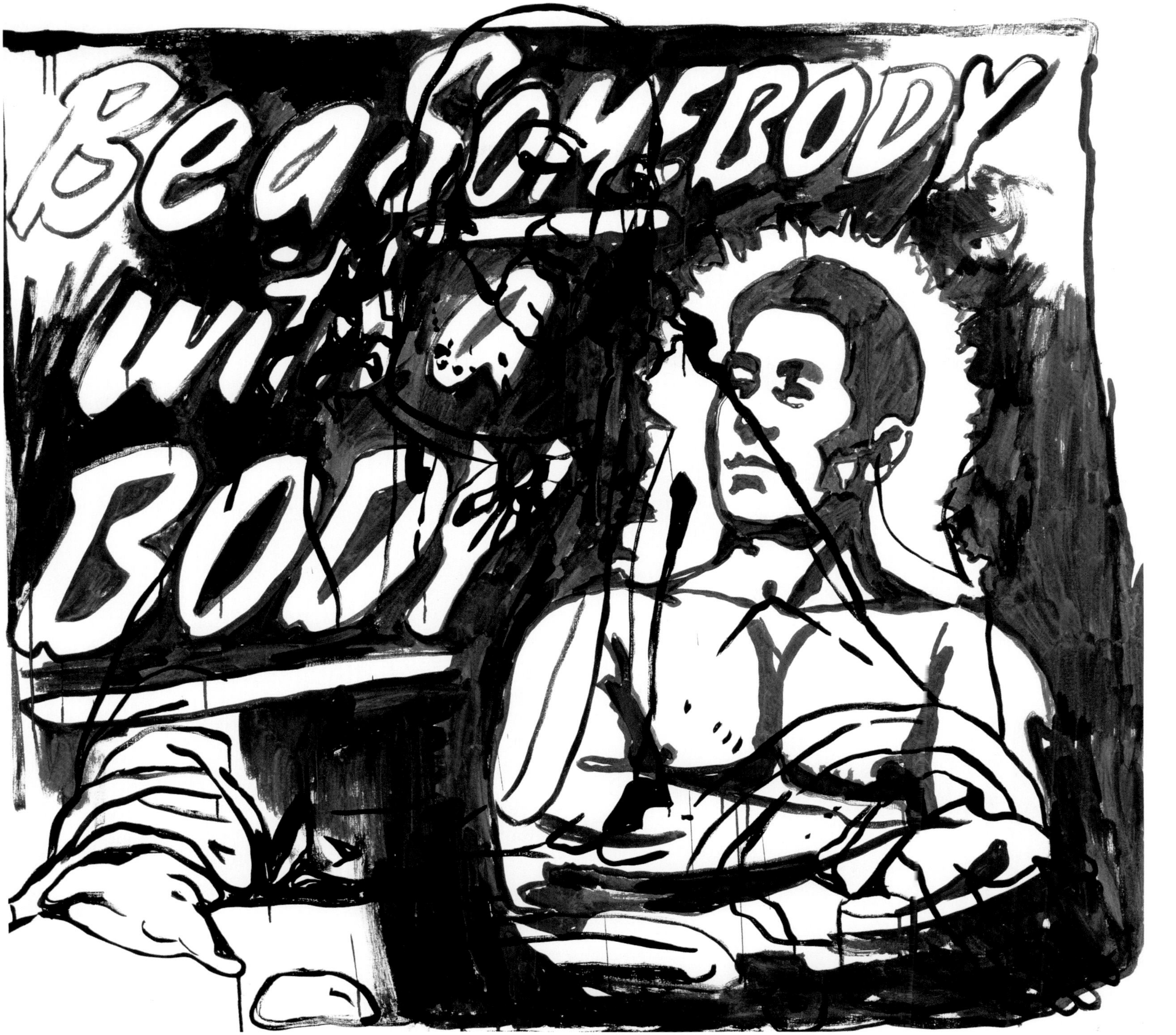
Be a SOMEBODY

60. *Self-Portrait*, 1986. Acrylic and silkscreen ink on linen, 40 x 40 in. (101.6 x 101.6 cm). Mugrabi Collection

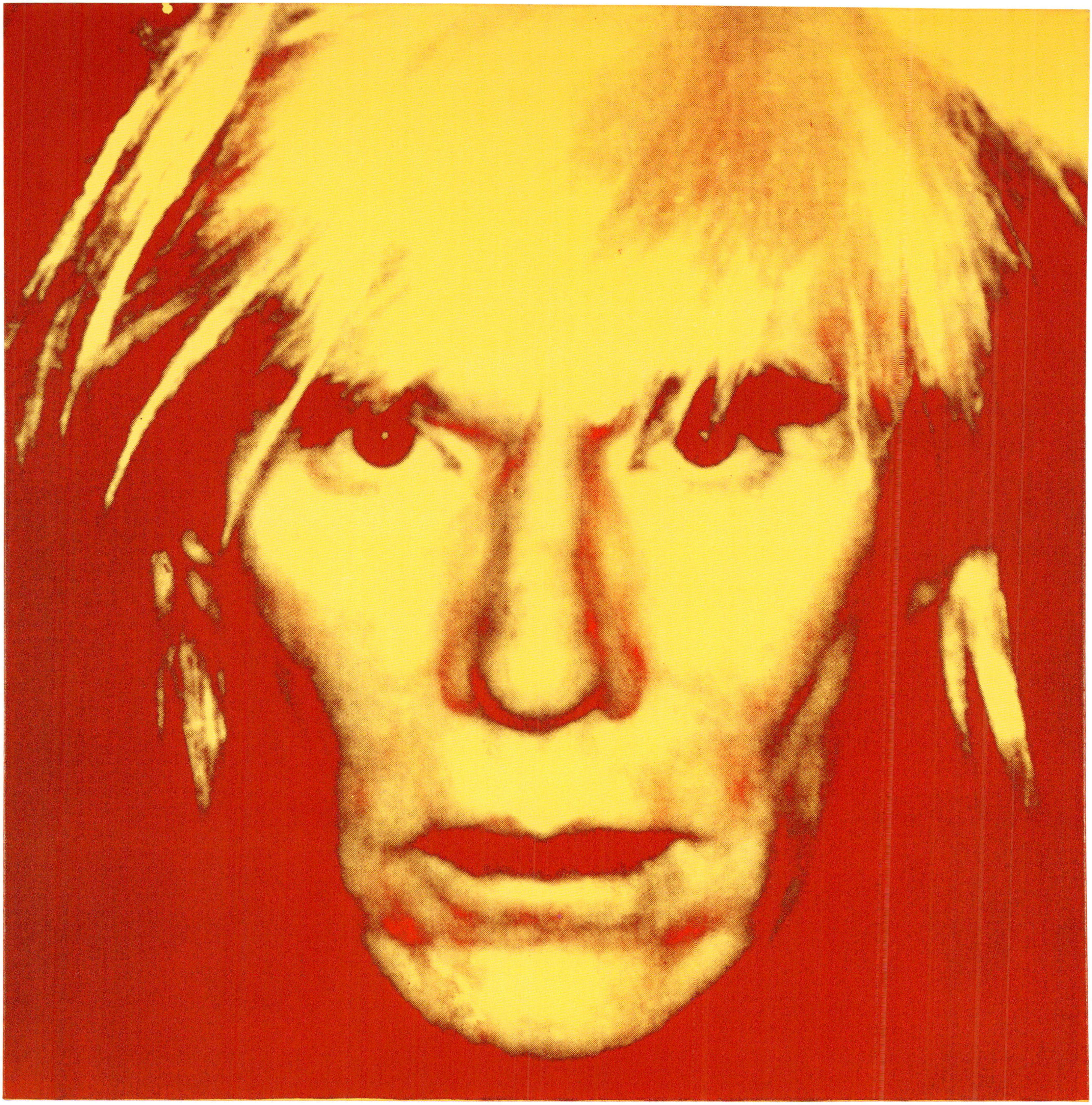

61. *Self-Portrait*, 1986. Acrylic and silkscreen ink on canvas, 108 x 108 x 1½ in. (274.3 x 274.3 x 3.8 cm). The Andy Warhol Museum, Pittsburgh; Founding Collection, Contribution The Andy Warhol Foundation for the Visual Arts, Inc.

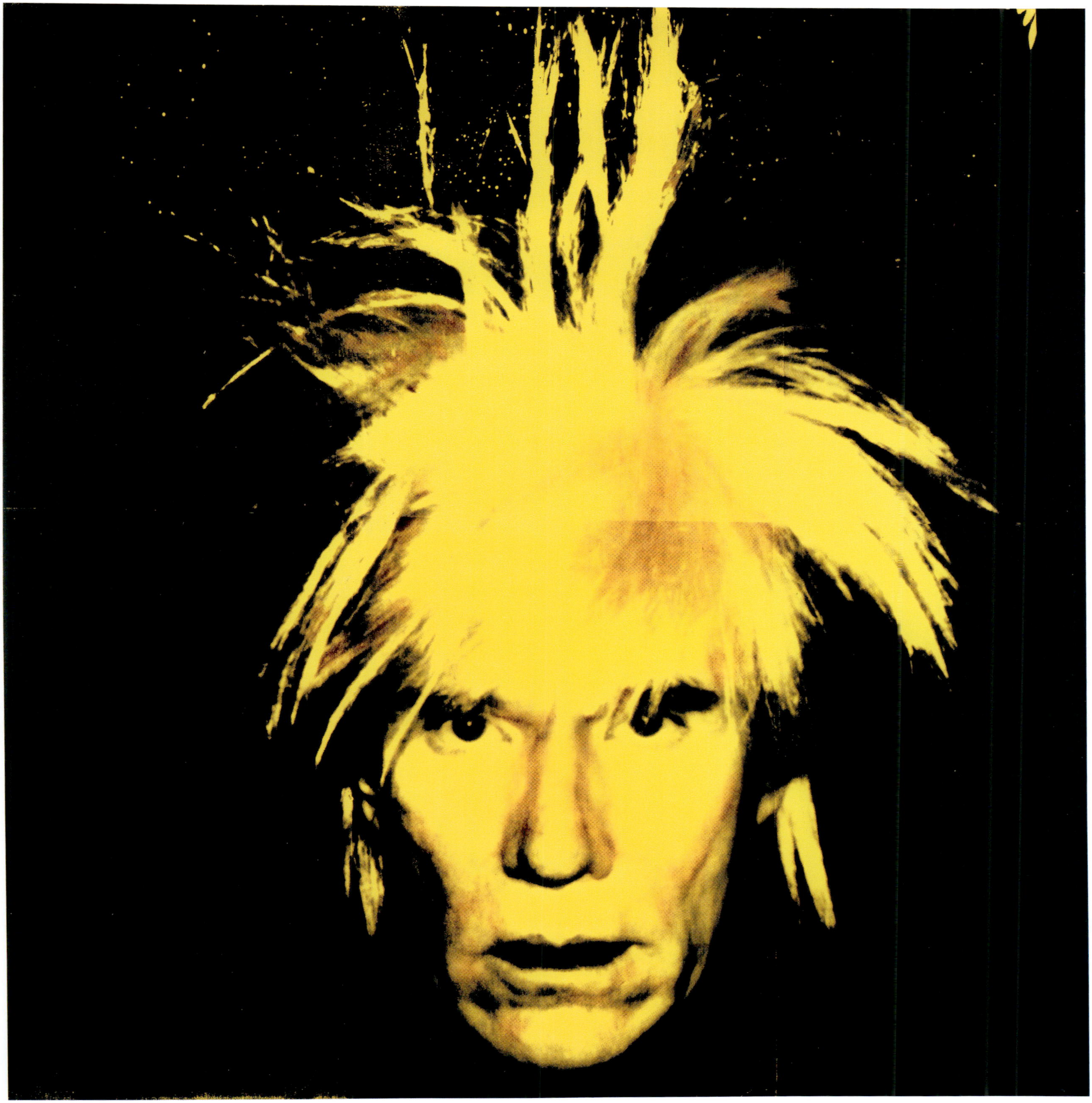

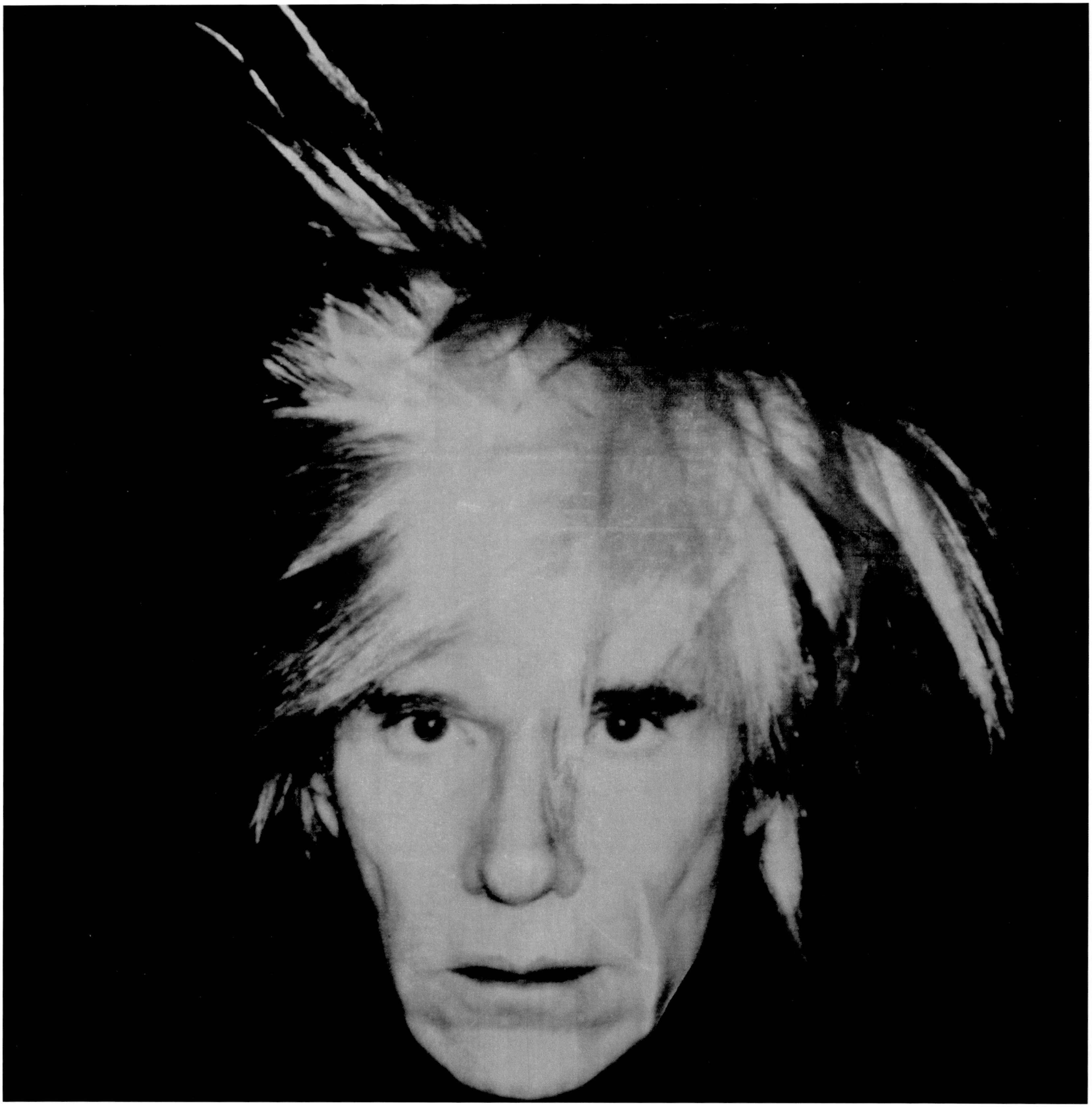

62. *Self-Portrait*, 1986. Acrylic and silkscreen ink on canvas, 80⅛ x 80⅛ in. (203.5 x 203.5 cm). Carnegie Museum of Art, Pittsburgh; Fellows Fund

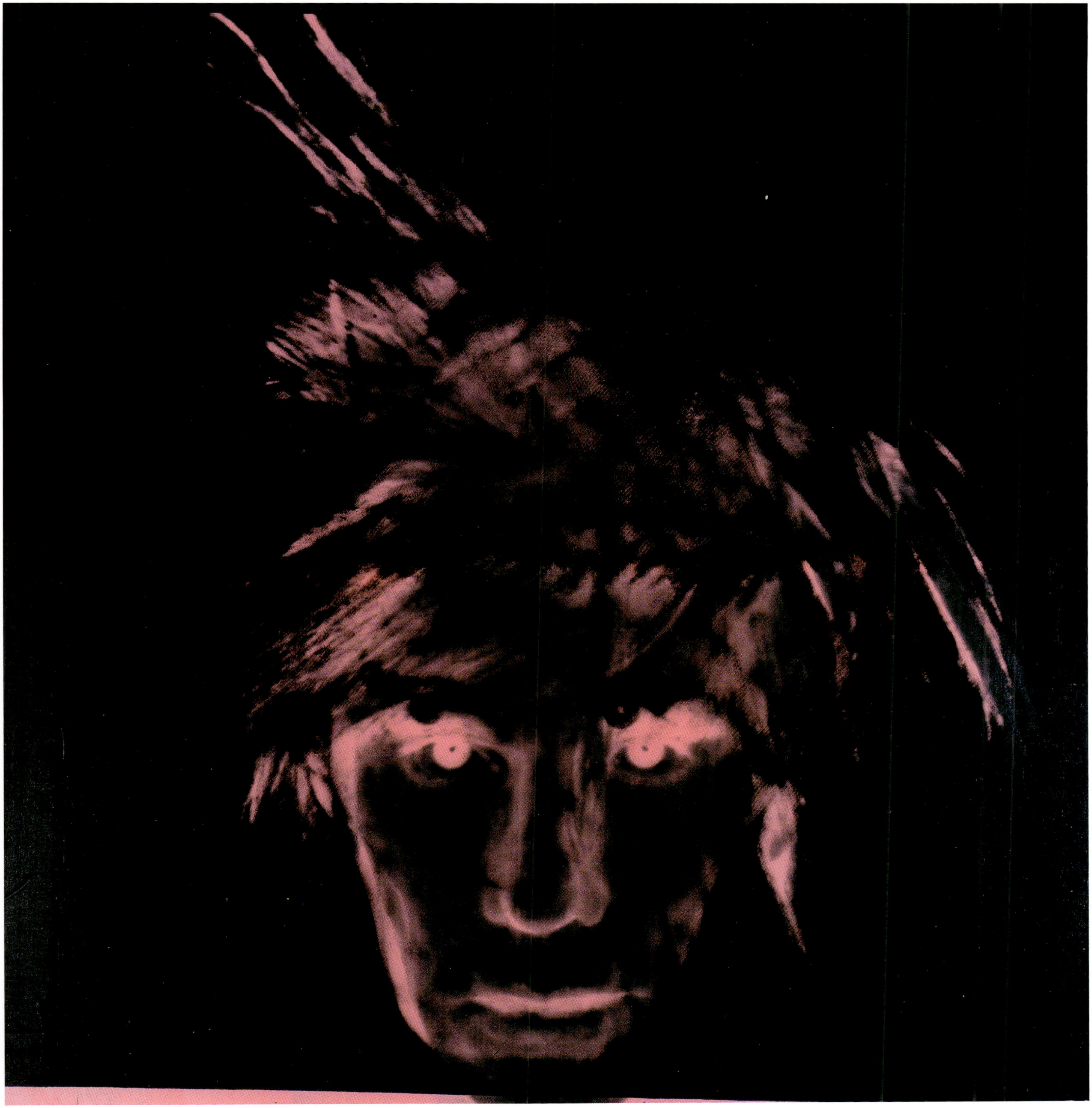

63. *Self-Portrait*, 1986. Acrylic and silkscreen ink on canvas, 80 1/16 x 80 in. (203.4 x 203.3 cm). The Baltimore Museum o Art: Purchase with exchange funds provided from Bequest of Saidie A. May; and partial gift of The Andy Warhol Foundation of the Visual Arts, Inc.

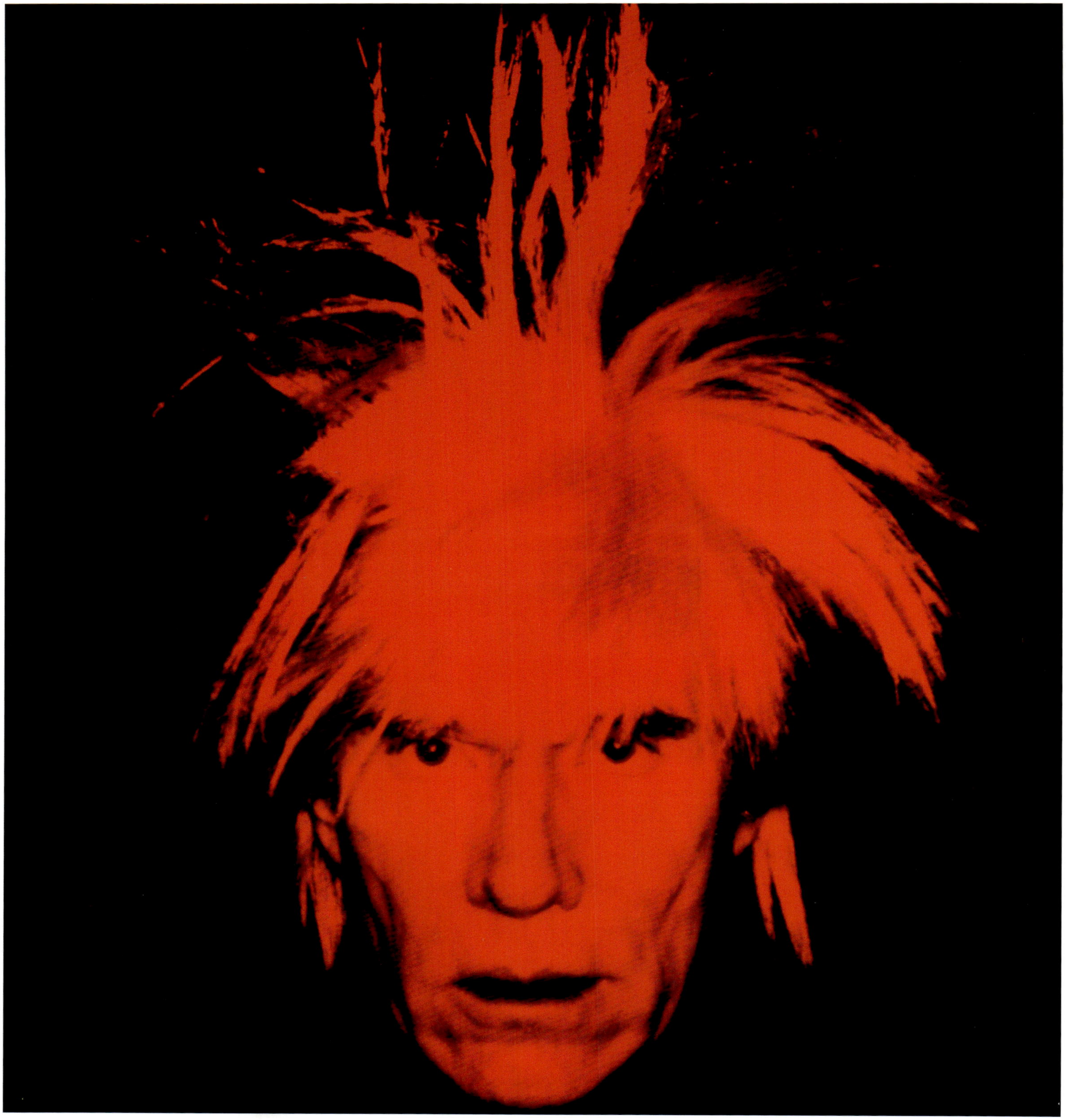

64. *Self-Portrait*, 1986. Acrylic and silkscreen ink on linen, 80 x 76 in. (203.2 x 193 cm). The Andy Warhol Museum, Pittsburgh; Founding Collection, Contribution The Andy Warhol Foundation for the Visual Arts, Inc.

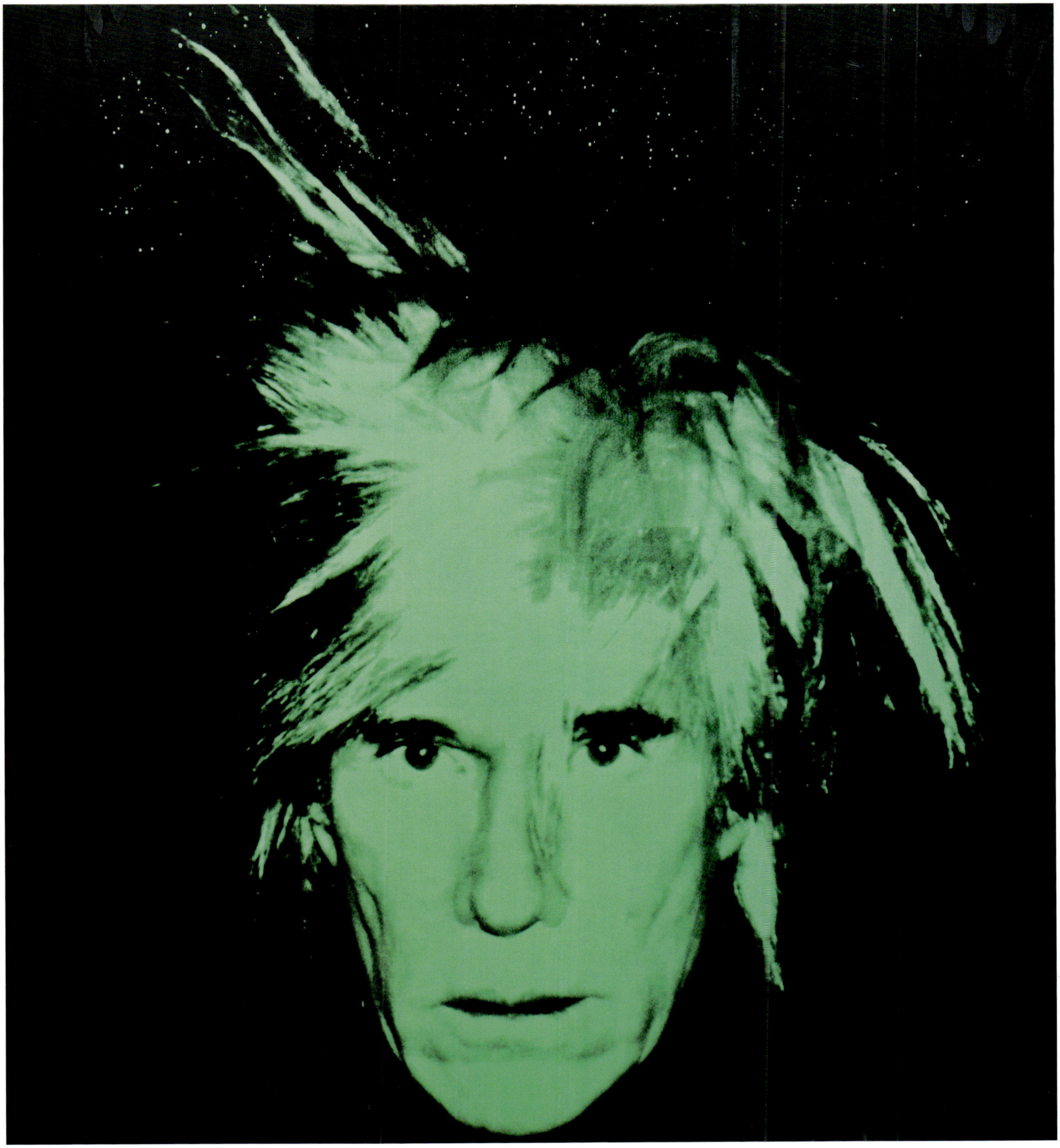

65. *Self-Portrait*, 1986. Acrylic and silkscreen ink on canvas, 106 x 106 in. (269.2 x 269.2 cm). Solomon R. Guggenheim Museum, New York, Gift, Anne and Anthony d'Offay, 1992

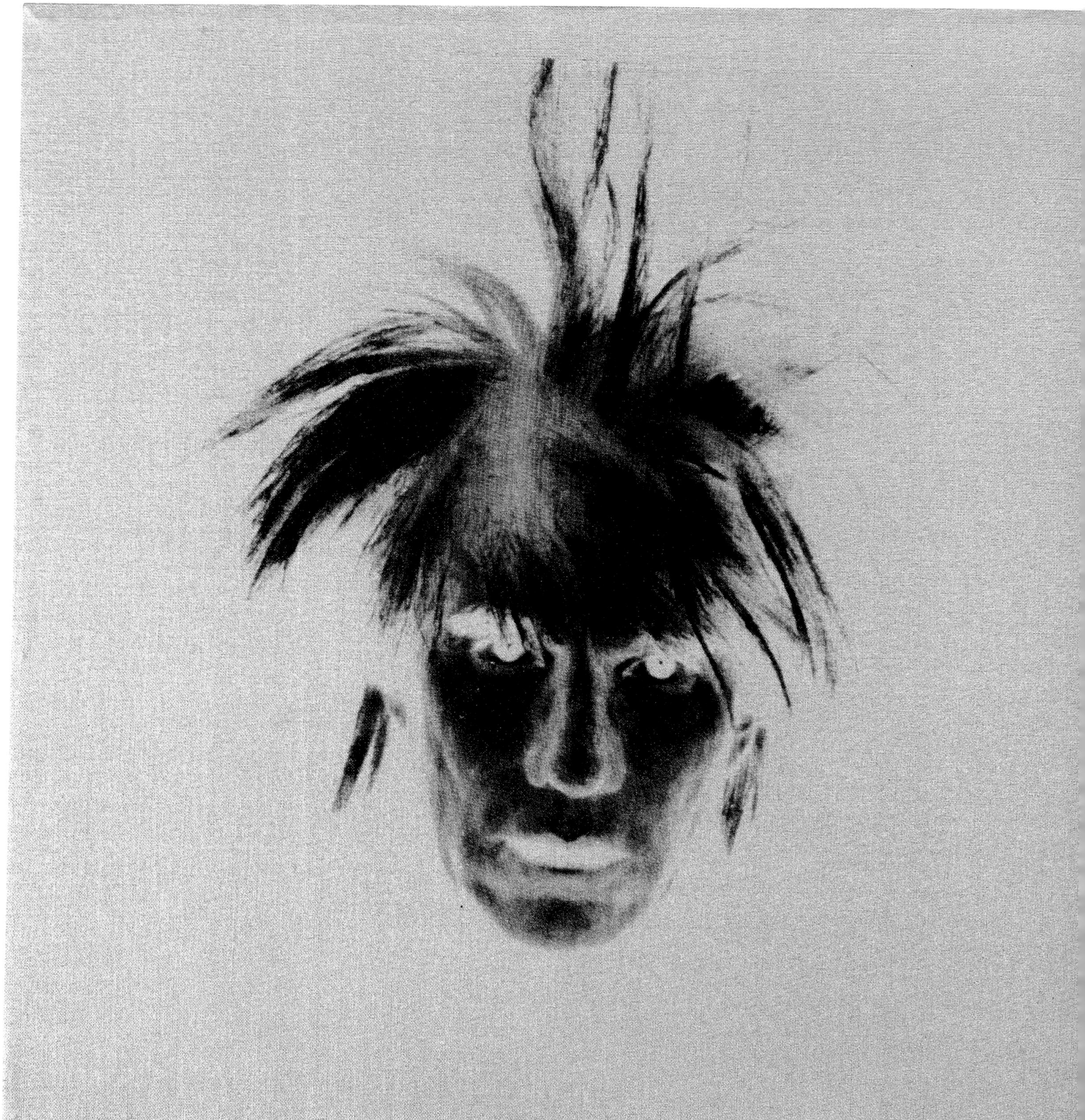

66. *Self-Portrait*, 1986. Acrylic and silkscreen ink on linen, 14 x 14 in. (35.6 x 35.6 cm). The Andy Warhol Museum, Pittsburgh; Founding Collection, Contribution The Andy Warhol Foundation for the Visual Arts, Inc.

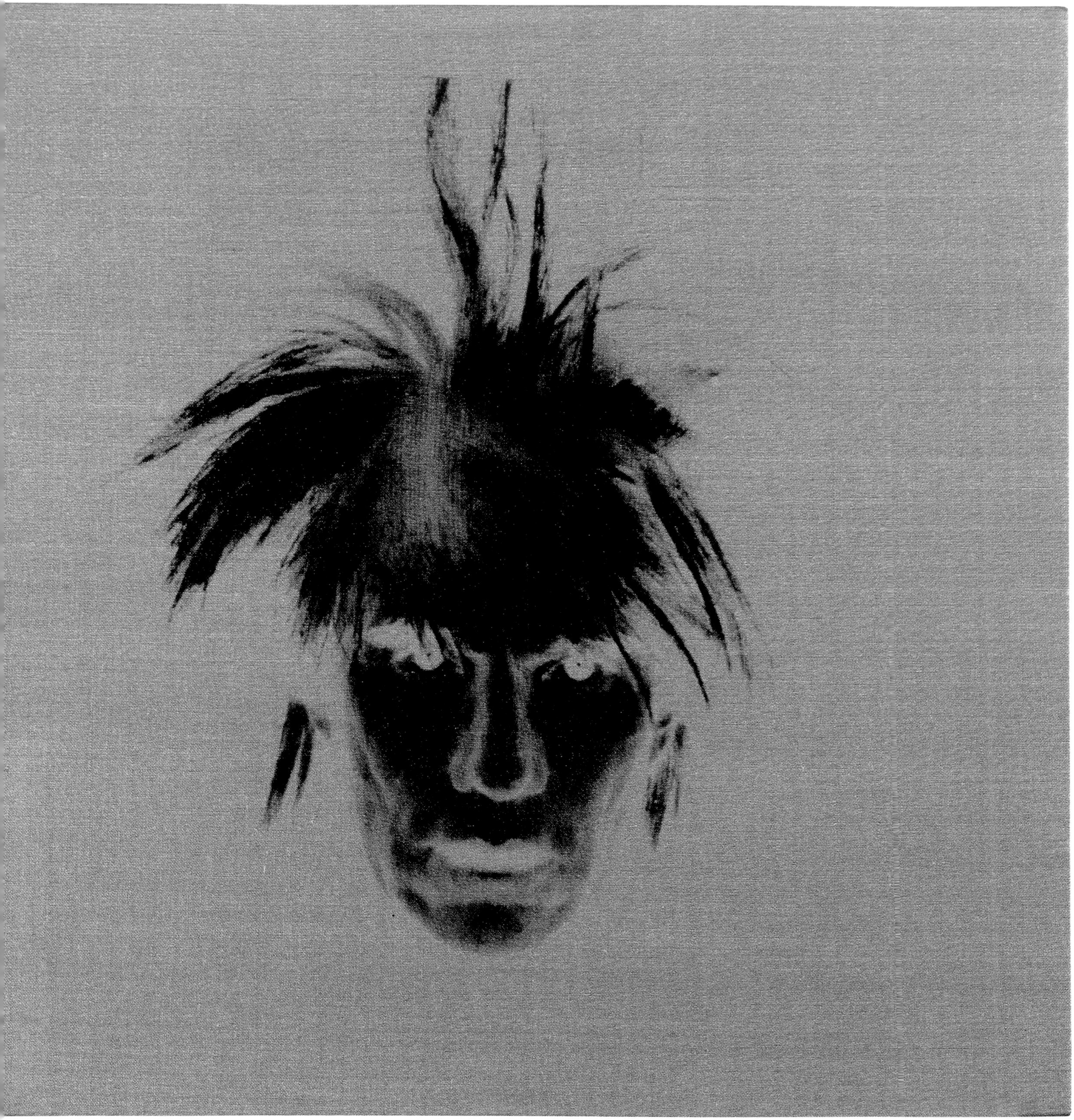

67. *Self-Portrait*, 1986. Acrylic and silkscreen ink on linen, 14 x 14 in. (35.6 x 35.6 cm). The Andy Warhol Museum, Pittsburgh; Founding Collection, Contribution The Andy Warhol Foundation for the Visual Arts, Inc.

68. *Self-Portrait*, 1986. Acrylic and silkscreen ink on linen, 80 x 76 in. (203.2 x 193 cm). The Andy Warhol Museum, Pittsburgh; Founding Collection, Contribution The Andy Warhol Foundation for the Visual Arts, Inc.

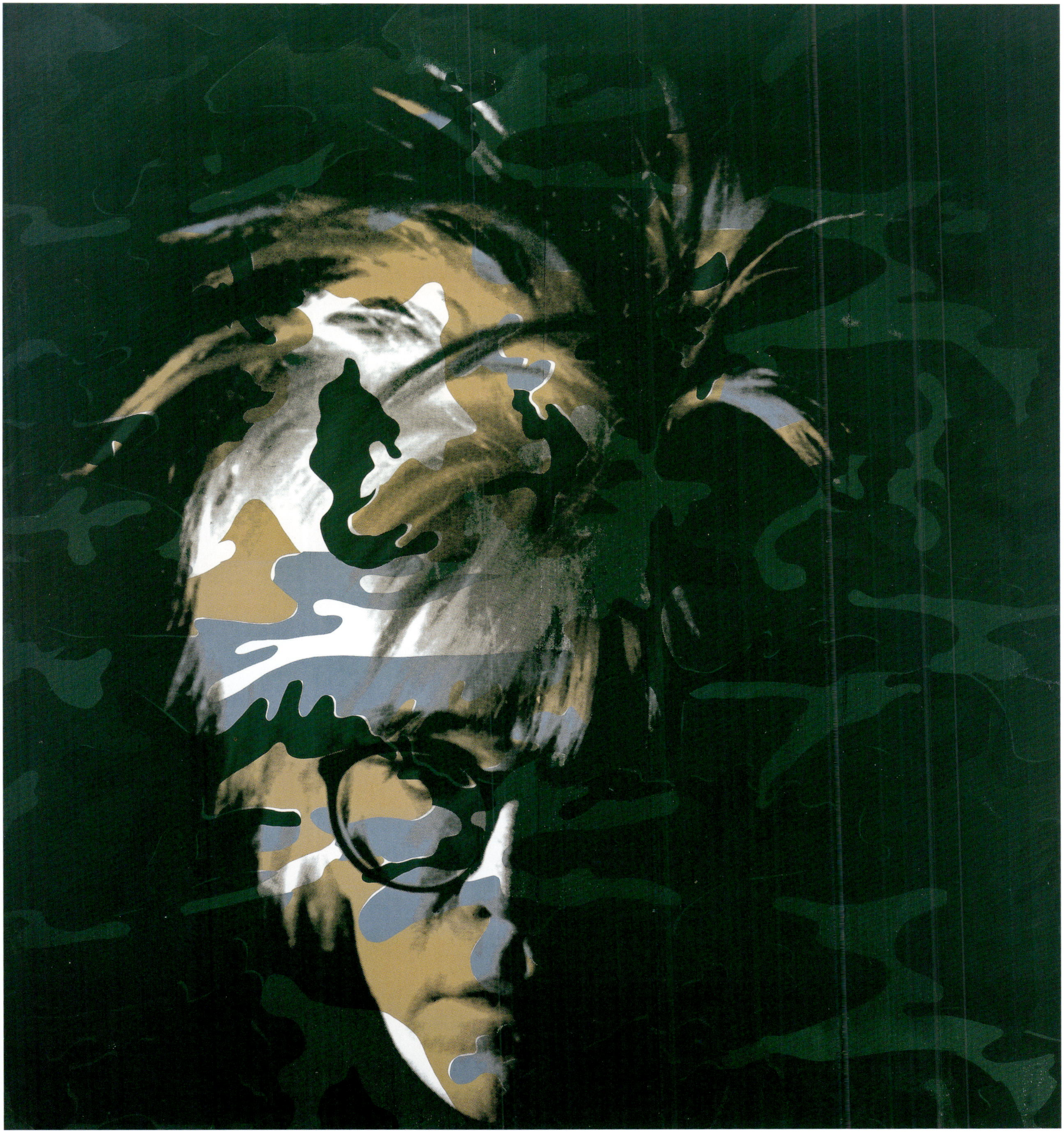

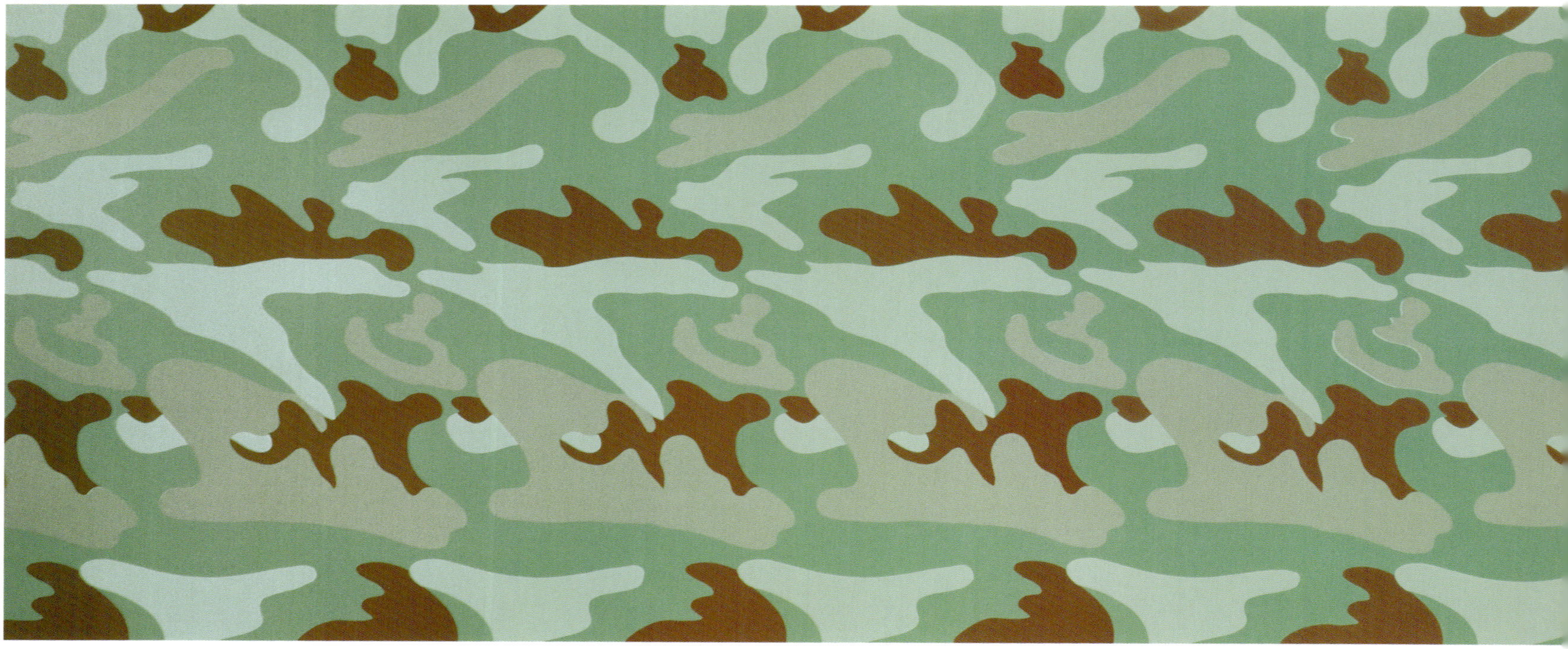

69. *Camouflage*, 1986. Acrylic and silkscreen ink on canvas, 79⅞ x 400 in. (203 x 1016 cm). Private collection

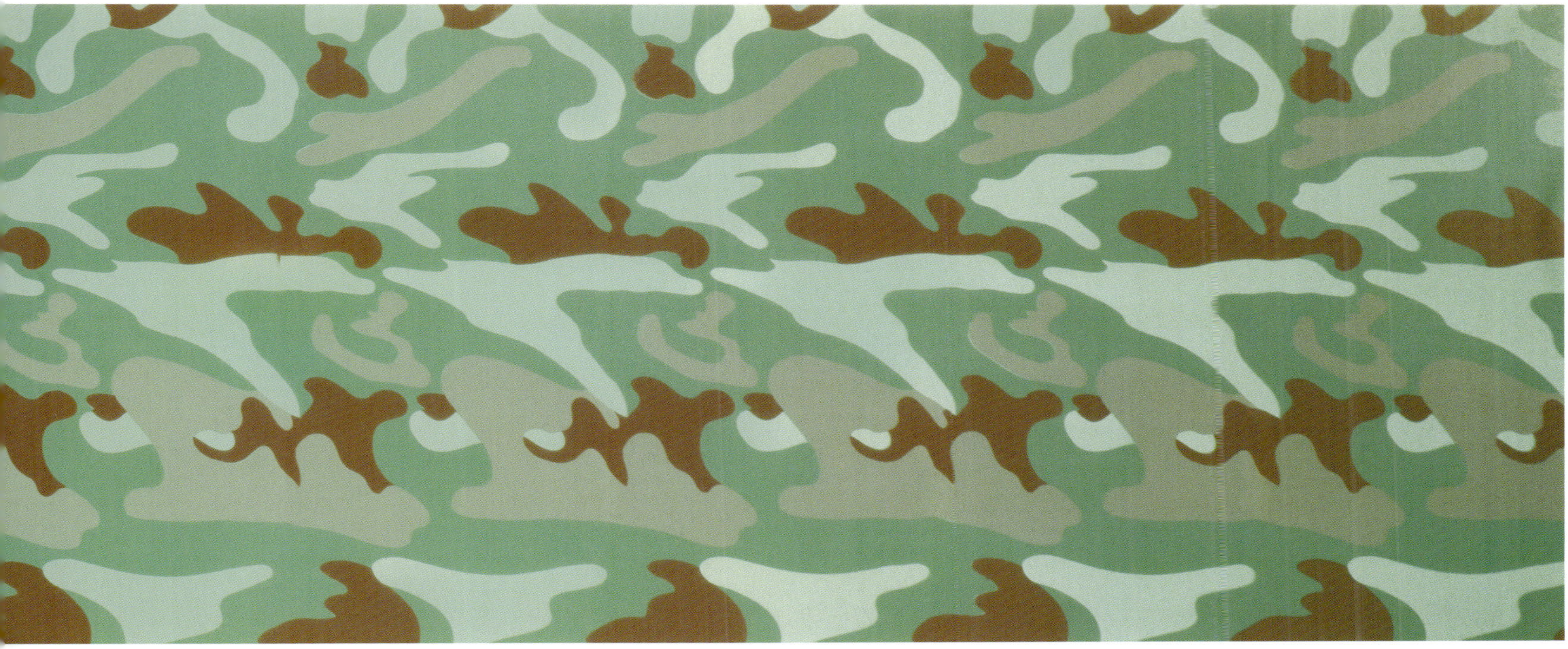

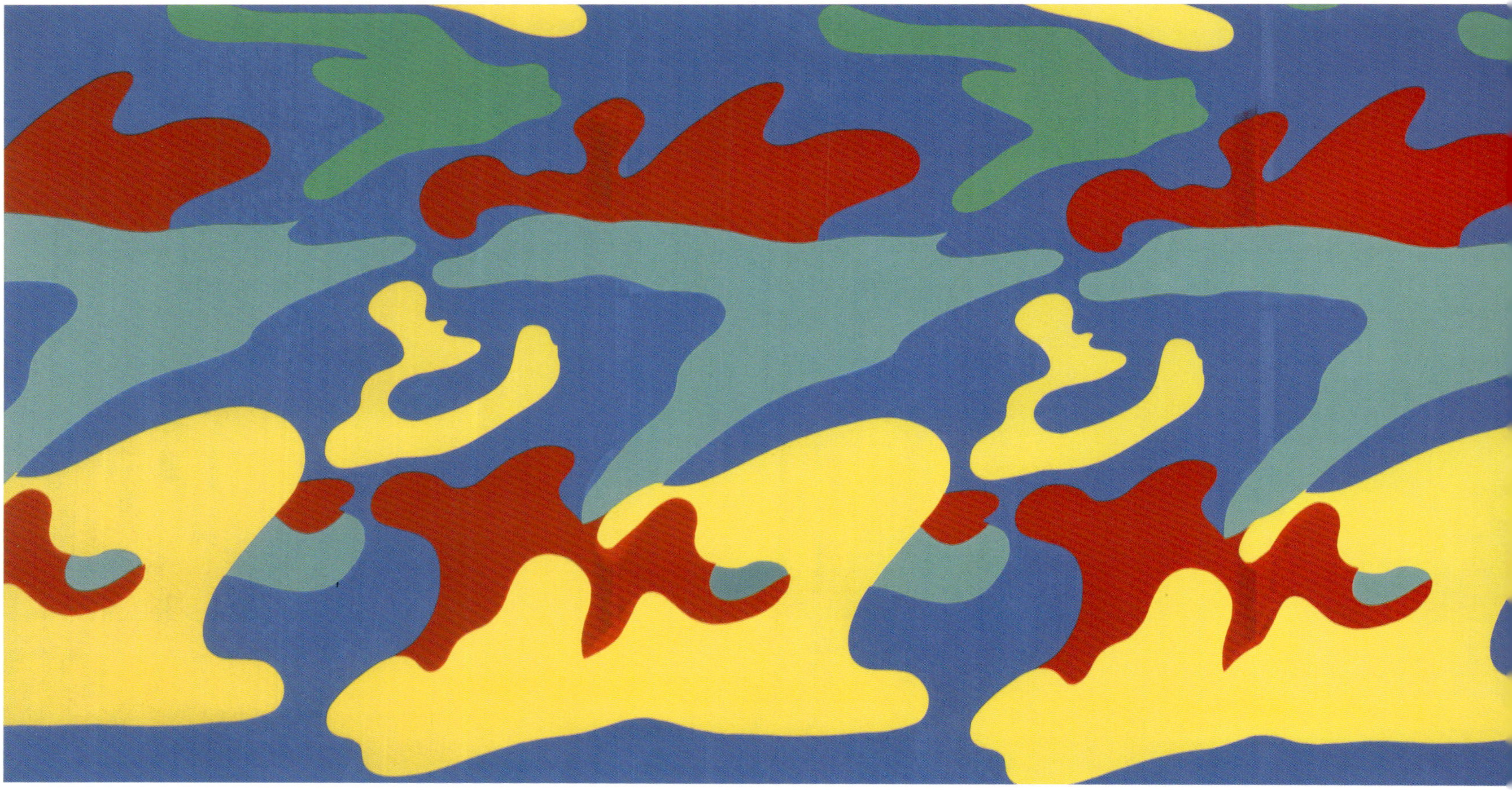

70. *Camouflage*, 1986. Acrylic and silkscreen ink on canvas, 50 x 198 in. (127 x 502.9 cm). Private collection

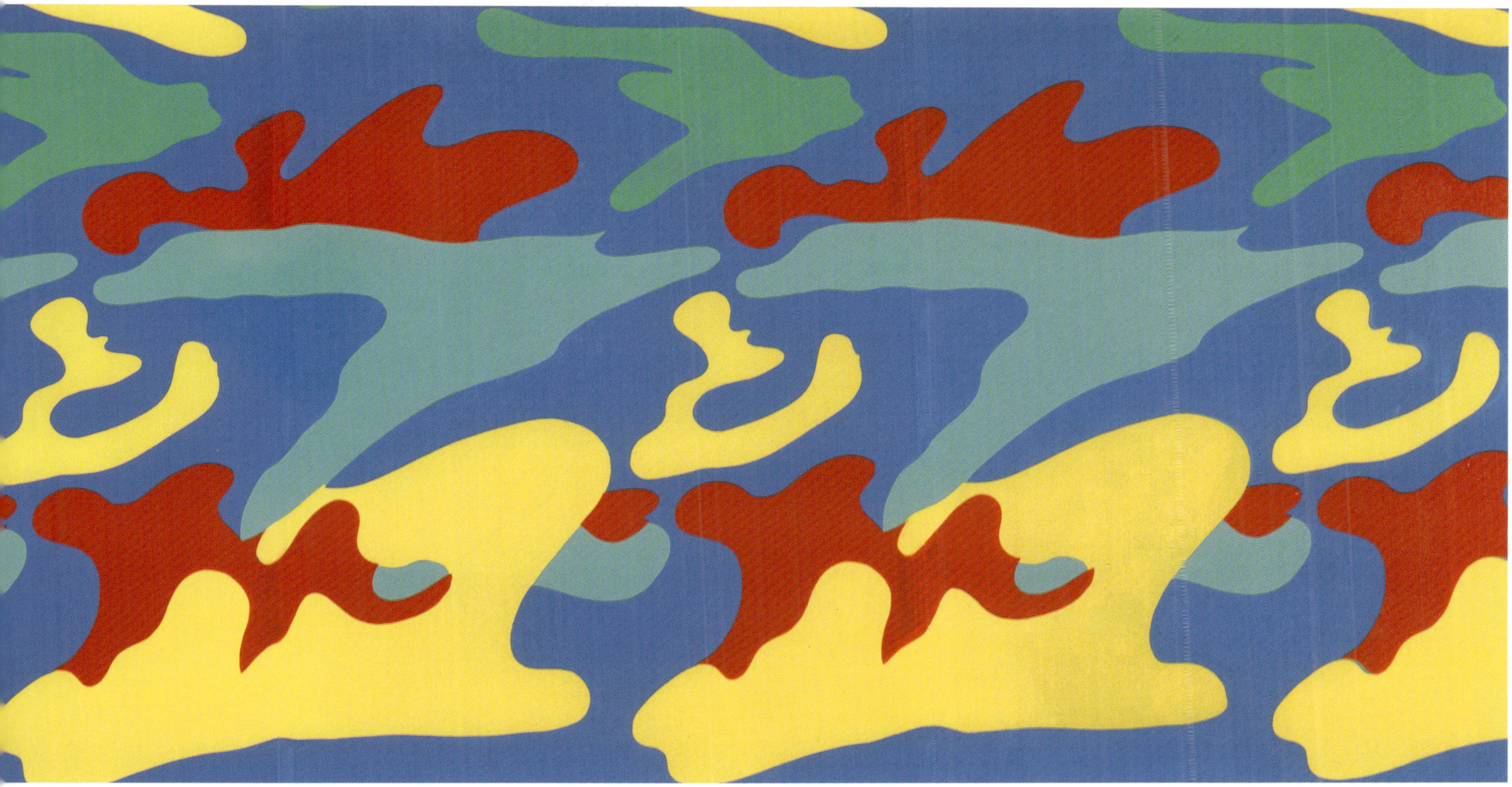

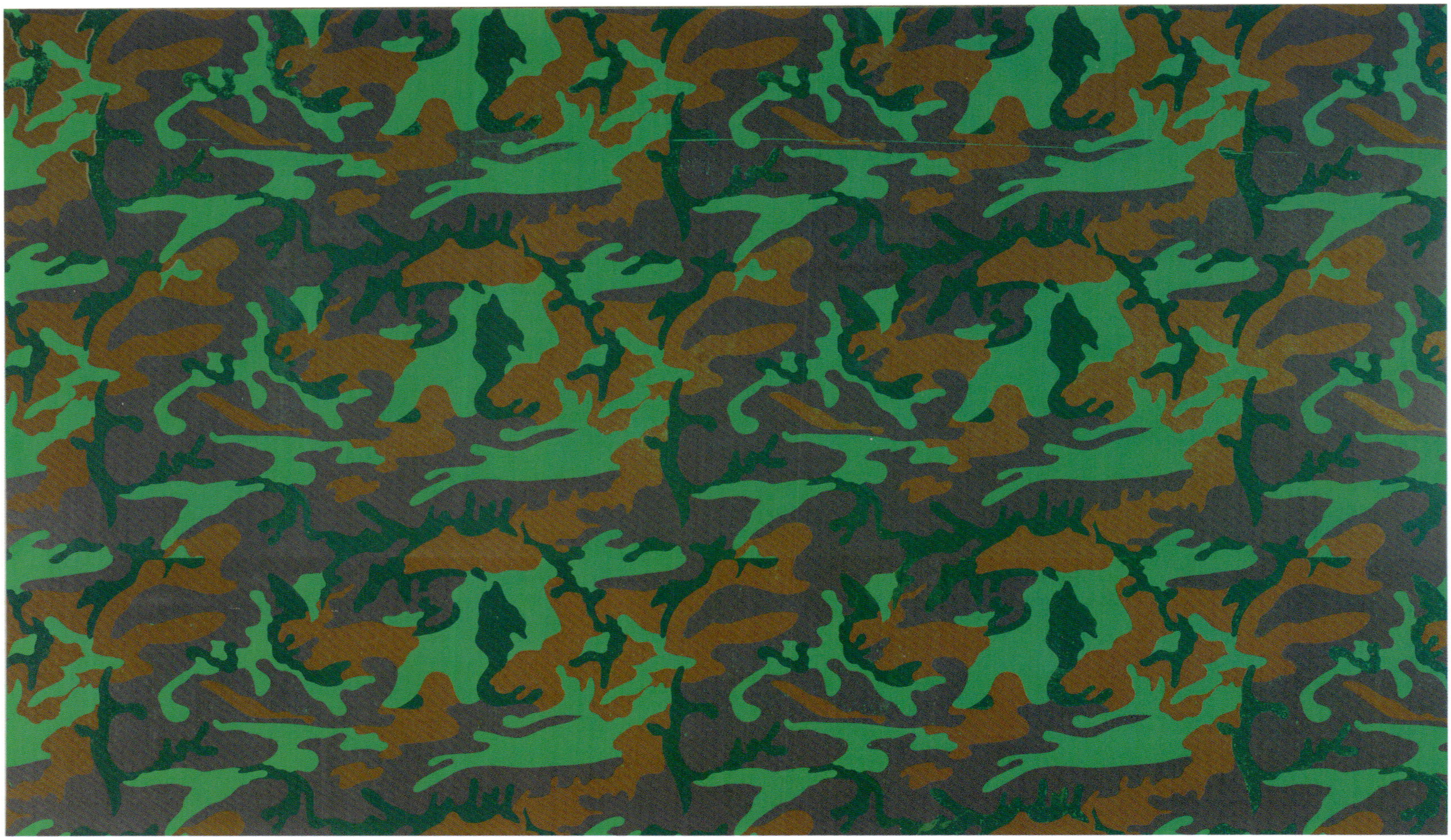

71. *Camouflage*, 1986. Acrylic and silkscreen ink on canvas, 116 x 200 in. (294.6 x 508 cm). The Baltimore Museum of Art: Purchase with funds provided by Esther and Richard Pearlstone through the Pearlstone Family Fund; and partial gift of The Andy Warhol Foundation for the Visual Arts, Inc.

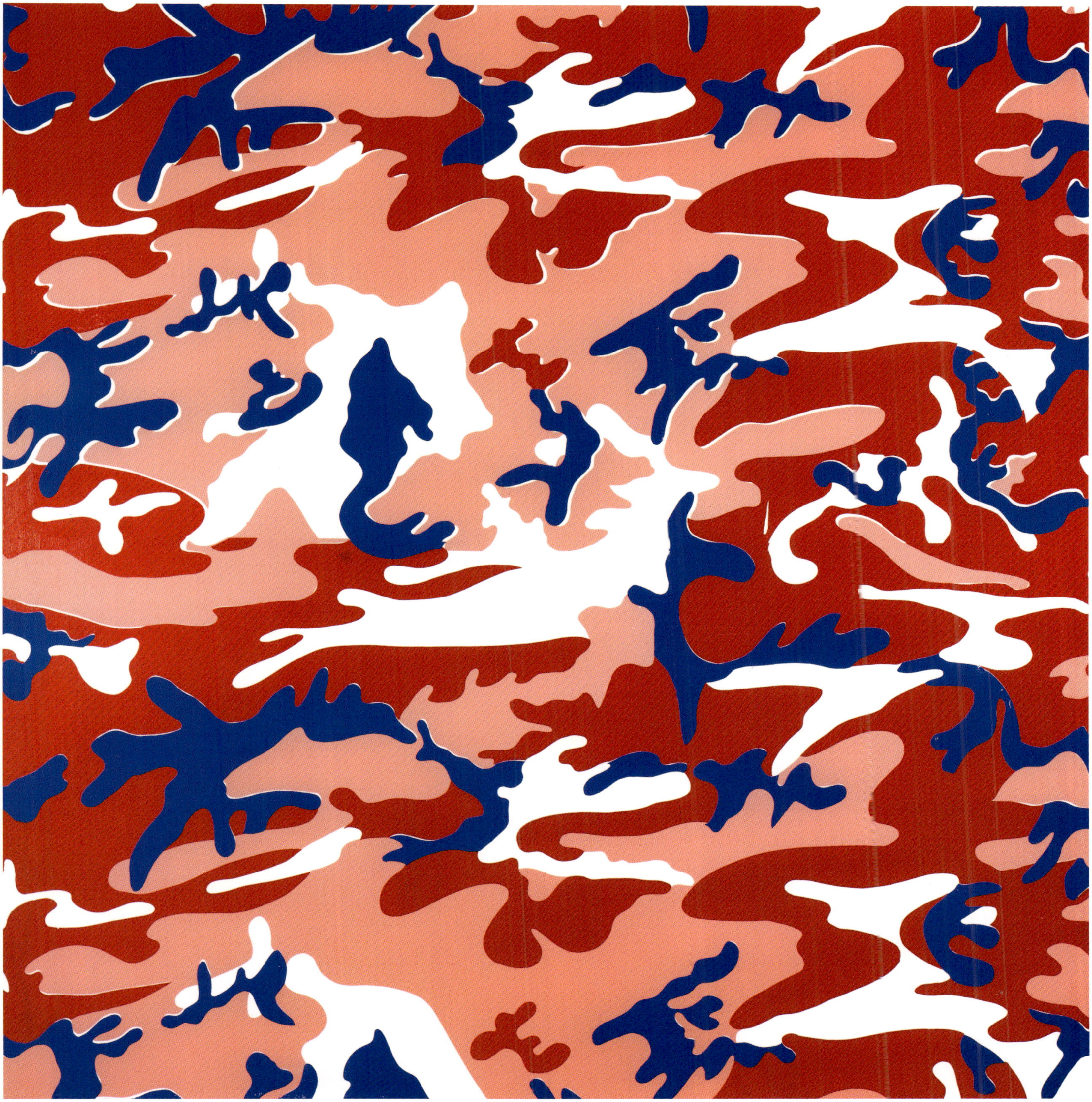

72. *Camouflage*, 1986. Acrylic and silkscreen ink on linen, 80¼ x 76¼ in. (203.8 x 193.7 cm). The Andy Warhol Museum, Pittsburgh; Founding Collection, Contribution The Andy Warhol Foundation for the Visual Arts, Inc.

73. *Camouflage*, 1986. Acrylic and silkscreen ink on linen, 76 x 76 in. (193 x 193 cm). Collection of Ealan Wingate and Batsheva Ostrow

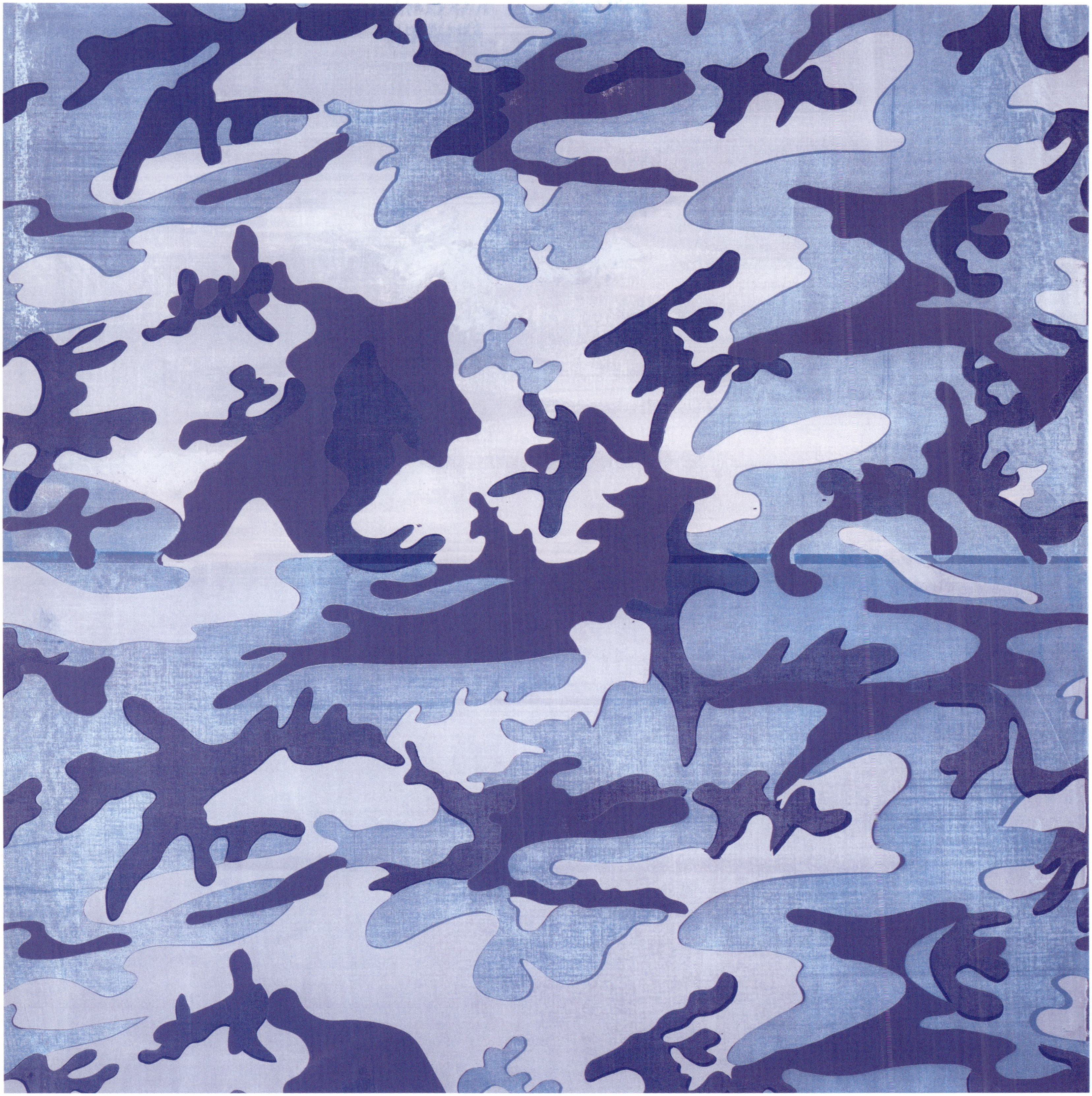

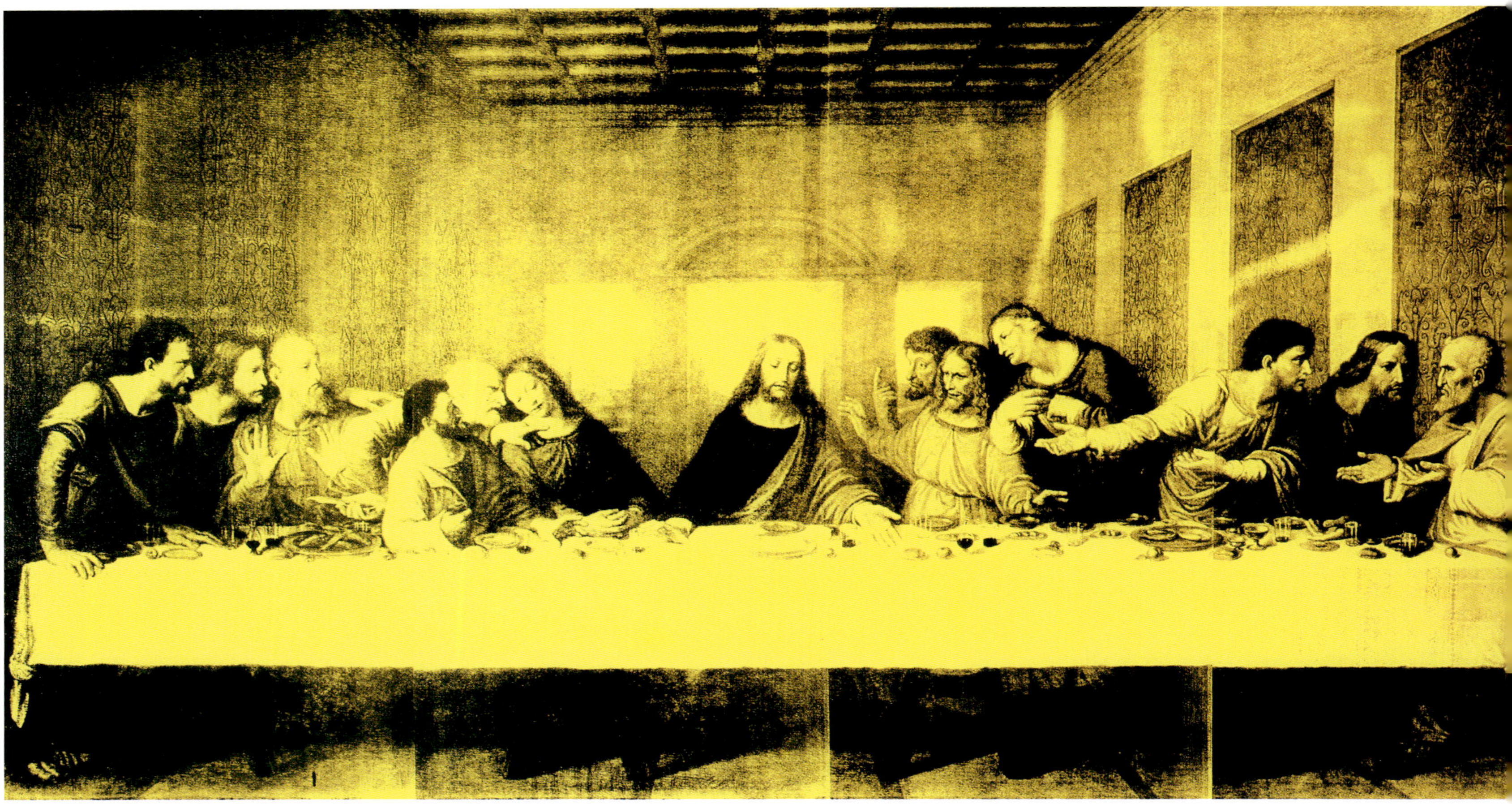

74. *The Last Supper*, 1986. Acrylic and silkscreen ink on linen, 78 x 306 in. (198 x 777 cm). The Baltimore Museum of Art: Harry A. Bernstein Memorial Collection, by exchange

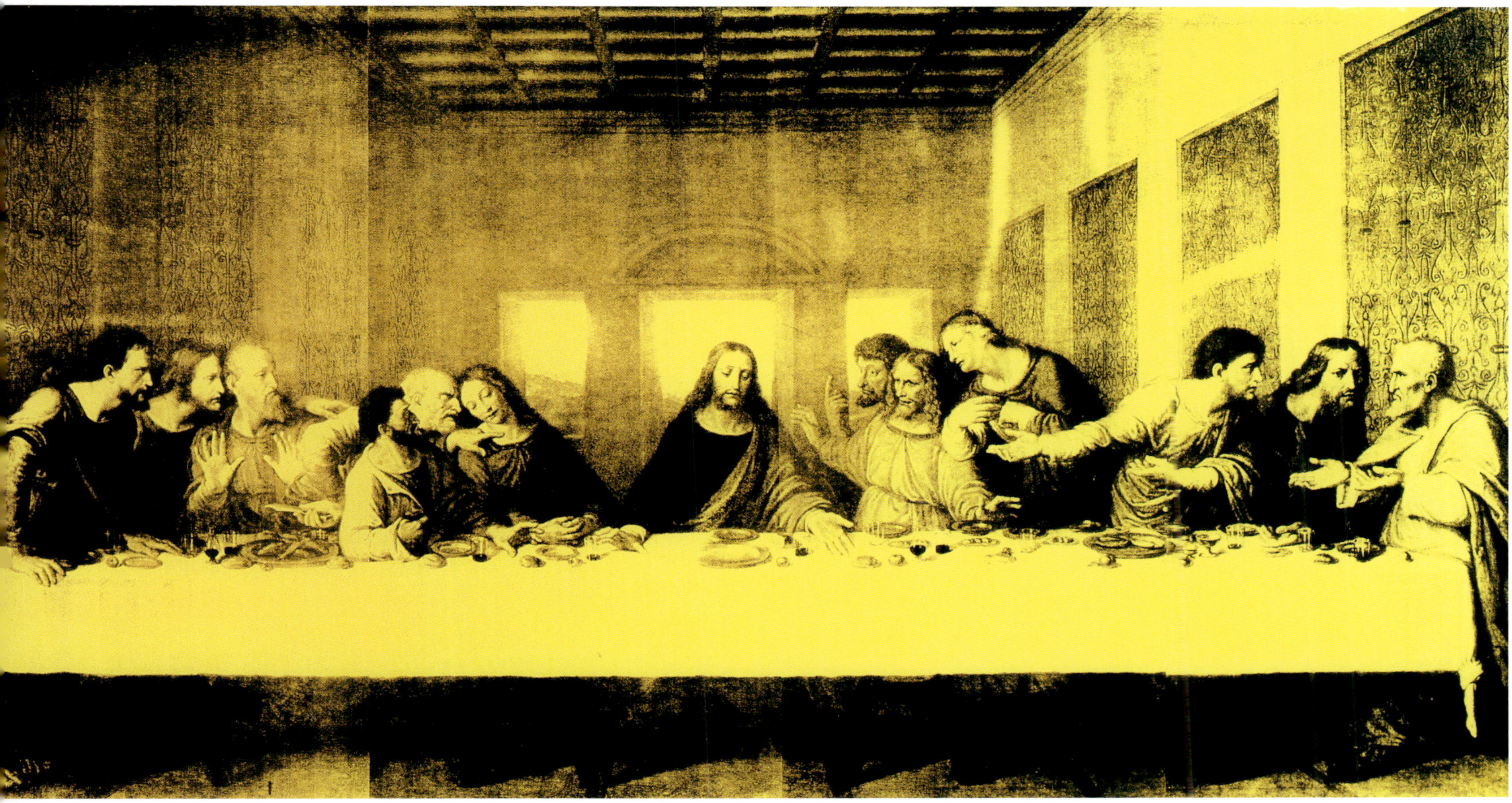

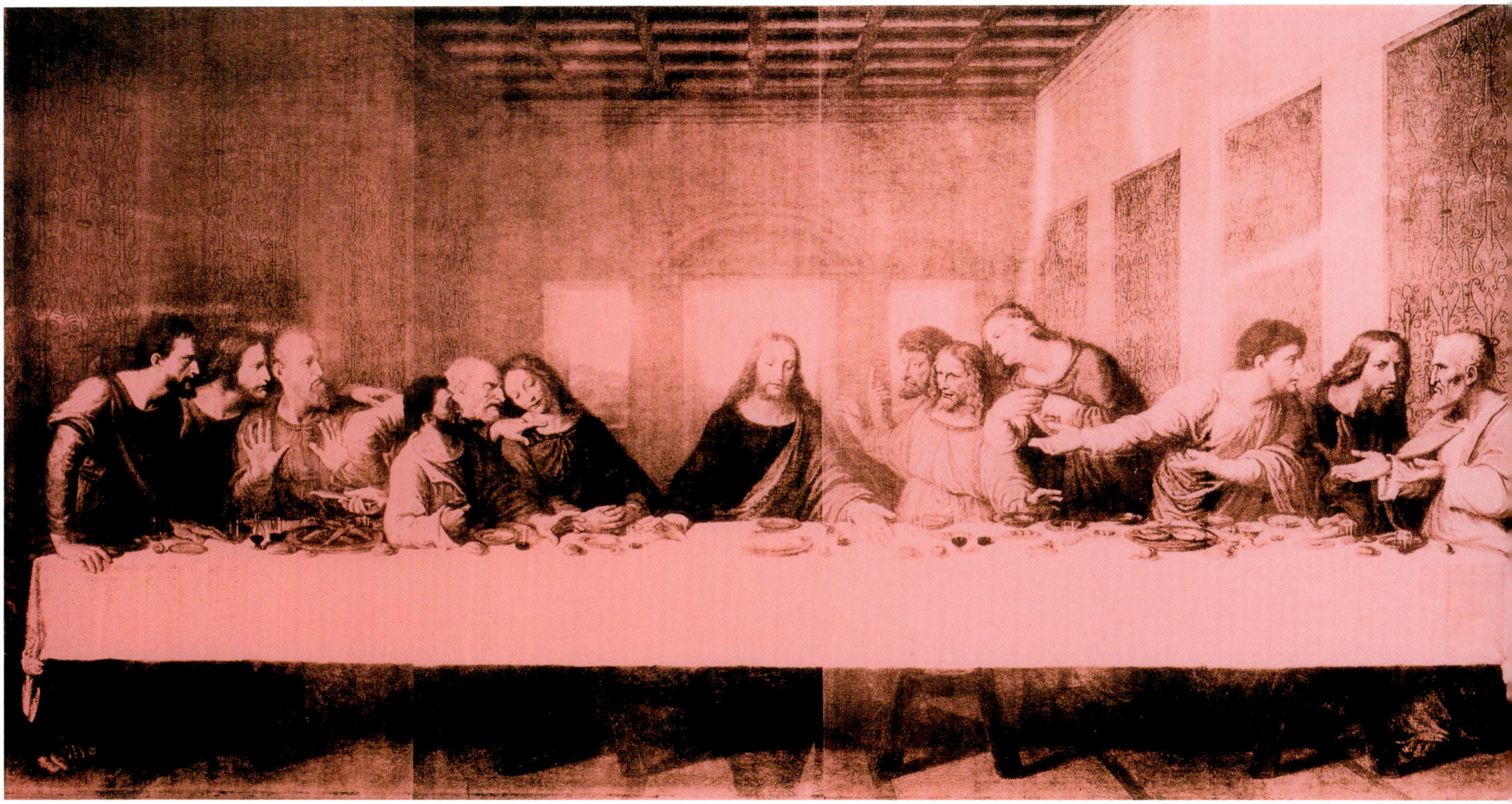

75. *The Last Supper*, 1986. Acrylic and silkscreen ink on linen, 78 x 306 x 2 in. (198.1 x 777.2 x 5.1 cm). The Andy Warhol Museum, Pittsburgh; Founding Collection, Contribution The Andy Warhol Foundation for the Visual Arts, Inc.

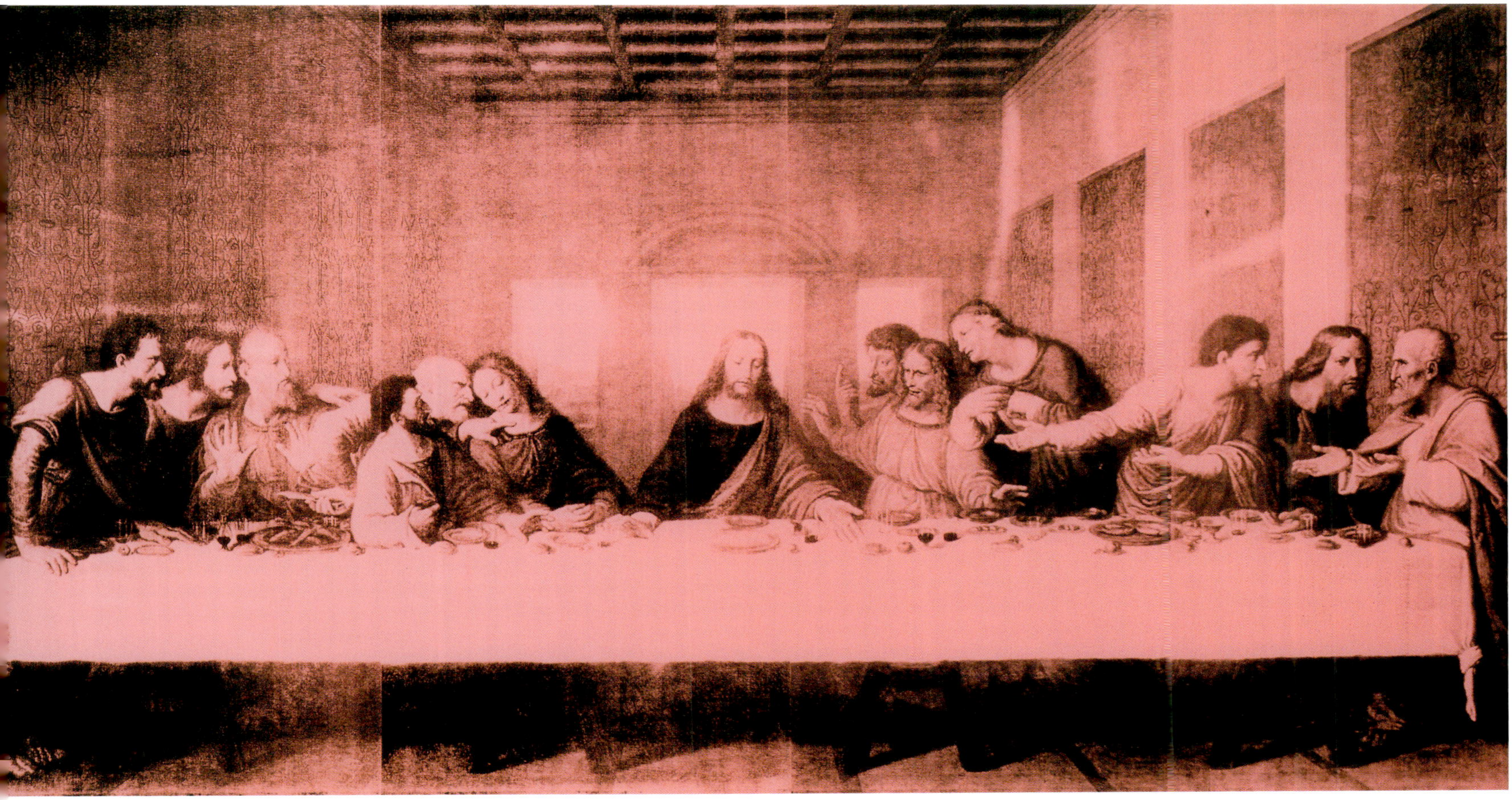

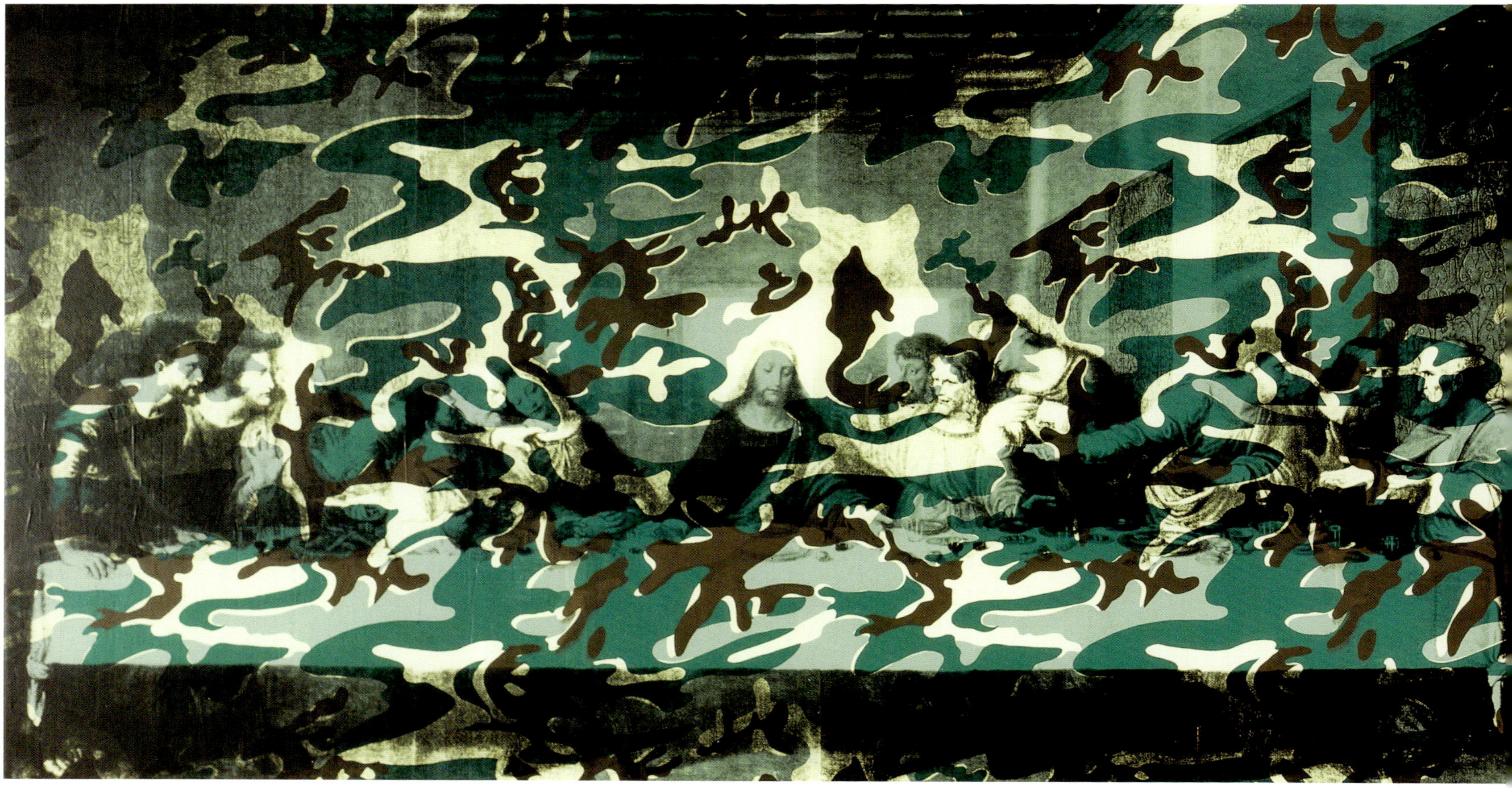

76. *Camouflage Last Supper*, 1986. Acrylic and silkscreen ink on canvas, 78 x 306 in. (198.1 x 777.2 cm). The Menil Collection, Houston, gift of The Andy Warhol Foundation for the Visual Arts, Inc.

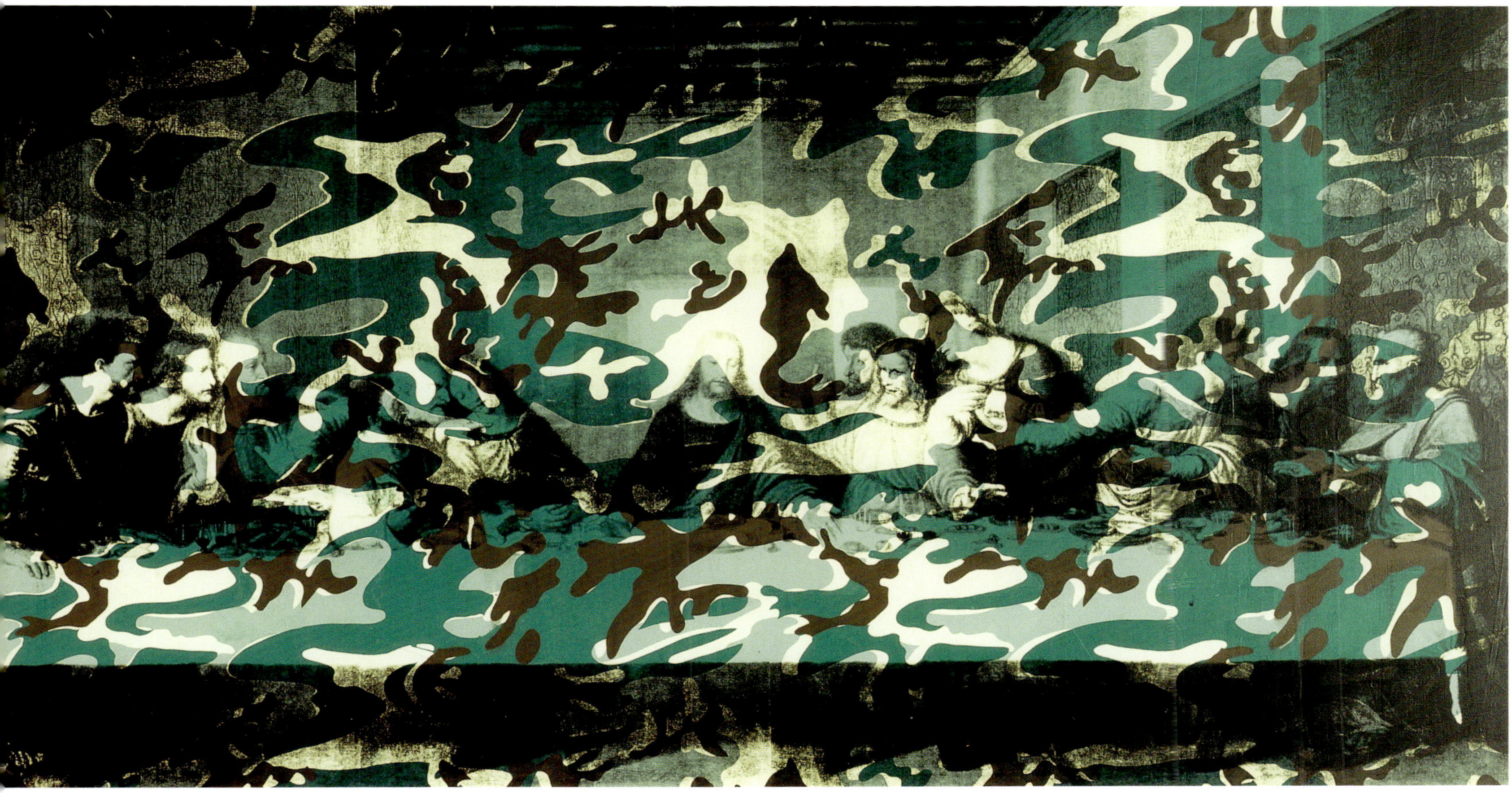

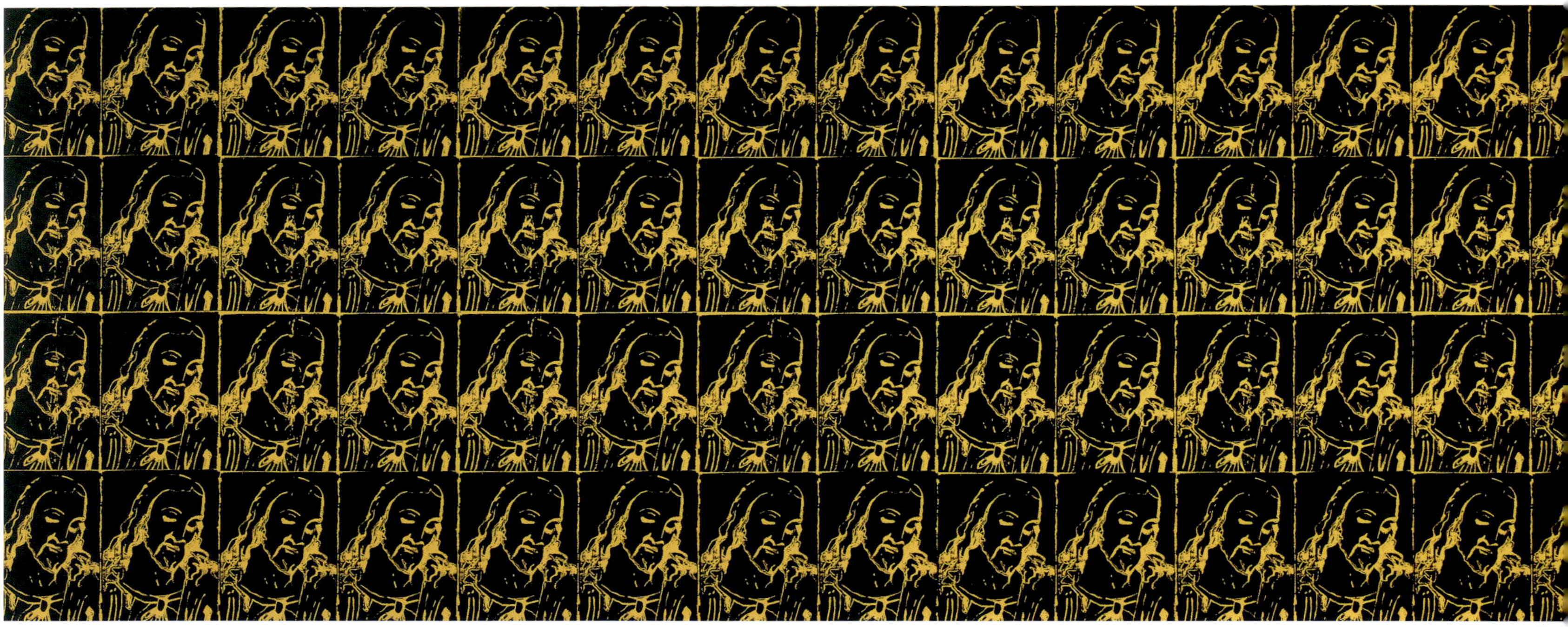

77. *Detail of the Last Supper (Christ 112 Times)*, 1986. Acrylic and silkscreen ink on canvas, 80 x 421 in. (203.2 x 1069.3 cm). Mugrabi Collection

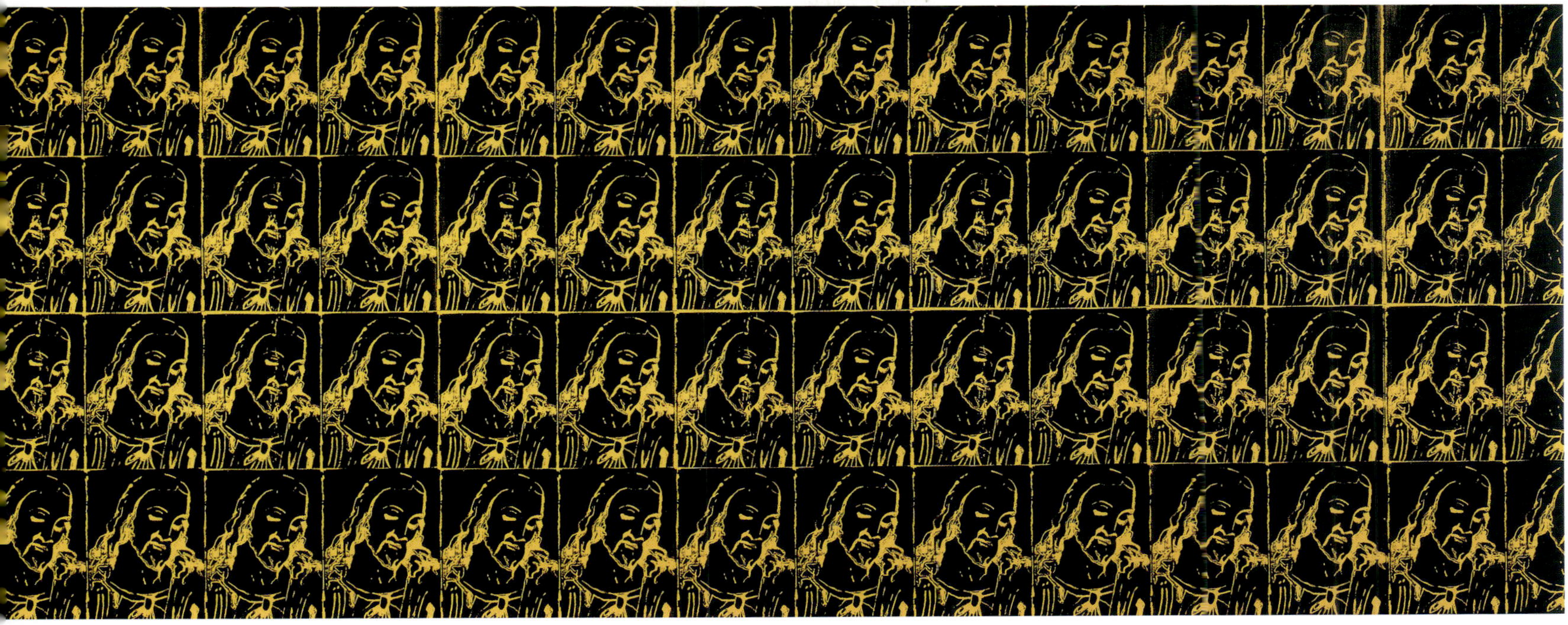

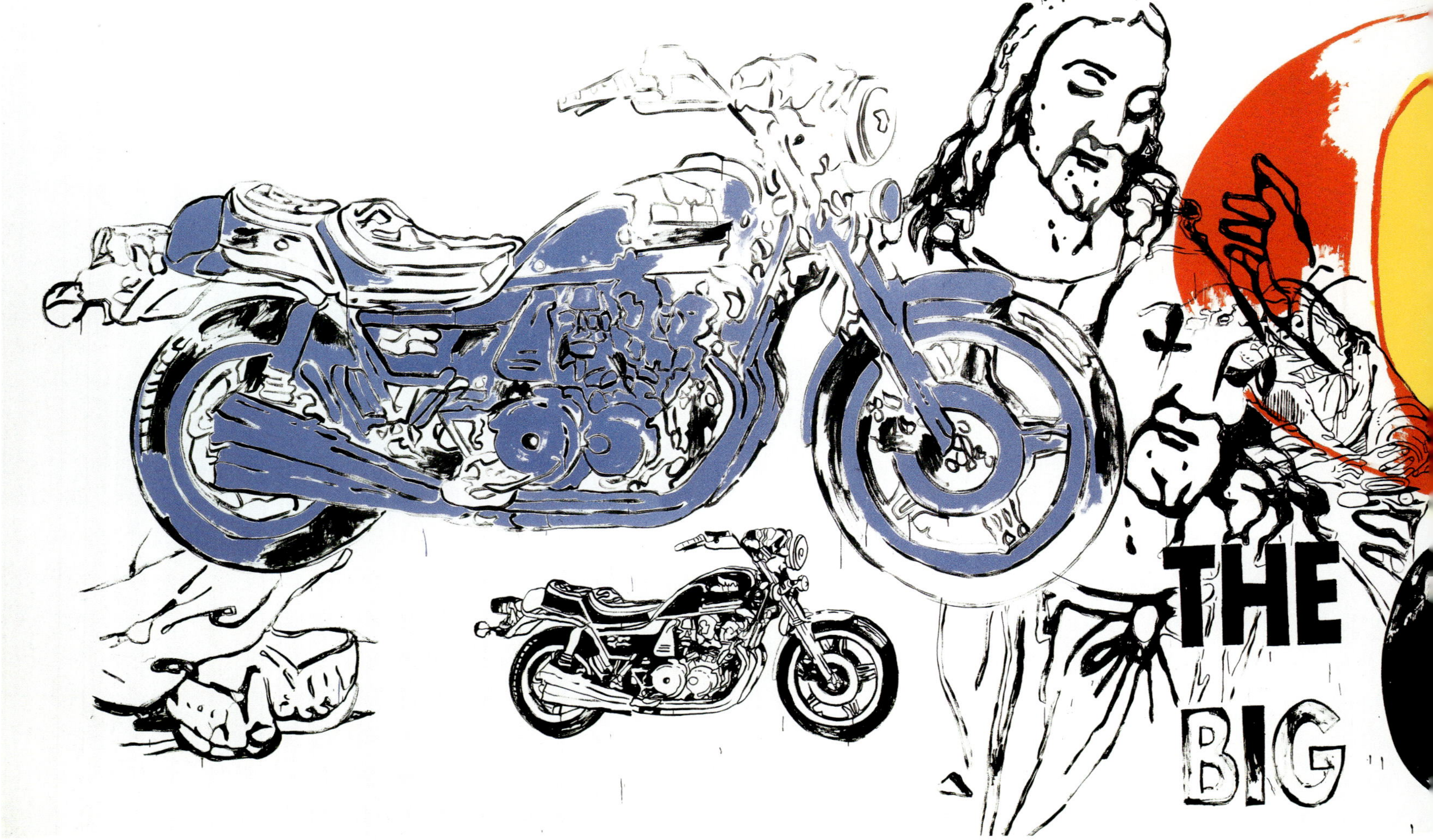

78. *The Last Supper*, 1986. Acrylic and silkscreen ink on linen, 116 x 390 x 2 in. (294.6 x 990.6 x 5.1 cm). The Andy Warhol Museum, Pittsburgh; Founding Collection, Contribution The Andy Warhol Foundation for the Visual Arts, Inc.

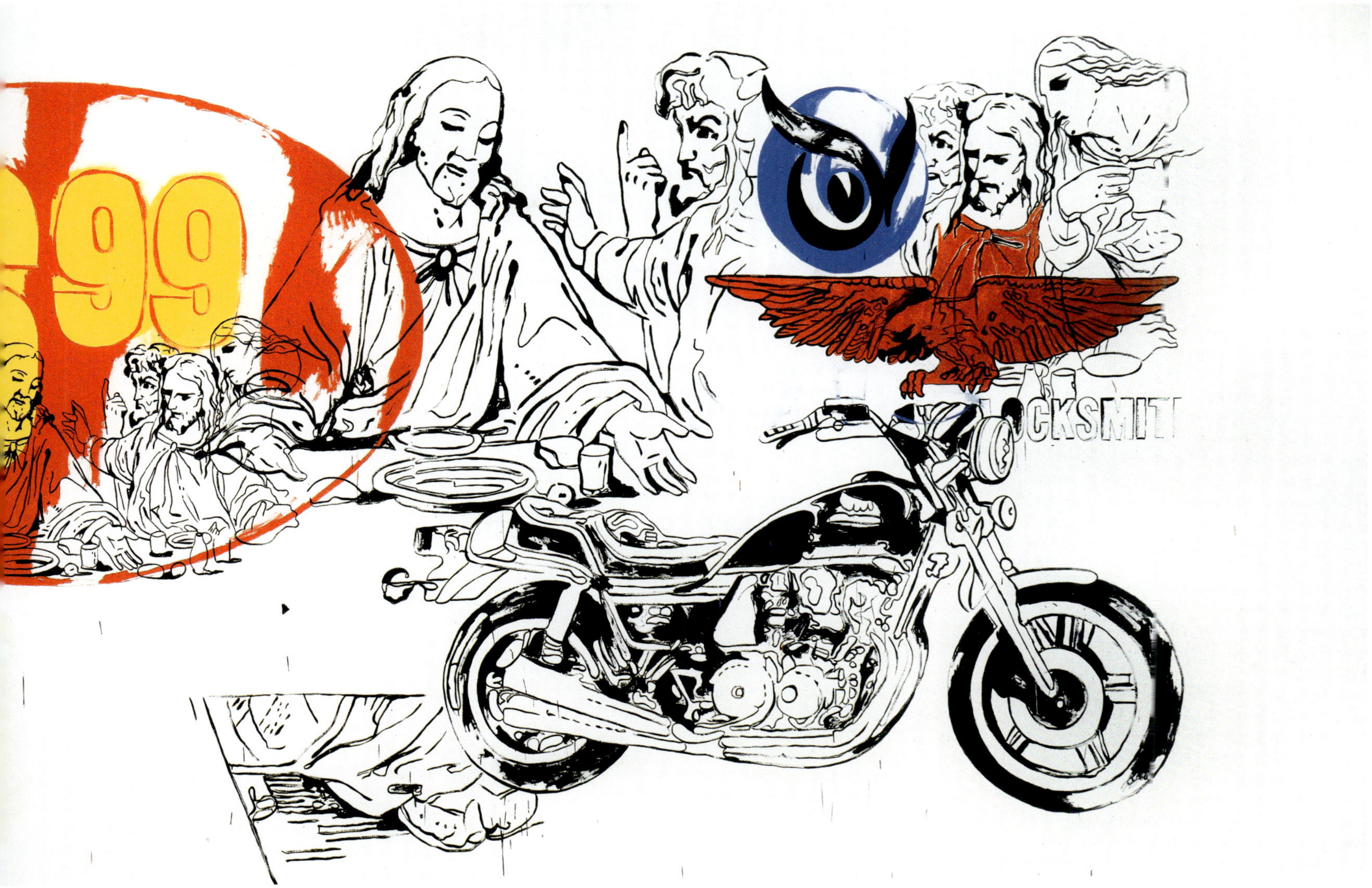
99

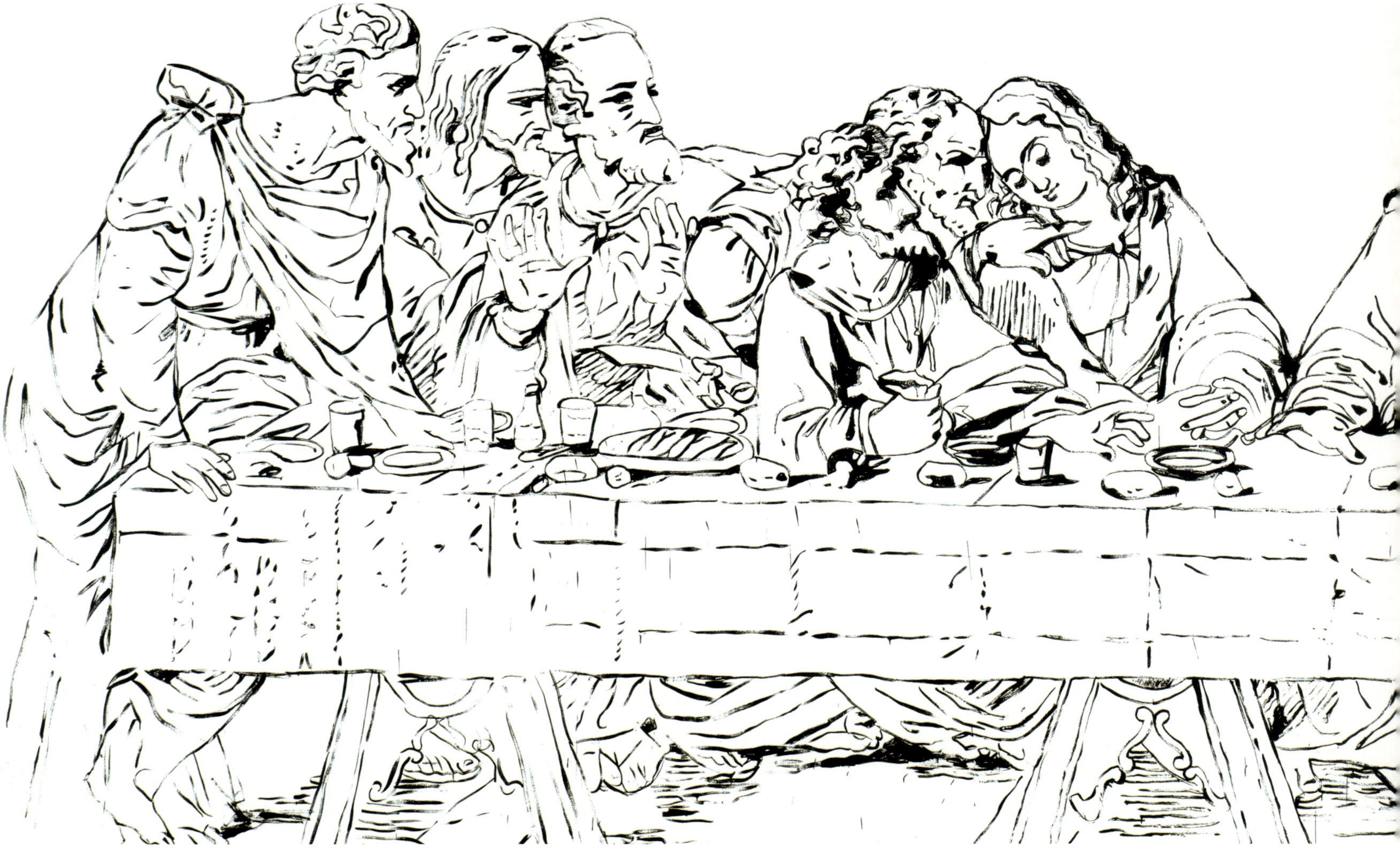

79. *The Last Supper*, 1986. Acrylic on canvas, 116 x 396 in. (294.6 x 1005.8 cm). The Stephanie and Peter Brant Foundation, Greenwich, Connecticut

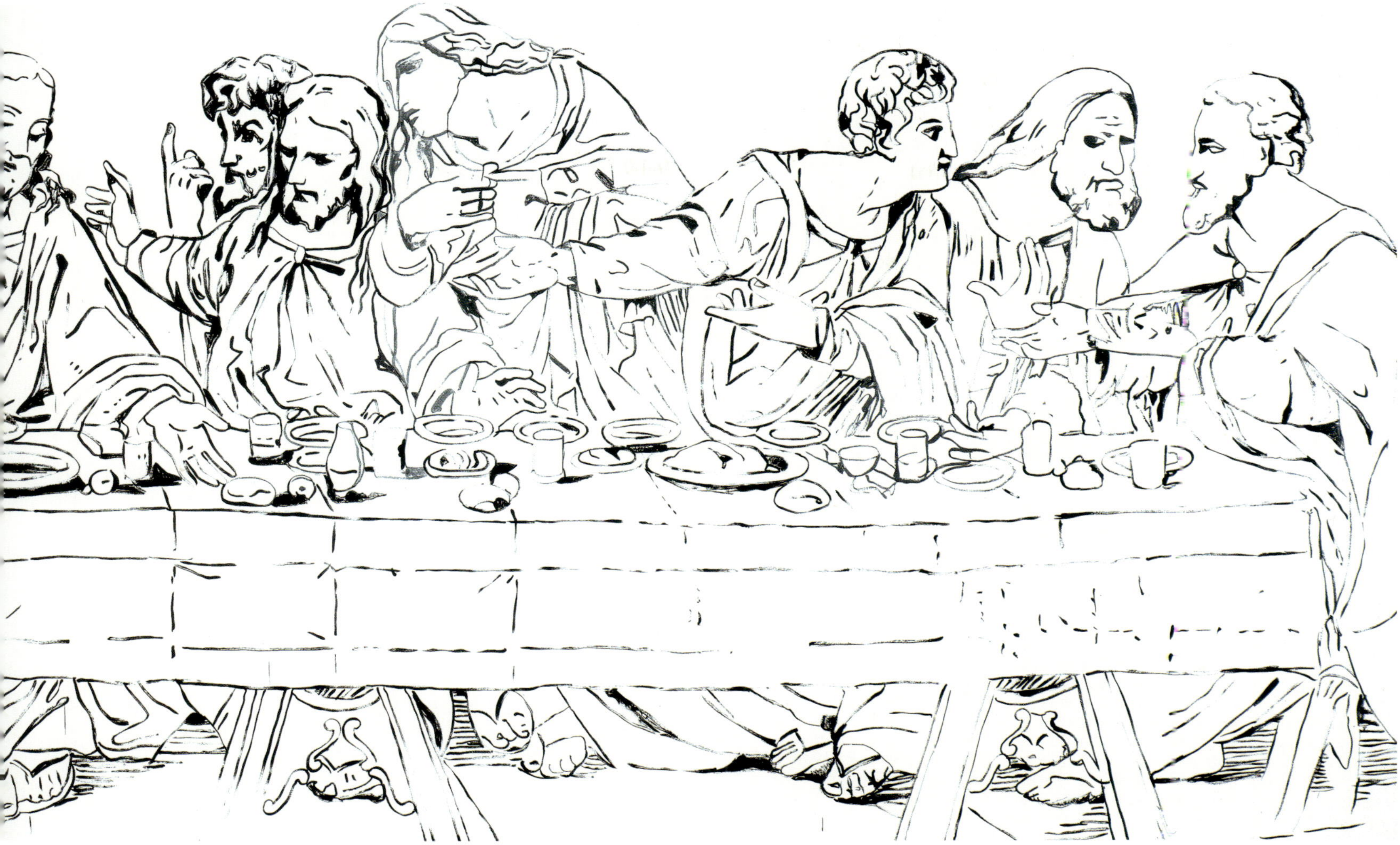

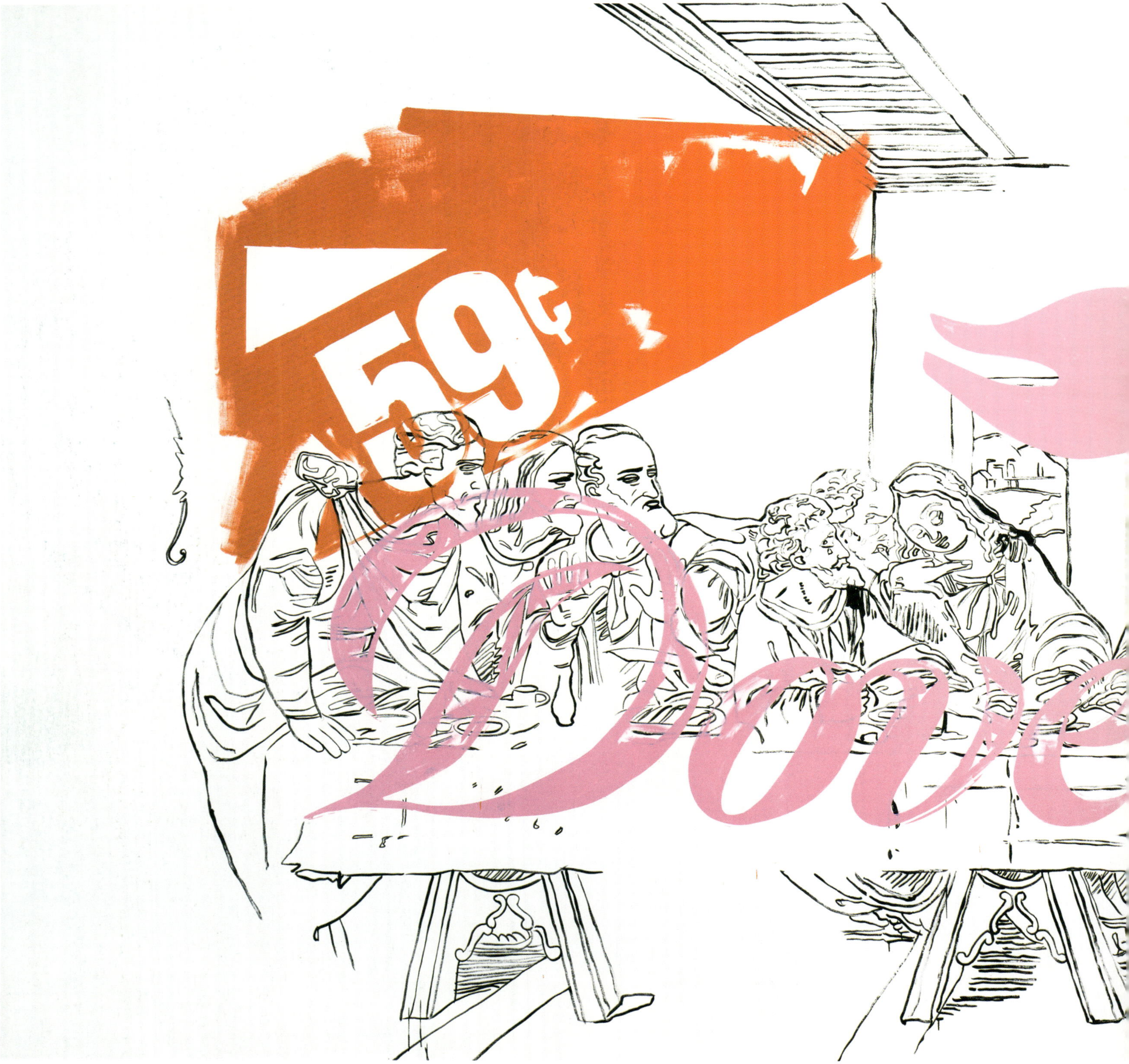

80. *The Last Supper*, 1986. Acrylic on canvas, 119¼ x 263¼ in. (302.9 x 668.7 cm). The Museum of Modern Art, New York, Gift of the Andy Warhol Foundation for the Visual Arts

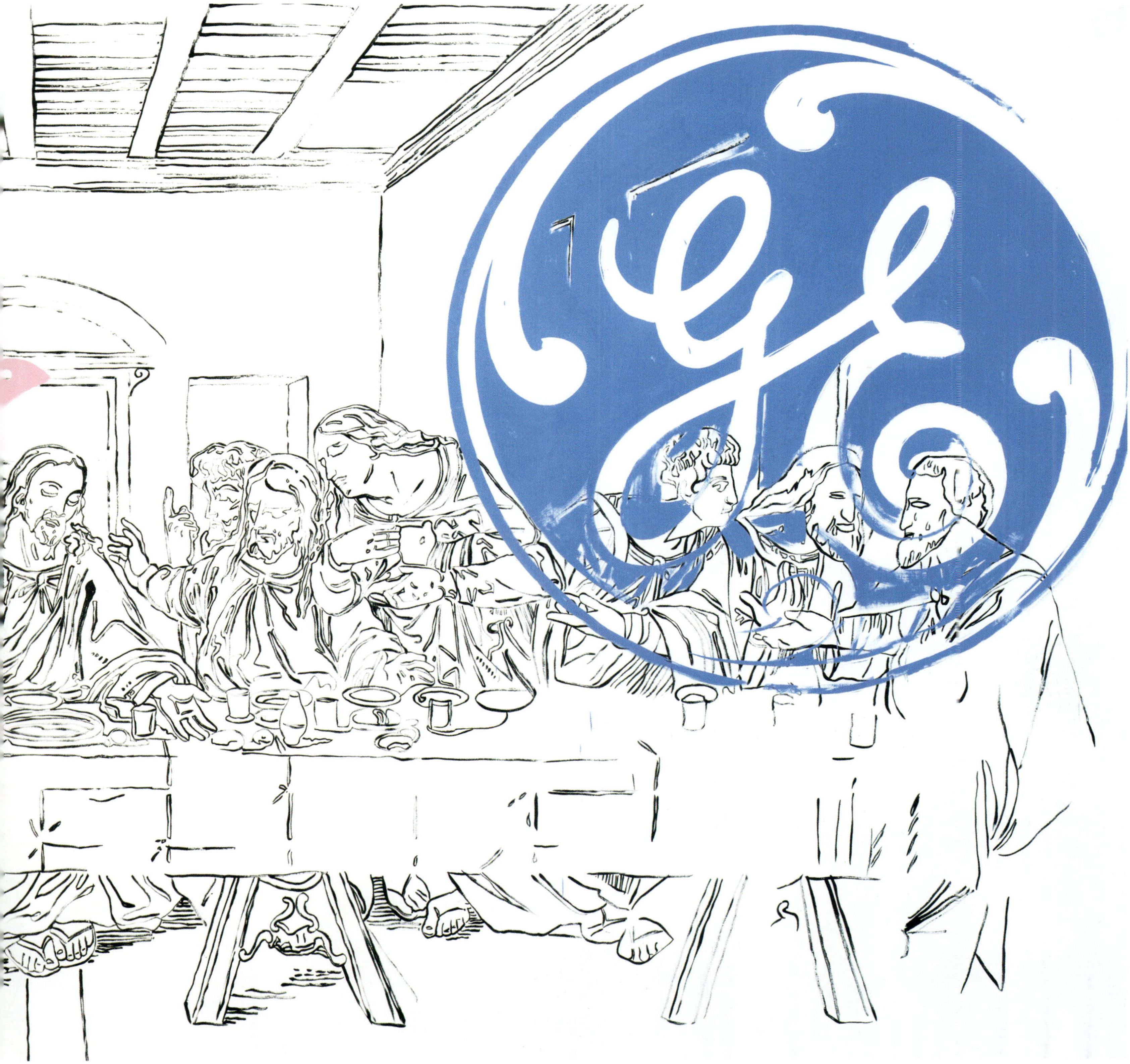

Shadow Paintings

Julian Schnabel

When Larry Gagosian sent me the photographs of the unseen *Shadow* paintings, I held them up to the light and all of my language about Andy Warhol's work seemed to disappear. There is almost nothing on them. Yet they seem to be pictures of something and as full of imagery as any of Andy's other paintings. These paintings embody the art historical landscape of postwar American painting as well as any other landscape I can think of; the rings around Saturn, fog lifting off a lake near Mount Fuji, the edge of the world or any other psychological one for that matter. There is not that much paint on them. And as is always the case, some would say they are not even paintings. In order to understand Andy's work, it is not enough just to show his versatility crowded together, the way they did in his retrospective at the Museum of Modern Art [1989], as if to say, look at all the stuff he thought up. Just because Andy made Pop art, it didn't mean his work had to be shown in a supermarket. You need enough space around it to understand the sublime gesture of its diamond bullet to the brain.

We can thank the Museum of Modern Art for assembling so many of Andy's great paintings. Better late than never, but the exhibition failed in unearthing anything that we didn't already know about his work. Although the catalogue contained many of Andy's late paintings, it is remarkable what a poor understanding and lack of attention and space were given to this work in the show. Why not just nail the guy's coffin shut and say he was good in the sixties? Not true. There was more consideration given to the wallpaper than to a perspective into the painterly concerns of an artist who was also a great painter.

Andy's paintings seem self-explanatory, simple but beyond definition. They have usually been described or appreciated by critics and curators in terms of the images he selected to paint and to their connection to the photographic image: a gangster painting, a movie star painting, an atomic bomb painting. Sometimes there are no brushstrokes. The only trace of paint other than a cover coat for the surface—also the ground—is the color for the photographic image printed on top of it.

This lack of luscious paint and obvious handmade marks has often served to mislead the audience as to the image of Andy's paintings—they are not just printed pictures that are on canvas.

Much of the discussion of Andy's work is based on the mass-produced, the multi-image, the recognizable subject, a Marilyn, a soup can, Mao, flowers, a hammer and sickle, any subject you pick it, and he might say, okay I'll make you

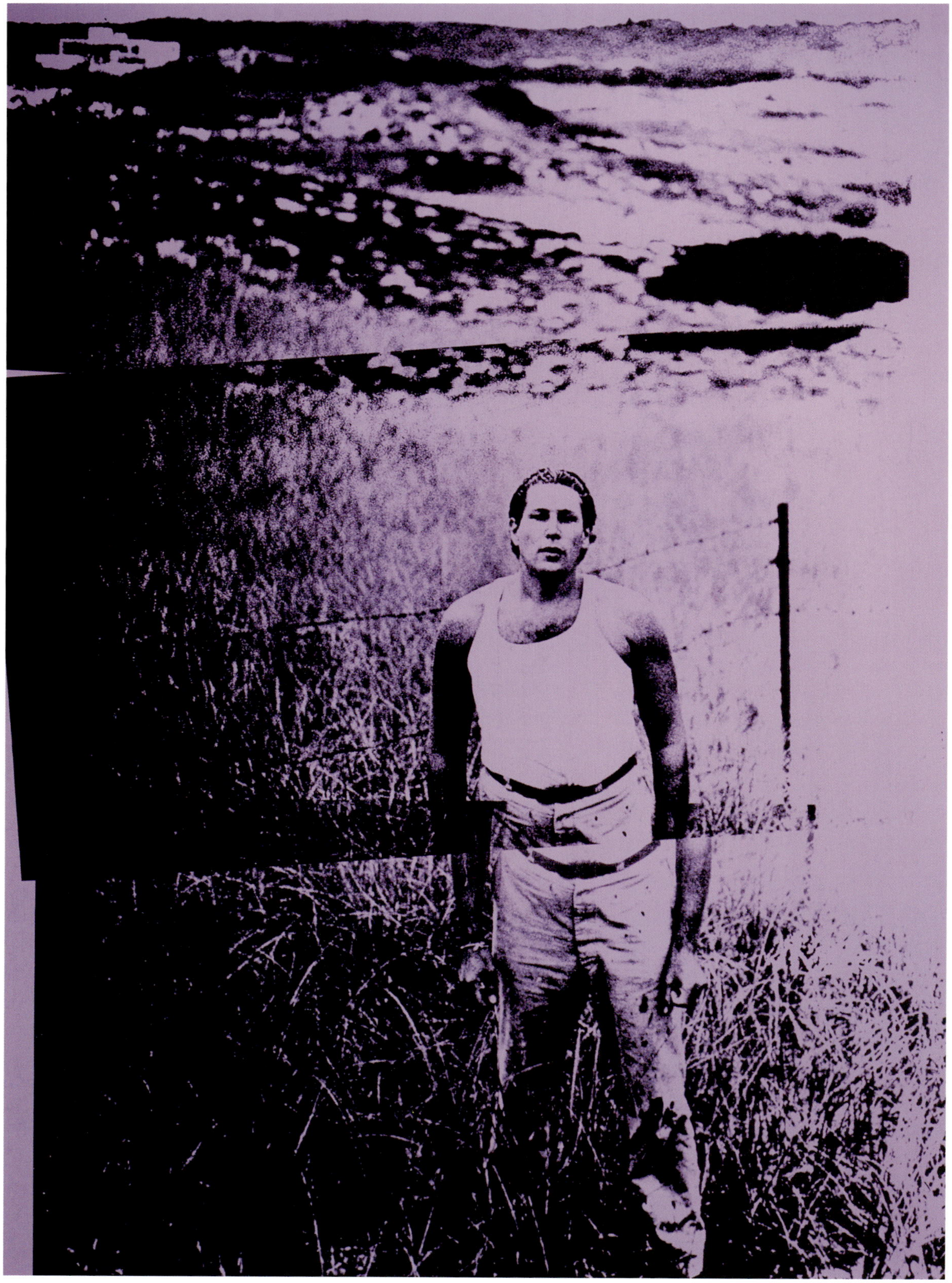

Fig. 65. *Julian Schnabel*, 1982. Acrylic and silkscreen ink on linen, 108 x 80 in. (274.3 x 203.2 cm). The Andy Warhol Museum, Pittsburgh; Founding Collection, Contribution The Andy Warhol Foundation for the Visual Arts, Inc.

one of those, He was a great listener (until the diaries came out, we didn't know what a great talker he was).

Andy's greatest contribution is in the traditional area called painting, but there was more written about his cookie jar sale at Sotheby's than his show of *Skull* paintings at Dia Art Foundation [1987–88]. As a matter of fact, these paintings were exhibited for a year and were not even reviewed in this country. They were some of the best paintings I've seen from this century. These in particular, happened to have a lot of brushstrokes.

What is it that constitutes the essence of his painting? An image maker is not necessarily a painter. A painter is someone who paints—it almost doesn't matter what. That is not to say that I would minimize the genius selection of a refrigerator or a double Liz as an element in a painting. But, all of the recognizable imagery that we know as Andy's work may at times serve to distract from, and be a veil for, his true accomplishment as a painter.

Many painters painted Christ on the Cross, but what differentiates Giotto's version from some obscure Italian painter is the way the thing is done, painted.

In Andy's case, the way he used the screen as an additional brush is the printed emblem of his behavior, the symbol of a philosophy of a distance whose radicality lies in its straightforwardness. His decision to select and to act without interpretation, without explanation, was the utter denial of the sentimental. This gesture remains as the irreducible image of Andy's painting; the irreducible clarity of distance.

The paintings configure into their own images according to how much paint is on the screen, according to how many pictures overlap and make new images—smudging or breaking up the selected printed image. These clogs and defacements of images make up the new, distanced picture. They overrule and coexist simultaneously with the selected photographic image as part of the meaning of the painting.

No other painter has come close to this radicality of gesture and self-denial. This gives the paintings their quality of realness and the sense that they existed before he touched them.

When I first saw the *Shadow* paintings, I thought he just ran out of images to paint and these paintings just looked like Warhols. I think I was projecting my preconceptions of his paintings on to my expectations. With new paintings, if you're looking for what you've already seen, you can only be disappointed. The *Shadow* paintings were leaning toward being formed; they were a place one might recognize but couldn't name. I saw them for the first time in 1976. Ten years later, seeing them in Houston, I really saw them for the first time.

There are four large *Shadow* paintings in this exhibition that have never been seen before. They are the reason I wrote this catalogue text. It is amazing how much you can get out of paintings just by looking at them. These paintings hover as the shadow of life's edge. These paintings are Andy Warhol's touch, his distance; whereas the subject of many of Andy's paintings is a record of events in life, these are a record of the act of painting.

They are a brilliant emphatic view of everything and nothing. They were painted in 1978. There is a lot in them. All of the images of Andy's paintings have passed through the shadow and light of these paintings, bolstering up and heralding in this vision of the existential.

(Reprinted from Andy Warhol: Shadow Paintings. *New York: Gagosian Gallery, 1989.)*

Collaborations: Reflections on My Experiences with Basquiat, Clemente, and Warhol

Bruno Bischofberger

In the winter of 1983–84, on the occasion of one of Jean-Michel Basquiat's many visits to our home in St. Moritz, we spoke about works that artists had done together, so-called collaborations. There were several reasons why we began talking about them. Basquiat had done a 120-by-120-centimeter acrylic-on-canvas painting in our garage with my daughter Cora, who was not quite four years old at the time. During the same visit Basquiat drew a double-page drawing, also with Cora, in my guest book. My daughter's childlike, primitive technique and Basquiat's independently chosen "primitive" style were a perfect fit. During my first visit to his New York studio in 1982, he had already answered my question about which artists had influenced him: "What I really like and what has influenced me are works by three- to four-year-old children." The same guest book shows, immediately preceding, a two-page colored pastel, a collaboration between Francesco Clemente and Cora dating from the previous winter (January 1983) and signed by Francesco with both names. Some pages earlier, one finds two drawings by Walter Dahn and Georg Dokoupil dated March 1982. During their stay, these artists had painted a small group of collaborations in our garage using acrylic on canvas, one of which was hanging in our house in the winter of 1983–84.

I personally had been fascinated by collaborations for some time. I knew about collaborations of painters dating from the fifteenth to the nineteenth century and the *cadavre exquis* of the Surrealists. For more than twenty years I had owned a collaboration, dating from 1961, made by Jean Tinguely, Niki de Saint-Phalle, and Daniel Spoerri. I also owned a painting that had been painted jointly by Enzo Cucchi and Sandro Chia. And in 1983 I had bought my first works by the New York artists David McDermott and Peter McGough. What fascinated me about these paintings was that through the voluntary act of collaborating a certain conceptual aspect became more apparent than in works the artists created individually.

I had noticed that in the works of the so-called post-modern movement a certain kind of conceptual collaboration was taking place. Artists were referring to other artists' works or integrating parts thereof in their own paintings. From many diverse examples let me mention: Julian Schnabel quoting Caravaggio in several early works from 1980–81 (fig. 66); David Salle referencing Watteau and Giacometti; and Warhol revisiting his own early works in his series of *Reversal* paintings from 1978 to 1979 (pls. 23, 24).

When I asked Sandro Chia in Venice in 1980 why he had copied fairly exactly, yet admittedly in his own style,

Ernst Ludwig Kirchner's shower painting in the Museum of Modern Art in New York, he responded: "Naturalmente, pesco nella pittura [Of course, I fish around in the history of painting]." This programmatic statement was valid for many works of the then-new painting and culminates in the conceptual work of Mike Bidlo, the radical finishing point of this development. The artist reproduces in the most direct way the work of other artists, which the uninitiated observer could interpret as simply copying. This too is a kind of ultracollaboration (fig. 67).

I had already developed the idea to ask Andy Warhol, whose main dealer I had become in 1968, if he would collaborate with one or two younger artists I represented. During our conversation in St. Moritz I asked Jean-Michel if he would be interested in making some collaborative paintings with Warhol and perhaps another artist. He was exceptionally receptive to new ideas and immediately agreed. He was surely also interested in creating works with the famous Warhol.

In the autumn of 1982 I brought Jean-Michel to meet Andy Warhol at the Factory on Union Square, and this is how they really got to know each other. I had a firm agreement with Warhol that I could propose young artists for articles in *Interview*, which we had founded together in 1969. Warhol also let me decide which young artists I could bring to the Factory to have a portrait done, for which they could swap one of their works. Warhol trusted my judgment. It was of no consequence that the works he received in exchange were often worth much less than his portraits. In this way Andy established a relationship with the generation of younger artists. When I told him that the next day I would bring Jean-Michel Basquiat for a portrait session and the usual buffet lunch at the Factory, he seemed rather surprised and asked me, "Do you really think that Basquiat is such an important artist?" Warhol was not familiar with Basquiat's new work and told me that he remembered having met the artist on one or two occasions, and thinking he was too forward. Basquiat had been trying to get to know Warhol and had offered to sell him his art off the street, small drawings on paper of which Warhol had been very skeptical.

Warhol photographed Basquiat with his special Polaroid portrait camera. Jean-Michel asked Warhol if he could also take a photo of him, took some shots, and then asked me to take some photos of him and Warhol together.

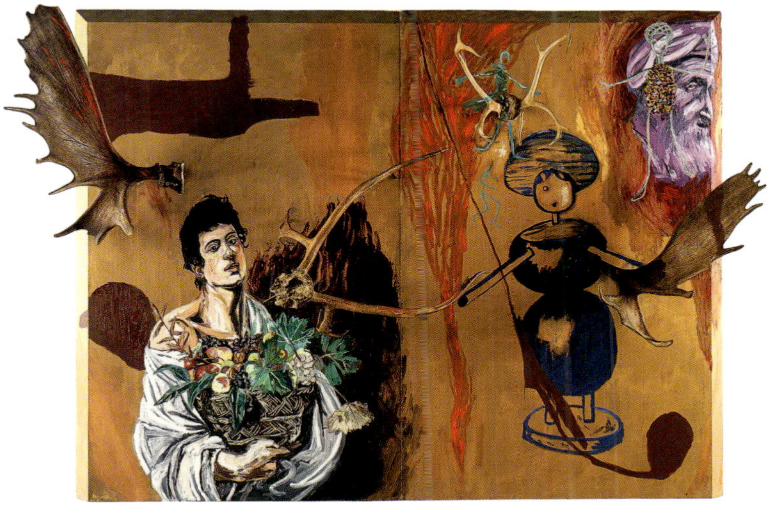

Fig. 66. Julian Schnabel, *Exile*, 1980. Oil, antlers, gold pigment, and mixed media on wood, 90 x 120 x 25 in. (229 x 305 x 63 cm). Bischofberger Collection, Switzerland

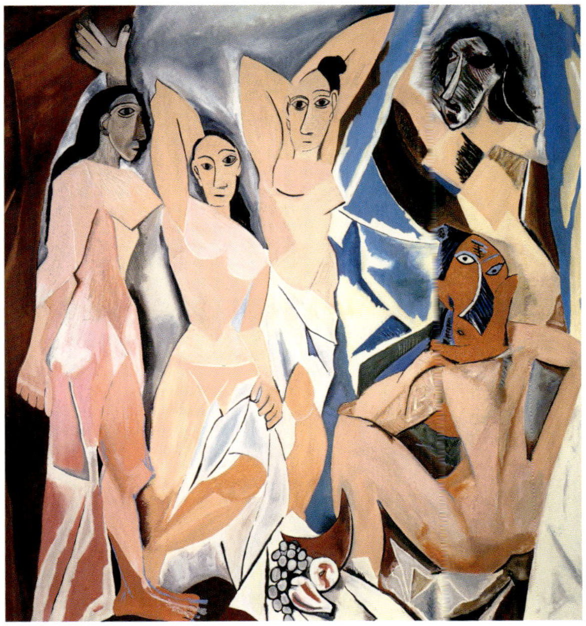

Fig. 67. Mike Bidlo, *Not Picasso (Les demoiselles d'Avignon, 1907)*, 1984. Oil on canvas, 96 x 92 in. (244 x 234 cm). Bischofberger Collection, Switzerland

We then wanted to go next door to have the customary cold buffet lunch. Basquiat did not want to stay and said goodbye. We had hardly finished lunch, one or at most one and a half hours later, when Basquiat's assistant appeared with a 150-by-150-centimeter work on canvas, still completely wet. It was a double portrait of Warhol and Basquiat: Andy on the left in his typical pose, resting his chin on his hand, and Basquiat on the right with the wild hair he had at the time. The painting was titled *Dos Cabezas*. The assistant had run the fifteen or so blocks from Basquiat's studio on Crosby Street to the Factory on Union Square with the painting in his hands because it wouldn't fit into a taxi.

All of the visitors and employees at the Factory flocked around to see the painting, which everyone admired. Most astonished of all was Andy, who said: "I'm really jealous—he is faster than me." Soon thereafter Warhol made a portrait of Basquiat, sporting his wild hairdo, on several equally large canvases: his images was screenprinted onto a background of the "oxidation" type, the same as the *Oxidation* or *Piss Paintings* of 1978 (pls. 10–15). Basquiat subsequently painted another two portraits of Warhol: one in 1984, titled *Brown Spots* (fig. 68), which depicts Andy as a banana; and the other in 1984–85, which shows Warhol in glasses and a large white wig working out with a barbell in each hand.

Basquiat and I soon started to speak of Francesco Clemente as the third artist for the collaborations project, and we decided together to invite him to join in. First, of course, we wanted to know if Warhol would agree to do the project.

Jean-Michel knew and respected Clemente, whose studio was only two blocks away from his own. In the following years he became great friends with him and his wife, Alba. In the summer of 1983 Clemente had painted a group of twelve large paintings in Skowhegan, Maine, which I was able to purchase. These works were also a sort of collaboration: he stretched fragments of theater backdrops made of painted cloth and added his own inventions to those already there. Interestingly, in 1986 Schnabel also

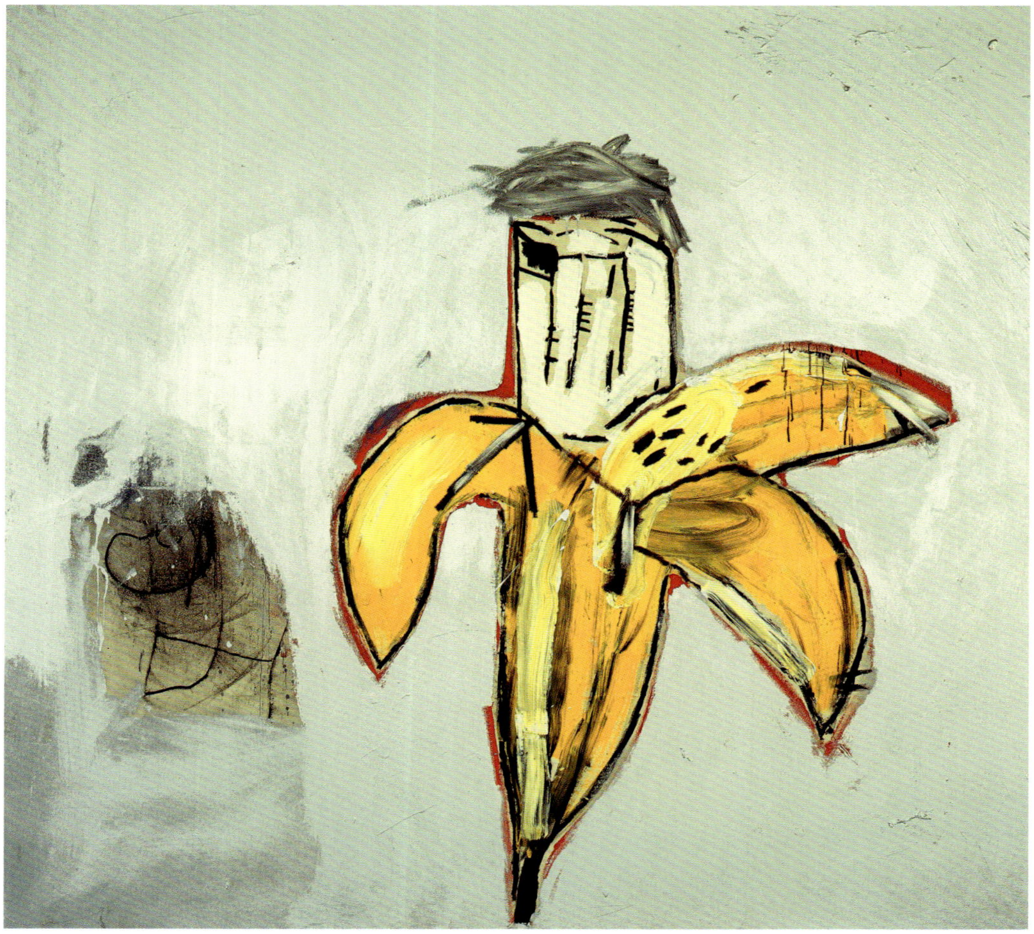

Fig. 68. Jean-Michel Basquiat, *Brown Spots (Portrait of Andy Warhol as a Banana)*, 1984. Acrylic and oil stick on canvas, 76 x 84 in. (193 x 213 cm). Private collection

painted on surfaces that had a clearly defined structure, a series of Japanese Kabuki theater backdrops, and in 1987 Enzo Cucchi painted on four Italian theater backdrops.

To get the most spontaneous work into the collaborations I suggested to Basquiat that each artist should, without conferring with the others about iconography, style, size, technique, etc., independently start a number of paintings—of course, with the knowledge that two more artists would be working on the same canvases, and that enough mental and physical space should be left to accommodate them. I further suggested to him that each artist should send one half of the started collaborations to each of the others for their contributions, after which the works would be passed on to the remaining artist. Basquiat liked my proposal and agreed.

On my next visit to New York I proposed the project to Warhol and Clemente, who both found it interesting and a new challenge. Each artist began four works with oil or acrylic, and one on paper.

From September 15 to October 13, 1984, I showed the group of fifteen works at my Zurich gallery in an exhibition titled *Collaborations—Basquiat Clemente Warhol*, accompanied by a publication of the same name. In all of the works on canvas Warhol used a screenprint technique that he had been using since 1962. In two of the works he repeated the first panel, which had been done by Basquiat and Clemente, five times in the same size using screen-printing. In three of the works Basquiat also used screeprinting.

The order in which the artists worked was different in each of the three large drawings. The finished works were mounted on canvas with the agreement of the artists so that they could be exhibited without glass. In the drawing for which Warhol was the last artist he again repeated the two other artists' work using the screenprint technique. On the drawing that he started himself he drew, using a projector, two GE (General Electric) logos and a spaceship, the latter an image from a series of children's paintings that I had

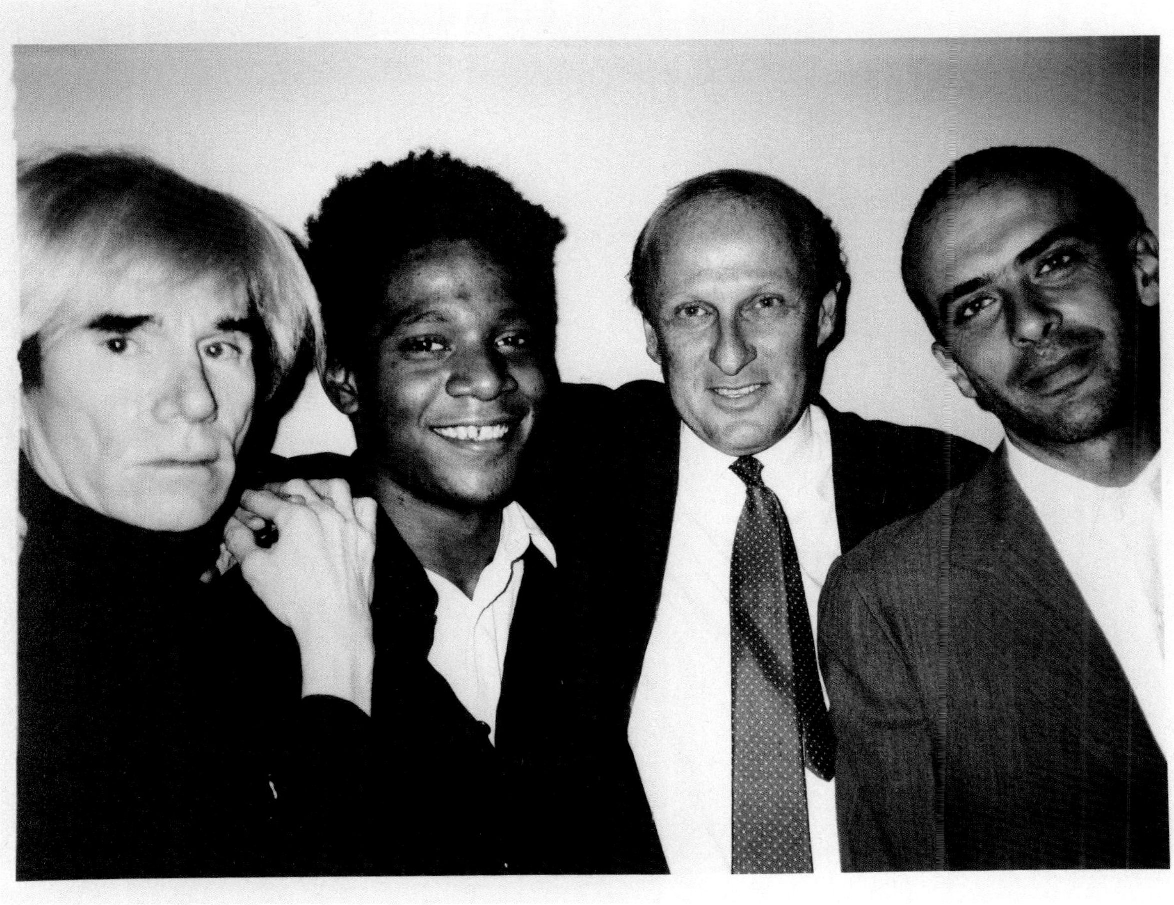

Fig. 69. Andy Warhol, Jean-Michel Basquiat, Bruno Bischofberger, and Francesco Clemente, New York, 1984. Photograph by Beth Philipps

commissioned from him for an exhibition the year before. In the third work on paper, *Alba's Breakfast* (pl. 38), which had been started by Clemente, Warhol painted a GE logo and a washing machine, both in red, very much in the style of the hand-painted works of the early 1960s.

At my request, Warhol left titling the works to Basquiat and Clemente. In the summer of 1984 my family and I, joined by Basquiat, flew to Rome to have a family portrait done by Clemente. During a break in the portrait session Basquiat, Clemente, and I went to the nearby restaurant Casa del Popolo, which lent its name to one of the paintings (pl. 40). The artists discussed possible titles for all of the fifteen works on the basis of the transparencies I had brought with me. One of the works was titled *Ex-Ringeye* (pl. 41). This work was started by Warhol. Basquiat, the last artist to work on the painting, put a white ring around the head of the central figure, which was done by Clemente, and also painted white rings around its eyes. After a discussion between the two and with mutual consent, the circle around the head and the circles around the eyes were removed.

During this trip, which took us to see Enzo Cucchi in Ancona and Miquel Barceló in Majorca, Basquiat said to me, mentioning Warhol's hand painting in *Alba's Breakfast*: "Andy is such a fantastic painter! His hand painting is as good as it was in his early years. I am going to try and convince him to start painting by hand again."

When I next saw Warhol about six months later, in the spring of 1985, he revealed to me that he and Jean-Michel had been working together at the Factory for several months on a large number of further collaborations. He seemed a bit embarrassed, presumably because they had not mentioned it to me earlier. He also said that both he and Basquiat felt that I was not in a privileged position regarding these paintings, since they were not a commission of mine as the three-way collaborations had been. I had to accept his point. He immediately agreed, however, that as his and Basquiat's dealer I was nevertheless the person best suited to purchase the paintings, and they entrusted me with them.

He showed me a large number of these paintings—large-scale works, most of which measured approximately 200 by 300 centimeters, some 300 by 500 or 600 centimeters, and a few 200 by 150 centimeters—and I was both extremely surprised by and enthusiastic about them. Warhol's entire contribution was in a kind of poster style, featuring heraldically hand-painted enlargements of advertising images, headlines, and company logos, but partly in painterly brushstrokes, similar to that seen in some of his works of 1961 and early 1962. Basquiat was usually the second painter to work on the canvases and had fused his spontaneous, expressive, and effusive iconography with that of Warhol. It was also surprising that Basquiat had used screeprinting in a large number of the paintings. In these works it was almost always Warhol who was the second artist to work on the paintings. I purchased a large group of the works from the two artists, and we decided to exhibit them in New York; our mutual choice was Tony Shafrazi's gallery. Andy was especially interested in showing the collaborations downtown and not uptown because, as he put it, there was a livelier and younger art scene there. Held at the end of September 1985, the show included sixteen of the paintings that I had purchased and had given to Tony Shafrazi on consignment. The critiques of the show were almost uniformly negative. Vivien Raynor described the works in the *New York Times* as Warhol's manipulations and claimed that Warhol was using Basquiat as his mascot.

After twenty years as an art dealer I was used to the fact that practically all my best and most important exhibitions had received almost entirely negative critiques. I have always believed that this helps keep an artist's creative and fighting spirit strong, and prevents risking that, because of the general acclaim for his art, the artist becomes less involved, rests on what he has already created, and, in the worst case, repeats and imitates himself.

Warhol had been familiar with this phenomenon for many years. On the other hand, Basquiat, who had hoped to gain a higher status with this exhibition and through this "baptism" by the famous Warhol, was unhappy about the critical reaction and broke off, almost entirely, the painting sessions in the Factory that had become so frequent. Andy was not very happy about this, since he had apparently planned further work. Many of Warhol's late paintings, the large, hand-painted works that have been shown by his estate on various occasions after his death, seem to me, for stylistic and iconographic reasons, to be started collaborations in which Basquiat's contribution is missing.

Painting the Third Mind

Keith Haring

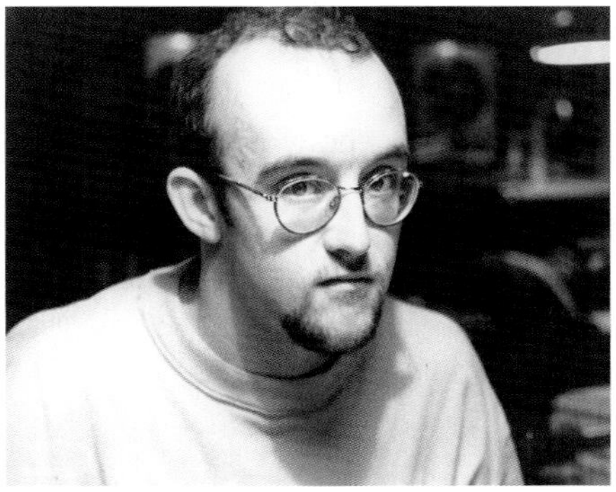

Fig. 70. *Keith Haring*, 1980–84. Gelatin silver print, 8 x 10 in. (20.3 x 25.4 cm). The Andy Warhol Museum, Pittsburgh; Contribution The Andy Warhol Foundation for the Visual Arts, Inc.

Jean-Michel Basquiat and Andy Warhol were from different generations and different sociological backgrounds. They had radically different painting styles and equally different aesthetics. They were at different stages of their lives and different levels of their own development. Physically, the only trait they had in common was their hair. Somewhere, though, they found a common ground and established a healthy relationship. Their personalities complemented each other. Jean was aggressive and point-blank, while Andy was shy and polite. Jean had the nerve to do anything he felt like doing, anywhere he felt like it, and Andy loved to watch. It was a wonderful kind of give-and-take that enabled each of them to fulfill his own secret desires. The relationship was built on mutual respect. Jean had sought after Andy since he was a teenager and by 1980 had been to the Factory several times. In time, Andy grew to respect Jean-Michel. The more he saw his work, the more he loved it. Andy eventually trusted Jean to the point that he would actually let him cut and sculpt his "hair." The respect ran deeper than just aesthetics. Each had a fascination with the other's impenetrable shell. The mystery that was Warhol was challenged by the complexities that were Basquiat. Their projected "images" were powerful and uncompromising, while they both harbored a vulnerable, humble spirit that endowed both of them with a sense of humor. They "understood" each other.

A successful collaboration is always the result of a successful relationship. The paintings are the physical proof of the harmony that existed beyond the canvas. I'm not sure if their collaboration was a deliberate, planned strategy or if it simply "happened."

Jean was spending more and more time visiting the Factory and eventually started painting there. This is not hard to imagine, since Jean painted anywhere he found himself. He would create with whatever materials were readily available on whatever surface would sit still long enough to draw on. Andy was also a workaholic and loved the added incentive of having Jean around. They exercised together, ate together, and laughed together. The great thing about visiting Andy was that he was always working. Whether or not there may have been endless interruptions from phone calls and visitors, there was still a sense that in between, a lot of things were getting done. There were always new paintings leaning against the wall, new piles of Polaroids, and new clippings or photostats of prospective projects. For an artist, the most important and most delicate relationship he can have with another artist is one in which he is constantly challenged and intimidated. This is

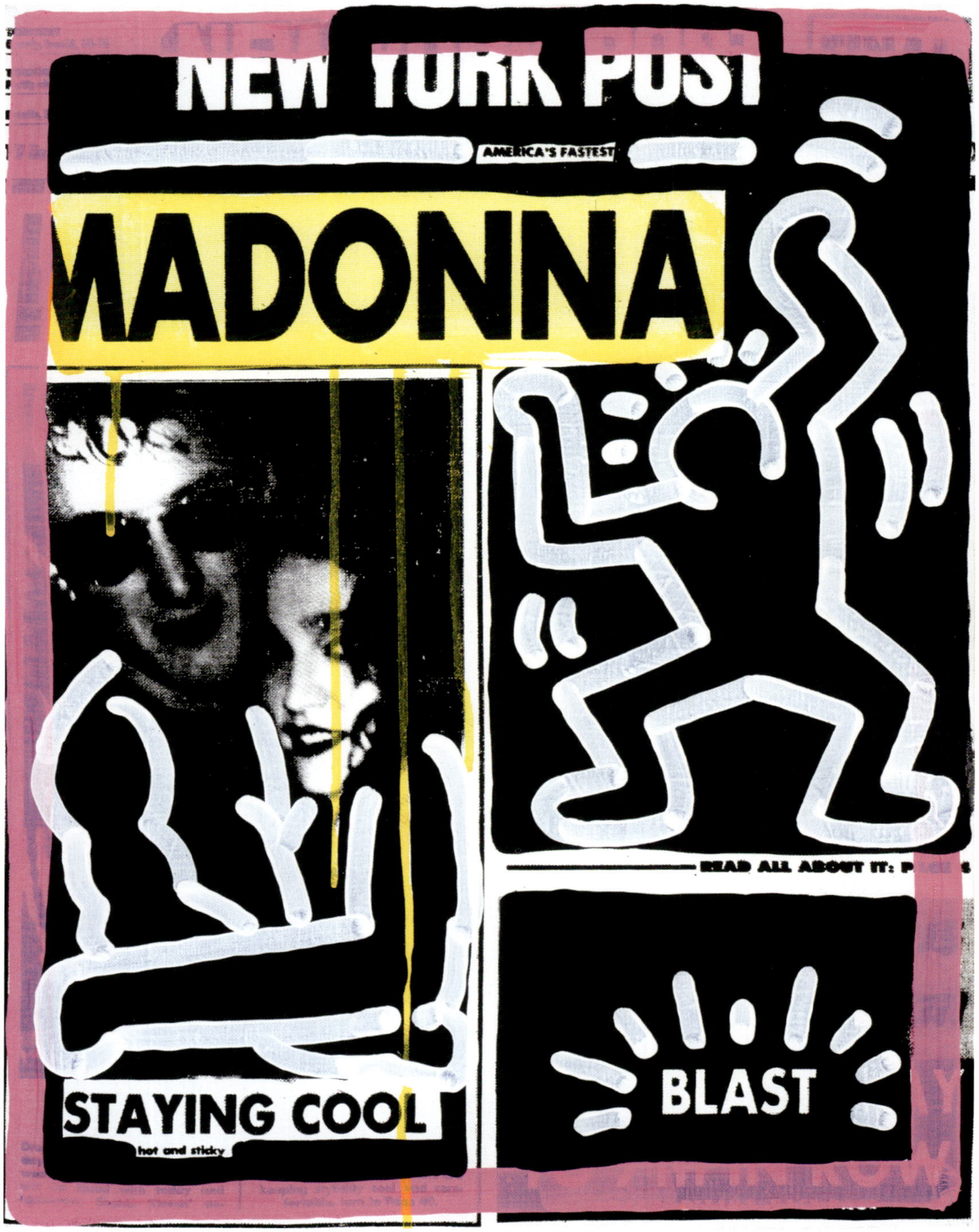

Fig. 71. Andy Warhol and Keith Haring, *Untitled (New York Post front page—Madonna)*, 1984–85. Acrylic and silkscreen ink on linen, 20 x 16 in. (50.8 x 40.6 cm). The Andy Warhol Museum, Pittsburgh; Founding Collection, Contribution The Andy Warhol Foundation for the Visual Arts, Inc.

probably the only productive quality of jealousy. The greatest pleasure is to be provoked to the point of inspiration. Most artists only admit to one or two others whom they feel are equal to themselves. Very few would accept the notion that their peers are actually superior. However, in the privacy of their own thoughts, they must admit to themselves that these thoughts arise and usually lead to a kind of unspoken competition. This provocation, coupled with a little self-confidence, can create an intense working atmosphere.

Jean-Michel and Andy had achieved a healthy balance. Jean respected Andy's philosophy and was in awe of his accomplishments and mastery of color and images.

Andy was amazed by the ease with which Jean composed and constructed his paintings, and was constantly surprised by the never-ending flow of new ideas. Each one inspired the other to outdo the next. The collaborations were seemingly effortless. It was a physical conversation happening in paint instead of words. The sense of humor, the snide remarks, the profound realizations, the simple chitchat all happened with paint and brushes. I visited them at the Factory several times while they were painting together. The atmosphere was playful and intense at the same time. Jean-Michel's painting posture and disregard for technique created a mood of unnerving spectacle. There was a sense that one was watching something being unveiled and discovered for the first time. Andy was intrigued and intimidated at the same time. It seemed to push him to new heights. Andy returned to painting with beautiful, delicate lines, carefully laid on to the canvas. The drips and gestures immediately reminded me of the earliest Warhol paintings I had seen. The new scale had forced him to develop an even richer draftsmanship. The lines flowed on to the canvas.

Painting with Jean-Michel was not easy. You had to forget any preconceived ideas of ownership and be prepared to have anything you'd done completely painted over within seconds. It was a kind of total abandon that required total trust and respect. Andy loved the energy with which Jean would totally eradicate one image and enhance another. It was truly an event. There were canvases hanging all over the Factory. They worked on many at the same time, each idea inspiring the next. Layers and layers of images and ideas would build toward a concise climax. It was exciting to visit the Factory at this time.

Many of the staff members were not so delighted by Jean-Michel's presence. He disrupted their schedules and filled the Factory with sweet-smelling pot smoke. Andy seemed happy to defend Jean and to challenge their conservatism. Jean brought back a much-needed touch of mischief that had been disappearing from the Factory agenda. But, he also brought an atmosphere of obsessive production that left its mark long after the collaborations had stopped. The ramifications of this investigation left obvious traces in Jean-Michel's paintings. He handled scale with a new sense of confidence and introduced several new Pop icons into his work. Many people believe that Jean was the sole reason Andy returned to his brushes. Both of them benefited immeasurably.

For me, the paintings that resulted from this collaboration are the perfect testimony to the depth and importance of their friendship. The quality of the paintings mirrors the quality of the relationship. The sense of humor that permeates all of the works recalls the laughter that surrounded them while they were being made. They are truly an invention of what William S. Burroughs called "the Third Mind"—two amazing minds fusing together to create a third, totally separate and unique mind.

Reprinted from Collaborations: Andy Warhol, Jean-Michel Basquiat. *London: Mayor Rowan Gallery and David Grob Limited, 1988.)*

Works in the Exhibition

All works are by Andy Warhol unless otherwise noted.
Dimensions are in inches followed by centimeters. Height precedes width precedes depth.
Each work will travel to all participating museums unless otherwise indicated.

Oxidation Painting (in 12 parts), 1978
Acrylic and urine on linen, 48 x 49 in. (121.9 x 124.5 cm)
The Andy Warhol Museum, Pittsburgh; Founding Collection, Contribution The Andy Warhol Foundation for the Visual Arts, Inc.
[11]

Oxidation Painting, 1978
Urine and metallic pigment in acrylic medium on canvas, 76 x 52 in. (193 x 132 cm)
The Baltimore Museum of Art: Purchase with funds provided by Esther and Richard Pearlstone through the Pearlstone Family Fund; and partial gift of The Andy Warhol Foundation for the Visual Arts, Inc.
[15]

Self-Portrait, 1978
Acrylic and silkscreen ink on canvas, 40 x 40 in. (101.6 x 101.6 cm)
The Andy Warhol Museum, Pittsburgh; Founding Collection, Contribution The Andy Warhol Foundation for the Visual Arts, Inc.
[1]

Self-Portrait, 1978
Acrylic and silkscreen ink on canvas, 40 x 40 in. (101.6 x 101.6 cm)
The Andy Warhol Museum, Pittsburgh; Founding Collection, Contribution The Andy Warhol Foundation for the Visual Arts, Inc.
[2]

Self-Portrait (Strangulation), 1978
Acrylic and silkscreen ink on canvas, ten parts, 16 x 13 in. (40.6 x 33 cm) each
Collection of Anthony d'Offay
[6]

Self-Portrait Wallpaper, 1978
Screenprint on wallpaper, 180 x 28 in. (457.2 x 71.1 cm) each roll
The Andy Warhol Museum, Pittsburgh
[9]

Self-Portrait with Skull, 1978
Acrylic and silkscreen ink on canvas, two parts, 16 x 13 in. (40.6 x 33 cm) each
Collection of Anthony d'Offay
[5]

Shadow, 1978
Acrylic (black), diamond dust, and silkscreen ink on canvas, 78 1/16 x 50 1/16 in. (198.4 x 127.2 cm)
The Baltimore Museum of Art: Purchased with funds provided by Laura R. Burrows-Jackson, Baltimore; and partial gift of The Andy Warhol Foundation for the Visual Arts, Inc.
[19]
Brooklyn and Baltimore only

Shadow, 1978
Silkscreen ink on linen, 76 x 52 in. (193 x 132 cm)
Private collection
[18]
Milwaukee only

Marilyn (4), c. 1978
Acrylic and silkscreen ink on canvas, 36 x 28 in.
(91.4 x 71.1 cm)
The Andy Warhol Museum, Pittsburgh; Founding Collection, Contribution The Andy Warhol Foundation for the Visual Arts, Inc.
[23]

Shadows, 1978–79
Acrylic, variously silkscreened and painted on canvas, four parts, 76 x 52 in. (193 x 132 cm) each
Anonymous collection

Shadow, 1979
Acrylic, diamond dust, and silkscreen ink on canvas, 77¾ x 52 in. (197.6 x 132.1 cm)
The Baltimore Museum of Art: Purchased with exchange funds from the Samuel and Tobie Miller Memorial Collection
[20]
Brooklyn and Baltimore only

Mona Lisa, c. 1979
Acrylic and silkscreen ink on canvas, 80 x 100 x 1½ in.
(203.2 x 254 x 3.8 cm)
The Andy Warhol Museum, Pittsburgh; Founding Collection, Contribution The Andy Warhol Foundation for the Visual Arts, Inc.
[24]

Eggs, 1982
Acrylic and silkscreen ink on linen, 90 x 70 in.
(228.6 x 177.8 cm)
The Andy Warhol Museum, Pittsburgh; Founding Collection, Contribution The Andy Warhol Foundation for the Visual Arts, Inc.
[Fig. 19]

Eggs, 1982
Acrylic and silkscreen ink on canvas, 90 x 70 in.
(228.6 x 177.8 cm)
The Baltimore Museum of Art: Purchase with funds provided by the Fanny B. Thalheimer Memorial Fund; and partial gift of the Andy Warhol Foundation for the Visual Arts, Inc.
[Fig. 20]

Yarn, 1983
Acrylic and silkscreen ink on linen, 40 x 40 in.
(101.6 x 101.6 cm)
The Andy Warhol Museum, Pittsburgh; Founding Collection, Contribution The Andy Warhol Foundation for the Visual Arts, Inc.
[27]

Yarn, 1983
Acrylic and silkscreen ink on linen, 40 x 40 in.
(101.6 x 101.6 cm)
The Andy Warhol Museum, Pittsburgh; Founding Collection, Contribution The Andy Warhol Foundation for the Visual Arts, Inc.
[28]

Yarn, 1983
Acrylic and silkscreen ink on canvas, 54 x 206 in.
(137 x 523 cm)
Staff Stiftung, Lemgo, permanent loan at Kunsthalle Bielefeld
[25]

Rorschach, 1984
Acrylic on canvas, 164¼ x 115 in. (417 x 292 cm)
Promised Gift of Virginia and Bagley Wright in honor of the 75th anniversary of the Seattle Art Museum
[32]

Rorschach, 1984
Acrylic on canvas, 158 x 110 in. (401 x 279.4 cm)
The Baltimore Museum of Art: Purchase with funds provided by Laura R. Burrows-Jackson, Baltimore; and partial gift of The Andy Warhol Foundation of the Visual Arts, Inc.
[33]

Andy Warhol, Jean-Michel Basquiat, and Francesco Clemente
Alba's Breakfast, 1984
Mixed media on paper, mounted on canvas, 46 x 59 in. (117 x 150 cm)
Bischofberger Collection, Switzerland
[38]

Andy Warhol, Jean-Michel Basquiat, and Francesco Clemente
Origin of Cotton, 1984
Mixed media on canvas, 48 x 66 in. (122 x 167.7 cm)
Private collection
[37]

Andy Warhol and Jean-Michel Basquiat
Untitled (Heart Attack), 1984
Acrylic on canvas, 76 x 156 in. (194 x 396 cm)
Mugrabi Collection
[36]

Andy Warhol and Jean-Michel Basquiat
Arm and Hammer II, 1985
Acrylic on canvas, 76 x 112 in. (193 x 285 cm)
Galerie Bruno Bischofberger, Zurich
[39]

Campbell's Soup (Tomato), 1985
Acrylic and silkscreen ink on canvas, 20 x 16 in. (50.8 x 40.6 cm)
Collection of Debbie and Mark Attanasio
[45]

Mount Vesuvius, 1985
Acrylic and silkscreen ink on linen, 78 x 82 in. (198.1 x 208.3 cm)
The Andy Warhol Museum, Pittsburgh; Founding Collection, Contribution The Andy Warhol Foundation for the Visual Arts, Inc.
[Fig. 28]

Are You "Different"? 1985–86
Acrylic and silkscreen ink on linen, 20 x 16 in. (50.8 x 40.6 cm)
The Andy Warhol Museum, Pittsburgh; Founding Collection, Contribution The Andy Warhol Foundation for the Visual Arts, Inc.
[48]

Double $5/Weightlifter, 1985–86
Acrylic on linen, 116 x 216½ in. (294.6 x 549.9 cm)
The Andy Warhol Museum, Pittsburgh; Founding Collection, Contribution The Andy Warhol Foundation for the Visual Arts, Inc.
[44]

Energy, 1985–86
Acrylic and silkscreen ink on linen, 20 x 16 in. (50.8 x 40.6 cm)
The Andy Warhol Museum, Pittsburgh; Founding Collection, Contribution The Andy Warhol Foundation for the Visual Arts, Inc.
[47]

Heaven and Hell Are Just One Breath Away! 1985–86
Acrylic and silkscreen ink on linen, 20 x 16 in. (50.8 x 40.6 cm)
The Andy Warhol Museum, Pittsburgh; Founding Collection, Contribution The Andy Warhol Foundation for the Visual Arts, Inc.
[51]

The Last Supper (Be a Somebody with a Body), 1985–86
Acrylic on linen, 50 x 56 x 1½ in. (127 x 142.2 x 3.2 cm)
The Andy Warhol Museum, Pittsburgh; Founding Collection, Contribution The Andy Warhol Foundation for the Visual Arts, Inc.
[59]

The Mark of the Beast, 1985–86
Acrylic and silkscreen ink on linen, 20 x 16 in.
(50.8 x 40.6 cm)
The Andy Warhol Museum, Pittsburgh; Founding Collection, Contribution The Andy Warhol Foundation for the Visual Arts, Inc.
[53]

Repent and Sin No More! 1985–86
Acrylic and silkscreen ink on linen, 20 x 16 in.
(50.8 x 40.6 cm)
The Andy Warhol Museum, Pittsburgh; Founding Collection, Contribution The Andy Warhol Foundation for the Visual Arts, Inc.
[55]

Self-Defense, 1985–86
Acrylic and silkscreen ink on linen, 20 x 16 in.
(50.8 x 40.6 cm)
The Andy Warhol Museum, Pittsburgh; Founding Collection, Contribution The Andy Warhol Foundation for the Visual Arts, Inc.
[50]

Steaks 99 [cents], 1985–86
Acrylic and silkscreen ink on linen, 20 x 16 in.
(50.8 x 40.6 cm)
The Andy Warhol Museum, Pittsburgh; Founding Collection, Contribution The Andy Warhol Foundation for the Visual Arts, Inc.
[46]

Reagan Budget, c. 1985–86
Acrylic and silkscreen ink on canvas, 20 x 16 in.
(50.8 x 40.6 cm)
The Andy Warhol Foundation for the Visual Arts, Inc.
[49]

Camouflage, 1986
Acrylic and silkscreen ink on canvas, 116 x 200 in.
(294.6 x 508 cm)
The Baltimore Museum of Art: Purchase with funds provided by Esther and Richard Pearlstone through the Pearlstone Family Fund; and partial gift of The Andy Warhol Foundation for the Visual Arts, Inc.
[71]

Camouflage, 1986
Acrylic and silkscreen ink on linen, 80¼ x 76¼ in.
(203.8 x 193.7 cm)
The Andy Warhol Museum, Pittsburgh; Founding Collection, Contribution The Andy Warhol Foundation for the Visual Arts, Inc.
[72]

Camouflage, 1986
Acrylic and silkscreen ink on linen, 76 x 76 in.
(193 x 193 cm)
Collection of Ealan Wingate and Batsheva Ostrow
[73]

Detail of the Last Supper (Christ 112 Times), 1986
Acrylic and silkscreen ink on canvas, 80 x 421 in.
(203.2 x 1069.3 cm)
Mugrabi Collection
[77]

The Last Supper, 1986
Acrylic and silkscreen ink on linen, 78 x 306 in.
(198 x 777 cm)
The Baltimore Museum of Art: Harry A. Bernstein Memorial Collection, by exchange
[74]

The Last Supper, 1986
Acrylic and silkscreen ink on linen, 116 x 390 x 2 in.
(294.6 x 990.6 x 5.1 cm)
The Andy Warhol Museum, Pittsburgh; Founding
Collection, Contribution The Andy Warhol Foundation
for the Visual Arts, Inc.
[78]
Fort Worth and Brooklyn only

The Last Supper, 1986
Acrylic on canvas, 119¼ x 263¼ in. (302.9 x 668.7 cm)
The Museum of Modern Art, New York, Gift of the Andy
Warhol Foundation for the Visual Arts
[80]
Milwaukee only

Self-Portrait, 1986
Acrylic and silkscreen ink on linen, 40 x 40 in.
(101.6 x 101.6 cm)
Mugrabi Collection
[60]

Self-Portrait, 1986
Acrylic and silkscreen ink on canvas, 80 1/16 x 80 in.
(203.4 x 203.3 cm)
The Baltimore Museum of Art: Purchase with exchange
funds provided from Bequest of Saidie A. May; and partial
gift of The Andy Warhol Foundation of the Visual Arts, Inc.
[63]

Self-Portrait, 1986
Acrylic and silkscreen ink on linen, 80 x 76 in.
(203.2 x 193 cm)
The Andy Warhol Museum, Pittsburgh; Founding
Collection, Contribution The Andy Warhol Foundation
for the Visual Arts, Inc.
[68]

Selected Bibliography

Exhibition Catalogues

Andy Warhol B&W Paintings: Ads and Illustrations, 1985–1986. London and New York: Gagosian Gallery, 2002.

Andy Warhol: Camouflage. Brenda Richardson. New York: Gagosian Gallery, 1998.

Andy Warhol: Diamond Dust Shadow Paintings. Essay by Rosalind Krauss. New York: Gagosian Gallery, 2000.

Andy Warhol: Diamond Dust Shoes. New York: Gagosian Gallery, 1999.

Andy Warhol $. New York: Gagosian Gallery, 1997.

Andy Warhol: Dollar Signs. Essay by Trevor Fairbrother. New York: Van de Weghe Fine Art, 2004.

Andy Warhol: Early Hand-Painted Works. New York: Gagosian Gallery, 2005.

Andy Warhol: Fifteen Abstract Paintings. New York: Anton Kern Gallery, 1998.

Andy Warhol Jean-Michel Basquiat: Collaboration Paintings. Los Angeles: Gagosian Gallery, 2002.

Andy Warhol: The Late Work. Düsseldorf: Museum Kunst Palast; Munich and New York: Prestel, 2004.

Andy Warhol: Oxidation Paintings, Piss Paintings. Munich: Galerie Daniel Blau, 1998.

Andy Warhol: Piss & Sex Paintings and Drawings. New York: Gagosian Gallery, 2002.

Andy Warhol: Stitched Photographs. Milan: Galeria Lawrence Rubin; New York: Paul Kasmin Gallery, 1999.

Andy Warhol's Time Capsule 21. Pittsburgh: The Andy Warhol Museum; Frankfurt am Main: Museum für Moderne Kunst, 2003.

Andy Warhol: The Record Covers, 1949–1987. Catalogue Raisonné. Montreal: The Montreal Museum of Fine Arts; Munich and New York: Prestel, 2008.

Andy Warhol: Rorschach Paintings. Essay by Rosalind Krauss. New York: Gagosian Gallery, 1996.

Andy Warhol: Shadow Paintings. New York: Gagosian Gallery 1989.

Aquin, Stéphane, ed. *Warhol Live: Music and Dance in Andy Warhol's Work*. Montreal: The Montreal Museum of Fine Arts; Munich and New York: Prestel, 2008.

Baal-Teshuva, Jacob, ed. *Andy Warhol, 1928–1987: Works from the Collections of José Mugrabi and an Isle of Man Company*. Vienna: KunstHausWein; Munich and New York: Prestel, 1993.

Bastian, Heiner. *Andy Warhol Retrospective*. London: Tate Publishing; Los Angeles: Museum of Contemporary Art, 2001.

Cast a Cold Eye: The Late Work of Andy Warhol. Commentary by Vincent Fremont and essay by Boris Groys. New York: Gagosian Gallery, 2006.

Collaborations: Andy Warhol, Jean-Michel Basquiat. London: Mayor Rowan Gallery and David Grob Limited, 1988.

Collaborations: Jean-Michel Basquiat/Francesco Clemente/ Andy Warhol. Zurich: Edition Galerie Bruno Bischofberger, 1984.

Elger, Dietmar, ed. *Andy Warhol: Selbsportraits/Self-Portraits*. Ostfildern-Ruit, Germany: Hatje Cantz, 2004.

Fogle, Douglas. *SUPERNOVA: Stars, Deaths, and Disasters, 1962–1964*. Minneapolis: The Walker Art Center, 2005.

Heinrich, Christoph. *Andy Warhol: Photography*. Zurich and New York: Edition Stemmle, 1999.

Hopps, Walter, and Neil Printz. *Andy Warhol: Death and Disasters*. Houston: The Menil Collection, 1988.

Iolas, Alexandre. *Warhol Il Cenacolo*. Milan: Arnoldo Mondadori Editore/Edizioni Philippe Daverio, 1987.

Jean-Michel Basquiat—Bilder, Zeichnungen, Collaborations. Essay by Robert Farris Thompson. Hannover: Kestner-Gesellschaft, 1986.

Kellein, Thomas. *Andy Warhol: Abstrakt*. Basel: Kunsthalle Basel; Munich and New York: Prestel, 1993.

Koch, Stephen. *Andy Warhol Photographs*. New York: Robert Miller Gallery, 1989.

McShine, Kynaston, ed. *Andy Warhol: A Retrospective*. New York: The Museum of Modern Art, 1989.

Meyer-Hermann, Eva, ed. *Andy Warhol. Other Voices, Other Rooms*. Rotterdam: NAi Publishers, 2007.

Osterwold, Tilman. *Collaborations: Warhol—Basquiat—Clemente*. Kassel: Museum Fridericianum; Munich: Museum Villa Stuck, 1996.

Schultz-Hoffmann, Carla, ed. *Andy Warhol: The Last Supper*. Munich: Bayerische Staatsgemäldesammlungen/ Staatsgalerie Moderner Kunst, 1998.

Stuckey, Charles. *Andy Warhol: Heaven and Hell Are Just One Breath Away! Late Paintings and Related Works, 1984–1986*. New York: Gagosian Gallery and Rizzoli, 1992.

Warhol. London: Tate Gallery, 1971.

Warhol/Basquiat Collaborations. Paris: Didier Lambert Fine Arts, 1989.

Warhol '80: Serie Reversal. Vienna: Museum Moderner Kunst/Museum des 20. Jahrhundert, 1981.

Warhol Shadows. Houston: The Menil Collection, 1987.

Whitney, David, ed. *Andy Warhol: Portraits of the Seventies*. Essay by Robert Rosenblum. New York: Whitney Museum of American Art, 1979.

Books

Bockris, Victor. *The Life and Death of Andy Warhol*. New York: Bantam Books, 1989.

Bockris, Victor. *Warhol*. Harmondsworth, England: Penguin, 1990.

Bourdon, David. *Warhol*. New York: Harry N. Abrams, Inc., 1989.

Collacello, Bob. *Holy Terror: Andy Warhol Close Up*. New York: HarperCollins, 1990.

Coplans, John. *Andy Warhol*. With contributions by Jonas Mekas and Calvin Tompkins. New York: New York Graphic Society, 1970.

Crone, Rainer. *Andy Warhol: A Picture Show by the Artist*. New York: Rizzoli, 1987.

Dillenberger, Jane Daggett. *The Religious Art of Andy Warhol*. New York: The Continuum Publishing Company, 1998.

Feldman, Frayda, and Jörg Schellmann. *Andy Warhol Prints: A Catalogue Raisonné, 1962–1987*, 4th ed. New York: D.A.P., 2003.

Frei, Georg, and Neil Printz, eds. *The Andy Warhol Catalogue Raisonné: Paintings and Sculpture.* Vol 1: 1961–63; Vols. 2A and 2B: 1964–69. London and New York: Phaidon, 2002 and 2004.

Garrels, Gary, ed. *The Work of Andy Warhol*. Dia Art Foundation, Discussions in Contemporary Culture, no. 3. Seattle: Bay Press, 1989.

Geldzahler, Henry, and Robert Rosenblum. *Andy Warhol: Portraits of the Seventies and Eighties.* London: Anthony d'Offay Gallery in association with Thames and Hudson, 1993.

Goldsmith, Kenneth, ed. *I'll Be Your Mirror: The Selected Andy Warhol Interviews, 1962–1987*. New York: Carroll & Graf Publishers, 2004.

Hackett, Pat, ed. *The Andy Warhol Diaries*. New York: Warner Books, 1989.

Hartley, Keith. *Warhol: A Celebration of Life . . . and Death*. Edinburgh: National Galleries of Scotland, 2007.

Kattenberg, Peter. *Andy Warhol, Priest: The Last Supper Comes in Small, Medium, and Large*. Leiden, The Netherlands: Brill, 2001.

Kornbluth, Jesse. *Pre-Pop Warhol*. New York: Random House, 1988.

Makos, Christopher. *Warhol: A Personal Photographic Memoir*. New York: New American Library, 1988.

Michelson, Annette, ed. *Andy Warhol: October Files 2*. Cambridge, Mass., and London: The MIT Press, 2001.

O'Connor, John, and Benjamin Liu. *Unseen Warhol*. New York: Rizzoli, 1996.

Pratt, Alan R., ed. *The Critical Response to Andy Warhol*. Westport, Conn., and London: Greenwood Press, 1997.

Richardson, John. *Sacred Monsters, Sacred Masters: Beaton, Capote, Dalí, Picasso, Freud, Warhol, and More*. New York: Random House, 2001.

Schellmann, Jörg, ed. *Andy Warhol Art from Art*. Cologne and New York: Edition Schellmann, 1994.

Smith, Patrick S. *Andy Warhol's Art and Films*. Ann Arbor, Mich.: UMI Research Press, 1981, 1986.

Smith, Patrick S. *Warhol: Conversations about the Artist*. Ann Arbor, Mich.: UMI Research Press, 1988.

Warhol, Andy. *America*. New York: Harper and Row, 1985.

Warhol, Andy. *The Philosophy of Andy Warhol (from A to B and Back Again)*. New York: Harcourt Brace Jovanovich, 1975.

Warhol, Andy, and Bob Colacello. *Andy Warhol's Exposures*. New York: Grosset & Dunlap, 1979.

Warhol, Andy, and Pat Hackett. *POPism: The Warhol '60s*. New York and London: Harcourt Brace Jovanovich, 1980.

Wünsche, Hermann. *Andy Warhol: Das Graphische Werk, 1962–1980*. Bonn: Bonner Universitäts-Buchdruckerei, 1981.

Articles

Affentranger-Kirchrath, Angelika. "Improvisation für sechs Hände. Die Collaborations von Andy Warhol, Francesco Clemente und Jean-Michel Basquiat." *Artis*, no. 9 (1993), pp. 40–45.

"Andy Warhol 1928–87: A Collage of Appreciations from the Artist's Colleagues, Critics and Friends." *Art in America*, 75 (May 1987), pp. 137–43.

Anfam, David. "Handy Andy." *Art History,* 14, no. 2 (June 1991), pp. 270–74.

Antin, David. "Warhol: The Silver Tenement." *Art News*, 65 (1966), pp. 47–48, 58.

Blinderman, Barry. "Modern Myths: An Interview with Andy Warhol." *Arts Magazine*, 56 (Oct. 1981), pp. 144–47.

Bourdon, David. "Dia Art Foundation and Larry Gagosian Gallery, New York." *Art in America*, 75 (Apr. 1987), pp. 213–14.

Cone, Michèle. "Warhol's Risk: Voyeurism or Exposure?" *Arts Magazine*, 63 (Summer 1989), pp. 51–55.

Cone, Tim. "The Most Fascinating Kind of Art: Andy Warhol and the Right of Publicity." *Arts Magazine*, 64 (Jan. 1990), pp. 25–26.

Cooke, Lynne. "Andy Warhol: The Last Supper Portraits." Dia Art Foundation, 1994–95, www.diabeacon.org/exhibs/warhol/lastsupper/essay.html.

Cooke, Lynne. "Andy Warhol *Shadows.*" Dia Art Foundation, 1995–2000, www.diacenter.org/exhibits/warhol/shadows/essay.html.

Cooke, Lynne. "Dia's Andy: Through the Lens of Patronage." Dia Art Foundation, 1995–2000, www.diacenter.org/exhibits/warhol/shadows/essay.html.

Crow, Thomas. "Saturday Disasters: Trace and Reference in Early Warhol." *Art in America*, 75 (May 1987), pp. 128–36.

Danto, Arthur. "Andy Warhol's Smirking Genius." *The Nation*, Sept. 16, 2006, www.alternet.org/story/41684.

Danto, Arthur. "Who Was Andy Warhol." *Art News*, 86 (May 1987), pp. 128–32.

De Duve, Thierry, and Rosalind Krauss. "Andy Warhol, or the Machine Perfected." *October*, 48 (Spring 1989), pp. 3–14.

De Sanna, Jole. "Andy Warhol, The Last Supper, Galleria Refeltorio delle Stelline." *Artforum*, 25 (Summer 1987), pp. 131–32.

Ehrenstein, David. "The Filmmaker as Homosexual Hipster: Andy Warhol Contextualized." *Arts Magazine*, 63 (Summer 1989), pp. 61–64.

Edenbaum, Seth. "Parody and Privacy." *Arts Magazine*, 62 (Oct. 1987), pp. 44–45.

Fineman, Mia. "Andy Warhol: Rorschach Paintings." *Artnet*, Oct. 15, 1996, http://www.artnet.com/Magazine/FEATURES/fineman/fineman10-15-96.

Foster, Hal. "Death in America." *October*, 75 (Winter 1996), pp. 36–59.

Gardner, Paul. "Gee, What's Happened to Andy Warhol?" *Art News*, 79 (Nov. 1980), pp. 73–77.

Glaser, Bruce. "Oldenburg, Lichtenstein, Warhol: A Discussion." *Artforum* (Feb. 1966), pp. 20–24.

Grundberg, Andy. "Photography View: Warhol Sews a Subversive Pattern in Black and White." *The New York Times*, Jan. 11, 1987.

Haden-Guest, Anthony. "Warhol's Last Supper." *Artnet*, Aug. 3, 1999, www.artnet.com/magazine_pre2000/features/haden-guest/haden-guest8-3-99.asp.

Haring, Keith. "Warhol & Basquiat: Kunstlermannepaare." *Kunstforum International*, 107 (Apr.–May 1990), pp. 181ff.

Heartney, Eleanor. "Basquiat/Warhol: Tony Shafrazi." *Flash Art*, no. 125 (Dec. 1985–Jan. 1986), p. 43.

Hughes, Robert. "The Rise of Andy Warhol." *The New York Review of Books*, Feb. 18, 1982, pp. 6–9.

Hughes, Robert. "A Caterer of Repetition and Glut, Andy Warhol: 1928–1987." *Time*, Mar. 9, 1987, p. 90.

Kageneck, Christian von. "Andy Warhol's Cars—Die Letzen Bilder." *Das Kunstwerk*, 41 (May 1988), pp. 89–90.

Kalina, Richard. "Andy Warhol at Anton Kern—New York, New York." *Art in America*, 86 (Nov. 1998), p. 130.

La Ferla, Ruth. "The Selling of St. Andy." *The New York Times*, Oct. 26, 2006, pp. E1, E5.

Lawson, Thomas. "Andy Warhol." *Artforum*, 20 (Apr. 1982), p. 75.

Lawson, Thomas. "Andy Warhol/Heiner Friedrich." *Flash Art*, nos. 88–89 (Mar.–Apr. 1979), p. 23.

Lurie, David. "Andy Warhol/*Disaster Paintings*." *Arts Magazine*, 60 (June 1986), pp. 117–18.

Magnani, Gregorio. "Dia Foundation, New York: Exhibit." *Flash Art*, no. 134 (May 1987), p. 87.

Mahoney, Robert. "Andy Warhol/Jean-Michel Basquiat." *Arts Magazine*, 60 (Nov. 1985), p. 135.

Mahoney, Robert. "The Quaint and Charming (Early) Andy: Notes on the MoMA Retrospective." *Arts Magazine*, 63 (Summer 1989), pp. 65–66.

McGonigal, Thomas. "Andy Warhol." *Arts Magazine*, 54 (Jan. 1980), p. 17.

McGuigan, Cathleen. "New Art, New Money." *The New York Times Magazine*, Feb. 10, 1985, p. 20.

Michelson, Annette. "Where Is Your Rupture? Mass Culture and the Gesamtkunstwerk." *October*, 56 (Spring 1991), pp. 42–63.

Morgan, Stuart. "Andy Warhol: Whitney Museum." *Artforum*, 18 (Feb. 1980), p. 96.

Morgan, Stuart. "Andy & Andy, the Warhol Twins: A Theme and Variation." *Parkett*, no. 12 (1987), pp. 35ff.

"New Talent USA," *Art in America* 50, no. 1 (1962), p. 42.

Nikas, Robert. "Andy Warhol's Rorschach Tests." *Arts Magazine*, 60 (Oct. 1986), pp. 28–32.

Papanani, Demetrio. "Collaborations: Warhol/Basquiat/Clemente." *Tema Celeste* (Nov. 1985).

Pincus-Witten, Robert. "Entries: Big History, Little History." *Arts Magazine*, 54 (Apr. 1980), pp. 183–85.

Pincus-Witten, Robert. "Pre-entry: Margins of Error." *Arts Magazine*, 63 (Summer 1989), pp. 56–60.

Pogrebin, Robin. "A Portrait of an Artist Both Loved and Hated." *The New York Times*, Sept. 20, 2006, pp. B1, B8.

Pomeroy, Ralph. "An Interview with Andy Warhol." *Afterimage*, 2 (Fall 1970), pp. 34–39.

Priess, Holger. "Der Tod im Konsumzeitalter." *Die Kunst Noll*, no. 11 (Nov. 1987), p. 874.

Ratcliff, Carter. "Master of Modern Paradox." *Art International*, 7 (Summer 1989), pp. 74–83.

Raynor, Vivian. "A Basquiat–Warhol Pas de Deux." *The New York Times*, Sept. 20, 1985, p. B5.

Russell, John. "Art View: When Art Came out of the Studio and Mingled." *The New York Times*, Oct. 28, 1984, p. 33.

Saltz, Jerry. "Swish Myth." *Artnet*, May 12, 2000, www.artnet.com/magazine/FEATURES/saltz/saltz5-12-00.asp.

Saussy, Haun. "A Note on Warhol's Mao." *Arts Magazine*, 63 (Summer 1989), p. 66.

Schuweiler, Daat Zum. "For Heaven's Sake: Warhol's Art as Religious Allegory." *Religion and the Arts, a Journal from Boston College*, 1 (Autumn 1996), pp. 15–31.

Schwabsky, Barry. "Dia, Gagosian, Robert Miller, Galleries, New York." *Arts Magazine*, 61 (Mar. 1987), p. 106.

Smith, Roberta. "Warhol's 15 Minutes Tick On, in Abstraction Shows." *The New York Times*, Dec. 4, 1998, p. E31.

Smith, Roberta. "Take a Museum. Do Something with It." *The New York Times*, Sept. 3, 1999, p. E33.

Smith, Roberta. "Art: A Collaboration, Tim Rollins and K.O.S." *The New York Times*, Nov. 2[illegible], 1986), p. C28.

Smith, Roberta. "7 of Warhol's Final Paintings." *The New York Times*, July 10, 1987, p. C4.

Smith, Roberta. "Andy Warhol 'Rorschach Paintings,' Gagosian Gallery." *The New York Times*, Oct. 4, 1996, p. C29.

Stuckey, Charles. "Warhol Backwards and Forwards." *Flash Art*, no. 101 (Jan.–Feb. 1981), pp. 10–18.

Swenson, G. R. "What Is Pop Art? Answers from 8 Painters, Part 1." *Art News*, 62 (Nov. 1963), pp. 24–27.

Taylor, Paul. "The Last Interview: Andy Warhol." *Flash Art*, no. 133 (Apr. 1987), pp. 40–44.

Tuchman, Phyllis. "Pop! Interviews with George Segal, Andy Warhol, Roy Lichtenstein, James Rosenquist, and Robert Indiana." *Art News*, 73 (May 1974), pp. 24–29.

Wallis, Brian. "Absolute Warhol." *Art in America*, 77 (Mar. 1989), pp. 25–31.

Warhol, Andy. "Painter Hangs His Own Paintings." *New York Magazine*, Feb. 5, 1979.

Wechsler, Max. "Reviews: Collaborations, Gallery Bruno Bischofberger." *Artforum*, 23 (Jan. 1985), p. 89.

Welzenbach, Michael. "Speakeasy." *New Art Examiner*, 14 (Apr. 1987), pp. 11–12.

Whiting, Cécile. "Andy Warhol: The Public Star and the Private Self." *The Oxford Art Journal*, 10, no. 2 (1987), pp. 58–75.

Lenders to the Exhibition

Debbie and Mark Attanasio
The Baltimore Museum of Art
Bruno Bischofberger
Anthony d'Offay
Kunsthalle Bielefeld, Germany
Mugrabi Collection
The Museum of Modern Art, New York
Virginia and Bagley Wright
The Andy Warhol Museum, Pittsburgh
Ealan Wingate and Batsheva Ostrow
One anonymous collection
Two private collections

Photograph and Reproduction Credits

All Andy Warhol artwork © 2009 Andy Warhol Foundation for the Visual Arts/Artists Rights Society (ARS), New York

Courtesy Thomas Ammann Fine Art, Zurich: 172–73; © The Art Institute of Chicago: 16; Artwork © 2009 The Estate of Jean-Michel Basquiat/ADAGP, Paris/Artists Rights Society (ARS), New York: 200; Artwork © 2009 The Estate of Jean-Michel Basquiat/ADAGP, Paris/Artists Rights Society (ARS), New York. © 2009 Andy Warhol Foundation for the Visual Arts/Artists Rights Society (ARS), New York: 134–35, 141, 144, 145; Artwork © 2009 The Estate of Jean-Michel Basquiat/ADAGP, Paris/Artists Rights Society (ARS), New York. © Francesco Clemente. © 2009 Andy Warhol Foundation for the Visual Arts/Artists Rights Society (ARS), New York: 136–37, 138–39, 142, 143; Artwork © Mike Bidlo. Courtesy Hal Bromm Gallery, New York: 199 bottom; Courtesy Galerie Bruno Bischofberger, Zurich: 112–13, 136–37, 142, 200; Courtesy Mary Boone Gallery, New York: 22; Courtesy the Stephanie and Peter Brant Foundation, Greenwich, Connecticut: 190–91; © Christie's Images Ltd/ARTOTHEK: 18, 24; Max Ernst artwork © 2009 Artists Rights Society (ARS), New York/ADAGP, Paris. Photo © The Museum of Modern Art/Licensed by SCALA/Art Resource, NY: 55, 130; Courtesy Ronald Feldman Fine Arts. Photo by D. James Dee: 77 top; Courtesy Gagosian Gallery, New York: 34 bottom, 174–75; Artwork © Keith Haring Foundation: 204; Mitro Hood: 17, 105, 110 right; Bill Jacobson. © Dia Art Foundation: 21, 106–107; Artwork © Ellsworth Kelly: 58; Paul Klee artwork © 2009 Artists Rights Society (ARS), New York/VG Bild-Kunst, Bonn: 50 top; Bob Kolbrener: 19; Kunstmuseum Basel. Photo by Martin P. Bühler: 51 top; *Life* Magazine © 1949 Time Inc., Used with Permission. Photographs Arnold Newman/Arnold Newman Collection/Getty Images: 52; Marilyn Monroe™ is a trademark of Marilyn Monroe LLC: 112–13, 114; © The Museum of Modern Art/Licensed by SCALA/Art Resource, NY: 192–93; © 1984 Beth Philipps: 201; Artwork © 2009 Estate of Pablo Picasso/Artists Rights Society (ARS), New York. Photo © The Metropolitan Museum: 62; Artwork © 2009 Pollock-Krasner Foundation/Artists Rights Society (ARS), New York: 52, 67; Artwork © Julian Schnabel, courtesy PaceWildenstein, New York: 22, 199 top; Harry Shunk: 23 top; Lee Stalsworth: 51 bottom; Richard Stoner: 77 bottom, 80, 83; © 2009 Arthur Tress: 66

Notes on the Contributors

Bruno Bischofberger is an art dealer and gallery owner based in Zurich, Switzerland. He cofounded *Interview* magazine with Andy Warhol in 1969 and produced Warhol's 1970 film *L'Amour*. Bischofberger is a well-known supporter of Pop art and other contemporary movements and has held solo shows for major artists such as Jean-Michel Basquiat, On Kawara, Donald Judd, Julian Schnabel, and George Condo.

Keith Haring (1958–1990) was one of the most prominent artists of the 1980s. He began his career doing graffiti chalk drawings in New York City subways and went on to create simple, yet powerful, imagery that had widespread public appeal. In 1980 Haring began organizing exhibitions at the popular Club 57 and the next year had his first solo exhibition at the Tony Shafrazi Gallery He participated in numerous exhibitions worldwide.

Keith Hartley is the deputy director of the Scottish National Gallery of Modern Art in Edinburgh. He has curated numerous exhibitions on modern and contemporary art and edited and written their accompanying catalogues, including *Andy Warhol: A Celebration of Life . . . and Death* (2007), *Douglas Gordon* (2006), *Robert Mapplethorpe* (2006), *Century City—Vienna* (with Richard Calvocoressi, 2001), *The Romantic Spirit in German Art* (1994), *Otto Dix* (1992), and *Scottish Art Since 1900* (1989).

Joseph D. Ketner II, the Henry and Lois Foster Chair in Contemporary Art at Emerson College, Boston, has worked for the past thirty years as a museum curator and director specializing in modern and contemporary art. Formerly, he was the chief curator at the Milwaukee Art Museum; director of the Rose Art Museum, Brandeis University; and director of the Washington University Gallery of Art, St. Louis (now the Mildred Kemper Museum). Ketner has curated, organized, and published catalogues on many exhibitions, including *Elusive Signs: Bruce Nauman Works with Light* (2006), *Co-Existence: Contemporary Cultural Production in South Africa* (2003), *Roxy Paine: Second Nature* (2003), *A Gallery of Modern Art at Washington University in St. Louis* (1994), and *The Emergence of the African American Artist: Robert S. Duncanson (1821–1872)* (1993).

Julian Schnabel is a well-respected artist and filmmaker. His first solo show, at the Mary Boone Gallery in 1979, received much critical acclaim, and today his work is in numerous museum and private collections around the world. Schnabel has directed films such as *Basquiat* (1996), *Before Night Falls* (2000), and most recently *The Diving Bell and the Butterfly* (2007), for which he was given the award for Best Director at the Cannes Film Festival in 2007.

Gregory Volk is a New York–based art critic and freelance curator. He writes regularly for *Art in America*, and his articles and reviews have also appeared in *Parkett* and *Sculpture*. He has contributed to numerous books, including *Vito Acconci: Diary of a Body* (2007), *Elusive Signs: Bruce Nauman Works with Light* (2006), and *Roxy Paine: Second Nature* (2003). He is also associate professor in the School of the Arts at Virginia Commonwealth University.

Index

Page numbers in *italics* refer to illustrations.